The Impact of Legislation and Regulation on the Freedom of Movement of Capital in Estonia, Poland and Latvia

The Impact of Legislation and Regulation on the Freedom of Movement of Capital in Estonia, Poland and Latvia

By

Graeme Baber

CAMBRIDGE SCHOLARS

PUBLISHING

The Impact of Legislation and Regulation on the Freedom of Movement of Capital
in Estonia, Poland and Latvia,
by Graeme Baber

This book first published 2010

Cambridge Scholars Publishing

12 Back Chapman Street, Newcastle upon Tyne, NE6 2XX, UK

British Library Cataloguing in Publication Data
A catalogue record for this book is available from the British Library

ISBN (10): 1-4438-2113-6, ISBN (13): 978-1-4438-2113-1

To my family, especially my mother, for loyalty and support in the preparation for and writing of this work.

Europe stands on the threshold of a new millennium. We face the challenge of integrating the continent's various countries and regions, and of modernising our societies.

—Dr. Vaira Vīķe-Freiberga, 6th President of Latvia 1999-2007

CONTENTS

LIST OF FIGURES

List of Tables

PREFACE

The idea behind the research described in this book represents a convergence of two professional subject interests – the laws describing the Internal Market of the European Union and the economic development of countries. The following paragraphs show how this confluence occurred.

One of the fundamental freedoms of the Internal Market is the free movement of capital. According to Article 56 of the Treaty Establishing the European Communities, (which has recently been recategorised as Article 63 of the Treaty on the Functioning of the European Union), restrictions on the movement of capital and payments between European Union Member States and between these countries and those outside the European Union shall be prohibited, subject to certain exceptions. This inspired piece of legislation should, in theory at least, improve conditions for cross-border business to take place, both within the Union and between the Union and countries outside it. But does it do so in practice?

A method for considering this issue is to relate the removal of national restrictions to the free movement of capital to the cross-border capital flows to and from selected Member States of the European Union. Countries that are advanced in terms of economic development tend to have higher cross-border capital flows per person than those that are less industrialised, other things being the same. The countries of the former Soviet Union and Warsaw Pact have been, and are still in some instances, transition economies from a less-developed command system to a more-developed free market system. Several of these countries have recently joined the European Union, including the three Member States that are the subject of this book.

The study of the movement of capital to and from Estonia, Latvia and Poland in this context provides the link being sought – between the Internal Market and economic development. First, ascertain the precise details of the European Union Law governing the free movement of capital. Second, develop a method to compare these provisions with the national laws limiting such movement. Third, identify the Estonian, Polish and Latvian laws restricting it. Fourth, develop a method to compare the national laws. Fifth, make this comparison, and from it, construct a legal index that measures national legal restrictions to cross-border capital movement. This index can then be compared with the capital flows to and from the three Member States. Some other factors affecting these flows are identified, too, and a reasonable explanation is given as to the role that the removal of national restrictions might have had on cross-border flows in the period 1998-2007.

This is exciting new ground, which is potentially extendible to other European Union Member States, and provides a framework for concentrated study of some of the business sectors in which the restrictions to the free movement of capital were identified. One senior professor of economics at the School of Oriental and African Studies, University of London, at which the research was conducted, was sceptical of this cross-disciplinary approach. His main objection was that a rigorous econometric analysis with panel data should have been undertaken, and, therefore, in the absence of such a method, the conclusions did not have the generality claimed.

This type of comment, whilst valid in itself, misses the whole point of the exercise. The research is exploratory, and connects two related items but in different orders. The first is the literal concept of deviation in the national legislation and regulations of Member States from the free movement of capital provisions of European Union Law. The second is the numerical concept of cross-border capital flows. The common theme is that both concepts relate to the same subject matter – the cross-border movement of capital. The research described does indeed explore the relationship between these concepts in some depth, and, by doing so, adds a considerable input to the research base in this developing area.

Econometric studies have been performed to measure the impact of laws on economic variables. Some of these by Dr. Raphael La Porta and his colleagues, leading proponents of this approach, are included in Appendix F. There are some technical shortcomings in the methodology, which are outlined there. Consequently, one would hesitate to follow it before a more thorough approach has been conceived, tested and applied.

Please feel free to come to a view on the value of this research, both in its methodology and in its findings. Improvements can always be made. If there are any specific issues which the reader wishes to raise concerning the work, then I am available at gb23@soas.ac.uk. In the meantime, I hope that the contents of this book at least equal, and even exceed, your expectations.

ACKNOWLEDGEMENTS

The author and publishers wish to thank the following, who have kindly given permission for the use of copyright material:

The Federal Trust for Education & Research and Alison Sutherland for the epigraph on page iv, which is from: Vīķe-Freiberga, V. (2000), 'Latvia's place in a new Europe', *The Federal Trust: European Essay No. 13*, page 15.

Elsevier Science Publications B.V. and the Copyright Clearance Center's Rightslink service for: Cardoso and Dornbusch (1989), 'Foreign Private Capital Inflows', figure 26.6, page 1418, *in* Chenery, H. And Srinivasan, T. N. *eds.*, *Handbook of Development Economics, Volume II* (Amsterdam: Elsevier Science Publications B.V.), which is adapted to become Fig. 1-1.

LIST OF ABBREVIATIONS

Annex I	Annex I to Directive 88/361/EEC
CPI	Consumer Price Index
EBRD	European Bank for Reconstruction and Development
ECJ	European Court of Justice
ECR	European Court Reports
EC Treaty	Treaty Establishing the European Communities
EEA	European Economic Area, comprising the European Union, Iceland, Liechtenstein and Norway
ELLC	Estonian Legal Language Centre
EU	European Union
FCMC	Latvian Financial and Capital Market Commission
FDI	Foreign Direct Investment
FSA	Estonian Financial Supervision Authority
FSC	Polish Financial Supervision Commission / Authority
GDP	Gross Domestic Product
IMF	International Monetary Fund
LTTC	Latvian Translation and Terminology Centre
Member State	Member State of the European Union
MNCs	Multinational corporations
NEER	Nominal Effective Exchange Rate
OECD	Organisation for Economic Cooperation and Development
PAAS	Prior Administrative Authorisation Scheme
PPP	Purchasing Power Parity
Third countries	Countries outside the European Economic Area
VLTL	Vorarlberg Land Transfer Law
WTO	World Trade Organisation

Abbreviations for Estonian legislation and regulations

Chapter 3 and section 8.2.1

CIA	Credit Institutions Act 1999
IAA	Insurance Activities Act 2004
IFA	Investment Funds Act 2004
ITA	Income Tax Act 1999
LPA	Law of Property Act 1993
PILA	Private International Law Act 2002
Regulation No.73	Regulation No.73 of the Minister of Finance of 19 November 1997
SMA	Securities Market Act 2001

Sections 1.3.2, 4.1.7, 4.3.3, 5.1.8, 5.3.3 and 7.2.2

ECIA	Credit Institutions Act 1999
EIAA	Insurance Activities Act 2004
EIFA	Investment Funds Act 2004
EITA	Income Tax Act 1999
ESMA	Securities Market Act 2001

Abbreviations for Polish legislation and regulations

Sections 2.5.2 and 8.2.2, and chapter 4, excluding section 4.1.7

AIPFPA	Act of 24 March 1920 on the Acquisition of Immovable Properties by Foreign Persons
BL	Act of 29 August 1997: Banking Law
FEAA	Act of 28 February 2004 on Freedom of Economic Activity
FEL	Act of 27 July 2002: Foreign Exchange Law
IAA	Act of 22 May 2003 on Insurance Activity
IFA	Act of 27 May 2004 on Investment Funds
IMA	Act of 22 May 2003 on Insurance Mediation
LPITA	Act of 15 February 1992 on Legal Persons' Income Tax
NPITA	Act of 26 July 1991 on Natural Persons' Income Tax
POA	Act of 29 July 2005 on Public Offers and the Conditions for Introducing Financial Instruments to the Organised Trading System, and on Public Companies
RGFEP	Regulation of the Minister of Finance of 3 September 2002 on General Foreign Exchange Permits

TFIA	Act of 29 July 2005 on Trading in Financial Instruments

Sections 1.3.2, 4.1.7, 5.1.8, 5.3.3, 5.4.6, 6.2.1 and 7.1.4

PAIPFPA	Act of 24 March 1920 on the Acquisition of Immovable Properties by Foreign Persons
PBL	Act of 29 August 1997: Banking Law
PIAA	Act of 22 May 2003 on Insurance Activity
PIFA	Act of 27 May 2004 on Investment Funds
PIMA	Act of 22 May 2003 on Insurance Mediation
PLPITA	Act of 15 February 1992 on Legal Persons' Income Tax
PNPITA	Act of 26 July 1991 on Natural Persons' Income Tax
PPOA	Act of 29 July 2005 on Public Offers and the Conditions for Introducing Financial Instruments to the Organised Trading System, and on Public Companies
PTFIA	Act of 29 July 2005 on Trading in Financial Instruments

Abbreviations for Latvian legislation and regulations

Section 8.2.3 and chapter 5, excluding sections 5.1.8 and 5.3.3

AIRIL	Activities of Insurance and Reinsurance Intermediaries Law 2005
CIL	Credit Institution Law 1995
FIML	Financial Instrument Markets Law 2003
FPRL	The Free Port of Riga Law 2000
FPVL	The Free Port of Ventspils Law 1996
LEIT	Law on Enterprise Income Tax 1995
LIC	Law on Investment Companies 1997
LICST	Law on Insurance Companies and Supervision Thereof 1998
LLRCRL	Law on Land Reform in the Cities of the Republic of Latvia 1991
LPIT	Law on Personal Income Tax 1993
LPLRA	Law on Privatization of Land in Rural Areas 1992
LPPF	Law on Private Pension Funds 1997
LSFP	Law on State Funded Pensions 2000
RICIOL	2002-08-15 Regulations on the Issue of Credit Institution and Credit Union Operating Licences

Sections 5.1.8 and 5.3.3

LAIRIL	Activities of Insurance and Reinsurance Intermediaries Law 2005
LCIL	Credit Institution Law 1995
LFIML	Financial Instrument Market Law 2003
LLEIT	Law on Enterprise Income Tax 1995
LLIC	Law on Investment Companies 1997
LLICST	Law on Insurance Companies and Supervision Thereof 1998
LLPIT	Law on Personal Income Tax 1993
LRICIOL	2002-08-15 Regulations on the Issue of Credit Institution and Credit Union Operating Licences

Legal subsidiary indices in chapter 7 and appendix A

D:I	legal restrictions on capital inflows
D:O	legal restrictions on capital outflows
L:EEA	legal restrictions on intra-EEA capital flows
L:TC	legal restrictions on capital flows to/from third countries
S:InvF	legal restrictions on investment funds' capital flows
S:InvS	legal restrictions on capital flows concerning investment services
S:CI	legal restrictions on credit institutions' capital flows
S:InsS	legal restrictions on capital flows concerning insurance services
S:InsM	legal restrictions on capital flows concerning insurance mediation
S:T	legal restrictions on capital flows concerning taxation
S:L	legal restrictions on capital flows concerning real property transfers

Abbreviations used only in appendix F

F,G&S	French origin, German origin and Scandinavian origin regression variables
GNP	Gross National Product
IPO	Initial Public Offering of equity shares
LP1	La Porta et al. (2003a)
LP2	La Porta et al. (2003b)
LP3	La Porta, Lopez-de-Silanes, and Schleifer (2006)
OLS	Ordinary Least Squares regression
2SLS	2-Stage Least Squares regression

CHAPTER ONE

ISSUES CONCERNING THE EFFECT OF LAWS ON CAPITAL FLOWS

1.1 What is the purpose of the research?

On 1st May 2004, ten new Member States joined the EU. The majority of these countries were members of the Warsaw Pact until its abolition in 1990, and three were part of the Soviet Union.

In 1998, the EU entered into accession talks with these countries for membership. The main condition for membership was acceptance and implementation of the 'acquis communautaire' – the substantial body of Treaty provisions, Regulations, Decisions and Directives and case law already in force in the EU.[1]

One substantial part of the acquis communautaire consists of the legislation to create the Internal Market, which is characterised by the removal of barriers to the free movement of goods, persons, services and capital between Member States.[2] This book concerns the free movement of capital legislation (Articles 56–60) of the EC Treaty.

I selected three from the ten accession countries of 2004 to study the national legislation and regulations, identify differences between the EU and national laws, and compare those differences with the capital flows into and out of these countries. I chose Poland because it is the largest economy in Central and Eastern Europe,[3] Estonia because it is the most advanced country in the former Soviet Union,[4] and Latvia because it completes a triad of north-eastern European countries.

The national financial services legislation must comply with the corresponding Directives – 2004/39/EC for investment firms, 2006/48/EC

---

[1] See section 1.3.1.

[2] See section 1.2.3.

[3] This excludes Germany, since the reunified Germany's economy remains largely driven by the western region.

[4] Estonian gross domestic product per capita was US$ 9,598 in 2005, highest of the former Soviet republics (United Nations Statistics Division, 21 June 2007).

for credit institutions, and 73/239/EEC, 88/357/EEC, 2002/83/EC and 2002/92/EC for insurance companies.[5] As I analyse such legislation and its related regulations in chapters 3, 4 and 5 for barriers to the free movement of capital, it is but a step further to comment on compliance with these Directives. Both are important contributions to the alignment of national laws with the acquis communautaire, which, by joining the EU, constituent Member States are obliged to implement.[6]

The book compares the cross-border capital movement restrictions in Estonia, Poland and Latvia, and analyses the effect of the limitations on capital flows to and from these countries. As there are other determinants of such capital flows,[7] the effect of legal barriers is difficult to establish in practice. Nonetheless, it is interesting to investigate for the EU and, potentially for other regional trade blocks, whether free movement of capital laws increase cross-border flows. This research makes an initial attempt to do just that.

1.2 Why legislate to remove cross-border capital restrictions?

It must first be established whether, on balance, it is beneficial for a country or trade block to lift its barriers to cross-border capital flows. Since the free movement of capital is part of the Internal Market, Member States have an additional powerful incentive to remove restrictions to these flows.

1.2.1 Reasons in favour of the free movement of capital

The free movement of capital stimulates cross-border trade and investment, which may increase the rate of economic growth.[8] Investment

[5] These are described in section 2.4.

[6] If an Article of a Directive limits the free movement of capital, Member States tend to follow the Article. Conflict between the EC Treaty and Directives was discussed at the United Kingdom Association for European Law conference on 28 April 2007, but there were no firm conclusions to this debate. Section 8.2.4 discusses alternative solutions to a situation in which a provision of a Directive restricts the free movement of capital.

[7] See Appendix E.

[8] The Harrod-Domar and two-gap models incorporate the positive effect of capital inflows on growth, and the Solow growth model has been applied to international capital movements. There are also two groups of optimization models: the representative consumer approach in which the economy is treated as a single unit

may also fund training and/or raise the level of exports in the sector concerned, although the latter may cause the terms of trade to deteriorate.[9] Free capital movement across the EU also encourages the formation of companies with subsidiaries and branches in other Member States,[10] and lowers the cost of investment for financial asset providers in such States.[11]

Cardoso and Dornbusch describe the following effects of capital inflows.[12] Firstly, such inflows raise the economy's productive capacity, thereby potentially increasing welfare.[13] There is an increase in national income, whose size is quadratically related to the share of capital in the income accruing to domestic factors of production, and inversely correlated with the elasticity of substitution between capital and other such factors.[14]

Secondly, capital inflows may smooth consumption in two contexts. 1) Cyclical fluctuations: one can borrow when disposable income is lower than consumption, and repay when income rises. 2) Growth in per capita income: foreign loans can finance investment so that income exceeds consumption and domestic savings increase; later, such savings fund investment and the loans are repaid.

Thirdly, capital inflows lower the scarcity of capital, thereby raising the factor productivity for domestic factors as a whole. Where such inflows are accompanied by immigration, returns to land increase whilst the income of local capital and labour tend to fall – the effect on factor prices depends on technology and on the relative change in the domestic capital stock and labour supply.

Fourthly, if there is a foreign exchange gap, foreign capital goods are too expensive to be purchased by exports and the real exchange rate must depreciate. Capital inflows may alleviate real price rigidity and/or costly adjustments to relative prices, by providing foreign exchange and raising investment for economic growth. In the two-gap model, the capital inflow

---

over time, and the life-cycle approach in which 'younger' consumers earn and save and 'older' consumers do not.

[9] See section 1.2.2.

[10] The free movement of capital therefore complements the freedom of establishment.

[11] The cost of investment includes taxes and administration expenses.

[12] *Handbook of Development Economics*, Volume II, 1989, 1404–1419.

[13] Capital inflows may lower welfare: see section 1.2.2.

[14] The domestic gain is the following fraction of national income: $(1 - \alpha)\, \alpha x^2 / 2\sigma$, where x is the proportionate rise in the capital stock, α is the share of capital in income to domestic factors, and σ is elasticity of substitution. This neoclassical model also predicts a gain to foreign investors.

moves the foreign exchange constraint to the right, thereby raising the growth rate and the ratio of domestic to foreign prices.[15]

1.2.2 Reasons for retaining barriers to capital flows

Capital flows may destabilize macroeconomic conditions within a country. An example is Chile, which implemented a financial liberalization program in the 1970s–1980s. After a period of high growth, the capital account of the balance of payments was opened to medium and long-term international capital movements. There was a large capital inflow, causing the exchange rate to appreciate. Expenditure on imports rose, creating a current account deficit. As the rate of capital inflow declined, a real devaluation of the peso was required to raise the competitiveness of the export sector. Since the nominal exchange rate was pegged to the strong dollar, and since Chile had a law which prevented reduction in real wages, there was initially no devaluation, and output declined rather than prices. The next year, the government devalued the peso, causing a loss of international reserves and lower capital inflows. As inflation was relatively low, there was a real devaluation and competitiveness was regained.[16]

One factor present in Chile's experience is deterioration in the terms of trade, since the exchange rate appreciation made exports and import-competing products more expensive relative to imports.[17] Drs. Raúl Prebisch and Hans Singer believed that the terms of trade had moved against primary products during the early 20th century, a trend which continued into the latter half of the century.[18] A rise in capital inflows to a developing country in these circumstances is counterproductive, stimulating the purchase of imports with the additional burden of debt repayment.

---

[15] Fig. 1-1 is adapted from Cardoso and Dornbusch, *Handbook of Development Economics*, figure 26.6, 1418.

[16] Edwards (1985), *Economic Development and Cultural Change*, 33, 223–254.

[17] The terms of trade are the price of exports divided by the price of imports.

[18] Cypher and Dietz (2004), *The Process of Economic Development*, 162–169. Many developing countries have traditionally been net exporters of agricultural products, a trend which changed to some extent with the introduction of import substitution industrialization (ISI). ISI has been partially but not totally successful.

Fig. 1-1: The two-gap model: a capital inflow shifts the foreign exchange constraint to the right.

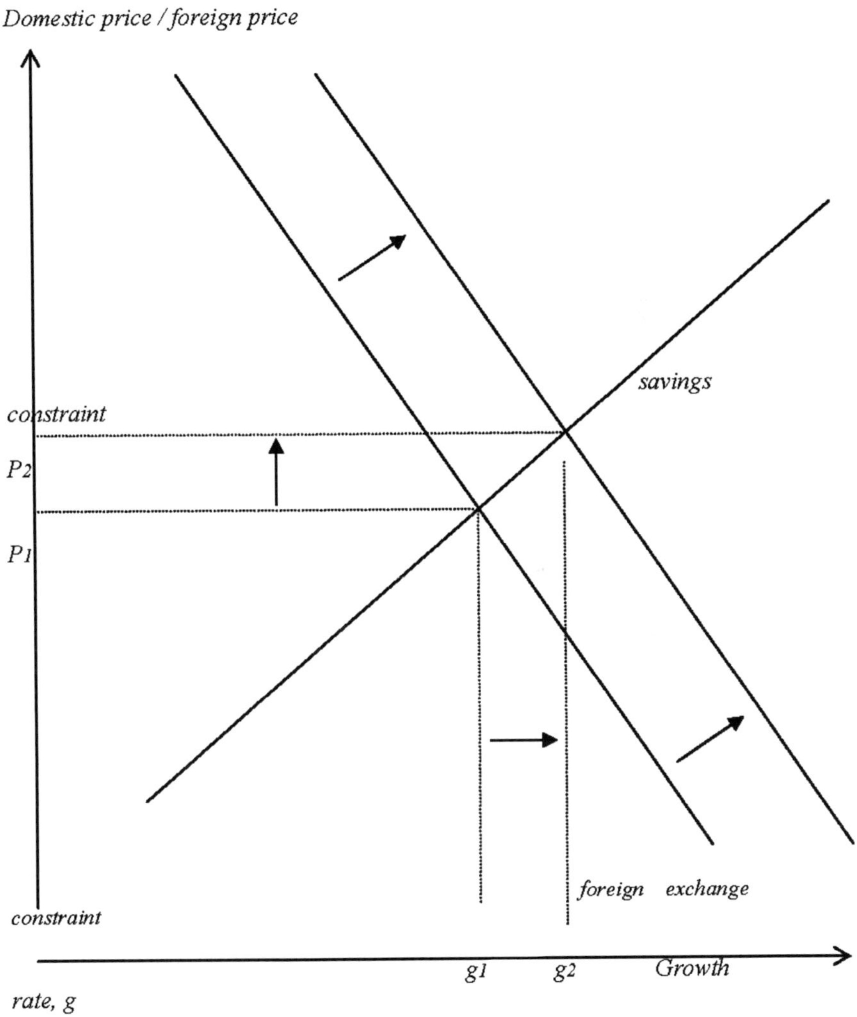

Cardoso and Dornbusch state two cases in which capital inflows reduce welfare.[19] 1) If capital inflows enable the expansion of an industry with monopoly power in the export sector, the terms of trade deterioration due to the rise in the price of exports may, in the absence of an optimum tariff, reduce national income. 2) Tariff or tax distortions may, through general equilibrium effects, cause capital inflows to contract an industry that is already underproductive. These welfare-reducing cases are an exception to the general principle that capital inflows tend to raise national income.[20]

Capital flight–the mass transfer of investment from domestic to foreign assets[21]–is a potential problem for countries in financial distress. The main determinants of capital flight are real exchange rate appreciation and/or currency overvaluation, a high and/or rising inflation rate, the expectation of currency devaluation, and a low domestic interest rate relative to the world interest rate.[22] Controls on capital outflows are essential for countries with these characteristics.[23] Investors may move their assets abroad in response to high domestic taxation or political risk (of expropriation, for instance),[24] or because local financial markets are volatile.

There are also difficulties with debt and FDI. Debtor countries may be unable to make debt repayments, especially after adverse economic shocks. The debt crisis of the 1980s was precipitated by the oil price rises

---

[19] *Handbook of Development Economics*, 1407–1408.

[20] See section 1.2.1.

[21] 'Capital flight' may be narrowly defined as short term capital outflows or broadly defined as the gross value of all capital outflows. The broad definition more accurately describes capital flight because many outflows are long term; for instance, some white South African residents invested abroad after termination of the apartheid regime to safeguard their assets. In estimating capital flight from selected countries from 1979–1982, the World Bank uses a broad definition: gross capital inflows plus the current account deficit less increases in official foreign reserves (Eaton (1989), *Handbook of Development Economics*, Volume II, 1353), leaving gross capital outflows as the residual term. The definition of 'capital flight' used by Cuddington (1986), *Princeton Studies in International Finance*, No. 58, 1–40 is more specific and his investigation covers 1974–1982, but both studies conclude that Argentina, Mexico and Venezuela displayed the highest levels of capital flight.

[22] Cuddington, *Princeton Studies*.

[23] Brazil, Chile and Peru retained some capital controls during 1974–1982, which prevented more extensive capital flight, given their inflation and exchange rate movements in this period (Cuddington, *Princeton Studies*).

[24] Cardoso and Dornbusch, *Handbook of Development Economics*, 1423.

of the 1970s and the worldwide economic recession of the early 1980s. In non-oil producing developing countries, export volumes and prices declined and the current account balance worsened. Real appreciation of the dollar raised the real value of developing countries' debt repayments, since their currencies were pegged to the dollar or to a basket of currencies. In Latin America, repayment problems were so severe that debt restructuring and forgiveness from the commercial lenders under the guidance of the Brady plan and market reforms supervised by the International Monetary Fund were required to restore economic health.[25]

Governments may incur problems by permitting FDI from MNCs. MNCs may 1) lower domestic savings and investment by smothering competition, extracting profits and providing income for people with a low propensity to save but a high propensity to import; 2) reduce foreign exchange earnings by importing intermediate and capital goods, and by repatriating profits, interest, royalties and management fees; 3) increase income inequalities by widening wage differentials, manufacturing advanced products for the local elites and operating in urban areas; 4) introduce inappropriate products and technologies and 5) use non-arm's length transfer prices in intra-firm transactions.[26]

1.2.3 The Internal Market

The free movement of capital is one of the four fundamental freedoms provided by the EC Treaty, the others being the free movement of goods, persons and services. These freedoms are part of the EU's Internal Market, whose completion by December 1992 also required the removal of internal frontier controls and the approximation of indirect tax rates.[27] Initially the free movement of capital was not intended to apply directly, but to facilitate, by way of Directives, the formation of a common market in financial services.[28] Today, the free movement of capital is stated by

---

[25] Pilbeam (2006), *International Finance*, 377–407. Although their export levels and inflation rates have recovered from the debt crisis, the total external debt in each of the four biggest debtor countries (Argentina, Brazil, Mexico and Venezuela) was higher in 2002 than it was in 1982, when the crisis began.

[26] Cardoso and Dornbusch, *Handbook of Development Economics*, 1413–1414. FDI may provide superior technology to local firms and economies of scale in marketing, and increase competition (ibid., 1407). The benefits and drawbacks are specific to each case.

[27] EC Commission (1985), 'Completing the Internal Market', COM(85) 310 final, 1–2, 9 and 51–54.

[28] Ibid., 32–33. This freedom was referred to as a 'secondary freedom'.

Article 63 of the Treaty on the Functioning of the European Union,[29] and stands on an equal footing with the other freedoms.

Comment

The requirement for Member States to remove barriers to capital flows to and from other States and third countries as part of implementing the Internal Market (with certain exceptions),[30] renders academic the question as to whether States should retain them. Nonetheless, the arguments in section 1.2.2 are persuasive for countries that wish to borrow to fund investment and which have, or expect to have, high or rising inflation rates and/or real exchange rates. Estonia, Poland and Latvia have not yet joined the Euro, so these conditions can still occur.[31]

1.3 The comparison of national law with European Law

1.3.1 Implementing the acquis communautaire

All aspiring EU Member States must implement the body of Treaty provisions, Regulations, Directives and case law that exists at the time of their accession to Membership – 1st May 2004 for Estonia, Poland and Latvia. This is a legal transplantation of EU law onto national law, and has implications of harmonisation of national law with that of other Member States. These issues are discussed below.

Legal transplants

Before the Enlightenment, European laws moved geographically, though usually with peoples – Germans into Poland, Normans into

---

[29] Until the recent implementation of the Lisbon Treaty, the relevant provision was Article 56 of the EC Treaty, which was identical to the new Article 63. Since all of the research for this book was undertaken before introduction of the Lisbon Treaty into EU law, this measure is referred to as 'Article 56, EC Treaty' throughout.

[30] See section 2.1.3.

[31] High Latvian inflation (8.5% annually to March 2007) may prevent Latvia from joining the Euro before 2011 (EUbusiness.com, 28 June 2007). Estonia's high inflation rate has caused it to postpone adoption of the Euro to beyond 2009 (Bank of Estonia (2007), 'Report on the Adoption of the Euro', 6). A recent Communication from the Commission of the European Communities confirms that Latvia and Poland have no target date for adopting the Euro, and that Estonia is aiming to join on 1 January 2011 (COM/2009/692 final, 3, 4 and 6).

England, English into Ireland, and all of these peoples into foreign territories as part of colonisation. However, this spatial movement of law was perceived by the participants as a growing area of influence rather than as a transplant. Legal rules were considered to be models that could be used or not in specific cases.[32]

Alan Watson considers that the growth of law is primarily to be explained by the transplantation of legal rules. Watson investigates the spread of Roman law across Europe, noting the persistence of Roman legal rules into the present time. He states that the rules of Roman law have been transplanted in bulk into most continental European countries and are the foundation of their legal systems.[33] Watson argues that legal transplants are the main method for legal change in Western countries because the law is conservative and backward-looking. The law is such because the legal profession tends to treat legal rules as ends in themselves, with the sources of law being regarded as given, almost sacrosanct.[34]

William Twining states that most literature on legal transplants is in the 'Country and Western Tradition' of comparative law,[35] and that a broader perspective is required. He perceptively observes that legal diffusion studies have shared origins with 19th century sociology and anthropology, but that such studies have lost touch with literature in other social sciences concerning the diffusion of innovations, language, music, religion and sport, which may enlighten enquiries into legal diffusion. Twining recommends adoption of a global view and a broad notion of law, covering different levels of ordering and relations.[36]

Twining's perspective of different levels is applicable to the implementation of EU law in Member States, for such law is of a higher level than the national rules of Member States, since these rules must

---

[32] Glenn (2006), *Journal of Comparative Law*, 1, 124–130.

[33] Watson (1974, 2nd edition 1993), *Transplants: An Approach to Comparative Law,* cited in Ewald (1995), *American Journal of Comparative Law*, 43, 489–510. These countries are 'civil law' families, a distinction used in contrast to 'common law' families by La Porta et al. in their leximetric studies – see Appendix F.

[34] Watson (1985), *The Evolution of Law*, cited in Ewald, *American Journal.*

[35] This tradition concerns positive laws and national legal systems, focuses on Western capitalist societies, is primarily concerned with common law / civil law differences, legal doctrine and private law, and involves description and analysis in preference to evaluation and prescription.

[36] Twining (2006), *Journal of Comparative Law*, 1, 3–26. Such different levels include, for example, the adoption of international norms into national law, such as the incorporation of the European Convention on Human Rights into the United Kingdom Human Rights Act 1998.

comply with it.[37] In as far as EU law has direct effect,[38] there is no change in the national law of Member States other than repealing incompatible provisions.

However, a more interactive legal transplantation occurs for Directives than for EU Treaty provisions and Regulations both because Directives must be transposed into national law and because of the principle of indirect effect.[39] Although the resulting national law must comply with EU law, it is in the context of the Member State's legal system, which may affect what form the domestic law takes – i.e. the transposed Directive may be transformed in the local environment.[40]

Harmonisation

The EC Treaty does not refer exclusively to 'harmonisation' of laws. Articles 94 and 95(1) use 'approximation' of laws instead, which conveys a lesser degree of uniformity than harmonisation. Confusion is caused, however, by the use of the term "harmonisation measure" in Articles 95(4) and 95(5), which refer to a measure adopted under Article 95(1).

Article 94 empowers the Council to issue Directives to approximate the laws, regulations or administrative provisions of Member States that "directly affect the establishment or functioning of the common market". The Council must act unanimously on a Commission proposal. By contrast, Article 95(1) authorises the Council acting by qualified majority on a Commission proposal (under the co-decision procedure)[41] to adopt

---

[37] In *Amministrazione delle Finanze dello Stato v Simmenthal SpA (No.2)* [1978] ECR 629, the ECJ stated that a national court must set aside a legal rule that conflicts with a provision of Community law.

[38] To have direct effect, an EU provision must 1) be clear and unambiguous, enabling the national court to identify the rights and obligations of individuals, 2) be unconditional, and 3) require no further action from EU and national authorities (*Van Gend en Loos v Nederlandse Tariefcommissie* [1963] ECR 1). The ECJ has extended the principal of vertical direct effect (i.e. rights conferred on individuals against national institutions) to Directives (*Van Duyn v Home Office* [1975] ECR 1337).

[39] The principle of indirect effect states that national courts are required to interpret their national law in the light of the purpose and wording of the Directive, especially if that law is specifically enacted to implement the Directive (*Von Colson v Land Nordrhein-Westfahlen* [1984] ECR 1891).

[40] The countries studied tend to transpose the financial regulation Directives (see section 2.4) into national law almost word for word (see sections 3.1, 4.1 and 5.1); i.e. there is little transformation of the Directives' content on placement in the national legal systems.

[41] Article 251, EC Treaty.

measures to approximate the laws, regulations or administrative provisions of Member States that "have as their object the establishment and functioning of the internal market".

Article 95(1) does not apply to fiscal provisions, which therefore require unanimity in the Council to be ratified.[42] Since unanimity is difficult to achieve, especially in relation to tax matters, the Council has passed few direct tax harmonisation measures.[43] Consequently EU developments in direct taxation have been by ECJ case law.[44]

Weatherill and Beaumont state that it would "likely to be fruitless" to introduce a single harmonised system, due to the diversity across the Community.[45] They express that replacing national rules by one Community rule is "a discredited option in most circumstances" because the accompanying "elimination" of the Member States' diversity would "stifle tradition and ... ossify existing practice, thereby deterring innovation by business".[46] The alternative taken is "to adopt different traditions within a flexible Community framework" and to emphasize "administrative cooperation".[47] Sometimes the Community may use a "minimum standard", which Member States can choose to exceed.[48] This differentiated pace of integration may be "inevitable and desirable" in a heterogeneous Community.[49]

Arnull, Dashwood, Dougan, Ross, Spaventa and Wyatt consider whether harmonisation facilitates the working of the Internal Market,[50] in particular company law and direct tax measures. The rationale of company law harmonisation is that it enables freedom of establishment, which different national rules of Member States would otherwise discourage.[51] Article 44(2)(g) of the EC Treaty supplies the legal basis for such harmonisation,[52] stating that the Council and Commission may "carry out the duties devolving upon them under the preceding provisions [the right of establishment] by coordinating ... the safeguards which ... are

[42] Article 95(2), EC Treaty. Unanimity is required for the "harmonisation" (not approximation) of indirect taxes (Article 93, EC Treaty).

[43] Directives 90/434/EEC (the Mergers Directive) and 90/435/EEC (the Parent/Subsidiary Directive) are examples.

[44] See section 2.3.

[45] (1999), *EU Law*, 556.

[46] Ibid.

[47] Ibid., 556–557.

[48] Ibid., 557.

[49] Ibid.

[50] (2006), *Wyatt and Dashwood's European Union Law*, chapter 20.

[51] Ibid., 850.

[52] Ibid.

required by Member States of companies or firms ... with a view to making such safeguards equivalent throughout the Community."

Arnull et al. explain that the company law harmonisation measures address the following issues: 1) differences between national rules that cause economic entities to be unfamiliar with those in another Member State, 2) differences between national rules that cause varying requirements for establishment, and 3) national rules or practices inhibiting cross-border establishment.[53] They conclude: "There has been a shift in emphasis [in recent years] from a model of the internal market in which the price of freedom of movement might be harmonisation, bringing with it uncompetitive levels of regulation, towards a model of the internal market in which freedom of movement, regulatory competition and overall competitiveness play a larger and more significant role".[54] Note the move away from harmonisation, also observed by Weatherill and Beaumont.[55]

By contrast, Arnull et al. argue that whilst the ECJ's interpretation of domestic tax legislation in restricting fundamental freedoms is consistent with its approach in other parts of "national regulatory competence", its consideration of justifications for these restrictions is "more questionable".[56] In particular, 1) the "cohesion of the tax system" defence has been defined "so narrowly as to deprive it of useful effect";[57] 2) the "mandatory requirements in the general interest" defence excludes national laws that aim to avoid tax revenue reduction or tax base erosion,[58] which has the outcome of making Member States treat tax collected in other States as equivalent to tax taken by them in the home State – this result has effects similar to those of positive harmonisation measures enacted under Article 94 of the EC Treaty,[59] rather than to those of the negative harmonisation resulting from applying directly effective Treaty rules.[60]

---

[53] Ibid, 865, 867 and 870. Discussion of the Directives is outside the scope of this section, which considers harmonisation of laws within the EU in general terms.

[54] Ibid., 875.

[55] See above in this subsection.

[56] *European Union Law*, 904–905.

[57] Ibid., 905. See section 2.3.1.

[58] This defence is referred to as "overriding reasons in the general interest" in section 2.3.

[59] See above in this subsection.

[60] Arnull et al., *European Union Law*, 905–906.

Comment

EU law has been superimposed on the national legal systems of Member States rather than transplanted. This is particularly true for the twelve States that joined the EU since 2000,[61] because they were required to implement an acquis communautaire developed over more than forty years by other decision-makers. In addition, most of these countries have legal systems that were shaped by communist rule during many of these years. By contrast, there was no communist input to the early development of Community law.

Wade Channell states that there are three core problems for postcommunist countries in implementing law that support the free market and democratic government:

1. *Lack of Ownership.* Foreign laws are often translated without sufficient attempt to adapt them to the local legal and commercial culture. Local users of such laws are not consulted and the reform agenda is decided by external donors.
2. *Insufficient Resources.* Law reforms are implemented too quickly and cheaply. The new laws are drafted, often by expatriate experts, passed by the legislature and explained to the legal community, culminating in no meaningful change. There should be wide-ranging public education and institutional reform as a basis for implementation.
3. *Excessive segmentation.* There may be hyperfocus on particular areas, which ignores systemic issues. For instance, judicial education in commercial concepts should be coupled with enforcement improvements.[62]

These issues are of concern in the transposition of EU Directives into Estonian, Polish and Latvian law. Since the relevant national rules have been enacted only recently, since information is sparse on enforcement in these countries, and since the focus of chapters 3, 4 and 5 is on compliance of national law with Community free movement of capital rules and with the financial regulation Directives, the comparison of national law with EU law concerns the content of these rules rather than their implementation.[63]

Harmonisation has become less of a crucial issue for the EU in recent years due to the trend away from it and towards free movement, regulatory competition and administrative cooperation.[64] However, one can argue

---

[61] Bulgaria, Cyprus, Czech Republic, Estonia, Hungary, Latvia, Lithuania, Malta, Poland, Romania, Slovakia and Slovenia.

[62] Channell (2005), *Carnegie Working Papers*, No. 57, 4–8.

[63] See section 1.3.2.

[64] See above in the subsection '*Harmonisation*'.

that whilst EU institutional policy has gone in this direction, the ECJ continues to harmonise direct tax law by allowing little scope for Member States to justify free movement restrictions.[65] Is this right, given that direct taxation is within Member States' area of national competence? It depends on one's priorities and perception of the Community. The EU institutions consider free movement at least as important as States' tax revenues (as long as the States are able to pay their dues to the EU budget), but States tend to emphasise taxation. Similarly, these institutions look to the Community as a unit, evident, for instance, in the Commission's proposal for a Common Consolidated Tax Base, whilst the Member States consider their national jurisdiction to be the unit, whose interests are pursued within the Community framework.

1.3.2 The methodology used for the comparison

Professor Vernon Palmer indicates that whilst comparative law has one method: "to compare and contrast norms, institutions, cultures, attitudes, methodologies and legal systems", it has many techniques which are called 'methods': "historical, functional, evolutionary, structural, thematic, empirical and statistical comparisons … from a micro or macro" perspective.[66] His four case studies show methods used in various breadth and depth. Although the first two cases concern Sotho law, the techniques used therein can be applied to Member States.

I. Inquiry into Sotho customary law, 1872

A commission of European magistrates put abstract questions to Basotho chiefs and councillors and to two French missionaries about Sotho law and custom. The questions were constructed in English and translated into Sesotho. They comprised Western legal concepts. The answers were translated back to English and revealed differences from English law in content, culture, language, history and religion. Although the method used was simple, inexpensive and ethnocentric,[67] it evoked a reasonable description of Sotho law and custom, and therefore a fairly accurate transfer of legal ideas, even though English and Sotho law in 1872 were very dissimilar.[68]

---

[65] Nine of the thirteen cases in section 2.3 are decided in favour of the taxpayer.

[66] Palmer (2005), *American Journal of Comparative Law*, 53, 262–263.

[67] The method was 'Eurocentric' and, in particular, 'Anglocentric'.

[68] Palmer, *American Journal*, 266–273.

II. Inquiry into Sotho family law, 1976

Sebastian Poulter's study into Sotho law involved:

1. reading the legal and ethnographic records of Sesotho law and society;
2. reviewing Sesotho family law judgments;
3. assembling an expert panel with judicial experience to discuss unsettled and unclear points of law;
4. conducting interviews with ladies in two villages about women's issues, such as widows' right to land and childbearing.

Poulter found that several versions of the law coexisted. He reconstructed all versions from 1850 to 1976, comparing and contrasting them with the judgments and panel discussions, thereby presenting a developmental history of Sesotho law over this period.[69]

III. Comparative study of pure economic loss in thirteen EU legal systems, 2003

An international team of tort/comparative lawyers drafted twenty factual hypothetical cases in English that explored different aspects of pure economic loss. This factual approach reduces distortions from the normative terminology of the enquiry's framework system. The three response levels from 'surface to core' are as follows.

1. *Operative Rules*, which state how judges have decided the case, whether doctrine agrees with the judgment, and whether solutions are the same as those in the past or are recent.
2. *Descriptive Formants*, which provide lawyers' reasons in support of the rules, each solution's degree of consistency with legislation and principles, how each solution is reasoned, and whether the solution relies on legal rules and/or public or procedural legal provisions.
3. *Metalegal Formants*, which are broader elements influencing each solution, such as economic factors and policy considerations.

This method yielded insights and knowledge about pure economic loss in the EU. However, it is on too large a scale to apply outside large harmonisation or codification projects.[70]

---

[69] Ibid., 273–275.

[70] Ibid., 276–281.

IV. European Code of Obligations

The Lando Commission, operating from 1982 to 1996, consisted of comparative law academics across Europe. Their objective was to construct a European Code of Obligations, which would form a foundation for a future European Code of Contracts, could be used by Member States, courts and arbitrators to govern their international contracts, and could be a model for legal development and harmonisation. The Commission formed a set of principles from sixteen legal systems using doctrinal works, national cases, codes and statutes, and international and EU legislation and conventions. The notes to each Article neither showed variations in this principle, nor why the Commissioners selected a particular rule; nor did they explicitly compare the laws of one country with another.[71]

Comment

The first method is subjective and investigatory as to Sotho law and custom. Given the limited resources, the study was successful, giving a general picture of Sotho legal practice. The second technique creates an historical record of Sotho law, especially family law. It is thorough and provides triangulation of different sources of evidence. Although conducted by just one researcher, it required substantial resources of his time, and input from other people in order to produce an accurate account.

The third method focuses in detail on one aspect of Member States' laws. It looks at the application of the specific provisions to cases, and at reasons behind the solutions proposed, including non-legal influences. It is the most comprehensive and unbiased technique of the four. However, it required many researchers, detailed analysis and considerable documentation.

The fourth method lacks both depth and objectivity. The Code of Obligations must be fair to all parties, and applicable in and acceptable to every Member State. Unlike the first three techniques, it creates new rules, rather than comparing existing laws on specific criteria. In these circumstances, subjectivity is unavoidable.

Each method is suitable for the objectives of each case study. The first study elicits a knowledge of Sotho law and custom from structured interviews. The second investigation produces a 126 year history of Sotho

---

[71] Ibid., 285–288. The principles are published in English by the Commission on European Contract Law (Lando Commission) at http://frontpage.cbs.dk/law/commission_on_european_contract_law/PECL%20engelsk/engelsk_partI_og_II.htm, and are "intended to be applied as general rules of contract law in the European Union" (Article 1:101(1)).

law from various sources. The third study provides a comprehensive examination of one legal aspect across European systems from in-depth case analysis. The fourth study produces a code applicable to all Member States from an inspection of black letter laws from these countries by European comparative lawyers of different nationalities.

I concur with Professor Palmer's conclusion.

> "There is not, and indeed cannot be a single exclusive method that comparative law research should follow. The tasks of teaching, research, law reform or historical investigation are too varied and contingent to be achieved by a single approach. ... [T]he best approach will always be adapted in terms of the specific purposes of the research, the subjective abilities of the researcher, and the affordability of the costs. ... [C]omparative law ... must be accessible and its methods must be flexible." [72]

Kötz' functional method and Legrand's critique

Professor Hein Kötz argues for the primary, but not exclusive, use of the functional method in comparative law.[73] Professor Pierre Legrand is its most ardent critic. Legrand proposes an alternative model that is rooted in and emerges from legal culture.[74] This model is difficult to apply due to its complexity.

Kötz states that comparative law investigations begin with a question or working hypothesis. From the fundamental methodological principle of functionality flow all the other rules that determine which laws to compare, the comparison's scope, and the creation of a comparative law system. "The question to which any comparative study is devoted must be posed in purely functional terms; the problem must be stated without any reference to the concepts of one's own legal system." [75]

The comparatist must consider statute, custom, trade usage, legal writing, general business conditions and standard-form contracts. He must learn about foreign civilizations, especially those whose law has generated the legal system families.[76] Except in moral and ethical areas of social life, such as divorce and adoption by unmarried people, "[d]ifferent legal systems give the same or very similar solutions, even as to detail, to the

[72] Ibid., 290.

[73] Zweigert and Kötz (1998), *An Introduction to Comparative Law*, chapter 3.

[74] Legrand (2006), *Journal of Comparative Law*, 1, 365–460.

[75] Zweigert and Kötz, *Comparative Law*, 34.

[76] Ibid., 36.

same problems of life, despite the great differences in their historical development, conceptual structure and style of operation".[77]

In general, developed countries fulfil the requirements of legal business in a similar way. Consequently, the comparatist can be satisfied if the conclusion of his research is that the systems he has compared produce similar practical outcomes. If he finds substantial differences, however, he must check that the terms of his original question were solely functional and that he has researched sufficiently widely.[78]

The comparatist should prepare separate reports for each legal system before the comparison. No report should contain critical evaluation.[79] To make the comparison, the solutions from the different jurisdictions must be freed from their conceptual context so that they may be seen in the light of their function to fulfil a specific legal need.[80]

Next, we must build a system that is flexible and has sufficiently broad concepts to include the functionally comparable heterogeneous legal entities. For example, a claim for unjust enrichment may be a claim for restitution, for rescission of contract and a claim in tort in three different legal systems. The comparative law system must find a higher concept for each of the functions of restitutionary claims, such as " 'restitution of payments gone wrong', 'restitution for appropriating the property of others', 'restitution for unjustifiably using another's thing' ".[81]

The comparatist must critically evaluate what he has discovered, stating whether the solutions are equally valid or one is superior. He may form a new solution from elements of different national solutions.[82]

Legrand describes 'functionalism' as "[d]iscarding the contents of experience and values, eliding the concrete law, lacking any critical vocation, betraying a fundamentally technical perspective, and accounting for a view of comparative legal studies as essentially utilitarian".[83] He also states:

> "Kötz's calculative goal is to overthrow difference, to coerce it, to manage it with a view to achieving the reformulation and the re-formation of the local law in terms of what is 'best'. Under Kötz's guardian eye and in the

[77] Ibid., 39.
[78] Ibid., 40.
[79] Ibid., 43.
[80] Ibid., 44.
[81] Ibid.
[82] Ibid., 46–47.
[83] Legrand, *Journal of Comparative Law*, 394–395.

name of 'bestness', disconcerting or distracting singularities will be overlooked, differences will be suppressed".[84]

The problem is Kötz's claim that functionality is the fundamental methodological principle from which flows all the other rules determining the laws to compare, the comparison's scope and the creation of a comparative law system.[85] Kötz has one goal: to compare the content of functionally similar legal rules of different jurisdictions in order to determine, outside the context of national culture, which solution is 'superior', which is not defined. Whilst this is plausible in some contexts, such as a methodology for producing the European Code of Obligations,[86] it is unsuitable in others, especially if the purpose of the study is to explain differences in national laws and/or legal systems. In these instances, legal culture is an integral component of the investigation.

Legrand states that the comparatist's goal is "to re-present a legal culture in ways that have greater interpretive power than is offered by the traditional rule-based model".[87] In the comparative study of pure economic loss,[88] the 'interpretive power' of legal culture is successfully applied. I choose a functional method for reasons set out below.

Reasons for selecting a functional method

The book is split into two sequential parts – identifying provisions of Estonian, Polish and Latvian law that do not comply with the EU free movement of capital rules (chapters 2–5), and investigating the effect of such restrictions on cross-border capital flows (chapters 6–7).[89] For the first part, I need to know what the national breaches of the free movement of capital are, rather than why they exist. It is therefore pertinent to identify them by comparing national law with EU law on the basis of the ECJ's approach,[90] which is preferable in this research to a literal

---

[84] Ibid., 394.

[85] See above in this subsection.

[86] See the subsection '*IV. European Code of Obligations*', above in section 1.3.2.

[87] Legrand, *Journal of Comparative Law*, 389. Legrand defines 'legal culture' as "the sub-culture that is constituted among law specialists, especially as regards the repository of those elements that partake in the stable, general and unconscious" (ibid., 388).

[88] See the subsection '*III. Comparative study of pure economic loss in thirteen EU legal systems, 2003*', above in section 1.3.2.

[89] See section 1.1.

[90] See chapter 2.

technique, an historic approach or a method based on the legal culture of the three countries concerned.

Two further reasons for applying a functional method concern the status of EU law relative to that of the Member States, which makes the comparison of national law with Community law unique among comparator systems. Firstly, EU law is supreme over the national laws of the Member States in the sense that the latter must comply with it. In *Costa v ENEL*,[91] the ECJ stated:

> "[T]he law stemming from the [EEC] Treaty,[92] an independent source of law, could not, because of its special and original nature, be overridden by domestic legal provisions ... without being deprived of its character as Community Law and without the legal basis of the Community itself being called into question."

The Court provided explicit guidance in *Amministrazione delle Finanze dello Stato v Simmenthal SpA (No.2)*:[93]

> "[EEC Treaty][94] provisions and [directly applicable] measures not only by their entry into force render automatically inapplicable any conflicting provision of current national law but ... also preclude the valid adoption of new national measures to the extent to which they would be incompatible with Community provisions."

Secondly, The ECJ applies EU law to Member States and their nationals in the same way, without distinction as to the legal system and culture in each specific State.[95]

The method

For each national provision which applies beyond the borders of the Member State concerned, I ask the three questions below in the order stated.

Is there a capital movement?

Is there a restriction on the free movement of capital?

---

[91] [1964] ECR 585.

[92] Treaty Establishing the European Economic Community; this treaty was incorporated into the EC Treaty, which recently became the Treaty on the Functioning of the European Union.

[93] [1978] ECR 629.

[94] See note 92.

[95] This consistency is present in the six 'Commission v Member State' cases in section 2.1.2.

Is there an acceptable reason for restricting the free movement of capital?

If the answer to the first two questions is 'yes' and the answer to the third question is 'no', then I conclude that the national rule in an unjustified restriction on the free movement of capital, which is contrary to Article 56 of the EC Treaty (requiring abolition on all restrictions on the movement of capital and on payments between Member States and between States and third countries). Any other combination of answers means that the national rule complies with Article 56.

Is there a capital movement?

'Capital movements' are defined by the nomenclature in Annex I to Directive 88/361/EEC.[96]

Is there a restriction on the free movement of capital?

If nationals of other Member States are treated less favourably than those of the home State, the measure in question restricts the free movement of capital, even if it is applied equally to both groups.[97] In direct tax cases, the non-resident taxpayer's situation must be 'objectively comparable' with that of a resident taxpayer in the Member State whose rule he/she is challenging.[98]

Is there an acceptable reason for restricting the free movement of capital?

The EC Treaty provides several justifications for restricting free capital movement, which are further developed by the ECJ's case law.[99] Property and direct tax cases have parallel but distinct judicial law.[100] Defences cannot permit arbitrary discrimination or covert restriction of free movement of capital and payments.[101]

A functional approach is also applied to the financial services legislation

I inspect all cross-border provisions of the national financial services legislation for compliance with the relevant regulatory Directive.[102] Occasionally, a national rule omits elements of the Directive or includes terms prohibited by the Directive.

---

[96] See section 2.1.1.
[97] See section 2.1.2.
[98] See section 2.3.
[99] See section 2.1.3.
[100] See sections 2.1.4 and 2.3 respectively.
[101] Article 58(3), EC Treaty.
[102] See section 2.4.

The method in action

1. Identify the provisions in the relevant Act with a cross-border element

Consider, for instance, the Estonian Insurance Activities Act 2004 (EIAA). The first measure with a cross-border element is s.29(5). The excerpt from the Act is as follows.

> "Division 2
> Activities of Estonian Insurance Undertakings in Foreign States
> s.29. Bases of activities of insurance undertakings in foreign state
> …
> (5) … ***Estonian insurance undertakings shall not engage in cross-border activities in third countries***."

2. Place each selected provision in the capital movement restrictions identification list

This list has the sections on the left with a description of their content, and three columns which correspond to the questions.[103] The answers at this stage are 'yes' (√), 'maybe/discuss' (?) and 'no' (X). I sometimes put a brief comment by the answer.

3. Review and expand the list entry to make a pertinent comment

The comment for s.29(5) of the EIAA states that Estonian insurance firms are not permitted to provide cross-border services to countries outside the EEA, and explains that this is an unjustified restriction on the free movement of capital since Articles 60(2) and 296(1)(b) of the EC Treaty are unlikely to apply.[104]

Comparator national law sections

Sections 4.1.7, 4.3.3 and 4.4.2 compare the free movement of capital restrictions in Polish law with those of Estonian law for financial services, taxation and property respectively. Sections 5.1.8, 5.3.3 and 5.4.6 compare capital movement restrictions in Latvian law with those of Estonian and Polish law over the same respective subjects. These comparisons are made on a functional basis in order to prepare this information for the construction of a legal index for each of the three Member States in section 6.1.[105]

---

[103] See the subsection '*The method*', above in section 1.3.2.
[104] See section 3.1.5.
[105] Section 1.4 shows how restrictions on cross-border capital movement are scaled for the legal index.

Table 1-1: Extract from capital movement restrictions identification list: Estonia

Description	Section No.	'Capital movement' as defined in Annex I	Restriction on capital movement amounts to a restriction on the free movement of capital	Derogation applicable
Prohibition of acquisition of immovable by foreign state in certain areas	6(2)	√	√	X
Insurance Activities Act 2004				
Estonian insurance undertakings shall not engage in cross-border activities in third countries	***29(5)***	√	√	***X Article 60(2) EC***
Refusal of authorisation to found branch in third country because of no legal basis etc.	33(5)	√	√ Potentially	X

The functional comparison identifies provisions from the national laws with similar content and assesses which is more restrictive of the free movement of capital. I compare s.29(5) of the EIAA with the equivalent part of the Polish Act of 22 May 2003 on Insurance Activity (PIAA) in section 4.1.7, concluding that Estonia and Poland equally restrict the free movement of capital because the PIAA does not consider the provision of cross-border insurance services to and from non-EEA countries.

Comment

The functional method used differs from that advocated by Professor Kötz in that it has two parts: 1) a comparison of EU law with national law, and 2) a comparison of national restrictions. The first step is designed to find differences between the EU and national free movement of capital rules; the questions asked for the comparison are based on the Community's position, especially that of the ECJ. By contrast, Kötz's method is intended to find similarities between national laws.[106]

Kötz's technique compares national rules on an equal basis in a functional system.[107] I use a comparative law system for the second part of the comparison with national laws having equal weight, but this is less specific than that of Kötz, and is used to identify differences in the national laws rather than similarities. For instance the Estonian and Polish financial services laws in section 4.1.7 are compared on the basis of their content within the national Acts, as follows.

Table 1-2: Comparison table for Estonian and Polish financial services legislation

<table>
<tr><th>Financial services area</th><th>Comparison content</th><th>Estonian legislation</th><th>Polish legislation</th></tr>
<tr><td>Investment funds</td><td rowspan="5">Extent of restriction on the cross-border free movement of capital over the particular financial services area</td><td>Investment Funds Act</td><td>Investment Funds Act</td></tr>
<tr><td>Securities</td><td>Securities Market Act</td><td>Public Offer Act
Trading in Financial Instruments Act</td></tr>
<tr><td>Credit institutions</td><td>Credit Institutions Act</td><td>Banking Law</td></tr>
<tr><td>Insurance activities</td><td>Insurance Activities Act</td><td>Insurance Activities Act</td></tr>
<tr><td>Insurance mediation</td><td>Insurance Activities Act</td><td>Insurance Mediation Act</td></tr>
</table>

[106] See the subsection '*Kötz' functional method and Legrand's critique*', above in section 1.3.2.
[107] Ibid.

My method is designed for a narrow application–the comparison of laws concerning the freedom of movement of capital, with a view to ascertaining their effect on cross-border capital movements. Consequently, it is less generally applicable than the functional technique proposed by Professor Kötz.

1.4 Determining the effect of legal barriers on capital flows

This section describes the methodology used to determine the impact of national laws restricting the free movement of capital on cross-border flows to and from Estonia, Poland and Latvia. As these flows are numerical, it is necessary to convert the language-based comparison described in section 1.3.2 to an index so that the magnitudes of legal restrictions and capital movements can be represented together.

Dr. Raphael La Porta and his colleagues apply legal indices in order to assess how national laws affect the depth and performance of stock markets. Appendix F describes three of their published papers and makes comments on the analysis and on the use of these indices. Dr. Mathias Siems' criticisms contained therein emphasise the need to take care with the comparison on which construction of each index is based.

Appendix F concludes that La Porta et al. should narrow their research objectives and use fewer indices in order to improve the statistical accuracy of their analysis. Although econometric methods are absent from section 7.1, this point relating research focus to accuracy also applies to the assessment made in that section. In addition, the investigation made there is concerned with one distinct relationship – the effect of national legal barriers on cross-border capital flows.

Accordingly, one legal index is constructed that measures the extent to which Estonian, Latvian and Polish laws comply with the EU's free movement of capital rules.[108] Legal enforcement is not considered due to lack of availability of information for these countries, and also because Article 234 of the EC Treaty provides a procedure for the ECJ to give national courts guidelines as to the compatibility of national law with EU law. It is in the interests of these courts, as legal institutions of the Member States, to ensure that Community law is implemented in practice.

[108] See the subsection '*Constructing the legal index*', below.

Constructing the legal index

In chapters 3, 4 and 5, I assess how much similar rules in Estonia, Poland and Latvia restrict the free movement of capital.[109] For each comparison, the following scale is applied:
0 = national law allows cross-border capital movement;
1 = national law imposes minor restrictions on cross-border capital movement;
2 = national law places major restrictions on cross-border capital movement;
3 = national law prevents cross-border capital movement.

The scores are added for each country, and this sum is divided by the number of national rules considered to obtain a value for its legal index. The functional basis of this comparison enables the application of a similar standard for 0–3 classification for Estonia, Poland and Latvia.[110]

Dividing the legal index into subsidiary indices

In table 6-2, subsidiary legal indices are calculated by direction of capital movement (inflow or outflow), by location of such movement (flows within the EEA or to/from third countries) and by national law topic. The legal areas that most restrict the free movement of capital to and from Estonia, Poland and Latvia correspond to the following industrial sectors: investment funds, investment services, credit institutions, insurance services, insurance mediation, taxation and real property.

The subsidiary indices are computed by dividing the total value of the relevant index scores by the number of corresponding cross-country comparisons. For example, in table 6-1, there are 3 observations relating to investment funds. For Estonia, the total index score for these funds is 4(=1+1+2); the subsidiary legal index for Estonian investment funds is therefore 1.33(=4/3). This process is repeated for Polish investment funds (the sub-index is 0.33(=(0+0+1)/3)), Latvian investment funds (the sub-index is 1.67(=(2+2+1)/3)), and for all other classifications for the three countries; table 6-2 shows the values of all the subsidiary legal indices.

Putting the legal index and subsidiary indices on a time basis

The indices are current values – they refer to the Estonian, Polish and Latvian legislative and regulatory position in 2007.[111] Since the data on

---

[109] Although chapter 3 reports specifically on Estonia, it is chapters 4 and 5 that compare national legal provisions.

[110] See section 6.1 for construction of the legal index for all three Member States.

[111] There are timing differences in the comparison of national law with EU law for the 3 countries. However, these variations are small in relation to the time period

cross-border capital flows are presented on an annual and/or quarterly basis, the indices must be placed on a timeline in order to make a meaningful comparison between such flows and national laws restricting the free movement of capital. This is done by assuming that there were no cross-border capital movements prior to the implementation of the particular national legal provision; consequently, the index value before the implementation date is 3. Although this assumption is not strictly true, it is sufficiently accurate for the laws/flows comparison in section 7.1 to be made.[112]

Comparing the legal index and subsidiary indices with cross-border flows using graphs

The legal index and its subsidiary indices are compared with the relevant cross-border capital movements by plotting each index and its corresponding flows against time. In section 7.1, this is done systematically, first by developing an overall position (section 7.1.2), then by considering capital inflows and outflows, capital movements within the EEA/between the EEA and third countries, and flows to and from the industrial sectors (sections 7.1.3, 7.1.4 and 7.1.5 respectively).

The capital flows data are taken from Estonian, Polish and Latvian international accounts and other statistical sources.[113] The data are placed in a Microsoft Excel spreadsheet, and, if not in Euros at source, are converted from national currency to Euros at the applicable exchange rate.[114] The relevant legal index/sub-index is added to the table of cross-border capital movements. A graph with two vertical axes–one for the capital flows and the other for the index–is plotted in Microsoft Excel from the data in this table. The completed graph is imported into the book and pertinent comments are made.

Illustrating non-legal determinants of cross-border capital flows using graphs

Appendix E identifies both economic, quantitative determinants of capital movements, such as the real interest rate and exchange rate expectations, and country-specific, qualitative factors affecting flows, such as infrastructure and institutional quality. Since the latter are difficult to

---

considered for assessment of whether Estonian, Polish and Latvian rules limit cross-border capital flows, which is 1997-2007 (or shorter period if data are unavailable).

[112] See section 7.1.1, especially note 9.

[113] The introduction to chapter 7 lists these sources.

[114] This is the average exchange rate for the quarter or year–see chapter 7 note 7.

define and measure, section 7.1.6, which considers non-legal factors affecting cross-border capital movements to/from Estonia, Poland and Latvia, uses those determinants identified in the 'economic indicators' subsection of Appendix E, namely the real interest rate, the inflation rate, the exchange rate against the Euro and against a basket of currencies, and the net barter terms of trade.[115]

In section 7.1.6, such factors are plotted against time along with cross-border capital flows for Estonia, Poland and Latvia.[116] There follows a description of the information conveyed by the graphs and an economic assessment for each of these Member States. This analysis is combined with information shown by the graphs in sections 7.1.2 and 7.1.3 to give an integrated portrait of how national legal provisions may have hindered cross-border capital flows to and from Estonia, Poland and Latvia in recent years. Although it is not possible to establish that restrictive laws cause smaller flows by this method, the comments in section 7.1.6 indicate that such a relationship is compatible with the data.

Comment

This methodology is used in preference to statistical analysis because of the exploratory nature of the research, and because of the need to find and investigate any observable correlation between national laws restricting the free movement of capital and the cross-border capital flows to/from Estonia, Poland and Latvia. As the comments on the La Porta et al. articles indicate,[117] considerable care is required with any subsequent statistical investigation. One would expect the association between the legal index and cross-border flows to be positive, other things being the same. However, a significant positive impact of the former on the latter would be surprising given the presence of several known determinants of capital flows.[118]

Chapter 7 contains the economic analysis investigating the effect of legal barriers in these Member States on cross-border capital movements. Chapter 8 draws conclusions from the research and makes suggestions for further investigation.

---

[115] Transaction costs are omitted–see chapter 7 note 86. GDP per capita is included as a control variable.

[116] See the subsection '*3. Non-legal factors affecting cross-border capital flows*' in section 7.1.6.

[117] See Appendix F.

[118] See Appendix E.

1.5 Canvassing the views of executives in the sectors most affected

1.5.1 Validation study methodology and profile of questionnaire returns

The purpose of the validation study

The validation study's objective is to confirm, refute and/or enrich the main research findings by investigating how national laws restricting the free movement of capital affect Estonian, Polish and Latvian organisations from the point of view of their executives. Combining the results from the study with those from the comparative law and descriptive economics increases the depth and robustness of the investigation into the impact of Estonian, Polish and Latvian law on cross-border capital movement.

Constructing the questionnaire

The first draft of the questionnaire consisted of 6 questions relating to the main research findings. It was piloted by providing it to a class of Ph.D. students for comment.[119] The suggestions made by the class and by my research supervisor were incorporated into the final draft, which contained 12 questions of greater precision with a tick-box format for most answers. A letter was written, which stated the purpose of the questionnaire and gave undertakings as to the confidentiality of the information sought. The questionnaire and letter were adapted to the recipient organisations according to their country and industrial sector.[120]

Selecting the recipient organisations

The questionnaire was sent to a stratified sample of Estonian, Polish and Latvian investment fund management companies, investment service providers, credit institutions, insurance service providers, insurance intermediaries and real property companies. Cross-border investment, financial, insurance and property service providers to Estonia, Poland and Latvia were also included. These industrial sectors were chosen as those most affected by national law restricting the free movement of capital.[121]

---

[119] The course topic of the class was question design for questionnaires and interviews.

[120] See Appendix C for the questionnaire and covering letter sent to organisations in each sector.

[121] In the research of national legislation and regulation undertaken for chapters 3, 4 and 5, most of the legal provisions concerning cross-border capital movements

The sample frame was each of the above Member States' financial regulator's lists of registered investment fund management companies, investment service providers, credit institutions, insurance service providers and insurance intermediaries. The population for the real property companies was those listed in the import/export directories for Estonia and Latvia, and those belonging to the British-Polish Chamber of Commerce.[122] Every 'nth' enterprise was selected from these lists after a random choice of the first organisation from 'n' options; the size of 'n' depended on the length of the list.

In addition to the 243 organisations selected in this way, the head offices of 10 large banks were contacted in order to provide an overview of investment in Estonia, Poland and Latvia. The response rate was 5.3%–a total of 13 replies, which was too few to provide a balanced sample. A follow-up e-mail with attached questionnaire and letter produced no further replies.

Sending translated questionnaires

The questionnaire was translated into Estonian, Polish and Latvian. A further 273 copies were sent to investment fund management companies, investment service providers, credit institutions, insurance service providers, insurance intermediaries and real property companies in these three Member States. The response rate was 9.2%–a total of 25 replies. 38 replies were produced from the two batches, which was an overall response rate of 7.2% from 526 questionnaires. This was a sufficiently large number from which to draw general conclusions.

The profile of questionnaire returns

Thirteen, sixteen and six responses were received from Estonian, Polish and Latvian enterprises respectively, with at least one reply from each Estonian industrial sector, from all but one Polish sector (investment fund management companies) and from three Latvian sectors (investment fund management companies, credit institutions and life assurance companies). There was just one reply from a cross-border service

---

related to these sectors and to direct taxation. As the latter affects all organisations, it was not included as a separate sector.

[122] No import/export directory for Poland could be accessed after reasonable investigation. Using the British-Polish Chamber of Commerce Membership List to select real property companies introduces a British bias to service provision in this sector for Poland. However, this is a minor issue both because these organisations are only a small part of the validation survey and because their professional business involves cross-border capital flows between Poland and other countries.

company–an investment fund management company based in Luxembourg, but further information was given by the head offices of the two major banks that responded. Overall, there were at least two replies from every sector and no major omissions.

Comment

The responses to the questionnaire give sufficient information concerning the impact of national laws on the free movement of capital as perceived by the directors of Estonian, Polish and Latvian businesses to enhance and, to an extent, to endorse, the findings from the substantive research.[123] The validation study's purpose is therefore fulfilled. The report sent to those company executives requesting it contains a numerical breakdown of the questionnaire responses, and summarises how, in their view, legal rules regulating the free movement of capital affect their organisations.[124]

1.5.2 Conclusions

This chapter explains what the purpose of the research is, how it is addressed and how the methodology builds upon and adapts existing methodologies in comparative law and economics to pursue the objective of establishing the effect of national legal restrictions to free capital movement on cross-border flows for Estonia, Poland and Latvia. A validation study is introduced to triangulate the outcomes from the main research. Chapter 2 determines what the free movement of capital rules are in the European Community.

---

[123] See section 7.2 for the validation study report.

[124] Appendix D contains the report sent to the executives.

CHAPTER TWO

THE EUROPEAN LEGAL FRAMEWORK

> "[F]or the last two thousand years ... human creations ... were of overwhelming importance in shaping the future. They acted ... upon the minds of generations, sometimes directing, sometimes inspiring, sometimes confining them, always leaving ineradicable signs of their influence on the history of Europeans and of Europe. ... The most important of them are to be found in ancient Greece, the world the Romans made, early Christianity, and the barbarian incursions into western Europe in the closing centuries of antiquity. Between them, they constituted the foundations of a future Europe".[1]

Europe as a cultural and geographical concept has survived centuries of territorial struggle between its constituent countries, culminating in the foundation of the European Economic Community (EEC) in 1957. The EEC originally had six Member States: Belgium, France, Italy, Luxembourg, the Federal Republic of Germany and the Netherlands. Today its successor organisation, the European Union (EU), has twenty seven Member States and includes most of the territory of Europe.

The EU has three constituent parts: the European Community (EC), the Common and Foreign Security Policy, and Justice and Home Affairs. The EC includes the Internal Market, which was introduced into Treaty Establishing the European Community (EC Treaty) in 1987 by the Single European Act. The Internal Market "shall comprise an area without frontiers in which the free movement of goods, persons, services and capital is ensured in accordance with the provisions of this Treaty".[2]

---

[1] J. M. Roberts (1996), *The Penguin History of Europe*, 1.

[2] Article 14(2), EC Treaty. See section 1.2.3 for a discussion of the Internal Market. The position stated is that immediately prior to the recent enactment of the Lisbon Treaty, which has had a modest effect on EU law provisions relating to the Internal Market. For instance, the post-Lisbon statement of Article 14(2) is contained in Article 26(2) of the Treaty on the Functioning of the European Union, with only the minor change of "this Treaty" to "the Treaties". All references are to the pre-Lisbon rules.

Section 2.1 discusses the EC Treaty provisions on the free movement of capital. Section 2.2 summarises Regulation 2560/2001 and the Directives on payments and settlement. Section 2.3 considers the Commission's tax policy and EU case law relating to the tax derogations from the free movement of capital. Section 2.4 states the EU requirements for financial service providers to be authorised by the national regulator and considers authorisation to provide cross-border financial services. Section 2.5 states EU transitional measures on the purchase of real estate for the countries studied in chapters 3 (Estonia), 4 (Poland) and 5 (Latvia).

2.1 The EC Treaty: Articles 56-60

Article 56(1) of the EC Treaty states "[w]ithin the framework of the provisions set out in this chapter, all restrictions on the movement of capital between Member States and between Member States and third countries shall be prohibited. The other Articles in Title III Chapter 4 provide exceptions to this unequivocal statement.

2.1.1 How are capital movements defined?

The EC Treaty does not define 'capital movements'. The ECJ held in *Trummer and Mayer* that the nomenclature in Annex I to Directive 88/361/EEC (hereafter 'Annex I') defines 'capital movements', but that the list contained therein is "not exhaustive".[3] This nomenclature of capital movements includes foreign direct investment, investment in real estate, shares, bonds, long-term loans, money market instruments, credits relating to commercial transactions, insurance premiums, gifts, endowments, dowries and legacies. Furthermore, capital movements cover "all the operations necessary for the purposes of capital movements".[4]

This definition is wide and has included much case law. For instance, liquidation of an investment in real property,[5] a shareholding,[6] and the purchase of real estate by non-residents,[7] constituted 'capital movements' in Annex I. Nonetheless, we must carefully interpret the explanatory notes in the Annex. For example, "bonds" are defined as "[n]egotiable securities with a maturity of two years or more from issues for which the

[3] [1999] ECR I-1661.
[4] Annex I.
[5] *Trummer and Mayer* [1999] ECR I-1661.
[6] *Commission v France* [2002] ECR I-4781.
[7] *Reisch and Others* [2002] ECR I-2157.

interest rate and terms for the repayment of the principal and the payment of interest are determined at the time of issue”.[8] Does this include bonds convertible to shares in less than two years or floating rate notes of more than one year duration? If not, they would probably be classified as “Miscellaneous” capital movements under Title XIII of the nomenclature.

2.1.2 The ECJ narrowly construes restrictions on the free movement of capital

There are restrictions on the free movement of capital if like situations are treated differently or dissimilar situations the same. In particular, national legislation restricts the free movement of capital if it treats residents of other EU Member States less favourably than those of the home country. In six recent cases brought by the European Commission against Member States for introducing rules that breach Article 56 of the EC Treaty, the ECJ ruled in the Commission’s favour in all but one.

Commission v France [9]

The French government passed Decree No 93-1298, attaching the following rights to the share it held in Société Nationale Elf-Aquitaine: Article 2(1)–any shareholding exceeding one tenth of the capital or voting rights must first be approved by the Minister of Economic Affairs; Article 2(3)–the government could oppose any decision to transfer or use as security the capital of Elf-Aquitaine’s subsidiaries. The ECJ held that these rules hindered the purchase of shares in Elf-Aquitaine and dissuaded investors in other Member States from investing in this group. They therefore constituted a restriction on the movement of capital.

Commission v Belgium [10]

The Royal Decrees of 10 and 28 June 1994 respectively attached to the share held by the Belgian government in Société nationale de transport par canalisations and in Société de distribution du gaz SA the following rights: Article 3–the Energy Minister can oppose within 21 days of prior notice the transfer, use as security or change in the company’s strategic assets if (s)he considers that this adversely affects the national interest in the energy sector; Article 4–the Minister may appoint two government representatives to the Board of Directors, who may propose to him/her the

---

[8] Annex I.

[9] [2002] ECR I-4781.

[10] [2002] ECR I-4809.

annulment of any Board decision which they consider contrary to Belgium's energy policy. The ECJ held that these rules restricted the movement of capital but upheld them as derogations.[11]

Commission v Portugal [12]

Portuguese Decree-Law 65/94 states that the foreign entities may hold no more that 25% of the capital of Portuguese re-privatised companies, unless the re-privatisation legislation provides otherwise. The Portuguese government claimed that it did not apply this provision in practice and that the provision referred solely to investors who are not EU nationals. The ECJ rejected this argument. It held that the incompatibility of national laws with EU Treaty provisions (including those directly applicable) required amendment by law; administrative practices do not fulfil Treaty obligations because they create uncertainty as to persons' rights guaranteed therein. The Portuguese legislation therefore breached Article 56 of the EC Treaty.

Commission v Spain [13]

Article 3 of Spanish Law 5/1995 specifies a procedure of governmental prior approval for decisions relating to the privatisation of Spanish commercial entities, including voluntary liquidation, mergers, demergers, changes in the object clause and share purchases. The ECJ held that, although the procedure applied equally to residents and non-residents, it constituted a restriction on the movement of capital because it affected the position of share purchasers and therefore was liable to deter nationals from other Member States from investing in the Spanish entities.

Commission v United Kingdom [14]

Article 10(2) of the British Airports Authority's (BAA) Articles of Association specifies a system of Ministerial prior approval for decisions including the voluntary liquidation of BAA or one of its subsidiaries, disposal of an airport or BAA's surrender of control of an airport-owning subsidiary. Article 40(1) of the Articles prohibits a person from acquiring more than 15% of the voting rights in BAA. The ECJ held that both these provisions amounted to a restriction on the movement of capital because

---

[11] These derogations are discussed in section 2.1.3, under the subsection '*Derogations in the Commission's cases introduced in subsection 2.1.2*'.

[12] [2002] ECR I-4731.

[13] [2003] ECR I-4581.

[14] [2003] ECR I-4641.

they affected the position of share purchasers and therefore were liable to deter investors from other Member States.

Commission v Italy [15]

Article 1 of Italian Decree-Law 192/2001 automatically suspends voting rights attaching to holdings exceeding 2% of the shares of companies in the electricity and gas sectors where such rights are acquired by public entities that dominate their domestic markets and are not quoted on a stock exchange. The ECJ held that since the Decree-Law's purpose was to prevent "anti-competitive attacks" by public organisations operating in these sectors in other Member States, it dissuaded such undertakings from acquiring shares in Italian companies. Therefore the suspension of voting rights constituted a restriction on the free movement of capital.

Comment

The ECJ's argument in these cases is that the national rules made potential shareholders in other Member States less likely to acquire shares in the national companies at issue. The Court held that there was a restriction on the free movement of capital, even when, as in the Spanish case, the national provisions were applied equally to residents and non-residents. In all these cases, the ECJ upheld the Commission's argument as to there being a restriction.

2.1.3 Derogations from the free movement of capital

EU law provides several legitimate reasons for restricting the free movement of capital. These include the right to apply national tax law,[16] the prevention of infringement of national law and regulations in the field of taxation,[17] the prudential supervision of financial institutions,[18] formulating procedures for the purposes of administrative or statistical information,[19] public policy,[20] public security,[21] general interest,[22]

[15] [2005] ECR I-4933.
[16] Article 58(1)(a), EC Treaty.
[17] Article 58(1)(b), EC Treaty.
[18] Ibid.
[19] Ibid.
[20] Ibid.
[21] Ibid.
[22] In *Commission v Portugal* [2002] ECR I-4731, the ECJ held that the free movement of capital may be restricted by national rules that are justified by

defence,[23] and unilateral measures against a third country "for serious political reasons and on grounds of urgency".[24] The EU case law concerns taxation (see section 2.3) and public policy/security, which I discuss next.

Public policy and public security

Article 58(1)(b) of the EC Treaty states "[t]he provisions of Article 56 shall be without prejudice to the right of Member States ... to take measures which are justified on grounds of public policy or public security". These measures cannot be "a means of arbitrary discrimination or a disguised restriction on the free movement of capital and payments" provided by Article 56.[25]

For Article 58 to apply, the measure must be proportionate, i.e. appropriate for accomplishing the objective it pursues without going beyond what is necessary to attain it.[26] More specifically, the ECJ held in *Albore* that the principle of proportionality must be observed for "the requirements of public security" to justify exceptions to Article 56, which means that any derogation be "appropriate and necessary for achieving the aim in view".[27]

Public policy, public security and prior authorisation

In *Eglise de Scientologie and Scientology International*,[28] Article 5-1(I)(1) of French Law No. 66-1008 stated that if the Finance Minister established that a foreign investment represented a threat to public policy, public health or public security, he/she may, if there is no request for prior authorisation required under Article 3(1)(c) of this law, order the investor to discontinue the investment, or modify or restore the previous position. The ECJ held that Article 58(1)(b) of the EC Treaty precluded a system of prior authorisation for direct foreign investments which defines the relevant investments as being those that represent a threat to public policy and public security, without providing additional guidance to help the

---

"overriding requirements of the general interest" and which apply to all persons in the Member State concerned, provided that they are suitable for securing that State's objective and are proportionate.

[23] Article 296(1)(b), EC Treaty: a Member State can take measures to protect "the essential interests of its security with the production of or trade in arms, munitions and war material".

[24] Article 60(2), EC Treaty.

[25] Article 58(3), EC Treaty.

[26] *Commission v Belgium* [2000] ECR I-7587.

[27] [2000] ECR I-5965.

[28] [2000] ECR I-1335.

persons concerned to ascertain the specific circumstances in which prior authorisation is required.

The ECJ made the following points.

1. A national provision requiring prior authorisation for a direct foreign investment is a restriction on the free movement of capital.
2. Grounds for public policy and public security must be interpreted strictly because they are derogations from the fundamental principle of free movement of capital.
3. No Member State may determine the extent of these derogations unilaterally.
4. For a Member State to rely on public policy or public security, there must be a "genuine and sufficiently serious threat to a fundamental interest of society" [paragraph 17]. These derogations cannot be used to protect economic interests.
5. Measures justified on public policy and public security grounds must be necessary to protect the interests which they are intended to guarantee, in so far as less restrictive provisions cannot attain these objectives.
6. Whilst a system of prior authorisation is not necessarily contrary to Community Law (*Konle*, section 2.1.4), the system established in *Eglise de Scientologie* is contrary to the principle of legal certainty because individuals are unable to ascertain the scope of their rights and obligations deriving from Article 56 of the EC Treaty.
7. For foreign direct investment, a system of prior declaration is inadequate to counter a genuine and sufficiently serious threat to public policy and public security because of difficulties in identifying and isolating capital that has entered a Member State.

Hence, in the case of foreign direct investments, the ECJ requires a system of prior authorisation which specifically makes clear when such authorisation is required, given explicit genuine and sufficiently serious threats to public policy or public security.

In *Analir and Others*,[29] the ECJ considers prior administrative authorisation schemes in the context of freedom to provide services. For a PAAS to be justified, the national authority must show that it is indispensable to the imposition of public service obligations, and that it is proportionate to the aim pursued–i.e. this aim cannot be attained by measures less restrictive of the freedom to provide services, especially a system of declarations. A PAAS cannot legitimize discretionary conduct

[29] [2000] ECR I-1271.

by the national authorities that may neutralise the effectiveness of EU law provisions, especially those concerning a fundamental freedom.

To be justified, therefore, a PAAS must be founded on objective, non-discriminatory criteria, known previously to those seeking authorisation, thereby ensuring that the national authorities do not exercise their discretion arbitrarily. Additionally, all persons affected by the restrictive measure must be able to obtain a legal remedy.

To summarize, national restrictions protecting discretionary conduct are forbidden. There must be a legitimate objective–to counter a genuine and sufficiently serious threat to a fundamental interest of society. The restrictions must not go beyond what is necessary to attain this objective.

Derogations in the Commission's cases introduced in subsection 2.1.2

In *Commission v France*,[30] the ECJ held that the objective pursued by the national legislation–safeguarding petroleum supplies in a crisis, is a legitimate public interest. The investors are not told "the specific objective circumstances" in which the Minister will refuse authorisation to buy a 10% shareholding in Elf-Aquitaine, or in which the government will prevent the transfer or use as security of the assets of Elf-Aquitaine's subsidiaries [paragraph 50]. Hence, investors do not know their rights and obligations under Article 56 of the EC Treaty. This system does not fulfil the requirements of legal certainty and goes beyond what is necessary to attain the objective specified because the PAAS includes no precise, objective criteria.

In *Commission v Belgium*,[31] the Court held that the national legislation's objective–safeguarding energy supplies in a crisis, is a legitimate public interest. The Energy Minister initiates control in each specific case. No prior approval is required. Furthermore, the Minister must exercise his/her power of opposition within time-limits. The regime only concerns companies' strategic assets, especially the energy supply networks, and specific management decisions affecting these assets. The Minister may only intervene if there is a threat that the energy policy's objectives may be obstructed, and must provide a formal statement of reasons for intervention. The national courts may review his/her decision. The scheme therefore guarantees, on the basis of reviewable objective criteria, that the lines and conduits providing the main infrastructures conveying energy products are available. It fulfils the requirements of legal certainty. The Commission has not established that less restrictive

[30] [2002] ECR I-4781.

[31] [2002] ECR I-4809.

measures could attain the objective pursued. The legislation is therefore justified by the objective of protecting energy supplies in a crisis.

In *Commission v Portugal*,[32] the Court stated that Portugal's general financial interests are inadequate justification because they are economic grounds for such restricting free capital movement. In *Commission v Spain*,[33] the ECJ held that the government's objective of providing petroleum or telecommunications and electricity services in a crisis may be a public security justification. The national rules went beyond this objective because the authorities had a particularly broad discretion as to whether to grant prior approval. In *Commission v Italy*,[34] the Court held that the government's objective to safeguard energy supplies may justify restrictions on the free movement of capital under certain conditions. But the national limitation of voting rights of just one category of public enterprises in gas and electricity companies is unnecessary to attain this objective.

Reasons why the ECJ accepted the justification only in Commission v Belgium

In *Commission v Spain*,[35] the ECJ distinguished its judgment in *Commission v Belgium*.[36]

1. The Belgian system was one of "ex post facto opposition", which is less restrictive than prior approval [paragraph 78].
2. The Belgium system specifically listed the relevant strategic assets and the challengeable management decisions in each case.
3. The administrative authorities only intervened in cases in which the energy policy's objectives were threatened.
4. The national legislation required the authorities to give a formal statement of reasons for their decision.
5. The decision was subject to judicial review.

The requirements for a successful public policy/security derogation

Firstly, there must be a genuine and sufficiently serious threat to a fundamental interest of society. In *Commission v Belgium*, the threat is to energy supplies. A crisis is unnecessary–the Court held in *Campus Oil and Others*[37] that public security considerations justifying an obstacle to

32 [2002] ECR I-4731.
33 [2003] ECR I-4581.
34 [2005] ECR I-4933.
35 [2003] ECR I-4581.
36 [2002] ECR I-4809.
37 [1984] ECR 2727.

the free movement of goods include the objective of providing a minimum supply of petroleum products at all times. This reasoning applies to the free movement of capital.[38]

Secondly, the restrictive measures must be necessary for the protection of interests which they are intended to guarantee. This requirement is satisfied in *Commission v Belgium* since intervention "was strictly limited to cases in which objectives of the energy policy were jeopardised" (*Commission v Spain*, paragraph 78).

Thirdly, the measures must be proportionate i.e. not attainable by less restrictive measures. The ECJ in *Commission v Belgium* states "[t]he Commission has not shown that less restrictive measures could have been taken to attain the objective pursued" [paragraph 53].

Fourthly, the measures must observe the requirements of legal certainty. They must be specific, objective and known to the parties beforehand. Those in *Commission v Belgium* fulfil this requirement, since they list "specifically the strategic assets concerned and the management decisions which could be challenged in any given case" (*Commission v Spain*, paragraph 78).

Finally, the persons affected by the measures must have access to legal redress. This is so in *Commission v Belgium*, as "intervention must be supported by a formal statement of reasons and [is] subject [to] review by the courts" [paragraph 51].

Comment

The five requirements constitute a stiff test, consistent with the ECJ's view that derogations from a fundamental freedom must be "interpreted strictly".[39] The first requirement is specific to the public policy/security justification. Economic and financial objectives are not acceptable under this defence. However, such objectives are relevant to the national right to "take all requisite measures to prevent infringements of national law and regulations, in particular in the field of taxation and the prudential supervision of financial institutions".[40] The lack of EU case law on the 'prudential supervision' derogation is problematical, but it is arguable that this exception includes the right of national financial regulators to uphold their supervisory rules, provided that the measures taken are neither discriminatory nor restrictive of free capital movement.[41]

---

38 *Commission v Belgium* [2002] ECR I-4809.

39 *Eglise de Scientologie and Scientology International* [2000] ECR-1335.

40 Article 58(1)(b), EC Treaty. The avoidance of double taxation is an acceptable objective for national tax law–see section 2.3.

41 Article 58(3), EC Treaty.

The last four requirements extend to derogations from Article 56 of the EC Treaty other than public policy/security. Directive 2006/48/EC states that Member States must specify grounds for authorising credit institutions to provide services,[42] and that national regulators must give reasons for refusing or withdrawing authorisation.[43] Financial supervision must be proportionate, depending on the "nature, scale and complexity" of financial institutions' activities.[44] I apply the requirements to land cases in the next subsection.

2.1.4 The real property cases

Konle v Austria [45]

Article 70 of Austria's Act of Accession to the EU states that Austria may keep its existing legislation on secondary residences for five years from its date of accession.[46] The ECJ made the following points.

1. National laws concerning land purchase must comply with Articles 56–60 of the EC Treaty. Article 222 of the Treaty (which upholds national rules governing property ownership) does not preclude this requirement.
2. A Member State can justify its prior authorisation procedure by depending on a town and county planning objective, such as "maintaining, in the general interest, a permanent population and an economic activity independent of the tourist sector in certain regions" [paragraph 40].
3. To comply with Article 56, national measures must not be "applied in a discriminatory manner" and must be the least restrictive to achieve the objective [paragraph 40].
4. Since the applicant cannot provide indisputable proof of the land's future use, the authorities have latitude in determining the value of the information received which is "closely related to a discretionary power" [paragraph 41].
5. The ECJ did not permit discretion by the administrative authorities in the exercise of prior authorisation relating to currency exports. In this context, an "adequate system of declaration" would suffice [paragraph 44].

---

[42] Article 6. This reflects the fourth requirement.

[43] Articles 13 and 17(2). This reflects the fifth requirement in part.

[44] Guidelines on the Application of the Supervisory Review Process under Pillar 2.

[45] [1999] ECR I-3099.

[46] Austria joined the EU on 1 January 1995. *Konle* was therefore decided before the end of the transition period, which expired on 1 January 2000.

6. However, where property is acquired, prior verification reflects not only a need for information but can precipitate "refusal to grant authorisation, without necessarily being contrary to Community law" [paragraph 45].
7. A declaration procedure is therefore insufficient. Member States must be able to act if a breach of the agreed declaration is established after property purchase.
8. A fine or prior declaration that the sale is void if property use is unlawful would suffice. A prior authorisation system for land purchase contains an inherent "risk of discrimination" [paragraph 49].[47]
9. The derogation permitted by Article 70 only applies to legislation passed after the accession date if it is identical in substance to previous legislation or removes obstacles to the exercise of Community rights and freedoms in this legislation. Legislation establishing new procedures cannot be treated as legislation existing at the accession date.

Reisch and Others [48]

The ECJ held that a prior declaration procedure for the purchase of building plots with penalties for non-observance was compatible with Community law, but that a prior authorisation procedure for declarations suspected to be untrue or inconsistent with the Austrian legislation was not so compatible. Points from *Reisch* are as follows.

1 The exercise of "the right to acquire, use or dispose of immovable property" in another Member State creates capital movements [paragraph 29].

2 The prior declaration/authorisation procedures restrict the free movement of capital but are permitted if the national measures "pursue in a non-discriminatory way, an objective in the public interest" and are proportionate [paragraph 33]. 'General interest' in *Konle* is refined to 'public interest'.

[47] The judgment in *Salzmann* [2003] ECR I-4899 clarifies that this risk emerges from the scope that the administrative authority has to act in a discriminatory way under an authorisation procedure for the purchase of land. See the subsection '*Salzmann*', below in this section.

[48] [2002] ECR I-2157.

Salzmann [49]

The Court held that a prior authorisation procedure for land purchased for holiday purposes was contrary to Article 56 of the EC Treaty. The objective was in the public interest, but the authorisation procedure gave latitude to the administrative authority that amounted to a discretionary power and therefore "could be applied in a discriminatory way" [paragraph 47]. Additionally, prior authorisation was not proportionate to the objective. Although a system of prior declaration alone was insufficient to achieve this objective, it may have been if linked with "appropriate legal instruments" [paragraph 50]. Such instruments were available under the Vorarlberg Land Transfer Law – pecuniary sanctions, an action for annulment of the sale contract and a penalty entailing compulsory sale of the land.

Ospelt and Schlössle Weissenberg Familienstiftung [50]

The ECJ held that Article 56 of the EC Treaty did not preclude prior authorisation for acquiring agricultural land, but did preclude such authorisation being refused in every case in which the acquirer does not himself farm this land. The national measures restricted the free movement of capital, but were permitted provided that they "pursue in a non-discriminatory way an objective in the public interest" and "are appropriate for ensuring that the aim pursued is achieved and do not go beyond what is necessary for that purpose" [paragraph 34]. This is familiar from *Konle, Reisch* and *Salzmann.* But the judgment also incorporates the reasoning in *Analir and Others* (see section 2.1.3); measures stipulating prior authorisation must be "based on objective criteria which are known in advance and which allow all persons affected [to have recourse to] a legal remedy" [paragraph 34].

The Court held that paragraph 5(1)(a) of the VLTL was not discriminatory because it did not distinguish between Austrian nationals and those of other Member States. Furthermore, the national law "pursues public-interest objectives which are such as to justify restrictions on the free movement of capital" [paragraph 38]. These objectives are preserving agricultural communities, maintaining a suitable distribution of rural land ownership and preventing natural disasters.

A prior authorisation system may be "necessary and proportionate to the aims pursued, if the same objectives cannot be attained by less restrictive measures, in particular by a system of declarations" [paragraph

---

[49] [2003] ECR I-4899.

[50] [2003] ECR I-9743.

41]. The objective of developing and sustaining "viable agriculture on the basis of social and land planning considerations entails keeping land intended for agriculture in such use" [paragraph 43]. Prior authorisation ensures that agricultural land transfer will not lead to long-term incompatible use.

A system of declarations with legal remedies "could not prevent a transfer which ran counter to that function of continued agricultural use, and would thus not be appropriate to the objective" [paragraph 44]. Only the courts could decide actions to take after the land transfer, leading to "delays inconsistent with the requirements of continuity of use and sound land management", thus undermining legal certainty [paragraph 44]. Since the national law can only achieve its objectives if the land's agricultural use is "not irretrievably impaired", the principle underlying a system of prior authorisation is indisputable [paragraph 45].[51]

Paragraph 5(1)(a) of the VLTL goes beyond what is necessary to achieve the objective pursued if the national authorities interpret it as always requiring the acquirer to farm the land as part of a holding in which he is resident. This is because acquiring non-resident landlords with tenant farmers and legal persons such as farming associations would be refused authorisation. Other measures less restrictive of the free movement capital could contribute to the objective, including making acquirers who are legal persons let the agricultural land on a long lease and giving the first right of refusal to purchase agricultural land to tenant farmers. Non-farming owners could acquire title to the land, provided that they agree to keep it in agricultural use.

The second part of paragraph 5(1)(a) states that the acquisition is permissible if "it is not contrary to the preservation and creation of an economically healthy, medium and small-scale agricultural estate" [paragraph 13]. The ECJ concludes:

> "If, in view of that provision, the national authorities were to interpret the [VLTL] as meaning that prior authorisation may be granted, depending on the circumstances, to persons who are not farmers resident on the land concerned but who can give the necessary assurances that the abovementioned land will be kept in agricultural use, the [VLTL] would not fetter the free movement of capital beyond what is necessary in order to achieve its objectives" [paragraph 53].

---

[51] The ECJ held in *Konle* that a prior authorisation system for property transfer is "not necessarily contrary to Community law" [paragraph 45].

Although this conclusion is clear, it still leaves the national authorities with discretion as to whether or not to grant authorisation. This is shown by the language 'depending on the circumstances' and by what constitutes 'necessary assurances'. Further case law may clarify the authorisation requirements.

Burtscher[52]

The ECJ held that Article 56(1) of the EC Treaty precludes the application of paragraph 8(1) of the VLTL, according to which the required declaration of land acquisition is retroactively invalid if it is submitted after the due date. The penalty was not proportionate to the public interest objectives, which were "maintaining, increasing or creating a viable agricultural population" [paragraph 5], because it was automatically imposed on a late declaration, preventing the national authority from investigating whether the proposed acquisition complies with the planning rules. Measures with narrower consequences, such as fines, could be used instead. The applicant could be invited "to explain the reasons for his delay", or the authority could be permitted under certain conditions to accept "a late declaration, or to uphold the validity of the agreement" [paragraph 60].

Burtscher concerned the acquisition of secondary residences and the declaration that the land would not be used for holiday purposes. In *Salzmann*, a declaration system may have been sufficient to achieve the objective of town and country planning if "coupled with appropriate legal instruments" [paragraph 50]. The ECJ held in *Burtscher* that the penalty of invalidating the contract after two years in the absence of a declaration was "proportionate to the objective of preventing the unlawful use of land for holiday homes" since it "puts [the] authorities in a position to take the necessary control methods within a reasonable period" [paragraph 51]. It was the fact that the penalty was applied automatically after two years in the absence of a declaration that rendered it disproportionate.

Comment

The criteria for a national rule on real property that restricts the free movement of capital are the same as for the public policy/security derogation, except that there must be an objective in the public interest which is pursued in a non-discriminatory way. This contrasts with the public policy/security requirement for a genuine and sufficiently serious threat to a fundamental interest of society. The former standard is lower.

[52] [2005] ECR I-10309.

For instance, the objective of maintaining, increasing or creating a viable agricultural population is less rigorous than the need to maintain petroleum supplies at all times.[53]

The ECJ stated in *Ospelt* that measures requiring prior authorisation must be "based on objective criteria which are known in advance and which allow all persons affected [to have recourse to] a legal remedy" [paragraph 34].[54] None of the real property cases consider whether measures not concerning prior authorisation, such as a system of prior declaration and fines, must be based on such criteria. Since this standard is set in *Commission v Belgium* for public policy/security,[55] it is probable that it also applies to national rules relating to land that hinder the free movement of capital.

2.2 Payments

Article 56(2) of the EC Treaty states "[w]ithin the framework of the provisions set out in this chapter, all restrictions on payments between Member States and between Member States and third countries shall be prohibited".

2.2.1 Cross-border credit transfers

Directive 97/5/EC provides for minimum information requirements relating to cross-border credit transfers. A 'cross-border credit transfer' is

> "a transaction carried out on the initiative of an originator via an institution or its branch in one Member State, with a view to making available an amount of money to a beneficiary at an institution or its branch in another Member State" [Article 2(f)].

Mandatory prior information includes the time needed to credit the funds to the "account of the beneficiary's institution" and thenceforth to the beneficiary's account, the method of calculating commission fees and charges, the value date, "complaint and redress procedures" and "reference exchange rates" [Article 3]. Required information subsequent to a transfer includes a unique reference number, the amount of the transfer and of all charges and commission fees and the value date [Article 4]. After the transfer order is accepted, all institutions must perform the credit transfer

---

[53] *Burtscher* [2005] ECR I-10309; *Campus Oil and Others* [1984] ECR 2727.
[54] [2003] ECR I-9743.
[55] [2002] ECR I-4809.

for the full amount unless the originator has stated that its costs are to be paid by the beneficiary [Article 7(1)].

2.2.2 Cross-border payment in Euros

Regulation 2560/2001 unifies charges and specifies information requirements relating to cross-border payments in Euros. When Estonia, Poland and Latvia join the Euro, they must implement this Regulation. Cross-border payments include cross-border credit transfers, electronic payment transactions and cheques [Article 2]. Charges made by an institution for cross-border credit-transfers and cross-border electronic payments (but not for cross-border cheques) up to EUR 50,000 must equal the charges levied by the same institution for corresponding credit transfers in Euro transacted within the institution's Member State [Article 3]. The institution must provide prior information to its customers on charges made for cross-border payments, payments transacted within the Member State and exchange transactions into and out of Euros [Article 4].

2.2.3 The New Legal Framework for payments in the Internal Market

Further to a consultative document issued by the European Commission in 2003,[56] the EU proposes a Directive to harmonise the national rules for payment services.[57] The Directive applies to payment institutions, but excludes credit, electronic-money and post office giro institutions; 'payment institutions' are "other natural and legal persons [authorised by] this Directive to provide and execute services throughout the Community" [Article 1]. Authorisation requires submission of a written application with a list of information to the home Member State authorities [Article 5]. Payment institutions can provide payment services and ancillary services (such as foreign exchange services and safekeeping activities), and can operate payment systems to transfer, clear and settle funds [Article 6(1)]. Member States must notify the Commission of their designated authorities for monitoring payment institutions, which must be legally authorised and independent but not credit, electronic-money or post office institutions [Article 15(1)].

Article 26 stipulates conditions that the payment service provider and user must communicate before the payment, including their obligations

---

[56] COM/2003/0718 final.

[57] COM/2005/0603 final–COD 2005/0245.

and liabilities, charges payable, the applicable law and complaint and redress procedures. After acceptance, the payment institution must provide the payer with a unique reference and with the payment amount, commission fees and charges [Article 27]. It must furnish the payee, after he/she receives the payment, with the payer's reference, the payment amount and the payee's commission fees and charges [Article 28]. From January 2010, the payer's payment service provider must credit the payee's payment account with the amount ordered by the end of the first working day following acceptance, provided both payer and payee are situated in the Community [Articles 59–60].

Comment

The legislation in this section provides precise requirements for cross-border payments, thereby improving both transparency and consistency across Member States and with intra-State transfers. The New Legal Framework only applies to 'payment institutions' as defined therein. This excludes credit institutions, which must nonetheless comply with Directive 97/5/EC. [58]

2.3 Taxation

There are two ways in which national tax law may derogate from the freedom of movement of capital. Member States may

> "apply the relevant provisions of their tax law which distinguish between taxpayers who are not in the same situation with regard to their place of residence or with regard to the place where their capital is invested",[59]

and

> "take all requisite measures to prevent infringement of national law and regulations, in particular in the field of taxation and the prudential supervision of financial institutions".[60]

These provisions and measures

---

[58] Directive 97/5/EC and the New Legal Framework are both superseded by Directive 2007/64/EC, which came into force in November 2009. Directive 2007/64/EC is not discussed here because its predecessors are applied to the national legal provisions on cross-border payments.

[59] Article 58(1)(a), EC Treaty.

[60] Article 58(1)(b), EC Treaty.

"shall not constitute a means of arbitrary discrimination or a disguised restriction on the free movement of capital and payments as defined in Article 56".[61]

A Declaration states:

"[T]he right of Member States to apply the relevant provisions of their tax law as referred to in Article [58(1)(a) of the EC Treaty] will apply only with respect to the relevant provisions which exist at the end of 1993. However, this Declaration shall apply only to capital movements between Member States and to payments effected between Member States".[62]

This Declaration applies to new Member States either from their date of accession or retrospectively. In the former instance, Estonia, Poland and Latvia may not pass national tax laws which derogate from the freedom of movement of capital under Article 58(1)(a) of the EC Treaty from May 2004, in so far as these laws discriminate between EU nationals.

The Commission's 2001 communication on tax policy indicates that it intends to pursue a proactive approach in determining national direct tax laws which are contrary to the free movement of capital, and that the tax derogations will be interpreted narrowly.[63]

The ECJ's approach in the direct tax cases is to consider whether the situation between resident and non-resident taxpayers is objectively comparable, and, if so, to see whether the national rules treat residents and non-residents differently. Unless the overriding reasons in the general interest defence applies, rules treating objectively comparable situations differently breach the free movement of capital. Such reasons include the need to safeguard the cohesion of the tax system, the fight against tax avoidance and the effectiveness of fiscal supervision. The difference in treatment must be proportionate i.e. not go beyond what is required to attain the national legislation's objectives.[64]

---

[61] Article 58(3), EC Treaty.

[62] Treaty on European Union – Declaration on Article 73D of the Treaty establishing the European Community (1992).

[63] COM/2001/0260 final. The ECJ interprets the tax derogations narrowly. For instance, the 'need to safeguard the cohesion of the tax system' defence requires both a link between the tax and the tax relief and the maintenance of this link (see *Weidert and Paulus* [2004] ECR I-7379, in section 2.3.1)

[64] *Verkooijen* [2000] ECR I-4071, paragraph 43; *Lenz* [2004] ECR I-7063, paragraph 27. Discrimination involves applying different rules to similar situations and the same rules to dissimilar circumstances (*Kerckhaert and Morres* [2006] ECR I-10967, paragraph 19). The cases included in section 2.3, and

2.3.1 Cross-border dividend payments

Verkooijen [65]

The ECJ held that a Dutch law making a tax exemption on shareholders' dividend income dependent upon the company having its seat in the Netherlands was contrary to the freedom of movement of capital. The Dutch law restricts capital movements because it discourages Netherlands' residents from investing in companies whose seat is in another Member State and because it dissuades companies from other Member States from investing in the Netherlands due to unfavourable tax treatment on their dividends paid to Dutch residents.

Member States must apply areas within their competence, including direct taxation, consistently with EU law. Economic aims, including loss of tax revenue, are not overriding reasons in the general interest for restricting a fundamental freedom. Such aims cannot be justified by other tax advantages.

Commission v Belgium [66]

The ECJ held that a Belgian law prohibiting residents from acquiring certain Eurobonds was inconsistent with Article 56 of the EC Treaty. The Court rejected the Belgian government's arguments in reliance of Article 58(1)(b) of the Treaty. The contested law did not safeguard the cohesion of the tax system because there was "no direct link between any fiscal advantage and a corresponding disadvantage" [paragraph 35]. Furthermore, although the fight against tax evasion and the effectiveness of fiscal supervision may warrant restrictions on free capital movement, "a general presumption of tax evasion or tax fraud" cannot justify a fiscal provision that inhibits a fundamental freedom [paragraph 45].

Weidert and Paulus [67]

The ECJ found a Luxembourg law limiting tax relief to resident shareholders of resident companies to be contrary to Article 56. The 'safeguarding of the cohesion of the tax system' defence requires there to be a direct link between the tax and the tax relief, and that the link be maintained to preserve this cohesion. Here, there is no direct link between

---

subsequently applied to the tax laws of Estonia, Poland and Latvia, are judgments up to and including that of *Meilicke and Others*, 2007 E.C.R. I-1835, of 6 March 2007.

[65] [2000] ECR I-4071.

[66] [2000] ECR I-7587.

[67] [2004] ECR I-7379.

the tax relief and the subsequent taxation of any dividends paid. Furthermore, as the Belgium-Luxembourg Double Taxation Convention's aim is to "secure fiscal cohesion", it cannot be invoked to justify the taxpayer's unfavourable treatment [paragraph 26].

Lenz [68]

The Court held that a lower tax rate on dividends to Austrian shareholders from Austrian companies than from non-resident companies was contrary to Article 56 of the EC Treaty. The national legislation deterred Austrian taxpayers from buying shares of companies established in another Member State. Such legislation also discouraged non-resident companies from raising capital in Austria because their shares were less attractive to Austrian investors than those of resident companies.

The legislation's objective is to reduce the economic effects of double taxation of company profits, i.e. corporation tax on profits and income tax on distributed dividends. However, revenue from capital originating in another Member State is also subject to double taxation. Consequently, fully taxable Austrian shareholders receiving dividends from Austrian companies are in a situation comparable to fully taxable Austrian shareholders receiving dividends from companies established in other Member States.

In rejecting the claim that the national legislation was necessary to preserve the coherence of the tax system, the Court found no direct link between the corporation and income taxes. Furthermore, the legislation's aim of attenuating double taxation is unaffected by extending it to dividends paid in another Member State.

The ECJ dismissed the 'effectiveness of fiscal supervision' argument because the application of different tax rates according to the dividends' source does not make financial supervision more effective. Furthermore, mere administrative inconvenience of extending the lower tax rate to dividends from non-resident companies cannot justify an obstacle to a fundamental freedom.

Manninen [69]

The ECJ held that a Finnish law designed to avoid double taxation which provided a tax credit to resident shareholders on dividends paid to them by Finnish companies was contrary to Article 56. Shareholders fully taxable in Finland are in a comparable situation, whether they receive

[68] [2004] ECR I-7063.
[69] [2004] ECR I-7477.

dividends from Finnish organisations or from companies established in other Member States. Dividends paid by Finnish and Swedish companies may be subject to double taxation.

In rejecting the 'preservation of the coherence of the tax system' defence, the ECJ held that this coherence is assured provided the correlation between the shareholder's tax credit and the corporation tax is maintained. Extending the tax credit to dividends paid by Swedish companies would not threaten the coherence of the Finnish tax system and is less restrictive of the free movement of capital than the Finnish tax rule.

Bouanich [70]

The ECJ held that Article 56 of the EC Treaty precludes national legislation which (i) states that a payment in respect of a share repurchase to a non-resident shareholder is taxed as a dividend without deducting the cost of acquisition of these shares, whereas the same payment made to a resident shareholder is taxed as a capital gain after deducting the acquisition cost; (ii) derives from a Double Taxation Convention that puts a lower ceiling on the taxation of dividends for non-resident shareholders than for resident shareholders and permits deduction of the shares' nominal value from the share repurchase agreement, except where this national legislation does not treat non-resident shareholders less favourably than resident shareholders. Resident and non-resident shareholders are in an objectively comparable situation because the share acquisition cost is directly linked to payment from the share repurchase.

Kerckhaert and Morres [71]

The ECJ stated that Article 56 is compatible with Belgian legislation that taxes dividends to resident shareholders from resident and non-resident companies at the same rate, without the tax rebate provided for in the France-Belgium Double Taxation Convention to reduce French withholding tax levied at source. Resident and non-resident shareholders are in an objectively comparable situation, but one which differs from that in *Verkooijen*, *Lenz* and *Manninen* in that the national legislation does not distinguish between dividends from companies established in Belgium and those from companies located elsewhere in the EU. The problems arise from "the exercise in parallel by two Member States of their fiscal sovereignty" [paragraph 20]. As Community law lays down no general criteria for apportioning authority between Member States for eliminating

[70] [2006] ECR I-923.
[71] [2006] ECR I-10967.

double taxation, Member States must apply apportionment criteria used in international tax practice.

Denkavit International and Denkavit France[72]

Freedom of establishment includes a company's right to practice through a subsidiary, branch or agency,[73] and entails abolition of restrictions for nationals of a Member State or companies with a registered office in that State to form agencies, branches or subsidiaries in another State. The ECJ held that a French law taxing dividends paid to non-resident parent companies but exempting those to resident parent companies was a discriminatory restriction on the freedom of establishment, even though the relevant Double Taxation Convention limited the tax to a 5% withholding tax. Imposing the tax rendered comparable the situation of resident and non-resident shareholders.

Meilicke and Others[74]

The ECJ followed its judgment in *Manninen* on similar facts, holding that Article 56 of the EC Treaty precludes national legislation granting a tax credit on dividends paid to a fully taxable shareholder by a company established in the same Member State but not by one located in another State. Extending the tax credit to dividends paid by Danish and Dutch organisations is less restrictive of the free movement of capital than the German tax rule.

Comment

If a Member State imposes a tax on dividends paid by companies established there to residents of other States, or paid to residents by companies established in another State, then the situation is objectively comparable with dividends paid by companies to shareholders within a Member State. Consequently, if the State does not tax the latter dividends, or taxes them at a lower rate than cross-border dividends, there is a restriction on the free movement of capital which is not justified by Article 58 of the EC Treaty.

The national rule in *Kerckhaert and Morres* did not discriminate against companies established in other Member States, thereby distinguishing it as the only such law in this subsection's cases that was compatible with Article 56. Member States' parallel exercise of fiscal sovereignty is an acceptable derogation under Article 58(1)(a)–the fact

---

[72] [2006] ECR I-11949.

[73] This derives from Articles 43 and 48 of the EC Treaty.

[74] [2007] ECR I-1835.

that the Belgian Government had withdrawn a tax benefit provided for in the France-Belgium Double Taxation Convention did not enable the applicants to succeed.

2.3.2 Tax credits to residents

D. [75]

The ECJ held that Articles 56 and 58 of the EC Treaty allow legislation that enables a Member State to deny non-resident taxpayers holding most of their wealth in their state of residence the allowances which it gives to resident taxpayers. For income tax, a resident's situation differs from that of a non-resident because most of his/her income is in the State of residence, which possesses all the information needed to assess his or her overall ability to pay. This is also true for wealth tax. A taxpayer who holds a small part of his/her wealth in another Member State is not in a situation comparable to that of residents of that other State, and the authorities' refusal to grant him/her the allowance to which residents are entitled is not discriminatory.

Blanckaert [76]

The Court held that Articles 56 and 58 permit a national rule under which a non-resident taxpayer receiving only savings and investments income in a Member State and who is not insured under its social security system cannot claim tax credits for national insurance, whereas a resident taxpayer who is so insured can claim tax credits, even if he/she receives only income of the same kind and pays no social security contributions. Insured residents and non-residents are entitled to reductions in national insurance contributions, unlike residents and non-residents who are not insured. Granting tax credits to uninsured persons is treating different situations identically, since insured persons can only obtain tax credits if they cannot match reductions in contributions against contributions due, whilst uninsured persons pay no contributions and therefore would automatically receive a tax credit. The objective difference between insured and uninsured persons justifies the national rule, given the power in Article 58(1)(a) of the EC Treaty for States to apply different tax laws to persons who are not in the same situation as to residence or place of capital investment.

---

[75] [2005] ECR I-5821.
[76] [2005] ECR I-7685.

Comment

Residents and non-residents are not in an objectively comparable situation in either case, so the difference in treatment is justified by Article 58(1)(a) of the EC Treaty. In *Blankaert*, the national rule distinguishes between persons insured and uninsured under the Netherlands social security system, with residents and non-residents in both categories being treated similarly.

2.3.3 Inheritance tax

Barbier [77]

The ECJ held that EU law precludes a Member State's legislation assessing inheritance tax due on immovable property situated there, according to which the fact that the legal owner was unconditionally obliged to transfer it to the financial owner may only be considered if the former resided in that State when he or she died. The Dutch legislation constituted a disguised restriction on the free movement of capital under Article 58(3) of the EC Treaty.

van Hilten-van der Heijden [78]

The Court held that Article 56 of the EC Treaty permits legislation by which the estate of a national of a Member State who dies within 10 years of ceasing to reside there is taxed as if he or she had continued to reside in that State, whilst being exempted from inheritance taxes levied by other States. Its reasoning is as follows.

1. Measures breach Article 56 that both (i) reduce the value of the inheritance of a resident of a Member State other than the State containing the assets concerned and (ii) tax the inheritance of those assets.
2. Since the Dutch provision treats nationals who have transferred their residence abroad and those who have remained in the Netherlands similarly, it can neither discourage the former from making investments in the Netherlands nor the latter from doing so in another Member State; nor can it reduce the value of the estate of a national who has become resident abroad. As it only applies to nationals of one State, it cannot hinder the capital movements of other States' nationals.

---

[77] [2003] ECR I-15013.

[78] [2006] ECR I-1957.

3. The Dutch rule is justified by the need to prevent tax evasion whereby a national of a State, anticipating death, transfers his/her residence to another State with lower tax.
4. In this context, transferring residence to another State is not a 'capital movement' in Annex I.

Comment

The national rule in *Barbier* is discriminatory against non-residents because the information concerned may be material to the inheritance tax assessment.[79] In *van Hilten-van der Heijden*, the Dutch measure discouraged residence transfer to other Member States, but this was not sufficient to constitute a 'capital movement' in Annex I. The exemption from such States' inheritance tax renders the rule discriminatory, and its justification under Article 58(1)(a) on the ground of preventing tax evasion is only acceptable because it applies only to Dutch nationals and, outside this proviso, does not affect the capital movements of other States' residents.

2.4 Authorisation and the 'Single Passport' Regime

The Directives discussed in this section state the conditions under which the each Member State's financial regulator can grant authorisation for firms to provide financial services in another State. This is called the 'single passport' regime.[80]

Authorisation is provided for the free movement of services and for the freedom of establishment. However, as section 3.1 shows for Estonia, a refusal or revocation of authorisation potentially hinders the free movement of capital from the unauthorised entities to and from their branches and clients. I therefore investigate whether the national rules for authorisation of financial regulators are in accordance with the Directives.

---

[79] The reasoning behind this statement is as follows. It is possible that taking the fact that the legal owner was unconditionally obliged to transfer immovable property to the financial owner into consideration could reduce the amount of inheritance tax payable on the former's estate. Therefore, a national rule restricting the consideration of this fact to cases in which the legal owner resided in a particular Member State when he or she died is a "disguised restriction on the free movement of capital" (Article 58(3), EC Treaty), which discriminates against legal owners of immovable property resident in other States.

[80] In principle, authorised firms can provide services in other Member States without additional legal or administrative requirements. Hence, the authorisation is a 'passport' to these States.

Contracts agreed by telephone and those without significant movement of personnel between home and host Member State are supplied in the home Member State,[81] which is the location of the firm or branch. In these circumstances, there is no need for an authorisation to provide financial services in another Member State, so subsequent cross-border capital movements are unhindered.

2.4.1 Investment firms (Directive 2004/39/EC)

The home Member State designates a competent authority, which is empowered to authorise investment firms to provide one or more of the investment and ancillary services listed in Annex I of this Directive.[82] An investment firm must request an extension to its authorisation if it adds further services. The authorisation enables the firm to supply services throughout the Community, either by establishing a branch or directly from its head office [Article 6].

The national authority only grants authorisation if it is "fully satisfied" that the applicant complies with all requirements under the "provisions adopted pursuant to this Directive" [Article 7(1)]. The investment firm must provide all information, including a business and organisational plan, which satisfies the authority that the firm has already set up "all the necessary arrangements to meet its obligations" under the authorisation chapter [Article 7(2)]. Member States cannot impose further requirements for founding a branch or providing cross-border investment services [Articles 31(1) and 32(1)].[83]

---

[81] The 'home Member State' is the country in which the company providing services is registered. The 'host Member State' is the country to which this firm wishes to supply cross-border services and/or in which it wishes to establish a branch or subsidiary to provide its services there.

[82] 'Investment services' include the reception and transmission of client orders relating to 'financial instruments', the execution of orders for clients and on own account, portfolio management, investment advice, the underwriting and placement of 'financial instruments', and the operation of Multilateral Trading Facilities. 'Ancillary services' comprise those connected with 'investment services', such as custodianship of clients' 'financial instruments' and foreign exchange services. 'Financial instruments' include transferable securities, money market instruments, units in unit and investment trusts, options, futures, forward rate agreements, derivative contracts for the transfer of credit risk, and contracts for differences (Annex I, Directive 2004/39/EC).

[83] Article 32(7) permits the host Member State's financial authority to request branch operational and organisational changes that are "strictly needed" for it to enforce compliance with Directive 2004/39/EC and its implementing measures.

Investment firms intending to provide services in another Member State must provide its national authority with this State's name and a "programme of operations" that includes the proposed investment and ancillary services, and the names of "tied agents" [Article 31(2)]. This authority forwards the information to the competent authority of the host Member State [Article 31(3)].

Investment firms wishing to establish a branch in another State must provide its national authority with the name of this State and of the branch managers, the address for obtaining documents in this State, and a "programme of operations" that includes the proposed investment and ancillary services, the branch's organisational structure and the names of "tied agents" [Article 32(2)]. This authority communicates the information to the competent authority of the host Member State [Article 32(3)], and must provide reasons to the investment firm if it refuses to do so [Article 32(5)]. It may only refuse if has "reason to doubt the adequacy of" the firm's administrative structure or financial situation, given the branch's proposed activities [Article 32(3)].

2.4.2 Credit institutions (Directive 2006/48/EC)

Member States must ensure that credit institutions acquire authorisation before starting their activities; they must state the requirements for authorisation and impart these to the Commission [Article 6]. Applications for authorisation must be accompanied by a "programme of operations", which specifies the institution's structural organisation and types of business [Article 7]. To grant authorisation, capital and reserves must be at least EUR 5 million, and must remain above this level, unless the credit institution belongs to a particular pre-specified category, in which case capital and reserves must be at least EUR 1 million [Articles 9 and 10(1)]. The authority must give reasons for refusing an authorisation [Article 13], and must inform the Commission of every authorisation it grants [Article 14]. It must give reasons for withdrawing an authorisation and must notify the Commission [Article 17(2)].

A credit institution must inform the national authority of its home Member State of the activities in Annex I of this Directive which it wishes to provide in another State.[84] This authority passes this information to the

[84] This Annex specifies a "List of Activities Subject to Mutual Recognition" in other Member States. Items include the acceptance of deposits, lending, financial leasing, money transmission services, the issuance and administration of methods of payment, guarantees, participation in securities issues, trading on own account

other State's competent authority [Article 28]. A credit institution wishing to establish a branch in another Member State must provide the authority of its home State with the name of this other State and of the branch managers, the address for obtaining documents in the other State, and a "programme of operations" giving the types of business and the branch's organisational structure [Article 25(2)]. The authority forwards the information to the competent authority in the other Member State [Article 25(3)], and must give reasons to the credit institution for refusing to do so, which this institution may challenge in its home State's courts [Article 25(4)]. It may only refuse if has "reason to doubt the adequacy of" the credit institution's administrative structure or financial situation, given its branch's proposed activities [Article 25(3)].

2.4.3 Insurance companies

Insurance other than life assurance (Directives 73/239/EEC and 88/357/EEC) [85]

The competent authority of the home Member State must grant prior authorisation to undertakings established there to provide direct insurance services or to extend their business to other insurance classes [Article 6, Directive 73/239/EEC]. Authorisations are valid across the EU for insurance classes or groups of classes [Article 7]. An authorisation requires a "scheme of operations", which includes particulars of the risks, reinsurance principles, minimum guarantee fund, set-up costs, and resources intended to finance these costs [Articles 8 and 9]. Authorisation withdrawal must be "supported by precise reasons" [Article 22].

An insurance undertaking wishing to found a branch in another Member State must furnish the competent authority of its home State with the name of the other State and the branch's authorised agent, an address in that other State to which documents may be delivered to this agent and from which documents may be obtained, and a "scheme of operations" specifying the types of business and the branch organisation [Article 10(2), Directive 73/239/EEC]. The home State authority must communicate this information to the competent authority of the other State unless the former has "reason to doubt the adequacy of the administrative structure or the financial situation of the insurance undertaking" or the

---

or for customers in money market instruments, foreign exchange, transferable securities, futures, options and other derivatives relating to interest rates or exchange rates, and various ancillary activities (Annex I, Directive 2006/48/EC).

[85] As amended by Directive 92/49/EEC.

repute, qualifications or experience of the directors, managers or agent [Article 10(3)]. The home State authority must give reasons for refusing to so communicate the information, and the insurance firm may challenge this decision in the home State's courts [Article 10(3)].

An insurance undertaking wishing to provide cross-border insurance services in another Member State must inform the home State's competent authority, indicating "the nature of the risks" it will cover [Article 14, Directive 88/357/EEC]. This authority must communicate to the competent authority of the other Member State a certificate attesting to the required minimum solvency margin, the classes of insurance which the undertaking has been authorised to provide, and the "nature of the risks" to be covered in that State [Article 16(1)]. The home State authority must provide reasons for refusing to communicate this information; the insurance undertaking may appeal against the refusal in the home State's courts [Article 16(2)].

Life assurance (Directive 2002/83/EC)

Similar rules apply to Directive 73/239/EEC with minor differences.[86]

2.4.4 Insurance and reinsurance mediation Directive (2002/92/EC)

(Re)insurance mediation means undertaking work preparatory to concluding (re)insurance contracts, concluding such contracts and assisting in their administration and performance [Article 2(3)-(4)]. Insurance and reinsurance intermediaries performing these activities fall within this Directive, but insurance undertakings authorised under the Insurance Directives (see section 2.4.3) and reinsurance undertakings, which are entities that accept risks from insurance undertakings and other reinsurance undertakings, do not [Article 2(1)-(6)].

Insurance and reinsurance intermediaries must be registered by the competent authority in their home Member State [Article 5]. If an intermediary wishes to practice in another Member State for the first time, it must inform this authority, which, within one month, must notify the competent authority in the host Member State and the intermediary; the intermediary may start business a month later [Article 6(1)]. The latter

[86] Directive 2009/138/EC on the taking-up and pursuit of the business of Insurance and Reinsurance (Solvency II) will supersede Directives 73/239/EEC, 88/357/EEC, 92/49/EEC and 2002/83/EC from 1 November 2012. The new Directive provides a comprehensive legal framework for the operation of insurance and reinsurance services within the Internal Market.

authority may publish the conditions under which, "in the interests of the general good", the intermediary may practice in the host State [Article 6(3)].

2.4.5 Comment

The general principles are as follows:

1. An authorisation covers service provision across the EU.
2. A company must obtain a further authorisation to provide services not specified in the original authorisation.
3. Withdrawal of an authorisation must be accompanied by reasons.
4. An authorisation includes the freedom to provide cross-border services to, and to establish a branch in, another Member State.
5. The company must provide certain information to the competent authority of its home Member State in order to provide cross-border services or open a branch. This information includes a programme of operations in the latter case.
6. This authority must communicate the information to the competent authority of the host Member State within one month for cross-border services and within three months for establishing a branch.
7. Refusal to forward the information in the specified time must be accompanied by reasons, and is actionable in the home Member State's courts.

2.5 EU Transitional Measures on the Purchase of Real Estate

Article 24 of the Act of Accession to the European Communities 2003 provides transitional measures for new Member States, including Estonia, Latvia and Poland. These rules are exceptions to the free movement of capital.

2.5.1 Estonia

Appendix VI of the Act of Accession states that Estonia can keep its national provisions relating to the acquisition of agricultural land and forests in force for seven years from its date of accession to the EU (1 May 2004). Independent farmers from another Member State who have farmed in Estonia for at least three consecutive years are exempt from this restriction and must be treated as Estonian nationals.

2.5.2 Poland

Appendix XII of the Act of Accession upholds Articles 8(2) and 8(2a) of the Polish Act of 24 March 1920 on the Acquisition of Immovable Properties by Foreign Persons.

Agricultural and forest immovable properties

Article 46(1) of the Polish Civil Code defines ‘immovable property’ as follows.

> “An immovable property shall be part of the earth's surface which constitute a separate object of ownership (land) as well as buildings permanently attached to the land, or parts thereof, if by special provisions they are an object of ownership separate from the land”.[87]

This means land and buildings.

Article 8(2)(1) of the AIPFPA states:

> “[C]itizens or entrepreneurs … of the European Economic Area shall not be required to obtain a permit, excluding the acquisition of: agricultural and foreign immovable properties, within 12 years since the day of accession of the Republic of Poland to the European Union [1st May 2004]”.

Article 8(2a)(1) provides exceptions for specific districts within Poland. This provision, as clarified by Appendix XII of the Act of Accession, includes all independent EEA farmers who have legally resided in Poland and leased land there for at least 3 years, other than eight districts where the period required to continue farming without a permit is 7 years.

Second houses

Article 8(2)(2) of the AIPFPA states:

> “[C]itizens or entrepreneurs … of the European Economic Area shall not be required to obtain a permit, excluding the acquisition of: a second house, within 5 years since the day of accession of the Republic of Poland to the European Union”.

No permit is required if the EEA resident “has lawfully and continuously resided” in Poland for at least 4 years [Article 8(2a)(2)(a)], nor to provide

---

[87] Kierzkowski, Miller, and Wiśniewski *(eds.)* (2000), *The Polish Civil Code*, 8.

tourist services [Article 8(2a)(2)(b)], although Appendix XII of the Act of Accession omits the latter exception.

2.5.3 Latvia

Appendix VIII of the Act of Accession permits Latvia to retain its legislation on the acquisition of arable land and forests for seven years from its date of accession to the EU (1 May 2004). Independent farmers from another Member State who have practised agriculture in Latvia for at least three years running are not subject to this restriction and must be treated as Latvian nationals.

2.5.4 Conclusions

This chapter enables comparison of the laws of Member States with EU law for obstacles to the free movement of capital. The procedure is as follows. First, inspect Annex I to see whether there is a capital movement (subsection 2.1.1). If there is a movement of capital relating to real property that falls outside the transitional provisions (subsections 2.5.1–2.5.3) and if the national legislation provides for prior authorisation or declaration, apply the case law in subsection 2.1.4. If the movement of capital may be affected by a tax provision, apply the test in *Verkooijen* to determine whether this provision restricts capital movement;[88] then apply the subsequent case law in section 2.3 to determine if the restriction is permitted under Article 58(1) of the EC Treaty.

For other capital movements, apply the case law in subsection 2.1.2 to see if the national law causes a restriction; then, if there is a possible justification of public policy or public security, apply the case law in subsection 2.1.3 to the national provision(s) at issue. Check the other justifications provided by the EC Treaty in the first paragraph of subsection 2.1.3.

[88] The 'test in *Verkooijen*', stated in the first paragraph in the subsection '*Verkooijen*' in section 2.3.1, is to decide whether or not a national legal provision restricts the movement of capital on the basis of it discouraging residents of the home Member State from investing in companies registered in another State and/or it dissuading companies from other Member States from investing in the home State. Objectively comparable situations must be treated similarly. This is consistent with the case law in section 2.1.2 above, which applies to national laws without a tax element. Non-discriminatory tax rules are absent from section 2.3, although the principle in *Commission v Spain* [2003] ECR I-4581 should apply to such legal provisions (see the subsection '*Commission v Spain*' in section 2.1.2).

If there is a national law which may limit a cross-border payment, then compare it to the Regulation and Directives in section 2.2. The justifications in Article 58 of the EC Treaty are relevant to such restrictions; if a restriction is established, apply the case law in subsection 2.1.3, or in section 2.3 for tax provisions. In the next chapter, I use the method in this subsection to compare Estonian legislation on cross-border capital movements with the EU law discussed above.

CHAPTER THREE

ESTONIA: LEGAL ISSUES

> "Estonia consists mainly of boulder-strewn lowland, but also includes over 800 islands in the Baltic. It covers 45100 km² (17400 square miles), and until 1945 was noted mainly for its cattle and dairy produce. Its industries now include food processing, electrical engineering and shipbuilding, and its people now have the highest standard of living in the USSR".[1]

Estonia's forward looking adaptability applies equally to its legal translations. The Estonian Legal Language Centre (ELLC) has translated all the major Estonian Legislation from this Uralian language into English. The ELLC is a part of the Estonian Ministry of Justice. It provides

> "[h]igh-quality translations ... which accurately reflect the content, intent and feeling of the original, are correct in grammar, idiomatic and consistent in use of terminology and phraseology".[2]

Estonian legislation that affects or potentially affects capital flows into and out of Estonia has only been enacted in the last few years, in anticipation of and immediately following Estonia's accession to the European Union on 1 May 2004. This legislation is comprehensive. However, it leaves considerable interpretative capacity to the Estonian Financial Supervision Authority (FSA) and, in the case of tax law, to the Estonian Tax and Customs Board. I draw attention to possible inconsistencies with the European Union legislation in sections 3.1 to 3.4.

Section 3.1 discusses Acts overseen by the Financial Supervision Authority. Section 3.2 considers the settlement of payments. Section 3.3 concerns taxation, especially the Income Tax Act. Section 3.4 reports on the transfer of immovable property ownership to non-Estonians.

Some areas of Estonian law which I expected to contain provisions governing cross-border activities do not do so. These include, for instance, the Law of Property Act and the Saving and Loan Associations

---

[1] A. B. Mountjoy *(ed.)* (1987), *Readers Digest Guide to Places of the World*, 216.
[2] ELLC, 8 November 2006.

Act. I have not discussed laws that do not apply to activities outside Estonia.

3.1 Acts Regulated by the Financial Supervision Authority

The FSA is an independent agency which conducts state financial supervision over activities provided for in the Investment Funds, Securities Market, Credit Institutions, Insurance Activities and other Acts, and in legislation pursuant to these Acts.[3] Its functions include ensuring that its subjects comply with financial soundness requirements under the Acts, guiding subjects to manage prudently, applying the law to protect clients' interests and ensuring good administrative practice.[4]

'Contracting State' means a Contracting Party to the EEA agreement.[5] All other foreign countries are 'third countries'.[6] 'Cross-border services' are those provided by a management company or credit institution in a country where it or its branch is not registered.[7]

3.1.1 Investment Funds Act 2004 (IFA)

Management company

This is a public limited company which manages the assets of a fund.[8] A management company may also manage a portfolio of securities, provide advice on investment in securities and hold units of shares in a fund for clients.[9] Fund management includes investing the fund assets, issuing and redeeming fund units, issuing documentation to unit-holders, keeping account of the fund assets and distributing the fund income between unit-holders.[10]

Sections 28 to 38: authorisation for branch foundation

The FSA may refuse to authorise the foundation of a branch of an Estonian management company in a third country or of a foreign management company in Estonia where, in the FSA's view, the third

---

[3] ss.2(1) and 4, Financial Supervision Authority Act.
[4] Ibid., s.6.
[5] s.4(1), IFA; s.6(8), SMA; s.4(4)(1), CIA; s.18(1)(14), IAA.
[6] s.25(5), IFA; s.9(5)(2), CIA; s.29(5), IAA.
[7] s.25(3), IFA; s.19^1(3), CIA.
[8] s.9(1), IFA.
[9] s.9(2), IFA.
[10] s.10(1), IFA.

country's financial authority has no legal basis or is unable to exercise sufficient supervision over the branch.[11] Furthermore, the FSA may determine requirements which a management company in a Contracting State must fulfil to provide services through an Estonian branch.[12]

Establishment of a branch is a 'capital movement' under Title I(1) of Annex I. Prior authorisation for capital movements must be proportionate and be based on objective criteria for legal certainty. Authorisation for branch foundation leaves broad discretion with the FSA, which is unacceptable as a ground for derogation from a fundamental freedom in the EU Treaty.[13]

Sections 40 and 42: potential capital movements with authorisation problems

The FSA may refuse to authorise cross-border services from a third country management company if, in the FSA's view, the third country's financial authority has no legal basis or does not guarantee sufficient supervision over the company.[14] Additionally, the FSA may decide the conditions under which a management company of a Contracting State provides cross-border services in Estonia, including portfolio management, consulting and depositing.[15] This decision is based on the company's business plan and the investor protection scheme in the Contracting State.[16]

Cross-border services are 'capital movements' under Annex I. Refusing to grant authorisation for or imposing conditions on the provision of these services amounts to a restriction on the free movement of capital. The prior authorisation scheme is unlikely to be accepted as a derogation for public policy or public security due to the lack of objective criteria for refusing such authorisation to the applicant. Also, Estonia may

> "for serious political reasons and on grounds of urgency, take unilateral measures against a third country with regard to capital movements and payments".[17]

---

[11] ss.28(4) and 36(2), IFA.
[12] s.38(2), IFA.
[13] *Commission v Spain* [2003] ECR I-4581.
[14] s.40(2), IFA.
[15] s.42(3), IFA.
[16] s.42(1), IFA.
[17] Article 60(2), EC Treaty.

The financial authority's lack of legal basis may amount to 'serious political reasons' in a clear case, but inadequate supervision does not.

Imposing conditions on the provision of cross-border services may be an acceptable derogation for public policy or general interest if the conditions are specific, proportionate and known beforehand to the applicant company, and if judicial review is available.[18] However, there is not a genuine and sufficiently serious threat to a fundamental interest to society, such as the provision of energy supplies in a crisis. A Member State's financial interests are inadequate justification because they are economic grounds.[19] The ECJ would therefore reject the imposition of conditions.

Sections 229 and 233: capital movements without justification

A foreign management company must contract with a management company, investment firm or credit institution which, or whose branch is, registered in Estonia in order to "organise the purchase and sale of" foreign fund units.[20] The company need not do this if is it has founded a branch in Estonia to organise purchase and sale of its fund units.[21]

Such organisation is a 'capital movement' under Title IVA of Annex I, especially as the definition includes all operations necessary to a capital movement. Given the fact that the requirement to contract with an Estonian company is unlikely to be justified on public policy or security grounds, the issue is whether this requirement amounts to a restriction on the free movement of capital. On the balance of probabilities, it does not so amount, because the foundation of a branch under Estonian law removes the requirement. This is reasonable. The administrative conditions for founding a branch in another Member State are not onerous,[22] and an existing authorisation for providing investment services in the home State suffices for provision of such services in Estonia.

The FSA may refuse registration to an offer of foreign fund units if the offer prospectus contains misleading, incomplete or contradictory statements, if there is insufficient evidence of risk-spreading, or if the foreign financial authority inadequately supervises funds' activities, has no legal basis or cannot cooperate with the FSA, or if investors' interests are not sufficiently protected.[23] The admission of foreign units to the Estonian

[18] *Commission v Belgium* [2002] ECR I-4809.
[19] *Commission v Portugal* [2002] ECR I-4731.
[20] s.229(1), IFA.
[21] s.229(2), IFA.
[22] See section 2.4.1.
[23] s.233, IFA.

capital market is a 'capital movement' under Title IVB of Annex I. Refusing registration restricts the free movement of capital. Some of the grounds for withholding registration to foreign funds may be legal because of similar requirements for Estonian funds, such as the existence of misleading, incomplete or contradictory statements in the prospectus.[24] However, others discriminate against foreign funds, are disproportionate and are inconsistent with legal certainty–for instance, the FSA's subjective judgment as to whether it can cooperate with a foreign financial authority. These rules are contrary to Article 56 of the EC Treaty.

Section 297: infringement of national law

The FSA may revoke its authorisation of a foreign management company to establish a branch in Estonia or to provide cross-border services there if the company breaches the requirements of the IFA or other legislation.[25] If a management company of a Contracting State commits this violation, the FSA can prohibit its Estonian activities.[26] Exceptionally, to protect investors or in the public interest, the FSA can act against such a company without advance notice to its financial authority.[27] In both the latter instances, the FSA must inform the European Commission of the measures that it takes.[28]

Establishment of a branch and cross-border services are capital movements under Titles I and IVA to Annex I respectively. If the FSA terminates these services, it restricts the free movement of capital. The protection of investors or the public interest does not amount to a 'genuine and sufficiently serious threat to a fundamental interest of society' as required by EU case law on public policy/security.[29] However, Article 58(1)(b) of the EC Treaty permits Member States to "take all requisite measures to prevent" breaches of national law, especially regarding taxation and "the prudential supervision of financial institutions". The lack of EU case law on prudential supervision necessitates analogous

---

[24] Such non-discriminatory grounds may not be legal, i.e. they may amount to a restriction on the free movement of capital because they discourage foreign investment funds from investing in Estonia. See the subsection '*Commission v Spain*' in section 2.1.2, in which this principle is applied to share purchasers in privatised Spanish companies.

[25] s.297(3), IFA.

[26] s.297(6), IFA.

[27] s.297(8), IFA.

[28] s.297(9), IFA.

[29] *Eglise de Scientologie and Scientology International* [2000] ECR I-1335.

treatment to the taxation derogation, under which the ECJ permitted the economic objective of double taxation avoidance.[30]

Directive 2004/39/EC repeatedly mentions 'protection of investors' without explanation, and does not explicitly consider the public interest.[31] The protection of investors is a legitimate national objective for restricting the free movement of capital under Article 58(1)(b) of the EC Treaty, provided that it is proportionate and non-discriminatory.[32] The IFA should define 'public interest' because derogations from fundamental freedoms must be based on specific, objective criteria, known to the parties beforehand so that they know their rights and obligations deriving from Article 56 of the EC Treaty.[33] Moreover, there is no legal redress for investment firms who have their authorisation revoked.[34] The Estonian government must make these modifications to make section 297 of the IFA an enforceable derogation under Article 58(1)(b) of the EC Treaty to the free movement of capital.

3.1.2 Regulation No.73 of the Minister of Finance of 19 November 1997

The issue of this regulation was pursuant to the last Investment Funds Act, now repealed. However, the regulation is still in force.[35] The sections of interest are the lists of countries in which it is permitted to invest fund assets, and whose stocks or investment fund units may be publicly sold in Estonia. The countries on at least one of the three lists include all Member States, Australia, Canada, Japan, Norway, Russia Switzerland, Ukraine and the USA.

---

[30] *Lenz* [2004] ECR I-7063; *Manninen* [2004] ECR I-7477. However, the ECJ held in *Verkooijen* [2000] ECR I-4071 that economic aims, including loss of tax revenue, are not overriding reasons in the general interest for restricting a fundamental freedom.

[31] Section 297 of the IFA complies with Article 62 of Directive 2004/39/EC, which provides measures that a host Member State may take when an investment firm does not comply with national laws "adopted pursuant to this Directive".

[32] Financial supervision must be proportionate (see section 2.1.3), and must not be a "means of arbitrary discrimination" on free capital movement (Article 58(3), EC Treaty).

[33] See section 2.1.3.

[34] *Commission v Belgium* [2002] ECR I-4809.

[35] The FSA confirmed that Regulation No.73 was in force but should be modified or rescinded (personal letter, 4 April 2007). The Ministry of Finance stated that the regulation "is no longer valid" since the IFA came into force on 1 May 2004 (e-mail communication, 14 March 2008). However, it persists as Estonian law and is therefore included in this analysis.

The investment of fund assets is a capital movement under Title IVA of Annex I. Prohibiting or limiting such investment in or by countries absent from the lists restricts free movement of capital. Public policy, public security and Article 60(2) derogations will not apply to many of the absent countries, for instance, New Zealand, India and Singapore. The lists therefore breach Article 56 of the EC Treaty.

3.1.3 Securities Market Act 2001 (SMA)

This Act concerns securities' regulation and investment services. 'Securities' include shares, bonds, derivatives, investment fund units and money market instruments, but exclude cheques and bills of exchange.[36] Professional securities market participants include investment firms, credit institutions, and operators of the regulated securities market and of securities settlement systems.[37] An 'investment firm' is a public limited company that provides investment services to third parties.[38] Investment funds and insurance companies are not investment firms,[39] but may offer investment services.[40] 'Investment services' include buying, transferring and trading securities, receipt of securities transaction orders, securities portfolio management, underwriting, and organising securities for trading on a regulated market.[41] The FSA issues an activity licence for the provision of individual or all investment services.[42]

Sections 61 and 62: branch foundation

The FSA must grant permission to an Estonian investment firm to establish a branch or subsidiary in a third country.[43] There are seven reasons for refusing permission, including there being no cooperation agreement between the FSA and the third country's securities market supervisory agency, and no suitable legal framework there.[44] Furthermore, the FSA may revoke permission if the risks arising from the branch's activities are "significantly greater" than the investment firm's risks.[45]

---

[36] s.2, SMA.
[37] s.7(1), SMA.
[38] s.40(1), SMA.
[39] s.42, SMA.
[40] s.45(4), SMA.
[41] s.43, SMA.
[42] ss.49 and 51, SMA.
[43] s.59(1), SMA.
[44] s.61(7), SMA.
[45] s.62(5), SMA.

Title I(1) of Annex I classifies branch foundation as a 'capital movement'. Although permissions are not 'capital movements' in Annex I, the cross-border provision of investment services are; for instance securities' operations on the capital market are so defined in Title III of the Annex. The two restrictions in the paragraph above give the FSA more discretion than EU law allows–measures limiting the free movement of capital must provide legal certainty.[46]

If an Estonian investment firm wishes to found a branch or provide cross-border services in a Contracting State, the FSA may refuse to forward the relevant information to the supervision authority in that State if the firm's resources, indicated in its business plan, are "insufficient" for providing the services.[47] For cross-border services, the FSA may refuse to forward the information if the State's supervisory agency has no legal basis or capacity for cooperation such that the FSA cannot adequately supervise the provision of these services.[48] If such grounds exist, the FSA may issue a precept to prohibit the investment firm from providing cross-border services.[49]

Sections 64 and 65: forwarding of information by FSA to Contracting State

Although forwarding of information concerning the investment firm's business plan is not a 'capital movement' in Annex I, cross-border investment services are, and the precept to prohibit them is a restriction on the free movement of capital. Article 32(3) of Directive 2004/39/EC permits the FSA to refuse to forward the information if it has "reason to doubt the adequacy of" the investment firm's administrative structure or financial situation, if this firm is establishing a branch in another Member State. The Directive provides no grounds for such refusal if the firm is providing cross-border investment services. Consequently, the ECJ would accept section 64(5)(1) of the SMA as a derogation from the free movement of capital, but would refuse section 65(4)(2) of the SMA–the former section applies to the establishment of a branch and the latter to cross-border services.

The wide scope of section 65(4)(4) of the SMA does not provide legal certainty, and the prohibition may be disproportionate. Hence, *Commission*

---

[46] See, for instance, *Eglise de Scientologie and Scientology International* [2000] ECR-1335.

[47] ss.64(5)(1) and 65(4)(2), SMA.

[48] s.65(4)(4), SMA.

[49] s.65(8)(1), SMA.

v Belgium does not apply.[50] There is a breach of Article 56 of the EC Treaty.

Sections 69 and 70: investment services in Estonia

The FSA determines the conditions for the founding of a branch or the provision of cross-border investment services in Estonia. There is considerable discretion in these conditions–they include the "requirements applicable upon provision of investment services",[51] which are not specified, and "other circumstances considered to be necessary by the Supervision Authority".[52] If these conditions are unspecific and unknown beforehand to the applicant, and if there is not a genuine and sufficiently serious threat to a fundamental interest of society, they will be unacceptable as a derogation from the free movement of capital, which is restricted by their imposition. The conditions also breach Articles 31(1) and 32(1) of Directive 2004/39/EC.[53]

Section 236: termination of investment services in Estonia

The FSA may prohibit the activities of an investment firm, including the public offer of and trade in its securities if investors need protection, if the Contracting State's securities market supervisory agency takes "insufficient" measures to terminate the firm's violation of this Act or of other Estonian legislation.[54] The FSA must inform the supervisory agency beforehand,[55] and must promptly inform the European Commission.[56] In exceptional cases to protect investors or the public interest, the FSA may apply measures under Estonian legislation to an investment firm without informing the Contracting State's supervisory agency beforehand.[57] However, the FSA must promptly communicate these measures to the Commission.[58]

The FSA's prohibition of cross-border investment services restricts the free movement of capital. As for section 297 of the IFA,[59] the protection of investors is a legitimate national objective for restricting the free

---

[50] [2002] ECR I-4809.
[51] ss.69(3)(7) and 70(3), SMA.
[52] ss.69(3)(8) and 70(3), SMA.
[53] See section 2.4.1.
[54] ss.236^{1}(6) and 236^{1111}(3), SMA.
[55] Ibid.
[56] ss.236^{1}(9) and 236^{1111}(5), SMA.
[57] s.236^{1}(8), SMA.
[58] s.236^{1}(9), SMA.
[59] See the subsection '*Section 297: infringement of national law*' in section 3.1.1.

movement of capital under Article 58(1)(b) of the EC Treaty, provided that it is proportionate and non-discriminatory. The SMA must define 'public interest' because derogations from fundamental freedoms must be based on specific, objective criteria, known to the parties beforehand to provide them with legal certainty. Furthermore, there is no legal redress for investment firms whose activities are prohibited. Article 56 of the EC Treaty precludes the provisions of section 236 of the SMA.[60]

3.1.4 Credit Institutions Act 1999 (CIA)

A 'credit institution' is a company that receives repayable funds from the public and grants loans.[61] Cross-border credits are 'capital movements' within Annex I.[62] Companies receiving repayable funds from the public must hold an authorisation from the FSA.[63]

Section 15: bases of refusal to grant authorisation

Two grounds for refusing authorisation are that close links between the applicant and another person, or laws of the country where that person resides, "prevent sufficient supervision" of the applicant,[64] and that the applicant plans to operate primarily in another Contracting State.[65] The first ground gives discretion to the FSA in deciding what amounts to "sufficient supervision", which is problematical because of the EU legal requirement that measures restricting the free movement of capital must observe the requirements of legal certainty.[66] The ECJ may interpret the second ground as being discriminatory against nationals of other EU Member States, which is forbidden by Article 12 of the EC Treaty. The

---

[60] Section 236 of the SMA follows Article 62 of Directive 2004/39/EC, which gives a host Member State's financial authority the right to prevent further actions of other Member States' investment firms if they breach national law based on this Directive.

[61] s.3(1), CIA.

[62] Current and deposit accounts, commercial credits and financial credits are in Titles VI, VII and VIII respectively.

[63] s.13, CIA.

[64] s.15(5), CIA.

[65] s.15(6), CIA.

[66] *Commission v Belgium* [2002] ECR I-4809. Under Article 12(3) of Directive 2006/48/EC, the FSA may refuse authorisation if the links/foreign laws "prevent the exercise of" its supervisory functions. This phrase requires greater interference with the FSA's powers than "prevent sufficient supervision" of the applicant (s.15(5), CIA). Hence, s.15(5) exceeds the requirements of Directive 2006/48/EC, even allowing for the Estonian to English translation of the subsection.

"sufficient supervision" requirement also arises in relation to foreign supervision authorities over other companies in the same "consolidation group" as the credit institution.[67]

Section 20: Estonian credit institutions operating in foreign countries

The FSA may refuse to authorise the foundation of a subsidiary, branch or representative office in a foreign state if, in its view, the financial situation of the credit institution or its foreign representation is "not sufficiently sound", the representation's organisational structure is "not suitable for the intended activities" or the foreign state's legislation precludes "the exercise of sufficient supervision".[68] These phrases allow the FSA considerable discretion in deciding which credit institutions to authorise. By issuing specific guidelines on how to satisfy these requirements, the FSA would provide legal certainty.

Founding branches and wholly-owned subsidiaries are 'capital movements' under Title I(1) of Annex I. Refusing authorisation restricts the free movement of capital. Since section 20(4) of the CIA is unjustified for lack of legal certainty, it breaches Article 56 of the EC Treaty.

Section 20³: forwarding of information to branch in Contracting State

The FSA can decide to refuse to forward the name, business plan and address of a proposed branch of a credit institution in a Contracting State if, in the FSA's opinion, the credit institution's resources are "insufficient" to provide the services specified in the plan, if opening the branch or implementing the plan "may damage" its finances, activities or its clients' interests, or if the FSA cannot "exercise sufficient supervision" over the branch because the financial supervision authority of the Contracting State "has no legal basis or possibilities for cooperation with" the FSA.[69]

Forwarding of information is not a 'capital movement' under Annex I. Furthermore, Article 25(3) of Directive 2006/48/EC permits the FSA to refuse to forward the information if it has "reason to doubt the adequacy of" the credit institution's administrative structure or financial situation. Section 20³ potentially restricts capital movement, but does not contravene Article 56 of the EC Treaty.

---

[67] s.17(7), CIA. A consolidation group includes subsidiaries and associates with at least 20% of the shares or votes (s.9(1), CIA).

[68] s.20(4), CIA.

[69] s.20³, CIA.

Section 20^{1111}: cross-border services in Contracting States and third countries

The FSA may decide to refuse to forward the name and proposed cross-border services of a credit institution to the financial supervision authority of a foreign state if the institution's resources are "insufficient" for providing those services, if supplying cross-border services "is likely to damage" clients' interests, the credit institution's financial situation or "trustworthiness", or if the FSA cannot "exercise sufficient supervision" over the branch because the financial supervision authority of the Contracting State "has no legal basis or possibilities for cooperation with" the FSA.[70] Forwarding information about cross-border services is not a 'capital movement' as defined in Annex I. Nonetheless, this provision restricts the free movement of capital because it forestalls cross-border services.[71]

The FSA may issue a precept to prohibit a credit institution from providing cross-border services on the grounds stated in the paragraph above.[72] These services are 'capital movements' as described in Annex I. Issuing a precept restricts the free movement of capital, which is not justified by these grounds because they do not relate to a genuine and sufficiently serious threat to a fundamental interest of society, are too general to observe the requirements of legal certainty, and may be disproportionate. Consequently, the issuance of a precept under section 20^{1111} breaches Article 56 of the EC Treaty. Furthermore, since Directive 2006/48/EC provides the FSA with no reasons for refusing to forward information for cross-border services (in the absence of branch foundation), this subsection does not comply with the Directive.

---

[70] s.20^{1111}(5), CIA.

[71] Both the last paragraph in the previous subsection ('*Section 20^{3}: forwarding of information to branch in Contracting State*') and the first paragraph in this subsection ('*Section 20^{1111}: cross-border services in Contracting States and third countries*') concern the FSA's power to refuse to forward information to the financial regulator of another EEA state, but identify such refusal as a potential restriction on the free movement of capital and an actual restriction respectively. In the first instance, the forwarding of information precedes the establishment of the branch–section 20^{1}(1)(1) of the CIA includes as one of its informational requirements "the name of the Contracting State where the credit institution ***wishes to*** open a branch" (emphasis mine). The second instance refers to cross-border services, which are capital movements in Annex I.

[72] s.20^{1111}(8)(1), CIA.

Section 21: authorisation of foreign credit institutions in Estonia

The FSA may refuse to grant an authorisation to a foreign credit institution to found a branch or subsidiary in Estonia, if, in its view, the institution's financial situation is "not sufficiently sound", if the branch's or subsidiary's organisational structure is "not suitable for the intended activities", if the foreign financial supervision authority does not "exercise sufficient supervision", or if this authority "has no legal basis or possibilities for cooperation with" the FSA.[73] The FSA should define the quoted terms with more precision to provide legal certainty.

Section 21^{11111}: cross-border services in Estonia

A credit institution of another Contracting State must inform that State's financial supervision authority of its wish to provide cross-border services, which then informs the FSA.[74] It must indicate which cross-border financial services it intends to provide.[75] Then, the FSA may determine the conditions under which the credit institution must provide its services.[76]

These services are 'capital movements' in Annex I. The FSA's conditions may restrict the free movement of capital. The general principle under EU law is that

[73] s.21(5), CIA. The FSA cannot require authorisation of a credit institution licensed in another Member State (Article 16, Directive 2006/48/EC). A credit institution from a Contracting State requires no authorisation to form an Estonian branch (s.21^{1111}, CIA). In s.21 of the CIA, reference to "foreign" credit institution should be replaced by "third country", because "foreign" may include "Contracting State" and, if so, the authorisation requirement in s.21(2) of the CIA breaches Article 16 of the Directive.

[74] s.21^{11111}(1), CIA.

[75] 'Financial services' include deposit transactions, borrowing and lending services, leasing transactions, settlement and cash transfer, non-cash payments, guarantees, transactions in traded securities, foreign exchange and money market instruments, transactions relating to the issue and sale of securities, advice given to clients on economic activities, transactions relating to the merger and division of companies, money broking, portfolio management, consultation on investments, securities' safekeeping and administration, credit information processing and safe custody (s.6(1), CIA).

[76] s.21^{11111}(3), CIA.

> "discrimination may consist not only in the application of different rules to comparable situations but also in the application of the same rule to different situations",[77]

so the conditions must be assessed carefully in the light of the situations of non-residents and residents to see if they restrict the free movement of capital.

Section 97^2: supervision over branches and cross-border services in Estonia

If a credit institution of a Contracting State violates Estonian legislation, then the FSA may issue a precept to terminate the violation or to prohibit the institution's activities or cross-border services.[78] The FSA must inform the State's financial supervision authority beforehand,[79] unless measures are required in exceptional cases "in order to protect depositors, investors and the public interest".[80] The FSA must promptly inform the European Commission of the measures it has taken.[81]

Cross-border and foreign branch services are 'capital movements' in Annex I. If the FSA terminates them, it restricts the free movement of capital. The ECJ will not accept public policy/security or general interest defences because the protection of depositors, investors and the public interest is not a sufficiently serious threat to a fundamental interest of society, such as the preservation of petroleum supplies at all times.[82] Furthermore, the FSA must state the exceptions in specific terms, known beforehand to the credit institution, in order to provide legal certainty.[83] Section 97^2 of the CIA therefore breaches Article 56 of the EC Treaty.[84]

---

[77] *Kerckhaert and Morres* [2006] ECR I-10967, paragraph 19. The ECJ has not yet extended this principle to other free movement of capital cases.

[78] s.97^2(6), CIA.

[79] Ibid.

[80] s.97^2(8), CIA.

[81] s.97^2(9), CIA.

[82] *Campus Oil and Others* [1984] ECR 2727; *Commission v Belgium* [2002] ECR I-4809.

[83] *Commission v Spain* [2003] I-4581.

[84] Section 97^2 of the CIA follows Article 30 of Directive 2006/48/EC, which enables the host Member State's financial authorities to take "appropriate measures" to ensure that an investment firm authorised by another Member State terminates irregularities that breach national law based on this Directive.

3.1.5 Insurance Activities Act 2004 (IAA)

'Insurance activities' are an insurance undertaking's acceptance of the policyholder's risks under an insurance contract, which pays indemnities when an insured event occurs.[85] An 'insurance undertaking' is a company whose "main permanent activity" is to compensate for damage resulting from insured events or payment of agreed sums.[86] The IAA does not define 'insured events'. An insurance undertaking must hold an activity licence issued by the FSA in order to practise insurance activities.[87] 'Insurance mediation' includes concluding, the preparation for concluding, and administering insurance and reinsurance contracts.[88] Capital transfers in respect of insurance contracts are 'capital movements' in Title X of Annex I.

Chapter 2 Division 2: activities of Estonian insurance undertakings abroad

In this Division, 'cross-border insurance activities' are those of an Estonian insurance undertaking relating to "insurance risks situated in a Contracting State".[89] Such an undertaking is prohibited from providing cross-border insurance activities in third countries.[90] This is a restriction on the free movement of capital, and is only justifiable "for serious political reasons and on grounds of urgency" or "for the protection of the essential interests of [Estonia's] security with the production of or trade in arms, munitions and war material".[91] Both of these grounds are unlikely for most third countries.

Prohibiting cross-border insurance activities to third countries is mitigated by the ability of Estonian insurance undertakings to found a branch in these states, for which the FSA must grant an authorisation.[92] The FSA may refuse to award this licence, and may revoke such an authorisation, for several reasons including that the third country's financial supervision authority "has no legal basis or possibility to cooperate with" the FSA, resulting in the FSA being unable to supervise

[85] s.2(1), IAA.
[86] s.3(1), IAA.
[87] s.16(1), IAA.
[88] s.2(2), IAA.
[89] s.30(1), IAA.
[90] s.29(5), IAA.
[91] Articles 60(2) and 296(1)(b), EC Treaty.
[92] s.31(1), IAA.

the branch.[93] The ECJ is unlikely to accept these reasons if they cause a restriction in the free movement of capital because they do not provide legal certainty, as discussed above.

The FSA may revoke an authorisation if the risks arising from the branch's activities are "significantly greater" that the risks from the insurance undertaking's activities.[94] Termination of the branch's activities restricts the free movement of capital. The Court will require "significantly greater" to be defined with precision, in order to provide the insurance firm with legal certainty. Furthermore, reasons must be given for revoking a licence, with an available remedy in the Estonian courts, if this measure to be an acceptable derogation from free capital movement.[95]

Chapter 2 Division 3: activities of foreign insurance undertakings in Estonia

In Division 3, 'cross-border insurance activities' are those of a Contracting State insurance undertaking relating to "insured risks situated in Estonia".[96] Third country insurance undertakings are prohibited from providing cross-border insurance activities in Estonia.[97] This is a restriction on the free movement of capital, which is only justifiable for important political reasons with urgency or to protect Estonia's security with arms production and trading.[98] Both grounds are unlikely for most third countries.

Third country insurance firms wishing to practice in Estonia must found a branch there, which requires an authorisation from the FSA.[99] The FSA may refuse to grant a licence for several reasons including that the applicant "does not have the sufficient facilities or experience" to practice in the long run,[100] and that close connections between the applicant and another person (whether arising from legislation in that person's state of establishment or not), or the third country's financial supervision authority having "no legal basis or possibility to cooperate with" the FSA, results in the FSA being unable to supervise the applicant.[101]

---

[93] ss.33(5) and 34(1)(6), IAA.
[94] s.34(1)(7), IAA.
[95] *Commission v Belgium* [2002] ECR I-4809; Article 22(2), Directive 73/239/EEC.
[96] s.42(1), IAA.
[97] s.41(5), IAA.
[98] Articles 60(2) and 296(1)(b), EC Treaty.
[99] s.43(1), IAA.
[100] s.23(1)(2), IAA.
[101] ss.23(1)(4) and 44(2), IAA.

Establishing a branch is a 'capital movement' under Title I(1) of Annex I. Since refusing authorisation inhibits the free movement of capital, the FSA must specify the above grounds precisely for them to provide legal certainty, refusal must be proportionate, accompanied by reasons, and subject to appeal in the Estonian courts.[102]

Chapter 10 Division 6: Estonian intermediaries in foreign countries

Only insurance brokers entered in the list of intermediaries by the FSA or insurance agents entered there by an insurance undertaking may engage in insurance mediation abroad.[103] In this Division, 'cross-border mediation' means insurance mediation by an Estonian intermediary without a branch in a Contracting State.[104] Listed intermediaries may not practice cross-border mediation in a third country.[105] Given that the conclusion of insurance and reinsurance contracts involves 'capital movements' as defined in Title X of Annex I, this provision restricts the free movement of capital. For most third countries, it cannot be justified on political and defensive grounds.[106]

An intermediary wishing to found a branch in a third country must apply for an authorisation.[107] The FSA may refuse to grant such an authorisation if, in its view, the intermediary's resources are "insufficient for engaging in mediation" there,[108] or if the third country's financial supervision authority "has no legal basis or possibility for cooperation with" the FSA, resulting in the FSA being unable to supervise the branch sufficiently.[109] The FSA may revoke an authorisation and delete an intermediary from the list if its branch does not satisfy the authorisation requirements.[110]

Founding a branch and insurance mediation involve 'capital movements' in Annex I. Refusal and revocation of authorisation therefore restrict the free movement of capital. This is not justifiable on grounds of public policy/security or the general interest unless there is a "genuine and sufficiently serious threat to a fundamental interest of society", which

---

[102] See the subsection '*The requirements for a successful public policy/security derogation*' in section 2.1.3.
[103] ss.131 and 151(1), IAA.
[104] s.151(2), IAA.
[105] s.151(5), IAA.
[106] Articles 60(2) and 296(1)(b), EC Treaty.
[107] s.152(1), IAA.
[108] s.154(3), IAA.
[109] s.154(6), IAA.
[110] s.155(1)(3), IAA.

cannot be "purely economic ends".[111] Furthermore, the measures must be more specific and objective so as to observe "the requirements of legal certainty".[112]

Chapter 10 Division 7: activities of foreign intermediaries in Estonia

In Division 7, 'cross-border mediation' means insurance mediation by an intermediary of a Contracting State in Estonia without a branch.[113] Third country intermediaries may not practice cross-border mediation in Estonia.[114] This provision impedes the free movement of capital. For most third countries, it cannot be justified on political and defensive grounds.[115]

A third country intermediary wishing to found a branch in Estonia must apply to the FSA for an authorisation.[116] The intermediary must include a statement giving the types of insurance contracts that it plans to mediate,[117] and an authorisation from the third country's financial supervision authority to open an Estonian branch.[118] The FSA may refuse to grant an authorisation if, in its view, the intermediary's resources are "insufficient for engaging in mediation in Estonia",[119] or if the third country's financial supervision authority "has no legal basis or possibility for cooperation with" the FSA, thus causing the FSA to be unable to supervise the branch sufficiently.[120] The FSA may revoke an authorisation and delete an intermediary from the list if the branch does not meet the authorisation requirements.[121]

Since insurance mediation involves 'capital movements' under Title X of Annex I, revocation of authorisation may hinder the free movement of capital. This limitation cannot be justified on grounds of public policy/security or the general interest unless there is a "genuine and sufficiently serious threat to a fundamental interest of society", which

---

[111] *Eglise de Scientologie and Scientology International* [2000] ECR-1335.
[112] *Commission v Belgium* [2002] ECR I-4809.
[113] s.160(2), IAA.
[114] s.160(5), IAA.
[115] Articles 60(2) and 296(1)(b), EC Treaty.
[116] s.161(1), IAA.
[117] s.161(2)(6), IAA.
[118] s.162(3)(1), IAA.
[119] s.163(3), IAA.
[120] s.163(6), IAA.
[121] s.164(1)(3), IAA.

excludes pure economic aims.[122] Furthermore, the measures must be more specific and objective to provide legal certainty.

Sections 172 and 173: precepts

The FSA may issue a precept to prevent violation of the IFA, SMA, CIA, IAA and other legislation pursuant to section 2(1) of the Financial Supervision Authority Act,[123] and to counteract situations which endanger an insurance undertaking's or intermediary's activities, insured persons' or beneficiaries' interests, or "transparency of the insurance market".[124] Furthermore, by issuing a precept, the FSA "has the right" to forbid a Contracting State insurance undertaking or intermediary from engaging in insurance activities in Estonia and to prohibit an Estonian insurance undertaking or intermediary from practising such activities in a Contracting State.[125]

Capital transfers relating to insurance contracts that cross a national boundary are 'capital movements' in Title X to Annex I. Passing a precept restricts these capital movements. Issuing a precept to stop violation of Estonian legislation may be justified under Article 58(1)(b) of the EC Treaty–to take measures necessary to prevent breach of national law with respect to the "prudential supervision of financial institutions".[126] The situations described by section 172(3) of the IAA are too vague to provide legal certainty; furthermore, the IAA neither requires the FSA to provide reasons for issuing a precept, nor gives the insurance firm a remedy, such as an appeal in the Estonian courts.[127] Section 172(3) therefore contravenes Article 56 of the EC Treaty.

Section 180: violation of Estonian legislation

The FSA may revoke its authorisation for a third country insurance undertaking or intermediary to found a branch in Estonia if it breaches the requirements of the IAA or other legislation.[128] The FSA can demand termination of such violation if it is committed by an insurance company or intermediary of a Contracting State.[129] If this insurance company or

---

[122] *Eglise de Scientologie and Scientology International* [2000] ECR-1335.
[123] ss.172(1)-(2), IAA.
[124] s.172(3), IAA.
[125] ss.173(4)-(5), IAA.
[126] The EC Treaty does not define 'financial institution', but, in this context, insurance firms qualify.
[127] *Commission v Belgium* [2002] ECR I-4809.
[128] s.180(3), IAA.
[129] s.180(4), IAA.

intermediary continues to breach Estonian legislation, and if the Contracting State's financial supervision authority's measures are "insufficient", then the FSA may issue a precept to forbid the insurance undertaking or intermediary from practising insurance activities or mediation.[130] The FSA must inform the European Commission of the measures it takes.[131]

Section 180 of the IAA follows the procedure in Article 40 of Directive 92/49/EEC, but does not enact paragraph 40(9), which requires restrictions or penalties on "the conduct of insurance business" to be "properly reasoned". This section complies with Directive 2002/92/EC, other than Article 8(5), which requires a restriction on an insurance intermediary's activities to be "properly justified and communicated" to the intermediary and to be challengeable in the courts of the Member State adopting it.

If the FSA terminates insurance activities or mediation, it hinders the free movement of capital by preventing cross-border capital transfers. This is not justifiable under Article 58(1)(b) of the EC Treaty (taking measures necessary to prevent breach of national law with respect to the "prudential supervision of financial institutions") because section 180 of the IAA gives no specific, objective grounds for terminating insurance activities or mediation. Furthermore, such termination may be disproportionate to the violation. Hence, section 180 infringes Article 56 of the EC Treaty.

3.1.6 Summary and other considerations

The FSA has wide discretion in granting and revoking authorisations, refusing to forward information, issuing precepts and prohibiting cross-border services, which the European Commission and ECJ will not accept in derogation from the free movement of capital. This is a consequence of Estonia's recent accession to the European Union. Estonia has not yet had time to set in place a comprehensive legal and regulatory framework for its cross-border capital flows.

Nonetheless, the FSA is working hard to fulfil the EU requirements. The European institutions should suspend their judgment until the supervisory framework is more complete. The following factors are relevant.

---

[130] s.180(6), IAA.
[131] s.180(8), IAA.

1. History

Estonia has historical and cultural links with Finland and Sweden. Scandinavian organisations have established branches and subsidiaries in Estonia since its Declaration of Independence in 1991. For instance, Estonia has seven affiliated branches of foreign credit institutions, three of which are Finnish, one Swedish and one Danish.[132] Furthermore, the FSA may be modelled on the Finnish Financial Supervision Authority–the supervised institutions and guiding legislation are similar.[133]

2. FSA guidelines

The FSA produces advisory guidelines to explain legal norms, guide supervised entities and establish best practice in the financial sector. The guidelines cover operational matters rather than setting out requirements for authorisation or cross-border service provision in securities, credit and insurance markets.[134]

3. Changes in EU Directives

Changes in EU Directives regulating financial institutions should be reflected in implementing legislation, but there may be a delay.[135] For instance, Articles 17(4) and 18(2) of Directive 93/22/EEC provide that the host Member State's financial authorities may, on receiving forwarded information from the home State's competent authorities relating to an investment firm wishing to establish a branch or provide cross-border investment services in the host State, show this firm the conditions with which "in the interests of the general good" it must comply with there. Directive 2004/39/EC removes this clause, so national legislation enacted pursuant to it is illegal.

For instance, the analysis in section 3.1.3 above found that subsection 65(4)(2) of the SMA was not acceptable under Directive 2004/39/EC. This subsection entitles the FSA to refuse to forward information to another Contracting State if the investment firm's resources are "insufficient" to provide cross-border investment services in that State. Article 18(2) of Directive 93/22/EEC may allow this provision on the

---

132 Estonian Financial Services Authority, 14 February 2007. The other two branches belong to German and Latvian banks.

133 See, in particular, the Finnish Act on the Financial Supervision Authority.

134 Examples include requirements for outsourcing and for organising business continuity process of supervised entities.

135 Directives 2004/39/EC and 2006/48/EC replace Directives 93/22/EEC and 2000/12/EC respectively. Implementation delay is greatest for 2004/39/EC, with transposition to national law required by 1 November 2007.

ground that it would adversely affect investors if the firm could not follow their investment instructions or was at risk of bankruptcy.[136]

4. Memoranda of understanding with Contracting States

The FSA has memoranda of understanding with supervisory authorities of several other European countries. Areas covered include information exchange, capital adequacy requirements for institutions in each State, corrective action and penalties for cross-border establishments, and financial crime.[137] Unfortunately, not all Member States have these bilateral agreements with Estonia,[138] and no third countries do–hence the Estonian government's worry over cooperation with foreign financial supervision authorities, which is a regular feature of its legislation.

5. The Insurance Activities Act revisited

This Act has one particular feature which is of concern with respect to the free movement of capital–the prohibition of Estonian insurance companies to provide cross-border insurance services and mediation to third countries, and vice versa.[139] This is an area which should be addressed by the Commission and Estonian authorities with more care, not only because the Estonian rules breach the EU Treaty, but also because these rules lead to inconsistency across Member States.[140]

3.2 Instructions for the Settlement of Payments

An Estonian Decree gives instructions for the settlement of payments.[141] This differs from the requirements in Directive 97/5/EC on

---

[136] The most recent enactment of section 65 of the SMA is February 2005, which may have been for compliance with Directive 2004/39/EC. Estonian financial legislation is, in general, up-to-date.

[137] The Memorandum of Understanding between the FSA and the German Federal Banking Supervisory Office contains all of these sections.

[138] Articles 56-58 of Directive 2004/39/EC, 42, 131-2 and 140 of Directive 2006/48/EC and 62 of Directive 2002/83/EC provide for cooperation between Member States' supervision authorities and with the European Commission.

[139] The FSA stated that these prohibitions were compatible with the Directives (personal letter, 4 April 2007). I accept this point, but not in mitigation of my argument.

[140] There is a Memorandum of Understanding between the FSA and the Swiss Insurance Supervisory Authority on Cooperation and Exchange of Information, but this does not supersede Estonian law or create enforceable rights [Article A3].

[141] Eesti Pank Governor's Decree, 14 May 2001 No 2.

cross-border credit transfers.[142] Prior information for a cross-border credit transfer (or 'cross-border payment' in the Decree)[143] under the Decree must be given by the issuer of the payment order (the originator) to the payee's credit institution. Such information includes the name of the payer and payee and their credit institutions, their account numbers, and the payment amount, initiation date and purpose.[144]

The prior information requirements according to the Directive are by the credit institutions to their customers, which is a different emphasis to the Estonian Decree. Furthermore, the content of these requirements differs to those in the Decree, being more general. It includes the time needed to credit the funds to the beneficiary institution's and beneficiary's account, the method of calculating commission fees and charges, the value date, procedures for complaint and redress, and reference exchange rates.

In fact, the prior information in the Decree for a cross-border credit transfer is similar to the information required subsequent to a transfer under the Directive. This includes a reference number, the amount of the transfer and of all charges and commission fees, and the value date.

Part IV of the Decree states the information that the credit institution needs to provide to its users. This information closely reflects the prior information requirements in the Directive. It includes the time taken to credit the beneficiary institution and thenceforth the beneficiary with the payment, the calculation method and fees for the payment, complaint and redress procedures, and the procedure for exchange rate usage. Only the value date requirement in the Directive is missing. Hence, other than a difference in timing, the Estonian Decree reflects most of the prior and subsequent information requirements in the Directive.

3.3 Taxation

The state taxes in Estonia are income, social, land, gambling, value added and heavy duty goods taxes, customs duty and excise duties.[145] There are also local taxes.[146] Only the Income Taxes Act provides

---

[142] See section 2.2.1. The New Legal Framework in section 2.2.3 does not apply because the Decree considers 'credit institutions' (not defined), which are not 'payment institutions' in the Framework.

[143] The definition in the Decree is broader, including one party or a payment intermediary being located outside Estonia rather than, as in the Directive, in another Member State.

[144] Part II of the Decree.

[145] s.3, Taxation Act 2002.

[146] s.5, Local Taxes Act 1994.

possible discrepancies with the EU legislation on the free movement of capital.[147]

3.3.1 Income Tax Act 1999 (ITA)

Residence

Residents include individuals who live in Estonia or who stay there for at least 183 days over twelve months,[148] and legal persons deemed to be residents by Estonian law including European public limited companies and European associations.[149] Resident individuals pay income tax on all their income.[150] Non-residents only pay income tax on income from Estonian sources.[151]

Income tax exemptions for residents but not for non-residents

Income from land transfer during ownership reform,[152] from selling "privatisation vouchers" associated with a "public capital bond",[153] from selling the "employment share" from agricultural reform,[154] from selling "privatisation vouchers" issued on the basis of an "unlawfully expropriated property compensation order",[155] and compensation paid for illegally expropriated property and for "privatisation vouchers" not used by "an entitled subject of ownership reforms",[156] are income tax deductions for residents only. These are not objectively comparable for residents and non-residents, because non-residents are unlikely to be affected by such land and ownership matters.[157]

---

[147] There are no such discrepancies in the Taxation Act or Social, Land and Local Tax Acts. Indirect taxes are within EU competence and should be harmonised. The Internal Market requires harmonisation of indirect tax rates–see section 1.2.3.

[148] s.6(1), ITA.

[149] s.6(2), ITA.

[150] s.6(1), ITA. Sections 48-52 of the ITA provide a list of items on which resident legal persons are taxed (s.6(2), ITA).

[151] s.6(3), ITA.

[152] s.15(4)(5), ITA.

[153] s.15(4)(6), ITA.

[154] s.15(4)(7), ITA.

[155] s.15(4)(8), ITA.

[156] s.15(4)(8^1), ITA.

[157] However, they may be affected by these matters where Estonian exiles or their descendants have owned property in Estonia: a significant pattern in most of Central and Eastern Europe.

Under certain conditions,[158] gains from transferring immovable property are exempt from income tax to residents. This does not apply to non-residents. There is a 'capital movement' under Title IIA to Annex I 'Investments in real estate on national territory by non-residents'. If the gains are submitted from Estonia to a non-resident, then the taxation of those gains restricts the free movement of capital. Because both residents and non-residents are taxed from gains from transferring immovable property in Estonia, their situations are objectively comparable. The national law treats them differently. None of the defences apply.[159] Consequently, there is a breach of Article 56 of the EC Treaty.

Income tax to residents is not charged on gifts and donations, lottery prizes, benefits paid to crime victims, conscripts' allowances and compensation for sports assignments under the Sport Act.[160] There is no income tax to residents on insurance payments and indemnities other than funded pensions, on the payment made when terminating a life insurance contract, on insurance indemnities paid when a person dies who is insured under a life contract with an investment risk,[161] or under an insurance contract relating to a supplementary funded pension.[162] Non-residents are taxed on these items.

Although Estonian law does not permit cross-border insurance provision without a branch to third countries,[163] such insurance provision to non-residents is permitted through an authorised branch or subsidiary in the foreign country. Transfers of capital in respect of insurance contracts are 'capital movements' under Title X of Annex I. Charging these transfers to income tax restricts the free movement of capital. Since both residents and non-residents are taxed on income arising in Estonia, their situations are objectively comparable. The national provision treats non-residents less favourably than residents, so there is a breach of Article 56 of the EC Treaty.

---

[158] These conditions are stated in section 15(5) of the ITA. They include, for example, instances in which an essential portion of the immovable property is a dwelling that (i) was used as the taxpayer's permanent or primary residence until transfer (s.15(5)(1), ITA), or (ii) was transferred to the taxpayer through restitution of illegally expropriated property (s.15(5)(2), ITA).

[159] The defences are the need to safeguard the cohesion of the tax system, the fight against tax avoidance and the effectiveness of fiscal supervision; see section 2.3.

[160] ss.19(3)(6)-(10), ITA.

[161] ss.20(3) and 20(5), ITA.

[162] s.21(5), ITA.

[163] See section 3.1.5. Cross-border insurance services are permitted to and from EEA states.

Fringe benefits

Fringe benefits are goods, services and payments-in-kind to employees, company officers and under a contract.[164] Employers pay income tax on such benefits, whether they are resident or non-resident.[165] This is treating objectively similar situations the same, and consequently does not lead to a breach of Article 56.

Income tax withheld at source by foreign countries (withholding tax)

Income derived from abroad, such as interest and dividends, is a 'capital movement' in Annex I, and withholding income tax on this income restricts the free movement of capital. The issue is whether Estonian residents deriving income from abroad are treated the same for income tax purposes as Estonian residents with no foreign income. These situations are objectively comparable. If the national rules distinguish between them without an overriding reason in the general interest, then these rules illegally hinder free capital movement.

If the Estonian income tax calculated on income obtained in a foreign country exceeds the income tax paid there, the taxpayer must pay the difference to the Estonian authorities.[166] But if such calculated income tax is less than the income tax paid in the foreign country, or if the income tax calculated on income from all sources is less than the income tax paid in that country, then the overpaid amount is not refunded in Estonia.[167] In addition, if more tax is paid or withheld in a foreign state than is prescribed by its law or by an international agreement, only the compulsory part of the tax may be deducted from Estonian income tax due.[168]

The third provision in the above paragraph is not discriminatory. But there is inconsistency between the first two provisions–either excess tax paid abroad should be refunded in Estonia and a shortfall of foreign tax be charged in Estonia, or there should be no charge in Estonia for foreign income tax overpayments and underpayments. Estonian residents in these two situations are objectively comparable, and the discrepancy between them is a "disguised restriction" on free capital movement.[169]

164 s.48(4), ITA.

165 ss.48(1)-(2), ITA.

166 s.45(2), ITA.

167 s.45(3), ITA.

168 s.45(6), ITA. This subsection uses the phrase "mandatorily payable", but the ITA does not define or explain what this means in practice.

169 Article 58(3), EC Treaty. This interpretation is a step towards the harmonisation of direct taxes in the European Union because it equalises the claim

Withholding tax on interest payments

Interest withheld on the basis of Directive 2003/48/EC is deducted from Estonian income tax in the same period.[170]

Dividend payments

Resident companies pay income tax on dividends, but not if the dividend is paid from profits of its permanent establishment in an EEA state or Switzerland or, if such profits incur income tax, in a third country.[171] A resident company receiving dividends from a non-resident company, and a non-resident company receiving dividends from another non-resident company through its Estonian permanent establishment, may deduct the income tax withheld from such dividends from its Estonian income tax, but only to the extent that such withholding tax is mandatory under a foreign state's law or an international agreement.[172]

Assuming that dividends received in Estonia from abroad have been taxed at source, both of these provisions are consistent with treating Estonian dividends to Estonian residents similarly to foreign dividends to Estonian residents. Objectively comparable situations are treated the same, as required by EU case law.[173] Consequently, these Estonian rules do not breach Article 56 of the EC Treaty.

Comment

There are a few provisions in the Income Tax Act that are incompatible with Article 56 of the EC Treaty. But, for such a significant and complex area of national legislation, alignment with EU law for the free movement of capital is surprisingly good. There were further anomalies in the 2004 translation of the Income Tax Act. The government has worked hard to align taxation conditions for Estonian residents and non-residents and for cross-border and local capital flows.

---

of Estonian and foreign tax authorities on Estonian residents' income. It may be argued that the interpretation is incorrect because Article 58(1)(a) of the EC Treaty permits Member States "to apply the relevant provisions of their tax law which distinguish between taxpayers who are not in the same situation with regard to … the place where their capital is invested". I disagree. The contrast between sections 45(2) and 45(3) of the ITA concerns Estonia's tax take and is therefore a disguised restriction on the free movement of capital.

[170] s.45(8), ITA.

[171] ss.50(2) and 50(4), ITA.

[172] s.54(5), ITA.

[173] *Lenz* [2004] ECR I-7063. See the subsection '*Lenz*' in section 2.3.1.

3.4 Property

The Law of Property Act 1993 (LPA) and the Law of Property Act Implementation Act 1993 contain no international provisions. Prior authorisation requirements of the Restrictions on Transfer of Immovable Property Ownership to Aliens, Foreign States and Legal Persons Act 1996 restrict the free movement of capital and are disproportionate, thus breaching Article 56 of the EC Treaty. This Act is no longer in force, however.[174] The Private International Law Act applies to cross-border property transfers.[175]

3.4.1 Private International Law Act 2002 (PILA)

The law of the country in which immovable property is situated is used in granting authorisations for the transfer of rights of such property.[176] Estonian law applies to contracts concerning real rights in, or the use of, immovable property located in Estonia unless the contract specifies otherwise.[177] Compliance with Estonian law renders this contract valid.[178]

There is no requirement for official authorisation of land transfer in the Estonian legislation. Real rights are entered, amended and deleted in the land register by completing a registration application.[179] A party transferring immovable property or a real right encumbering it, must complete a notarised agreement with the other party.[180]

These provisions do not restrict the free movement of capital. Estonian and cross-border property transfers are treated similarly, and the legislation does not discourage non-residents from purchasing Estonian assets.[181] Estonia does not even rely on its transitional measures.[182]

---

[174] Its legal effect ended in March 2003, without replacement.

[175] The Ministry of Justice confirmed this (personal letter, 13 April 2007).

[176] s.9(3), PILA. 'Real rights' include, but are not restricted to, ownership, servitudes, superficies, pre-emption and security (Article 5, LPA). The LPA defines these rights.

[177] ss.33(1) and 33(4), PILA.

[178] s.36(3), PILA.

[179] ss.62 and 62[1](1), LPA.

[180] s.64[1], LPA. 'Notarised agreement' is not defined.

[181] See section 2.1.2.

[182] See section 2.5.1. The Forest Act 2006 contains no international provisions.

3.4.2 Conclusions

The Estonian financial legislation is fairly watertight as far as restrictions on the free movement of capital are concerned. It is prescriptive, following a similar format in all four Acts. This tends to give the FSA a wider discretion than free capital movement allows. The Acts should contain guidance on what precise criteria the FSA will be using in each case where an authorisation is required. Occasionally, the Estonian legislation breaches the relevant Directive.[183]

The payments and tax legislation are compliant with EU free movement of capital, other than a few exceptions for taxation. Increasing complexity in these areas will challenge Estonian legislators to keep new measures non-discriminatory against the nationals of other Member States. The thin capitalisation legislation in England and Wales is an example of an area of taxation where considerable modification took place in response to such discriminatory concerns.[184]

The Estonian property laws are compatible with free capital movement. Possible improvements in form include the passing an Act specifying the role of the land authority and the inclusion of cross-border provisions in the Law of Property Act. These modifications bring the property legislation in line with the financial legislation, and clarify the legal rights and obligations of foreign persons interested in transferring Estonian assets.

In the next chapter, Polish law is analysed for its compliance with the EU free movement of capital rules discussed in Chapter 2.

---

[183] For instance, s.70(3) of the SMA breaches Article 31(1) of Directive 2004/39/EC–see section 3.1.3.

[184] The crucial legislation was *Lankhorst-Hohorst GmbH v Finanzamt Steinfurt* [2002] ECR I-11779, analysed by the author elsewhere. Its effect led to the abolition of the thin capitalisation laws in England and Wales and extension of the transfer pricing legislation. The British government chose to increase registration requirements within England and Wales rather than to abolish the registration requirements applying to cross-border capital flows to and from other Member States.

CHAPTER FOUR

POLAND: LEGAL ISSUES

> "The history of Polish Parliamentarism dates back to the 15th century. In contrast, the history of Poland's constitutionalism is a little over 200 years old. It was only in 1791 that the so-called 'Constitution of the 3d of May' was adopted, an endeavor that would lead to a modern system of government. Unfortunately, the Constitution was never implemented due to the subsequent collapse of the Polish state in 1795. ... It was the rebirth of a fully independent Poland in the wake of World War One that paved the way for the development of a truly indigenous constitution, which was adopted in March of 1921".[1]

The fall of communism in 1989 led to substantial constitutional and legal changes as Poland prepared for its membership of the European Union in 2004. Poland implemented a new constitution in 1997, which replaced the largely redundant Soviet-imposed version of 1952. The codified legal system survived, with modifications. Many of the Acts are recent, but there is older legislation, such as the Act of 24 March 1920 on the Acquisition of Immovable Properties by Foreign Persons. The main source of translated acts is from Translegis Publishing's Polish Law Collection. This is a comprehensive body of Polish business and tax legislation.

Sections 4.1 and 4.2 discuss financial Acts; the former considers those regulated by the Financial Supervision Commission (FSC).[2] Section 4.3 considers the Natural Persons' and Legal Persons' Taxation Acts. Section 4.4 comments on the Acquisition of Immovable Properties by Foreign Persons Act. In sections 4.1.7, 4.3.3 and 4.4.2, I compare Polish laws with corresponding Estonian laws.

---

[1] S. Frankowski *(ed.)* (2005), *Introduction to Polish Law*, 1.

[2] The FSC authorises all forms of financial services in Poland, including investment services, banking and insurance. It is called 'Financial Supervision Commission' in the Polish Law Collection, but is also known as 'Financial Supervision Authority'.

4.1 Acts Regulated by the Financial Supervision Commission

4.1.1 Act of 27 May 2004 on Investment Funds (IFA)

An investment fund is a legal person that raises cash by issuing participation units or investment certificates in securities, money market instruments and other property rights in the IFA.[3] Open-end investment funds transfer and repurchase participation units.[4] Closed-end investment funds issue public or non-public investment certificates in bearer form, and the latter as registered securities.[5]

Article 93: open-end investment fund

An open-end investment fund must invest 90% or more of its assets in a regulated market in Member States, in an organised market in OECD Member countries, in short-term deposits with Polish banks and credit institutions, or in money-market instruments elsewhere provided that they or their issuer are subject to investor and savings protection regulations and meet other specified criteria.[6] The FSC must consent to investments in securities and money-market instruments traded on an organised market or purchased in a non-OECD Member country.[7]

Cross-border operations in securities on the capital and money markets are 'capital movements' under Titles III and V respectively of Annex I. Article 93 of the IFA restricts the free movement of capital between Poland and countries outside the EU that do not belong to the OECD. The consent required by Article 93(2) of the IFA is permitted by Directive 2004/39/EC. However, to be a justified restriction on the free movement of capital, this consent must be needed to protect the interests it is intended to guarantee, which are not stated, and be based on specific, objective criteria known to the applicants beforehand to provide legal certainty.[8] In

---

[3] Article 3(1), IFA.

[4] Article 82, IFA. These funds may also buy participation titles in foreign funds and joint investment institutions with a non-Polish seat (Article 101(1)-(2), IFA). A 'foreign fund' is "an open-end investment fund or investment company" with its seat outside Poland but within the EU (Article 2(9), IFA).

[5] Articles 117(1) and 121(1), IFA.

[6] Article 93(1), IFA. 'Regulated market' and 'organised market' are defined in Articles 2(22a) and 2(22) of the IFA respectively.

[7] Article 93(2), IFA.

[8] See the subsection '*The requirements for a successful public policy/security derogation*' in section 2.1.3.

Article 93(1) of the IFA, the interests are investor and savings protection and the criteria are specified. However, this subsection contains no requirement to give reasons if the FSC refuses the application for cross-border investment; nor is an appeal provided in the Polish courts.[9] Article 93 of the IFA must fulfil these requirements in order to comply with Article 56 of the EC Treaty.

Article 145: closed-end investment fund

The following provisions limit free capital movement. Deposits in one Polish bank, foreign bank or credit institution,[10] and foreign currency of one country (including the euro),[11] must be no more than 20% of the fund's assets. Securities, money-market instruments and debt issued by one entity may not amount to more than 20% of these assets,[12] other than securities issued by the Polish National Bank or Treasury, international financial institutions of which Poland is a member, or OECD Member countries.[13]

There is no justification for Articles 145(6)-(7) of the IFA because these restrictions should be applied only at the level of the investment fund rules and prospectus in offering choice to potential clients. Article 145(8) of the IFA discriminates against non-OECD Member countries, and may only be justified "for serious political reasons and on grounds of urgency",[14] or to protect Poland's security with respect to "the production of or trade in arms, munitions and war material".[15]

Articles 264 and 267: investment services in other Member States

The FSC may refuse to pass information on a proposed branch or on planned changes to a branch to the financial authority of the host Member State if, in the FSC's view, 1) the investment firm's financial position does not enable the branch to carry out the proposed services in its business plan, 2) the planned branch organisation "may" cause the branch to "carry on its activity" in breach of the principles of fair trading, or 3) the branch managers "do not warrant" that the branch will carry out the proposed

---

[9] Ibid.

[10] Article 145(6), IFA. A 'foreign bank' has its seat outside the EU (Articles 2(16), IFA and 4(1)(2), Banking Law). Article 145(6) does not include banks within the EU but outside Poland.

[11] Article 145(7), IFA.

[12] Article 145(3), IFA.

[13] Article 145(8), IFA.

[14] Article 60(2), EC Treaty.

[15] Article 296(1)(b), EC Treaty.

investment services.[16] The FSC may impose penalties, including prohibiting investment services in the host Member State, if the investment firm or its branch violates that State's law and fails to eliminate its irregularities within the time limit set by the host State's financial authority.[17]

Article 32 of Directive 2004/39/EC permits the first exception,[18] and may allow the second exclusion,[19] but there is no explicit reference in the Articles referred to in Article 32(7) to lack of capacity from the branch managers. The procedure for imposing penalties must follow Article 62 of Directive 2004/39/EC, which empowers only the host Member State's financial authority to prohibit the investment firm's activities there in the event of a breach of its law.

Founding and extending branches in another Member State are 'capital movements' in Title I(1) of Annex I. Refusing to forward information to the host Member State's financial authority prevents such foundation, thereby restricting free capital movement. Article 264 of the IFA allows the FSC wide discretion, which does not provide legal certainty to investment firms. The IFA must state the criteria for refusing to forward information specifically and objectively, provide reasons for such refusal and allow an appeal in the Polish courts for these Articles to be a justified exception to Article 56 of the EC Treaty.[20] Furthermore, such refusal must be proportionate,[21] which it is not for the second and third exceptions–monitoring the branch's activities with the option of prohibition in a serious case should suffice.[22]

Prohibiting investment services in the host Member State for breach of national law restricts the free movement of capital. This is justifiable under Article 58(1)(b) of the EC Treaty for the "prudential supervision of financial institutions", but not in this instance because the IFA neither

---

[16] Articles 264(6) and 264(10), IFA.

[17] Article 267, IFA.

[18] See section 2.4.1.

[19] Article 32(7) of Directive 2004/39/EC enables the host Member State's financial authority to "request such changes as are strictly needed" to enforce obligations under Articles 19, 21, 22, 25, 27 and 28 and "measures adopted pursuant thereto". This includes adhering to the principle of fair trading. However, a request from the host State's authority does not amount to the FSC's refusal to forward information.

[20] See the subsection '*The requirements for a successful public policy/security derogation*' in section 2.1.3.

[21] Ibid.

[22] The second and third exceptions of Article 264 are only persuasive that the branch will not reasonably provide investment services. Therefore, empowering the FSC to refuse to pass information to the financial authority of the host State if one of these exceptions applies is a severe penalty.

provides specific, objective criteria that constitute a breach, nor requires reasons to be given for such violation, nor provides an action in the national courts.

Articles 270 and 273: investment services in Poland

The FSC may prohibit a management company establishing a Polish branch from transferring participation titles of foreign funds in Poland 1) if the transfer does not meet the legal conditions there, 2) if a foreign fund does not ensure efficient payment for acquiring and redeeming such titles, or 3) if this fund gives insufficient access to information on it to its participants.[23] The FSC may prohibit the management company or its branch from providing investment services in Poland if it breaches national law, with an opportunity given for the home Member State to take action first unless the prohibition is "required for the protection of investors", in which case the FSC informs the European Commission.[24]

Establishing a branch is a 'capital movement' in Annex I. Prohibiting the transfer of foreign fund participation titles restricts the free movement of capital. The first exception would be justified under Article 58(1)(b) of the EC Treaty as a measure to prevent infringements of Polish law if the relevant conditions are specified to provide legal certainty and if reasons are given for the prohibition together with an appeal in the national courts.[25] The second and third exceptions are compatible with Article 32(7) of Directive 2004/39/EC. Nonetheless, they are not justifiable restrictions on free capital movement because they are not defined specifically enough to provide foreign investment firms with legal certainty.

Article 273 of the IFA is less rigorous than Article 62 of Directive 2004/39/EC. Article 62(1) requires the FSC to have "clear and demonstrable grounds" for finding a breach in national law for cross-border investment services; Article 62(2) requires the FSC to "ascertain" such a breach if the investment firm has a Polish branch. Article 273(1) of the IFA only requires the FSC to "find" a breach, whether there is a Polish branch or not.

Cross-border investment services are 'capital movements' in Annex I. The FSC's prohibition of these services hinders free capital movement. Article 273 of the IFA cannot be justified under Article 58(1)(b) of the EC

---

[23] Article 270(6), IFA. A management company is an entity with its seat in a Member State that manages foreign funds (Article 2(10), IFA). 'Foreign fund' is defined in note 4.

[24] Article 273, IFA.

[25] *Commission v Belgium* [2002] ECR I-4809. The restriction is proportionate.

Treaty because the IFA neither requires the FSC to give reasons for its prohibition nor permits an appeal in the Polish courts; prohibition may also be disproportionate. Furthermore, the IFA should provide more guidance to investment firms on what precise behaviour warrants the prohibition of services and on what actions induce a fine, in order to provide them with legal certainty.[26]

Articles 264, 267, 270 and 273 of the IFA also apply to branches of OECD Member countries outside the EEA that manage open-end investment funds,[27] causing restriction of the free movement of capital between Poland and these countries. There is no breach of Directive 2004/39/EC because the states concerned are third countries.

4.1.2 Act of 29 July 2005 on Public Offers and the Conditions for Introducing Financial Instruments to the Organised Trading System, and on Public Companies (POA)

Article 19(2) of the POA states that the FSC may take measures in Articles 16–17 of the POA to protect investors' interests where the home Member State's financial authority has taken no or ineffective action to prevent infringement of this Act, informing that authority and the European Commission of these actions.[28] The measures include prohibiting the initiation or completion of a public offer,[29] and cancelling the admission of securities to a regulated market.[30]

---

[26] See the subsection '*The requirements for a successful public policy/security derogation*' in section 2.1.3. Article 273(2) of the IFA empowers the FSC to fine the firm up to 500,000 zlotys, which is approximately £107,000 or 123,000 Euros (on 30 January 2010).

[27] Articles 277(1) and 279 of the IFA refer Articles 264-279 of the IFA (other than Article 270(9), which is not discussed above) to branches of non-EEA OECD countries.

[28] The home State is that in which the securities' issuer has its seat (Articles 4(6) and 11, POA) or head/registered office (Article 20, Directive 2004/39/EC). Poland is the host Member State, which is where a public offer of securities takes place or where the issuer or sponsor applies for securities to be admitted to a regulated market (Article 11(5), POA). 'Member State' means a party to the EEA Agreement (Article 4(21), POA).

[29] Article 16(2), POA.

[30] Article 17(2), POA. The Polish 'regulated market' comprises stock exchange(s), over-the-counter agreements and the "commodity market for contracts in financial instruments" (Article 15(1), TFIA).

Admission of and transactions in securities on the capital and money markets are 'capital movements' under Titles III and V of Annex I respectively. The above measures restrict the free movement of capital. To be justified, they must be necessary to protect the interests that they are intended to guarantee, in this case investors' interests, but must not be attainable by less restrictive provisions.[31] Articles 16(1) and 17(1) provide less restrictive measures–withholding a public offer or securities' admission to a regulated market for up to 10 days. This is good, but the POA does not specify objective criteria for the FSC to apply the measures, so the securities' issuer is without legal certainty. Furthermore, the FSC need not give reasons for its actions, which must be reviewable in the Polish courts.[32] Article 19(2) therefore breaches Article 56 of the EC Treaty.[33]

4.1.3 Act of 29 July 2005 on Trading in Financial Instruments (TFIA)

Article 96: brokerage activity by foreign subsidiaries in Poland

Subsidiaries or 20% associates of, or of the parent company of, investment firms, credit institutions and insurance undertakings authorised to conduct brokerage activity in another Member State, and of authorised brokers in an OECD Member country or WTO member state, require a permit from the FSC to pursue brokerage activity in Poland, the grant of which depends on a written opinion from the financial authority in the home country as to the firm's conduct of brokerage activity there and, in particular, compliance with national law.[34]

This Article complies with Article 60 of Directive 2004/39/EC, which requires the FSC to consult the home Member State's competent authority before authorising a subsidiary investment firm of an investment firm or credit institution authorised in that State to supply investment services in Poland. It also complies with Article 15 of Directive 2006/48/EC, which requires an authorisation for credit institutions that are subsidiaries of such

---

[31] *Eglise de Scientologie and Scientology International* [2000] ECR I-1335. See section 2.1.3.

[32] See the subsection '*The requirements for a successful public policy/security derogation*' in section 2.1.3.

[33] Article 19 of the POA complies with Article 62 of Directive 2004/39/EC.

[34] Article 96, TFIA. 'Member State' means a party to the EEA Agreement (Article 22(2), TFIA).

institutions of other Member States to provide services in the host State.[35] However, Article 13 of Directive 2006/48/EC requires the FSC to give reasons for refusing authorisation, which the TFIA omits.

'Brokerage activity' is a 'capital movement' in Annex I.[36] Article 96 of the TFIA restricts the free movement of capital. To be justified, prior authorisation must be proportionate, and the grounds on which it is given must be specified objectively to provide the applicant with legal certainty.[37] The TFIA does not provide such information. Consequently, Article 96 violates Article 56 of the EC Treaty.

Article 104: brokerage activity in other Member States

The conditions for authorised Polish institutions to carry out brokerage activity in other Member States,[38] either through a branch or directly, do not entail further authorisation from the host State,[39] and are consistent with Directive 2006/48/EC.[40] Article 104 of the TFIA does not restrict the free movement of capital.

Articles 115 and 117: brokerage activity through a Polish branch

A legal person carrying on brokerage activity in an OECD Member country or WTO member state (outside the EEA) requires authorisation from the FSC to open a branch in Poland, which depends upon a favourable written opinion from the host country's supervisory authority on the legal person's conduct of brokerage activity there, especially its compliance with national law.[41] Opening a branch is a 'capital movement'

---

[35] Article 96 of the TFIA also complies with the general authorisation requirement in Article 5(1) of Directive 2004/39/EC, Article 6 of Directive 2006/48/EC, and Article 6 of Directive 73/239/EEC. Directive 73/239/EEC does not specifically refer to the authorisation of subsidiaries.

[36] 'Brokerage activity' includes receiving, transmitting and executing orders to acquire or transfer, and acquiring, transferring, offering, underwriting or managing portfolios of, financial instruments, together with activities ancillary to these functions (Article 69, TFIA). In so far as such activity involves cross-border transactions in securities on the capital and money markets, it falls within Titles III and V of Annex I respectively.

[37] See the subsection '*The requirements for a successful public policy/security derogation*' in section 2.1.3.

[38] Article 104(2)-(10), TFIA.

[39] Article 104(1), TFIA.

[40] These conditions follow Articles 25 and 28 of Directive 2006/48/EC.

[41] Article 115(3), TFIA. Article 116 provides for a legal person to open a representative office in Poland, but the TFIA does not explicitly provide for cross-

under Title I(1) of Annex I. The authorisation requirement hinders the free movement of capital. This restriction is unjustified because the TFIA neither states specific, objective criteria to be satisfied by applicants, nor requires the FSC to give reasons for refusing an authorisation, nor provides an appeal in the Polish courts against such a refusal.[42]

An investment firm from another Member State can supply cross-border brokerage services in Poland, or open a Polish branch providing such services, without requiring a permit from the FSC;[43] this complies with Article 56 of the EC Treaty. However, there are additional requirements that exceed the scope provided by Directive 2004/39/EC.

Article 117(5)(2) of the TFIA states that Article 94(1)(1) of the TFIA applies to cross-border brokerage services, which empowers the Finance Minister to regulate the provision of these services. This contravenes Article 31(1) of Directive 2004/39/EC, which prohibits Member States from imposing additional requirements on investment firms or credit institutions "in respect of matters covered by this Directive". The definition of 'investment services and activities' in Annex I of Directive 2004/39/EC is similar to that of 'brokerage activity' in Article 62(2) of the TFIA, so the Directive applies.

Article 169: breach of Polish law

Article 169(1)-(3) of the TFIA follows the procedure in Article 62 of Directive 2004/39/EC for breach of Polish law by an investment firm from another Member State. However, the former has a lower standard for imposing penalties than the latter.[44] This provision restricts the free movement of capital, and is not justified under Article 58(1)(b) of the EC Treaty (taking measures to prevent breach of national law for the "prudential supervision of financial institutions") because it does not require the FSC to give specific, objective criteria for taking action against

---

border brokerage activity in Poland from third countries. If this omission renders such activity illegal, then there is a breach of Article 56 of the EC Treaty.

42 *Commission v Belgium* [2002] ECR I-4809. The prior authorisation is only justified "for serious political reasons or on grounds of urgency" (Article 60(2), EC Treaty) or to protect Poland's security "with production of or trade in arms, munitions and war material" (Article 296(1)(b), EC Treaty). See section 2.1.3.

43 Article 117(1), TFIA.

44 The relevant language is the same as for Article 273 of the IFA. See the subsection '*Articles 270 and 273: investment services in Poland*' in section 4.1.1.

a breach of national law or to give reasons for its decision, nor does it provide an appeal in the Polish courts.[45]

Article 169(7) of the TFIA enables the FSC to unilaterally suspend the investment firm's brokerage activity in Poland for up to a month "where the public interest needs to be protected", whilst informing the financial authority of the home Member State and the European Commission. This exceeds the authority granted by Directives 2004/39/EC and 2006/48/EC,[46] and restricts the free movement of capital. Since the TFIA does not define 'public interest', it cannot be established that Article 169(7) is necessary to achieve this objective. Suspending brokerage activity may be disproportionate in some cases, and the lack of specific, objective criteria for suspension does not provide foreign investment firms with legal certainty. This provision breaches Article 56 of the EC Treaty.[47]

4.1.4 Act of 29 August 1997: Banking Law (BL)

Articles 37 to 48j: authorisation

The FSC refuses to authorise the foundation of a bank in Poland if the law in the country of the founder's seat or residence, or its link with other entities, "might prevent effective supervision" of the bank.[48] The FSC must issue a permit to found a bank or branch abroad,[49] but this is not

---

[45] The reasoning is similar to that for Article 273 of the IFA. Article 169 of the TFIA also gives the FSC the option of imposing a fine.

[46] The definition of 'brokerage activity' in the TFIA (see note 36) is similar to that of 'investment services and activities' in Annex I of Directive 2004/39/EC (see chapter 2 note 82); therefore, this Directive applies. However, it neither mentions the suspension of an investment firm's activity, nor defines 'public interest'. There is overlap between the definition of 'brokerage activity' in the TFIA and the 'List of Activities Subject to Mutual Recognition' in Annex I of Directive 2006/48/EC (see chapter 2 note 84); hence, this Directive also applies. Article 31 of the Directive empowers host Member States to prevent credit institutions from conducting further transactions there if those organisations breach national rules enacted "in the interests of the general good". Given the similarity of the terms 'public interest' and 'general good' (neither defined), Article 31 gives the FSC authority to unilaterally suspend the investment firm's brokerage activity for up to one month, but on narrower grounds than the general statement in Article 169(7) of the TFIA (see above).

[47] See the subsection '*The requirements for a successful public policy/security derogation*' in section 2.1.3.

[48] Article 37, BL.

[49] Article 39(1), BL.

required to provide cross-border services in, or to establish a branch in, another Member State.[50] It must authorise the opening of a Polish branch of a third country bank,[51] but this is unnecessary for a bank of another Member State to found a branch in, or to provide cross-border services to, Poland.[52]

These provisions are consistent with Directive 2006/48/EC. The authorisation requirement for founding a third country bank's branch in Poland, and for establishing a Polish bank's branch in a third country, limits the free movement of capital.[53] This restriction is unjustified because the Banking Law does not specify objective criteria upon which authorisation is granted or refused that provide legal certainty to applicant banks. Furthermore, the Law does not require the FSC to give reasons for refusing an authorisation, and no appeal is available to the bank in the Polish courts.[54]

Article 48l and 48ł: banking services in Poland

A credit institution may commence cross-border services in Poland after receiving notification from the home Member State's financial authority of these services.[55] A credit institution's branch may provide services in Poland two months after the FSC has received the following information from the home State's financial authority: the branch's name and address, the surnames of its director and vice-director, a programme of activity specifying the branch's organisational structure and intended operations, and the amount of the credit institution's own funds and its solvency coefficient.[56] The FSC may, within these two months, specify the conditions that the branch must meet for "public benefit", especially to "protect consumers' interests, ensure safety of economic trading" or prevent legal infringements.[57]

---

[50] Articles 48a and 48b, BL. The services are banking and associated operations listed in Articles 5-6 BL, and are similar to those provided in Annex I to Directive 2006/48/EC (see chapter 2 note 84). 'Member State' means EU Member State (Article 4(1)(17), BL).

[51] Article 40(1), BL.

[52] Articles 48i and 48j, BL.

[53] Establishing a branch is a 'capital movement' under Title I of Annex I.

[54] For the requirements to give reasons and provide for appeal through the courts, see section 2.1.3.

[55] Article 48ł, BL.

[56] Article 48l(1), BL.

[57] Article 48l(2), BL.

The informational requirements for providing cross-border services and establishing a Polish branch follow Articles 28 and 25 of Directive 2006/48/EC respectively, and are compatible with Article 56 of the EC Treaty, as they do not require prior authorisation. However, Article 48l(2) of the BL restricts the free movement of capital,[58] and may breach Article 26 of Directive 2006/48/EC, depending upon its interpretation.[59] Refusing the branch permission to operate is an unjustified restriction on free capital movement because the objectives of protecting consumers' interests, ensuring safe economic trading and preventing legal infringements are not specified clearly enough for credit institutions to ascertain their rights and obligations under Article 56 of the EC Treaty, and the refusal may not be necessary to protect these interests.[60] Lesser measures may suffice, for instance the branch could be legally required to report its marketing policies to the Polish consumer association at regular intervals, which could then query particular items such as alleged overcharging on overdrafts.

Article 63g: cross-border transfers: compliance with Directive 97/5/EC [61]

Before accepting the customer's transfer order, banks must provide the time limit for "effecting" the transfer and the cost of "fees and commissions".[62] Article 3 of the Directive also requires the method of calculating commission fees and charges, the value date, reference exchange rates (e.g. EUR/PLN) and complaint and redress procedures.[63]

Article 4 of Directive 97/5/EC requires banks, after a cross-border transfer, to provide their customers with a unique reference number, the amount of the transfer and of charges and commission fees, and the value date. Article 63g of the BL does not implement Article 4. It does, however, implement Article 7(1) of the Directive, which requires all

---

[58] Establishing a branch is a 'capital movement' under Title I(1) of Annex I, which is hindered by imposing conditions.

[59] Article 26(1) empowers the FSC to indicate the conditions under which the credit institution must conduct its activities in Poland "in the interest of the general good". 'Public benefit' is commensurate with 'general good'. The three stated aims are in the public interest, but may lead the FSC to apply disproportionate measures to specific branches.

[60] *Eglise de Scientologie and Scientology International* [2000] ECR I-1335.

[61] See section 2.2.1.

[62] Article 63g(1), BL.

[63] To comply with Article 3, the time limit for 'effecting' the transfer must include the time needed to credit the funds to the beneficiary's credit institution, and then to the beneficiary's account.

institutions to perform the transfer for the full amount unless the originator has stated that the beneficiary is to pay the costs.[64]

Articles 141a and 141b: branch supervision

The FSC may limit the scope of the activities of a branch of a credit institution with its seat in another Member State if it breaches Polish law, although it must give the home State's financial authority the opportunity to act first other than in urgent cases.[65] The FSC may revoke the authorisation of a Polish bank, or limit its activities, if it violates another Member State's laws or regulations through a branch established there or in providing cross-border services.[66] In both cases, the institution may appeal against the decision in the Polish administrative court within 7 days.[67]

These provisions comply with Directive 2006/48/EC, provided that the measures are "appropriate measures" and are "properly justified".[68] Establishing a branch and providing cross-border banking services are 'capital movements' in Annex I. These penalties do not hinder the free movement of capital because the FSC may apply them to Polish banks for breaking Polish law[69]–provided that violations with a cross-border element are not treated more harshly than those without.[70]

4.1.5 Act of 22 May 2003 on Insurance Activity (IAA)

'Insurance activity' consists of insurance acts plus insurance cover for the risk of events.[71] Firms wishing to pursue insurance activity must possess a permit issued by the FSC.[72] 'Insurance acts' include agreeing

---

[64] Article 63g(2), BL.
[65] Articles 141a(1)-(3) and 138(3)(3), BL.
[66] Articles 141b(1), 138(3)(3) and 138(3)(4), BL.
[67] Articles 141a(5) and 141(b)(3), BL.
[68] Articles 30 and 32, Directive 2006/48/EC.
[69] Article 138(3), BL.
[70] See section 2.1.2. The measures may restrict the free movement of capital even if they are applied equally to residents and non-residents (*Commission v Spain* [2003] ECR I-4581). Note that the other 'breach of national law' provisions of Estonia, Poland and Latvia do not have comparable sanctions for the contravention of domestic law by national investment, financial or insurance service providers; therefore, those provisions discriminate against service providers that are registered in other Member States.
[71] Article 3(1), IAA.
[72] Article 6(1), IAA.

insurance and reinsurance contracts,[73] determining premiums and commissions,[74] risk evaluation,[75] payment of indemnity and other dues from the contracts,[76] and investing the insurance firm's funds.[77] Capital transfers in respect of insurance contracts are 'capital movements' under Title X of Annex I.

Article 93a: authorisation of a Polish subsidiary of an EU insurance group

Before issuing a permit, the FSC must write to the home Member State's competent authority for information concerning the insurance establishment, credit institution or investment firm it supervises, including its substantial shareholders, to assess whether the promoters, shareholders and managers of the proposed Polish insurance subsidiary will manage it well.[78] If the subsidiary is fully owned by the group, then its establishment is a 'capital movement' under Title I(1) of Annex I. Refusing a permit restricts the free movement of capital. To be justified, the authorisation requirement must be based on specific, objective criteria known beforehand that ensure that the FSC does not exercise its discretion arbitrarily, and must be proportionate to the aim pursued.[79] The objective is competent management of the insurance subsidiary.

Articles 104 to 122: foreign insurance establishments

A foreign insurance establishment requires a permit from the FSC to pursue insurance activity in Poland,[80] unless its seat is in a Member State.[81] A 'main branch' of such an establishment must fulfil rigorous conditions and submit proof to the FSC, before being granted a permit,[82]

---

[73] Article 3(3)(1), IAA.
[74] Article 3(3)(3), IAA.
[75] Article 3(4)(1), IAA.
[76] Article 3(4)(2), IAA.
[77] Article 3(4)(6), IAA.
[78] Articles 93a, 92(3)(23) and 2(1)(8)-(8a), IAA, and 4(14)-(15), POA.
[79] *Analir and Others* [2000] ECR I-1271.
[80] Article 104(3), IAA. A 'foreign insurance establishment' is a non-Polish firm pursuing insurance activity (Articles 2(1)(16), IAA and 5(2)-(3), FEAA).
[81] Article 128(1), IAA. Articles 104-122 of the IAA therefore comply with Directives 73/239/EEC, 88/357/EEC and 2002/83/EC. 'Member State' means a party to the EEA Agreement (Article 2(2), IAA).
[82] Article 107(3), IAA. Examples are the submission of a satisfactory career record and a clean criminal record for the proposed appointees for the posts of Director, Deputy Directors and Actuary of the main branch (Articles 107(3)(12)-(15), IAA). A 'main branch' is a branch of an insurance establishment with its seat

and the FSC will only issue a permit if it is satisfied that several other criteria are met.[83] The main branch must fulfil further conditions to commence business,[84] and to operate on an equal basis with EU insurance firms.[85]

The FSC may withdraw its permit for the foreign insurance establishment to pursue insurance activity in Poland if any of the conditions for granting it are breached,[86] if the establishment does not commence insurance activity within 12 months of authorisation,[87] or ceases such activity for more than 6 months,[88] or if the main branch breaches Polish law or the establishment's Articles of Association.[89] The FSC may liquidate the main branch if it performs insurance activity in violation of Polish law, the Articles or the business plan,[90] or does not "provide insurance benefits" in Poland, or partly or belatedly provides them.[91]

These provisions restrict the free movement of capital between Poland and third countries. Some of them are disproportionate, such as the FSC's power to liquidate the main branch on the grounds stated above. The FSC must state specific, objective criteria that a foreign insurance firm must satisfy to be granted a permit or to avoid its withdrawal, in order to accord legal certainty. For instance, the FSC could specify what should be present in the main branch's business plan to offer specific insurance services.[92] The IAA neither requires the FSC to give reasons for refusing or withdrawing authorisation, nor explicitly provides an appeal in the

---

in a non-EU country (Article 2(1)(3), IAA). 'EU' may extend to the 'EEA' (see note 80), i.e. include insurers with seats in Iceland, Liechtenstein and Norway.

[83] These include the foreign insurance establishment possessing sufficient financial means, the main branch's business plan being adequate to support its proposed insurance activity, and the pursuit of such activity not endangering "defence, State security and public security or order" (Article 114(1), IAA).

[84] Main branches must have a minimum solvency margin and security deposit (Articles 113 and 116, IAA).

[85] The FSC must grant permission to situate assets covering technical and underwriting reserves in Poland (Article 109(1)(3), IAA).

[86] Article 119(2)(1), IAA.

[87] Articles 119(2)(4) and 111, IAA.

[88] Article 119(2)(5), IAA.

[89] Article 119(2)(2), IAA.

[90] Article 122(1)(1), IAA.

[91] Article 122(1)(2), IAA.

[92] Class I provides 5 types of life assurance, and class II gives 18 categories of personal and property insurance (Annex, IAA).

Polish courts.[93] Articles 104-122 of the IAA therefore breach Article 56 of the EC Treaty.[94]

Articles 127 to 137: insurance activity between Poland and other EU Member States

An authorised Polish insurance undertaking may provide insurance services in another Member State without further permission.[95] An insurance firm authorised to pursue insurance activity in another Member State may supply insurance services to Poland.[96] This State's financial authority must provide the FSC with a certificate stating that the firm possesses assets to cover the solvency margin,[97] with information on types of insurance that the firm is authorised to provide,[98] and with information on the "kinds of risks" it covers in Poland.[99] This information is provided for both cross-border insurance services and for establishing a branch.[100] The latter also requires notification of the branch's organisational structure, business plan, address and agents' names, the host Member State's name, and the types of insurance activities and risks.[101]

A Polish insurance firm wishing to provide cross-border insurance services in another Member State must inform its financial authority,[102] furnishing it with the risks it intends to cover.[103] It must also provide the information in Article 132(1) of the IAA within 30 days of initial notification.[104] The FSC may refuse to forward this information if the

---

93 Polish common courts have jurisdiction over matters in Poland in which a foreign insurance establishment is a "party or participant" (Article 106(10), IAA).

94 These measures may be justified "for serious political reasons and on grounds of urgency" (Article 60(2), EC Treaty), but this cannot apply to all third countries.

95 Article 127(1), IAA.

96 Article 128(1), IAA.

97 Article 132(1)(1), IAA.

98 Article 132(1)(2), IAA.

99 Article 133(1)(3), IAA.

100 Article 131(1)(1), IAA. Article 16(1) of Directive 88/357/EEC only requires this information for providing cross-border insurance services (see section 2.4.3).

101 Article 135(1), IAA. Article 10(2) of Directive 73/239/EEC requires all this information, other than the last item (see section 2.4.3). The notification of insurance activities and risks may assist the FSC in assessing what the conditions are, "in the interest of the general good", that the branch must conduct business (Article 10(4), Directive 73/239/EEC).

102 Article 134, IAA.

103 Article 137(1), IAA.

104 Article 137(2), IAA. This provision complies with Article 16(1) of Directive 88/357/EEC.

insurance firm's financial position does not "allow" it to provide cross-border services.[105] Article 16 of Directive 88/357/EEC contains no such statement. The IAA requires the FSC to provide reasons for this refusal,[106] but does not give the firm the right to appeal against refusal in the Polish courts as required by Article 16(2) of the Directive.

The FSC must notify the host Member State's financial authority of the domestic insurance undertaking's intention to establish a branch there,[107] and must provide it with the information in Article 135(1) of the IAA within 3 months of initial notification.[108] The FSC may refuse to furnish such information if it considers that the insurance firm's financial position "does not permit" a branch to be opened,[109] that the branch's structure "does not ensure" satisfactory pursuit of insurance activity,[110] that the branch's managers are insufficiently qualified or experienced, do not guarantee good professional conduct or have a criminal record,[111] or that the branch's business plan does not enable it to perform its obligations.[112] The FSC must give reasons for this refusal.[113]

Opening a branch and capital transfers in respect of insurance contracts are 'capital movements' under Titles I(1) and X of Annex I respectively. If the FSC refuses to forward information to the host Member State's financial authority, it restricts the free movement of capital if the Polish insurance firm is establishing a branch there, and potentially hinders capital movement if this firm is to provide cross-border insurance services. Such restriction is unjustified because the grounds specified in the IAA give the FSC too much discretion. The Act should provide specific, objective criteria that provide legal certainty to the applicant insurance firms, which they must satisfy for the FSC to forward the required

[105] Article 137(3), IAA.

[106] Article 137(5), IAA. Article 16(2) of Directive 88/357/EEC requires the home State's financial authority to provide reasons for refusing to forward the information.

[107] Article 134, IAA.

[108] Article 135(2), IAA. Article 10(2) of Directive 73/239/EEC requires the FSC to provide all this information other than the types of insurance activities and risks.

[109] Article 135(3)(1), IAA.

[110] Article 135(3)(2), IAA.

[111] Article 135(3)(3), IAA.

[112] Article 135(3)(4), IAA. Article 10(3) of Directive 73/239/EEC does not explicitly allow this reason for refusal, but requires competent authority to "tak[e] account of the business planned" in deciding whether to forward the information.

[113] Article 135(5), IAA. See note 106.

information, and should give these firms the right to appeal in the Polish courts against a decision of the FSC to refuse to forward it.[114]

Article 139: breach of Polish law

If an insurance firm whose seat is in another Member State breaches Polish law, then the FSC asks it to remedy the infringement(s);[115] if it does not do so, then the FSC informs the home State's competent authority.[116] If this authority takes insufficient action to stop the infringement(s), then the FSC may, after informing it, apply measures granted to it by the IAA to prevent further violations of Polish law,[117] including prohibiting further insurance activity by the firm in Poland.[118]

Article 139 of the IAA follows Article 40 of Directive 92/49/EEC, with the following differences.

1. Preventing further insurance activity is "as is strictly necessary" in the Directive;[119] Article 139(4) IAA omits this phrase.
2. Article 40(9) of the Directive requires the FSC's measures to be "properly reasoned" and imparted to the insurance firm; this requirement is absent from the IAA.

Prohibiting insurance activity restricts the free movement of capital. It cannot be justified under Article 58(1)(b) of the EC Treaty,[120] because the IAA neither states the specific, objective grounds on which the FSC will take this action, nor requires the FSC to provide reasons for it, nor provides an appeal against it in the Polish courts.[121]

Article 214: limiting permits to third country insurance firms

The FSC may limit the number of permits issued to third country firms wishing to pursue insurance activity in Poland, if the European Commission takes an "appropriate decision" based on information given by Polish insurance companies intending to pursue such activity in those

---

[114] See the subsection '*The requirements for a successful public policy/security derogation*' in section 2.1.3.
[115] Article 139(1), IAA.
[116] Article 139(2), IAA.
[117] Article 139(3), IAA.
[118] Article 139(4), IAA.
[119] Article 40(5).
[120] Member States can "take all requisite measures to prevent infringement of national law and regulations" in particular for "the prudential supervision of financial institutions".
[121] See the subsection '*The requirements for a successful public policy/security derogation*' in section 2.1.3. Prohibiting insurance activity is disproportionate if the breach is insignificant.

countries.[122] Since capital transfers in respect of insurance contracts are 'capital movements' in Title X of Annex I, authorisation restrictions hinder the free movement of capital between Poland and the third countries concerned.

Article 60(2) of the EC Treaty enables a Member State to unilaterally restrict capital movements to/from third countries for "serious political reasons" and if urgent. If the restrictions are in line with the European Commission's decision, then, provided that the need for them is immediate, they are an acceptable derogation from free capital movement.

4.1.6 Act of 22 May 2003 on Insurance Mediation (IMA)

'Insurance mediation' involves the paid execution of "factual or legal acts" in the "conclusion and performance of" insurance contracts.[123] Insurance mediation must be performed by insurance agents or insurance brokers.[124] An 'insurance agent' is an "entrepreneur", entered in the insurance agents' register, which performs "agency activities" under a contract with an insurance company.[125] 'Agency activities' include seeking clients, preparing and concluding insurance contracts, and assisting both in matters relating to insurance contracts and in organising and supervising such activities.[126]

An 'insurance broker' is a natural or legal person, entered in the insurance brokers' register, which is authorised to perform "brokerage activities".[127] 'Brokerage activities' are conducted on behalf of persons seeking insurance coverage, and include preparing, concluding and participating in issues concerning, insurance contracts.[128]

An insurance agent registered as such in another Member State may "pursue agency activities" in Poland,[129] having notified the FSC,[130] upon

---

[122] Articles 214(1) and 214(3)(1), IAA.

[123] Article 2(1), IMA.

[124] Article 2(2), IMA. Reinsurance mediation must be undertaken by insurance brokers with a reinsurance permit (Article 2(3), IMA).

[125] Article 7, IMA. An 'entrepreneur' is a natural person, a legal person or an organisation with no legal personality but with legal capacity, which undertakes "economic activity" in its own name (Article 4, FEAA). 'Economic activity' is profit-making activity in specified fields (Article 2, FEAA), including insurance mediation (Article 5, IMA).

[126] Article 4(1), IMA.

[127] Article 20, IMA.

[128] Article 4(2), IMA.

[129] Article 16(1), IMA.

[130] Article 16(2), IMA.

the latter's receipt of confirmation by the home State's competent authority that the agent is so registered.[131] An insurance broker registered as such in another Member State may "pursue brokerage activities" in Poland under the same conditions.[132]

An insurance agent registered as such in Poland may "pursue insurance activities" in another Member State,[133] having informed the FSC of this intention.[134] Within 30 days of such notification, the FSC must inform the host State's competent authority that the agent is so registered.[135] An authorised Polish insurance broker may "pursue brokerage activities" in another Member State under similar conditions.[136]

These provisions follow Article 6(1) of Directive 2002/92/EC.[137] However, the IMA does not fully transpose the Directive. It omits Article 6(3), which empowers the host Member State's competent authority to take the required steps for publication of business conditions "in the interest of the general good". It also omits Article 8(5), which requires the FSC to "properly" justify, and to communicate to the insurance intermediary, measures it takes involving sanctions or limitations on the latter's activities, and which provides a right of appeal to the courts of the State adopting these measures.

Agency and brokerage activities are 'capital movements' in Title X of Annex I, because they are "operations necessary for the purpose of capital movements",[138] which the Annex includes as 'capital movements'. However, none of the above provisions restrict the free movement of capital; they only require confirmation that the insurance agent or broker is registered.

4.1.7 Comparison with Estonia

Estonian Investment Funds Act (EIFA) and Polish Investment Funds Act (PIFA)

The PIFA splits 'investment funds' into open-end and closed-end funds, and applies limitations to each on the percentage of assets that can

---

[131] Article 16(3), IMA.
[132] Article 31, IMA.
[133] Article 17(1), IMA.
[134] Article 17(2), IMA.
[135] Article 17(3), IMA.
[136] Article 32, IMA. The FSC must inform the host State's competent authority that the broker holds a permit to perform these activities (Article 32(3), IMA).
[137] See section 2.4.4.
[138] Annex I.

be invested in various categories (e.g. a maximum of 20% of closed-end fund assets may be invested as deposits in one bank).[139] The EIFA neither distinguishes between fund types, nor restricts investments in particular assets.[140]

The EIFA uses two categories of country for cross-border investment: EEA and third countries.[141] The PIFA has three such categories: EEA, OECD and non-OECD states.[142] An Estonian firm can legally invest only in selected third countries.[143] The Polish legislation is slightly less restrictive, and therefore is more compliant with Article 56 of the EC Treaty–open-end investment funds are required to invest at least 90% of their assets in EU or OECD countries.[144]

A foreign investment firm without an Estonian branch wishing to buy and sell its fund units in Estonia must contract with a management company, investment firm or credit institution which is, or whose branch is, registered there.[145] The PIFA does not require this. However, the Estonian requirement is not a restriction on the free movement of capital because the foreign firm can establish an Estonian branch to market its fund units.[146]

Estonian Securities Market Act (ESMA) and Polish Public Offer (PPOA) and Trading in Financial Instruments Acts (PTFIA)

The PPOA provides three measures for legal breach by a securities' issuer: publication of the violation, ten day suspension of the public offer or securities' admission to a regulated market, and cancellation of the

---

139 Article 145(6), PIFA.

140 See section 3.1.1.

141 Ibid. The distinction applies to Estonian firms investing abroad and to foreign companies investing in Estonia.

142 See section 4.1.1.

143 See section 3.1.2. Consequently, for outbound Estonian investment there are three categories: EEA, selected third country and non-selected third country. The 'selected' third countries are the states outside the EEA on at least one of the three lists of Regulation No.73 of the Minister of Finance of 19 November 1997; these are Australia, Canada, Japan, Russia, Switzerland, Ukraine and the USA.

144 Article 93(1), PIFA. The first list of countries in Estonian Regulation No.73 of the Minister of Finance of 19 November 1997 permits up to 10% of Estonian investment fund assets to be used to purchase the securities of non-selected third countries. However, the following OECD Member countries are not on that list: Iceland, Mexico, New Zealand, South Korea and Turkey, which makes it more restrictive than Article 93(1) of the PIFA.

145 s.229(1), EIFA.

146 See section 3.1.1.

public offer or securities' admission.[147] The ESMA gives just two remedies for breach of national law: terminating the contravention and prohibiting further activities.[148] The Polish approach is less restrictive of free capital movement than the Estonian legislation because the first two Polish measures may be sufficient to stop the violation, and because the Estonian legislation does not indicate what precise measures the FSA should take to apply the prescribed remedies.[149]

Both the Estonian FSA and the Polish FSC can apply unilateral measures for breach of national law to protect the public interest, but the latter may suspend the investment firm's activity for up to one month,[150] whilst the former may take any measures under Estonian legislation.[151] The Estonian legislation is more restrictive of the free movement of capital than the Polish law, because it provides the FSA with discretion as to which measures to apply.[152]

Estonian Credit Institutions Act (ECIA) and Polish Banking Law (PBL)

If a Polish bank breaches another Member State's laws and regulations, then the FSC may revoke its authorisation, limit the scope of its activities or impose a fine.[153] The ECIA does not provide an equivalent provision. The Polish rule does not restrict the free movement of capital, however.[154]

Whilst the FSC can fine, or "limit" the Polish activities of, a foreign credit institution for a contravention of Polish law,[155] the FSA can apply measures in the ECIA to stop a foreign credit institution's violation of Estonian law or to "prohibit" its activities or cross-border services.[156] The Polish rule hinders the free movement of capital less than the Estonian

[147] Articles 16-17, PPOA.

[148] s.236^{1}(6), ESMA.

[149] The FSA is authorised to "apply measures provided for in this Act" (s.236^{1}(6), ESMA). This does not provide investment firms with specific, objective criteria consistent with legal certainty, and the measures taken may be disproportionate to the breach (see '*The requirements for a successful public policy/security derogation*' in section 2.1.3).

[150] Article 169(7), PTFIA.

[151] s.236^{1}(8), ESMA. The FSA may also apply such measures to protect investors.

[152] See note 149.

[153] Articles 141b(1) and 138(3), PBL.

[154] See section 4.1.4.

[155] Articles 141a(2) and 138(3), PBL.

[156] s.97^{2}(6), ECIA.

provision because the former provides more specific, more proportionate measures than the latter.[157]

In Poland, the bank or credit institution may appeal against an FSC decision to limit its activities or to revoke its authorisation, although it has only 7 days to do so.[158] The ECIA provides no appeal against the FSA's decisions. Granting such an appeal is a necessary component of a justification for restricting the free movement of capital.[159]

Estonian Insurance Activities Act (EIAA) and Polish Insurance Activity Act (PIAA)

Estonian insurance firms are not permitted to provide cross-border insurance activities to countries outside the EEA.[160] Furthermore, insurance companies registered in a non-EEA country may not pursue cross-border insurance activities in Estonia.[161] The PIAA does not refer to the provision of cross-border insurance services to or from third countries.[162] It refers only to firms from such states pursuing insurance activity in Poland through a branch, and not vice versa.[163] Given this fact, it would appear that the absence of legal provisions in the PIAA on cross-border insurance services to or from third countries reflects the fact that such activity is not permitted by Polish law. If so, the Estonian and Polish positions on cross-border insurance services to and from non-EEA states equally restrict the free movement of capital.

Both EIAA and PIAA require authorisation for a third country insurance firm to found a branch in Estonia/Poland, but the conditions for establishing the Polish branch are more precise and more numerous.[164] The discretion that the EIAA gives to the FSA in deciding whether to grant an authorisation may enable it to refuse disproportionately, which hinders free capital movement.[165] Nevertheless, the Polish conditions limit such movement more than the Estonian rules because they make it

[157] See '*The requirements for a successful public policy/security derogation*' in section 2.1.3. The language in the PBL ('limit') is less likely to lead to disproportionate measures than that in the ECIA ('prohibit').

[158] See section 4.1.4.

[159] See '*The requirements for a successful public policy/security derogation*' in section 2.1.3.

[160] s.29(5), EIAA.

[161] s.41(5), EIAA.

[162] The freedom to provide insurance services only applies to EEA countries (Chapter 7, PIAA).

[163] Chapter 6, PIAA.

[164] See sections 3.1.5 and 4.1.5.

[165] See section 2.1.3.

difficult for a third country insurance company to establish a working branch in Poland.[166]

The PIAA makes no reference to a Polish insurance firm being able to found a branch in a non-EEA country. Since an Estonian insurance company may establish a branch there after obtaining an authorisation from the FSA,[167] the Estonian rule is less restrictive of the free movement of capital than the Polish position.

Whilst the FSC may limit the number of permits granted to third country insurance companies providing insurance services in Poland on the basis of a European Commission decision,[168] the EIAA contains no equivalent measure. Conversely, the FSA may apply precepts for the breach of Estonian law or to counteract situations that adversely affect the insurance market,[169] but the PIAA does not provide for the issue of precepts. The latter rule restricts the free movement of capital more than the former because of its wider scope–it applies both to third countries and to EEA states, and does not depend upon an EU decision.

EIAA and Polish Insurance Mediation Act (PIMA)

In both Estonia and Poland, insurance mediation must be undertaken by insurance intermediaries, which are either insurance agents or insurance brokers.[170] Only the former may practise agency activities, and only the latter brokerage activities.[171]

Estonian intermediaries may not provide cross-border insurance mediation to countries outside the EEA.[172] Intermediaries registered in a non-EEA state may not supply cross-border insurance mediation to Estonia.[173] The former intermediaries may provide insurance mediation to another EEA country, and the latter to Estonia, through a branch after being authorised by the FSA.[174] The grounds for refusing authorisation are neither specific nor objective, thereby denying legal certainty to applicants.[175]

---

[166] See section 4.1.5.
[167] s.31(1), EIAA.
[168] Article 214(3), PIAA.
[169] s.172, EIAA.
[170] ss.130(1)-(2), EIAA; Article 2(2), PIMA.
[171] s.130(3), EIAA; Articles 7 and 20, PIMA.
[172] s.151(5), EIAA.
[173] s.160(5), EIAA.
[174] ss.152(1) and 161(1), EIAA.
[175] See section 3.1.5.

The PIMA neither refers to Polish intermediaries providing insurance mediation to countries outside the EU, nor to intermediaries registered in non-Community states supplying these services to Poland. The Act's omission of third countries may prevent capital movements associated with insurance mediation to and from these states, and at least casts doubt on the legality of such movements. If the omission equates to the prohibition of those capital movements, the Polish position is identical to that of Estonia for cross-border insurance mediation to and from non-EEA countries, and more restrictive than the Estonian rules of the free movement of capital to and from these countries via a branch.

Comment

The Polish legislation is less well organised than the Estonian legislation. In Estonia, the FSA tends to have more discretion in granting and withdrawing authorisations than the FSC does in Poland. The broad, prescriptive Estonian rules may provide a more rigid framework for capital movement than the detailed Polish laws. It is essential that the FSA carefully considers the facts of each case in deciding whether or not to grant an authorisation, and that it gives reasons for its decision, thereby enabling the development of specific, objective criteria for authorisation known beforehand to applicant firms.

4.2 Other Financial Acts

4.2.1 Act of 28 February 2004 on Freedom of Economic Activity (FEAA)

The Minister for the Economy can prohibit a foreign entrepreneur from "conducting economic activity" in Poland through a branch or agency if the branch/agency "flagrantly" breaches Polish law,[176] if liquidation proceedings are commenced against the entrepreneur or if it "forfeits the right" to pursue economic activity,[177] or if the entrepreneur jeopardises state defence and security or "another important public interest".[178]

[176] Articles 91(1)(1) and 101(1)(1), FEAA. A 'foreign entrepreneur' is a natural person resident abroad, or a legal person (or organisation with no legal personality but with legal capacity) with its seat abroad (Articles 5(2)-(3), FEAA). 'Economic activity' is defined in note 125.

[177] Articles 91(1)(2) and 101(1)(2), FEAA.

[178] Articles 91(1)(3) and 101(1)(3), FEAA.

Establishing a branch is a 'capital movement' under Title I(1) of Annex I.[179] The Minister's prohibition hinders the free movement of capital.[180]

Article 91(1)(1) of the FEAA is an unjustified restriction

Article 58(1)(b) of the EC Treaty enables Poland to take all necessary measures to prevent violations of national law and regulations. A prohibition of profit-making activity for a 'flagrant' breach of Polish law may be proportionate, but the FEAA neither provides legal certainty by defining a specific, objective standard for 'flagrant' legal violation, nor provides redress in the Polish courts for a prohibition.[181]

Article 91(1)(2)

If liquidation proceedings are started against the foreign entrepreneur, its Polish assets should be frozen. Therefore, the prohibition of profit-making activity is proportionate. Since the FEAA does not explain what 'forfeiting the right' to conduct economic activity means, prohibition for this reason is unjustified for lack of legal certainty.[182]

Article 91(1)(3)

To be justified for public policy/security under Article 58(1)(b) of the EC Treaty, there must be a "genuine and sufficiently serious threat to a fundamental interest of society",[183] such as a threat to energy supplies in a crisis,[184] or to petroleum products at all times.[185] Article 91(1)(3) of the FEAA does not specify such a threat–it is drafted in general terms.

Poland may take measures to protect its security "with the production of or trade in arms, munitions and war material".[186] Article 91(1)(3) is justified in so far as the foreign entrepreneur threatens Poland's military security.

---

[179] Article 94 of the FEAA empowers an agency only to promote and advertise the foreign entrepreneur, which is not a 'capital movement' in Annex I.

[180] See section 2.1.2. The FEAA does not apply these provisions to domestic entrepreneurs.

[181] See '*The requirements for a successful public policy/security derogation*' in section 2.1.3.

[182] Ibid.

[183] *Eglise de Scientologie and Scientology International* [2000] ECR I-1335.

[184] *Commission v Belgium* [2002] ECR I-4809.

[185] *Campus Oil and Others* [1984] ECR 2727.

[186] Article 296(1)(b), EC Treaty.

4.2.2 Act of 27 July 2002: Foreign Exchange Law (FEL)

Articles 9 and 10: limitations on cross-border foreign exchange dealings

There are limitations on work-related payments from foreigners to residents in non-convertible currencies,[187] on exportation of domestic or foreign tenders exceeding 10,000 euros, gold and platinum except for those previously imported and declared to the customs authorities,[188] and on many transfers to and from third countries including securities, debts and the acquisition by residents of immovable property in third countries and rights in such property.[189]

Poland may introduce "special limitations" for ensuring balance of payments equilibrium or for enforcing decisions of international organisations.[190] The Council of Ministers may regulate to bring in these limitations.[191]

Cross-border foreign exchange flows are 'capital movements' in Annex I. Introducing limitations on them restricts the free movement of capital. Several elements are missing for Article 9 of the FEL to be justified, as follows. The term 'limitation' should be defined and connected with a public interest objective. The limitation must be necessary for the protection of the specified interest, and must be proportionate. Restricting so many capital flows to and from third countries is disproportionate. Furthermore, the FEL neither requires reasons to be given for limitation, nor provides an appeal in the Polish courts.[192] Article 9 of the FEL therefore breaches Article 56 of the EC Treaty.

For Article 10 of the FEL to be justified, the special measures must be necessary for the protection of the specified interest, and must be proportionate. The proposed regulations should provide specific,

---

[187] Article 9(1), FEL. The FEL does not define 'limitation'.

[188] Articles 9(2), 9(3) and 18(1), FEL. 'Domestic tenders' are Polish currency, securities and documents drawn in Polish currency whose function is a means of payment (Article 2(1)(6), FEL). 'Foreign tenders' are foreign currency and foreign exchange (Article 2(1)(9), FEL).

[189] Articles 9(5)-(13), FEL. 'Third countries' are those outside the EEA and OECD (Articles 2(1)(5) and 2(2), FEL).

[190] Article 10(1), FEL. Until 1 May 2004 but no later, special limitations could be introduced to ensure public order or security, and to keep the Polish currency stable (Articles 10(1) and 62, FEL).

[191] Articles 10(2)-(3), FEL.

[192] See '*The requirements for a successful public policy/security derogation*' in section 2.1.3.

objective criteria for capital flows to avoid restriction, and must give reasons for the restriction and an action against it in the national courts.[193]

Articles 19 and 23: export permits

Residents and non-residents exporting domestic or foreign tenders exceeding 10,000 euros or gold or platinum must present to the customs authorities documents confirming their right to export, or a foreign exchange permit granting them this right.[194] There is a 'capital movement', as defined in Annex I. These Articles restrict such movement.[195]

To be justified, the restrictions must be based on specific, objective criteria, in order to provide exporters with legal certainty. The Polish legislation must state reasons for refusing an export, and must permit an appeal against this refusal in the Polish courts.[196] Whilst the FEL does not satisfy these requirements, it allows the Finance Minister to determine by regulation the rules for importation and exportation, and to list the documents confirming the right to export domestic and foreign tenders.[197] This gives the Minister sufficient scope to justify Articles 19 and 23 of the FEL as a restriction on the free movement of capital. The Minister has passed one such regulation, which is discussed in section 4.2.3.

4.2.3 Regulation of the Minister of Finance of 3 September 2002 on General Foreign Exchange Permits (RGFEP)

This regulation provides an extensive list of circumstances under which cross-border foreign exchange dealings are permitted, which reduces the restrictions of Article 9 of the FEL, thereby enhancing cross-border capital movement.[198] It also states exceptions to the export permit

---

[193] Ibid.

[194] Article 19, FEL. Article 23 of the FEL replaces 'exporting' with 'sending abroad'.

[195] Since residents and non-residents are treated the same, there is no discrimination. Nonetheless, Articles 19 and 23 of the FEL deter nationals from other Member States from investing in Polish entities, and therefore restrict the free movement of capital (see section 2.1.2).

[196] See '*The requirements for a successful public policy/security derogation*' in section 2.1.3.

[197] Article 21, FEL. Article 24 of the FEL is similar but refers to 'sending abroad'.

[198] Article 3, RGFEP. The regulation identifies 'BIT countries' as third countries with which Poland has agreements on mutual support and investment protection (Article 1(1), RGFEP). It offers more favourable treatment to these countries, and

requirement of Articles 19 and 23 of the FEL.[199] There is greater precision than in the FEL concerning the documents required for export, thereby improving legal certainty for applicants.[200] However, export/import refusals are unjustified restrictions on the free movement of capital, due to the absence of an appeal procedure.[201]

4.3 Taxation

Two Polish taxation Acts contain provisions that restrict cross-border capital movement: the Natural Persons' Income Tax Act (NPITA) and the Legal Persons' Income Tax Act (LPITA). Resident taxpayers are taxed on worldwide income.[202] Non-resident taxpayers are taxed on Polish income.[203]

4.3.1 Act of 26 July 1991 on Natural Persons' Income Tax

Article 30b: residents' tax deductions on income from foreign securities

Residents' income from securities and derivative financial instruments of Polish and foreign companies is combined, and the foreign tax due is deducted from the tax calculated for the total.[204] The excess foreign tax

---

to Algeria, Armenia, Georgia, Kyrgyzstan, the Russian Federation, South Africa and Turkmenistan, than to other third countries (Article 1(2), RGFEP). For example, Polish residents may acquire immovable property or rights in such property for profit- making purposes, shares, investment fund units, and debt securities of at least one year maturity in BIT countries (Article 3(5), RGFEP), but not in other third countries.

[199] For instance, residents and non-residents may export domestic or foreign tenders exceeding 10,000 euros withdrawn from a bank account (Article 4(1), RGFEP).

[200] For example, Article 6(2) of the RGFEP requires precious metal dealers wishing to export gold or platinum to furnish a certificate of entry to the industry or a copy of their record in the register of entrepreneurs confirming their status as such dealers.

[201] See '*The requirements for a successful public policy/security derogation*' in section 2.1.3.

[202] Articles 3(1), NPITA and 3(1), LPITA. The NPITA and LPITA refer to 'place of residence' and 'seat or management office' respectively.

[203] Articles 3(2a), NPITA and 3(2), LPITA.

[204] Article 30b(5a), NPITA. 'Securities' include shares, rights to shares, warrants, depositary receipts, bonds, mortgage bonds and investment certificates (Articles 5a(11), NPITA and 3(1)(a), TFIA). 'Derivative financial instruments' include participation titles in collective investment institutions, money-market instruments,

over 19% is non-deductible.[205] This rule is applied when residents earn all such income abroad.[206] This income cannot be combined with that from other sources.[207]

Income tax paid by Polish residents on the sale, return or redemption of the shares or units of investment funds (or joint investment enterprises outside the EU) that have invested more than 40% of their assets in Treasury securities, bonds or notes, is deducted from residents' income from securities and derivative instruments.[208] The income must be from Andorra, Austria, Belgium, Luxembourg, San Marino or Switzerland,[209] or from dependencies and associated territories of the UK or the Netherlands with which Poland has an agreement on the taxation of savings income.[210]

The foreign income to residents is a 'capital movement' in Annex I. Article 30b of the NPITA does not refer to non-residents. The situations of residents and non-residents receiving dividends from Polish companies are objectively comparable, as are those of residents receiving dividends from Polish and foreign companies.[211] Although Article 30b considers more than dividend payments, it is limited to investment income, so objective comparability applies.

Since Poland taxes investment income at 19% regardless of its source or destination, there is no discrimination against non-residents. However, residents receiving dividends or interest taxed at source at more than 19% from foreign companies are treated less favourably than residents receiving investment income from Polish companies. Article 30b of the NPITA therefore restricts the free movement of capital.[212]

---

forwards, futures, swaps, options and commodities derivatives (Articles 5a(13), NPITA and 2(1)(2), TFIA). The NPITA does not define 'foreign'.

[205] Article 30b(5a), NPITA. Income from securities and derivative financial instruments are taxed at 19% (Article 30b(1)), NPITA.

[206] Article 30b(5b), NPITA.

[207] Article 30b(5), NPITA.

[208] Articles 30b(5c) and 42c(5)(4), NPITA.

[209] Article 30b(5c)(1), NPITA.

[210] Article 30b(5c)(2), NPITA. Article 30b(5c) discriminates against the other Member States in breach of Article 12 of the EC Treaty, which prohibits discrimination based on nationality.

[211] See section 2.3.1.

[212] An alternative interpretation is that the taxes on investment income arise from "the exercise in parallel by two Member States of their fiscal sovereignty" (*Kerckhaert and Morres* [2006] ECR I-10967). However, Article 30b of the NPITA charges incremental income tax to 19% on foreign investment income, without repaying excess foreign withholding tax over 19%. This is a "disguised restriction" on free capital movement (Article 58(3), EC Treaty).

Article 30c: residents' tax deductions from on foreign non-agricultural income

Residents' income from non-agricultural economic activity in Poland and abroad is combined, and foreign tax payable is deducted from the tax computed for the total.[213] The excess foreign tax over 19% is non-deductible.[214] This rule is applied when residents earn all such income abroad.[215] This income cannot be combined with that from other sources.[216]

Transfers concerning the provision of services are 'capital movements' in Annex I. Residents receiving income from economic activity in Poland and abroad are in an objectively comparable situation.[217] Since residents taxed at more than 19% at source on this income earned abroad are treated less favourably than those earning such income at home, Article 30c NPITA limits the free movement of capital.[218]

4.3.2 Act of 15 February 1992 on Legal Persons' Income Tax

A Polish company that receives dividends from a 75% subsidiary located in a third country may deduct the foreign tax payable on these dividends from its national tax bill.[219] A Polish company receiving dividends from a 10% associate in a Member State may deduct the tax due on the dividends in that State from its national tax assessment.[220] The deduction may not exceed the Polish tax due on the dividend payment.[221]

---

213 Article 30c(4), NPITA.

214 Article 30c(4), NPITA. Income from non-agricultural economic activity is taxed at 19% (Article 30c(1), NPITA).

215 Article 30c(5), NPITA.

216 Article 30c(6), NPITA.

217 This claim is incorrect if Polish residents' income from non-agricultural economic activity falls within the second leg of Article 58(1)(a) of the EC Treaty, which states that Member States may "apply the relevant provisions of their tax law which distinguish between taxpayers who are not in the same situation with regard to their place of residence or with regard to the place where their capital is invested." Furthermore, residents and non-residents are not objectively comparable for income from economic activity (Article 58(1)(a), EC Treaty).

218 See note 212: 'income from non-agricultural economic activity' replaces 'investment income'.

219 Article 20(2), LPITA.

220 Article 20(3), LPITA. This deduction is allowed for a 10% associate of a 10% associate (Article 20(4), LPITA).

221 Article 20(1), LPITA.

Dividends are 'capital movements' in Annex I. Polish companies receiving dividends from Polish associates and subsidiaries are in an objectively comparable situation to Polish companies receiving dividends from foreign associates and subsidiaries.[222] Dividends from 10% associates in Member States are treated more favourably than those from Polish companies.[223] Dividends from 75% subsidiaries in third countries may be similarly treated to those from Polish companies.[224] However, dividends from 0.01%–74.99% associates/subsidiaries in third countries, and from 0.01%–9.99% associates in Member States, are treated less favourably than those from Polish companies. Article 30c of the LPITA restricts the free movement of capital by refusing double taxation reductions to these associates and subsidiaries.[225]

4.3.3 Comparison with Estonia

Neither the Estonian Income Tax Act (EITA) nor the NPITA refunds foreign income tax withheld at source in excess of the domestic tax on this income.[226] Both rules equally restrict the free movement of capital.

Whilst income tax withheld at source on dividends paid by a foreign firm to an Estonian company may be deducted from the latter's Estonian tax assessment,[227] income tax withheld at source on dividends to a Polish company from 0.01%–9.99% associates in Member States, and from 0.01%–74.99% associates/subsidiaries in third countries, may not be deducted from that company's Polish tax assessment.[228] The Polish law hinders free capital movement; the Estonian rule does not.

---

222 See section 2.3.1.

223 There is no withholding tax on dividends from 10% associates in Member States (Directive 2003/123/EC). Dividends from Polish companies are taxed at 19% (Article 22(1), LPITA).

224 The LPITA does not provide a tax rate for dividends on non-resident companies. All stated dividend rates in NPITA and LPITA are 19%.

225 See section 2.3.1.

226 s.45(3), EITA; Articles 30(b)(5a) and 30(c)(4), NPITA.

227 s.54(5), EITA.

228 Articles 20(2)-(3), LPITA.

4.4 Property

4.4.1 Act of 24 March 1920 on the Acquisition of Immovable Properties by Foreign Persons (AIPFPA)

A foreign person must apply to the Minister for Internal Affairs for a permit to obtain immovable property in Poland.[229] The Minister issues the permit provided that such acquisition does not threaten public defence, security, order, health or social policy,[230] as long as the applicant is able to prove that he/she has Polish links,[231] such as Polish nationality or birth,[232] marriage to a Polish citizen,[233] a permit to reside in Poland,[234] or membership of the managing body of a Polish organisation.[235] The immovable property's area for living needs may not exceed 0.5 hectares.[236] The Minister may define "special conditions" that the foreign applicant must satisfy to acquire the property.[237] The permit is valid for two years.[238]

A foreign person who acquires control of a company or partnership with its seat and immovable property in Poland must apply to the Minister for a permit.[239] This is issued on the terms above.[240] A foreign person does not need a permit to acquire "individual living accommodation" or "individual business premises" connected with such accommodation.[241]

Investments in real estate on national territory by non-residents are 'capital movements' under Title IIA of Annex I. The requirement for a

---

[229] Article 1(1), AIPFPA. 'Immovable property' is defined in section 2.5.2, which contains the EU/Polish transitional provisions on the acquisition of such property. 'Foreign person' means an individual without Polish citizenship, a partnership or legal person with its seat abroad, or a Polish company controlled by a foreign person (Article 1(2), AIPFPA).

[230] Article 1a(1)(1), AIPFPA.

[231] Article 1a(1)(2), AIPFPA.

[232] Article 1a(2)(1), AIPFPA.

[233] Article 1a(2)(2), AIPFPA.

[234] Article 1a(2)(3), AIPFPA.

[235] Article 1a(2)(4), AIPFPA.

[236] Article 1a(5), AIPFPA.

[237] Article 2(2), AIPFPA.

[238] Article 3(2), AIPFPA.

[239] Article 3e(1)-(2), AIPFPA.

[240] Article 3e(4), AIPFPA.

[241] Article 8(1)(1)-(1a), AIPFPA.

permit restricts the free movement of capital, and must be based on an objective in the public interest that is pursued in a non-discriminatory way.[242] The AIPFPA contains public interest aims, but these are not based on objective criteria known beforehand, and there is no recourse to a legal remedy.[243] Furthermore, these aims are pursued in a discriminatory way because they specifically require 'foreign persons' to obtain authorisation to acquire immovable property. EEA citizens and entrepreneurs do not require such authorisation,[244] except under the EU/Polish transitional measures.[245] Consequently, the AIPFPA's requirement for non-EEA persons to obtain a permit to acquire immovable property in Poland breaches Article 56 of the EC Treaty.

4.4.2 Comparison with Estonia

Estonia has repealed the property legislation that restricted the free movement of capital.[246] The AIPFPA should be modified so that authorisation to acquire Polish immovable property is proportionate and based on objective criteria in the public interest known beforehand to applicants who have a legal remedy, which do not discriminate against non-EEA residents or legal persons.[247]

4.4.3 Conclusions

The Polish legislation is detailed and complex, but, with the exception of the AIPFPA, tends to be compatible with the free movement of capital and to comply with the relevant Directives. Other than simplification and clarification, the main concern is the authorisation requirement of the AIPFPA. A real property system that may be compatible with the free movement of capital is one which requires all applications for immovable property transfer to be submitted to a specialised government agency for its information. Authorisation would be unnecessary because this provides the agency with discretionary power and may disproportionately restrict free capital movement.[248] Instead, the agency would be

---

[242] See the subsection '*Comment*' in section 2.1.4.

[243] See *Analir and Others* [2000] ECR I-1271, and *Ospelt and Schlössle Weissenberg Familienstiftung* [2003] ECR I-9743.

[244] Article 8(2), AIPFPA.

[245] See section 2.5.2.

[246] See section 3.4.

[247] See section 2.1.4.

[248] *Konle v Austria* [1999] ECR I-3099; *Salzmann* [2003] ECR I-4899.

empowered to ask the applicant questions and request further information, and to impose fines and/or annul the property transfer contract if it discovered that the transfer breached EU or Polish law.[249]

In Chapter 5, I analyse the compatibility of Latvian law with the EU free movement of capital rules, and compare the Latvian provisions with those of Estonia and Poland.

[249] *Salzmann* [2003] ECR I-4899; *Burtscher* [2005] ECR I-10309.

CHAPTER FIVE

LATVIA: LEGAL ISSUES

> "Riga [the capital city of Latvia] has been a major Baltic port since its foundation in the thirteenth century. It was successively a citadel of the Teutonic Knights, a leading member of the Hanseatic League and the largest city in the Swedish empire before being absorbed into the Russian empire in the eighteenth century. The Latvians have always been a distinct people with their own language and culture, but only in the twentieth century–between the Wars, and since 1991–has the country emerged as an independent state".[1]

Although Estonia, Poland and Latvia joined the European Union simultaneously in May 2004, accession negotiations for Estonia and Poland commenced two years earlier than those for Latvia.[2] Consequently, Latvia had four years to implement the acquis communautaire,[3] compared with six years for Estonia and Poland. This difference is evident in the presentation of Latvia's laws, which are more copious and less ordered than those of Estonia. Poland's laws are more similar to Latvia's than to Estonia's in presentation, however. Estonia's close relationship with Finland,[4] which joined the EU in January 1995, may also have contributed to the good organisation of its laws in preparation for its accession to the Community.

The Latvian Translation and Terminology Centre (LTTC) translates Latvian legislation and regulations into English, and is the main source of the materials used in this chapter.[5] The LTTC is a state institution, which

---

[1] M. D. V. Randall and F. M. Urquhart *(eds.)* (2007), *Martin Randall Travel 2007*, 135.

[2] Accession talks began in March 1998 for Cyprus, the Czech Republic, Estonia, Hungary, Poland and Slovenia, and in February 2000 for Bulgaria, Latvia, Lithuania, Malta, Romania and Slovakia (Polish Office of the Committee for European Integration, 22 October 2007).

[3] Section 1.3.1 discusses implementation of the acquis communautaire.

[4] See the subsection '*1. History*' in section 3.1.6.

[5] The Director of the LTTC, Professor Māris Baltiņš, stated that the English version of Latvian law published by the LTTC was only "informative" and "not

is "widely recognised nationally and internationally as Latvia's leading provider of high-quality translation and terminology services".[6]

Sections 5.1 and 5.2 consider financial laws; those in section 5.1 are regulated by the Financial and Capital Market Commission (FCMC).[7] Sections 5.3 and 5.4 discuss taxation and land laws respectively that limit cross-border capital movement. In sections 5.1.8, 5.3.3 and 5.4.6, I compare Estonian, Polish and Latvian legislation on financial regulation, taxation and property. I use the information yielded by these comparisons to build a legal index for each of the three Member States in the next chapter.

5.1 Laws Regulated by the Financial and Capital Market Commission

5.1.1 Law on Investment Companies 1997 (LIC)

An 'investment company' is a "financial and credit stock company" that manages investment funds, the provision of investment certificates and "activities directly related thereto".[8] It may also manage the resources of pension funds under the Law on Private Pension Funds and the Law on State Funded Pensions.[9]

Section 60: public circulation of foreign open-ended investment funds

Investment certificates of foreign open-ended funds may only be released into public circulation in Latvia by a brokerage company or credit

---

officially published in the government journal" (e-mail communication, 29 August 2007). Rather than citing and referencing the LTTC website for each Act, I accept his point whilst giving the official reference in the bibliography.

[6] LTTC, 4 October 2007.

[7] The FCMC authorises all forms of financial services in Latvia, including investment services, banking and insurance. It supervises private pension funds (s.28(1), LPPF), but state funded pension schemes are supervised by the Ministry of Welfare (s.9(1), LSFP).

[8] s.4(2), LIC. The LIC defines neither 'investment fund' nor 'financial and credit stock company'. A 'stock company' is a public company with publicly traded shares (s.134(4), The Commercial Law 2000). An 'investment certificate' is a security declaring a person's participation in an investment fund (ss.1(1) and 1(3), LIC).

[9] s.4(3), LIC. These laws are discussed in sections 5.1.7 and 5.2.1 respectively.

institution registered there.[10] The certificates may not be so released if, within one month of receiving documentation, the FCMC notifies the distributer that their release does not comply with the LIC.[11] Documents to be sent by the distributer to the FCMC include items not specified by Article 31(2) of Directive 2004/39/EC, such as the rules for managing the foreign fund,[12] and regulations for distributing the certificates in Latvia.[13]

The engagement of a Latvian-registered distributer to circulate investment certificates of foreign open-ended funds, required by section 60(1) of the LIC, is a 'capital movement' under Title IVA of Annex I of Directive 88/361/EEC (Annex I), since the definition includes all operations necessary for capital movements. It restricts the free movement of capital and is not justified for public policy or security. This conclusion differs from that for a similar provision in the Estonian Investment Funds Act,[14] because there is no exemption from section 60(1) if the foreign investment company has a Latvian branch.[15]

The FCMC's power under section 60(3) of the LIC to prevent release of the foreign investment certificates in Latvia, if it decides that such release does not comply with the LIC, is an unjustified restriction on the free movement of capital. As in *Analir and Others*,[16] a derogation from free movement is not permitted because the national authority is able to exercise its discretion arbitrarily.

---

[10] s.60(1), LIC. The LIC does not define 'foreign'. A 'foreign insurer' may be registered in the EEA or outside it (Articles 1(4), 1(12) and 1(14), LICST), indicating that 'foreign' means 'non-Latvian'. Conversely, ss.1(44)-(45) of the CIL define a 'foreign state' as a non-EEA country. An open-ended investment fund is distinguished from a closed-ended investment fund by the managing company of the former being empowered to repurchase investment certificates (ss.21(1)-(2), LIC). An 'investment brokerage company' is a "capital company" that regularly and professionally provides investment services (s.1(3), FIML). A 'credit institution' is a "capital company" that is a "bank", which accepts repayable funds, supplies credits in its own name and provides other financial services, or an "electronic money institution", which issues electronic money (s.1(1), CIL). A 'capital company' is a commercial company, the equity capital of which is the total par value of its equity shares (s.134(1), The Commercial Law 2000).

[11] s.60(3), LIC.

[12] s.60(2)(2), LIC.

[13] s.60(2)(6), LIC.

[14] s.229(1).

[15] See section 3.1.1.

[16] [2000] ECR I-1271. See the subsection '*Public policy, public security and prior authorisation*' in section 2.1.3.

Sections 62 to 65: investment types

Fund assets may be invested in transferable securities or money market instruments that satisfy one or more of the following conditions:[17] 1) they are officially listed on a stock exchange registered in an EEA or OECD state, or on a comparable list (hereafter 'official list'),[18] 2) they are traded on "other regulated and openly accessible financial instrument markets" (hereafter 'regulated markets') in the above countries;[19] 3) they are officially listed on a stock exchange or traded on a regulated market in other countries, provided that the fund prospectus permits such investment;[20] 4) they are to be listed/traded on one of the above stock exchanges/markets and fund assets are to be invested in them within one year of such listing/trading.[21] Fund assets may also be invested in money market instruments issued or guaranteed by the government or central bank of, or by a credit institution registered in, one of above countries,[22] or issued by a commercial company whose securities are listed/traded as in 1), 2) and 3) above or which belongs to a category approved by the FCMC and satisfying three further conditions.[23]

Fund resources may be deposited in a credit institution licensed in an EEA or OECD country and entitled to provide financial services there.[24] Fund assets may be invested in investment certificates of open-ended funds registered in an EEA state,[25] or in another country if 1) "the legal framework provides for the state supervision of such undertakings which

[17] 'Transferable securities' are stocks, bonds and other marketable securities that may be alienated without restriction (s.1(11), LIC). 'Money market instruments' are liquid, short-term debt instruments traded on the money market that can be precisely valued at any time (s.1(12), LIC).

[18] s.62(1)(1), LIC. The LIC does not define 'comparable list'.

[19] s.62(1)(2), LIC. The LIC defines neither 'regulated' nor 'openly accessible'. 'Financial instruments' derive from "an agreement, which concurrently creates financial assets for one person, but financial liabilities or capital securities for another person" (s.1(14), LIC; s.1(1), FIML). This is a broad definition synonymous with a commercial transaction in which money is the means of exchange.

[20] s.62(1)(3), LIC.

[21] s.62(1)(4), LIC.

[22] ss.62(2)(1), 62(2)(2) and 62(2)(4), LIC. This includes local and state governments, the European Central Bank, the European Investment Bank and other financial institutions of which several EEA countries are members.

[23] ss.62(2)(3) and 62(2)(5), LIC.

[24] s.63(1), LIC.

[25] s.64(1), LIC.

is of equal value with the supervision specified in this Law",[26] 2) the foreign funds' principles of operation are "analogous" to those for open-ended funds under the LIC,[27] and 3) they publish half-yearly financial reports.[28] Fund resources can be used to buy derivative financial instruments traded on the markets in section 62(1) of the LIC,[29] or on an over-the-counter market in which the underlying assets are included in sections 62, 63 and/or 64 of the LIC,[30] the counterparty is a credit institution satisfying section 63(1) of the LIC,[31] and the over-the-counter derivative is valued each day and can be sold for its fair value at any time.[32]

Investment of fund assets in foreign financial instruments is a 'capital movement' in Annex I.[33] Sections 62–65 of the LIC do not limit the free movement of capital between Latvia and other EEA countries because investments in Latvian and EEA financial instruments are treated the same.[34] The following restrictions exist on cross-border capital movement between Latvia and non-EEA countries.

1. Investments are not permitted in money market instruments not traded on regulated markets issued by governments, central banks and credit institutions of non-EEA, non-OECD countries.
2. Fund resources may not be deposited with such credit institutions.
3. The conditions under which fund assets may be invested in investment certificates of open-ended funds registered in a non-EEA country hinder the free movement of capital. Two of these restrictions require the exercise of the FCMC's discretion, and therefore deny legal certainty to investment funds.[35] The phrases "of equal value" and "analogous" in sections 64(2)(1) and

[26] s.64(2)(1), LIC.
[27] s.64(2)(2), LIC.
[28] s.64(2)(3), LIC.
[29] s.65(1), LIC. 'Derivative financial instruments' are financial instruments (see note 19) whose value changes with interest rates, exchange rates, security prices, credit rating or other similar variables and which transfer financial risks characteristic of the underlying asset between the parties to the transaction (s.1(14), LIC). See above for section 62(1) of the LIC.
[30] s.65(1)(1), LIC. See above for sections 62-64 of the LIC.
[31] s.65(1)(2), LIC. See above for section 63(1) of the LIC.
[32] s.65(1)(3), LIC.
[33] Securities, investment certificates, money market instruments and deposits are in Titles III, IV, V and VI of Annex I respectively. Derivative financial instruments are in Titles V or VI.
[34] See section 2.1.2.
[35] See section 2.1.3.

64(2)(2) of the LIC respectively,[36] without further specification, provide the FCMC with this discretion. Does 'equal value' mean that the relevant laws are identical? If the non-EEA country's supervisory laws are stricter on some points and looser on others than the LIC, is the state supervision in this country 'equal' to that in Latvia? Which laws in the LIC are to be considered supervisory? There are similar questions for 'analogous'. Further guidelines would reduce the risk of the FCMC making two opposite decisions under s.64(2) of the LIC on similar facts or the same decision in different circumstances.[37]

These limits on the free movement of capital are unjustified and consequently breach Article 56 of the EC Treaty, other than in exceptional cases where they are adopted "for serious political reasons and on grounds of urgency".[38]

Section 66: investment limitations

No more than 10% of fund assets may be invested in one issuer's transferable securities or money market instruments.[39] This limit is 35% if these financial instruments are issued or guaranteed by an EEA or OECD country,[40] or by an international financial institution to which several EEA states belong.[41] It may be raised further if the fund prospectus so provides,[42] stating the issuer,[43] and if there are at least six issues, none of which exceed 30% of the fund assets.[44]

---

[36] See above.

[37] EU legal provisions concerning regulation in non-EEA states may include unexplained comparative terms. For instance, The Third Money Laundering Directive states: "Member States shall require the credit and financial institutions covered by this Directive to apply, where applicable, in their branches and majority-owned subsidiaries located in third countries measures *at least equivalent to* those laid down in this Directive with regard to customer due diligence and record keeping (Article 31(1), Directive 2005/60/EC; emphasis mine). The Latvian legislature may have followed this practice.

[38] Article 60(2), EC Treaty.

[39] 41. s.66(1), LIC. The limit is 5% if the total value of investments exceeding 5% is greater than 40% of the fund assets (s.66(1), LIC).

[40] ss.66(2)(1) and 66(2)(2), LIC.

[41] s.66(2)(3), LIC.

[42] s.66(3)(1), LIC.

[43] s.66(3)(3), LIC.

[44] s.66(3)(2), LIC.

Up to 25% of fund resources may be invested in debt securities issued by one credit institution registered in an EEA or OECD country.[45] Investment in one credit institution is limited to 20% of the fund assets.[46] These provisions are inconsistent. Section 66(4) of the LIC permits 22% of fund assets to be invested in certificates of deposit issued by a German bank, but section 66(6) of the LIC forbids this transaction.

10% of fund resources may be invested in investment certificates of one open-ended fund.[47] Total investments with a single issuer from an EEA or OECD state may not exceed 35% of the fund assets.[48] This limit is 20% for a single issuer outside these countries.[49] Up to 10% of fund resources may be invested in transferable securities and money market instruments that do not satisfy section 62 of the LIC.[50] These restrictions may be disapplied by a closed-ended investment fund if its prospectus provides different limits.[51]

Investment of fund assets is a 'capital movement' in Annex I. Since investments in EEA and OECD countries are treated the same as those in Latvia, subsections 66(2)-(5), 66(10) and 66(12) of the LIC do not restrict the free movement of capital.[52] However, subsections 66(1) and 66(11) of the LIC do so restrict, because a smaller percentage of fund resources may be invested in a single issuer's financial instruments outside the EEA and OECD than inside these countries.[53] These provisions cannot be justified for public policy or security because there is no "genuine and sufficiently serious threat to a fundamental interest of society",[54] such as to the

[45] s.66(4), LIC. The limit is 5% if the total value of investments exceeding 5% is greater than 80% of the fund assets (s.66(5), LIC). The LIC does not define 'debt securities'.

[46] s.66(6), LIC.

[47] s.66(10), LIC.

[48] s.66(12), LIC. This limit does not apply if the conditions of s.66(3) of the LIC are fulfilled (see above).

[49] s.66(11), LIC.

[50] s.66(13), LIC. See the subsection '*Sections 62 to 65: investment types*' in section 5.1.1 for s.62 of the LIC.

[51] s.66(14), LIC.

[52] See section 2.1.2.

[53] Investment preference for EEA and OECD countries does not arise from the capital adequacy requirements of investment firms. Directives 2004/39/EC and 2006/49/EC mention neither the EEA nor the OECD. The Basel II Framework and Directive 2006/48/EC mention the OECD only, and this solely with reference to the methodology to be used by Export Credit Agencies in assigning country risk weightings.

[54] *Eglise de Scientologie and Scientology International* [2000] ECR I-1335.

provision of petroleum products at all times.[55] Unless adopted "for serious political reasons and on grounds of urgency",[56] subsections 66(1) and 66(11) breach Article 56 of the EC Treaty.

Subsection 66(14) of the LIC restricts the free movement of capital because it applies the investment limitations of section 66 of the LIC to closed-end investment funds whose prospectus lacks such limits. As stated in section 4.1.1, investment limitations should only be specified in the fund prospectus and regulations.[57]

Section 68: immovable property

Resources from a closed-ended investment fund invested may only be invested in immovable property in an EEA or OECD country.[58] Investments in real estate abroad by legal persons are 'capital movements' in Title IIA of Annex I. There is a restriction on the free movement of capital to other states. As the LIC gives no public interest objective for this measure, it may only be justified "for serious political reasons and on grounds of urgency",[59] or to protect Latvia's security in connection with "the production of or trade in arms, munitions and war material".[60]

5.1.2 Financial Instrument Market Law 2003 (FIML)

The FIML contains rules on the provision of investment services by investment brokerage companies and credit institutions,[61] but these are incomplete in their scope. Chapter IX provides for cross-border

---

55 *Campus Oil and Others* [1984] ECR 2727. See section 2.1.3.
56 Article 60(2), EC Treaty.
57 Investors voluntarily restrict cross-border movement of their capital by choosing one investment fund over another with different limitations. Such consumer choice is compatible with Article 56 of the EC Treaty.
58 s.68(1), LIC.
59 Article 60(2), EC Treaty.
60 Article 296(1)(b), EC Treaty.
61 'Investment brokerage company' and 'credit institution' are defined in note 10. 'Investment services' include the acceptance, transfer and execution of investors' orders for transactions involving financial instruments, the management of financial instruments in accordance with investors' authorisation, purchase and initial allocation of financial instruments, dealing in financial instruments on behalf of an investment brokerage company or a credit institution, and investment advice (s.3(4), FIML). This is similar to the investment services and activities listed in Annex I of Directive 2004/39/EC. The list of non-core investment services in section 3(5) of the FIML resembles the list of ancillary services in this Directive.

investment services within the EEA, but there are no equivalent laws for cross-border investment services to and from third countries. This omission, in the light of the wording of section 134(3) of the FIML,[62] is indicative that the provision of investment services between Latvia and non-EEA countries is not permitted.

The FIML also contains provisions on the public offer and circulation of financial instruments,[63] but few mention non-Latvian companies. These laws do not consider cross-border capital flows and are consequently not discussed here.

Section 112: EEA companies' investment services in Latvia

A branch of an investment brokerage company registered in a Member State may provide investment services in Latvia without requiring a licence to be issued under the FIML only after the competent authority in that State has furnished the FCMC with 1) certification of the company's licence for the provision of investment services, 2) the address and "operational programme" of the branch, 3) the branch manager's name, nationality, date of birth and personal identity number, 4) details of the investor protection system in which the company participates and 5) a written declaration concerning inspections of the company's Latvian branch(es).[64] If an investment brokerage company registered in a Member State wishes to provide cross-border investment services to Latvia, that State's supervisory authority must furnish the FCMC with a "relevant notification … regarding such brokerage company".[65]

The information to be given to the FCMC is in accordance with Article 32 of Directive 2004/39/EC. However, Article 31 of this Directive on the provision of cross-border investment services does not require items 3), 4) and 5) in the previous paragraph.[66] Section 112(4) of the FIML breaches Article 31 if 'relevant notification' means all the information specified in section 112(2)(1) of the FIML.[67] If this phrase means the information required by Article 31, then there is no such breach. Section 112(4) should specify the information to be furnished to the FCMC in order to provide cross-border investment services in Latvia.

---

[62] This section states that registration of a non-Latvian company in accordance with ss.134(1)-(2) of the FIML does not give it "the right ... to provide investment services and investment non-core services in the Republic of Latvia".

[63] 'Financial instruments' are defined in note 19.

[64] s.112(2)(1), FIML. 'Member State' means an EEA country (s.1(5), FIML).

[65] s.112(4), FIML.

[66] See section 2.4.1.

[67] See above in this subsection.

Establishment of a branch is a 'capital movement' under Title I(1) of Annex I. Although passing information to the FCMC is not a capital movement, cross-border investment services following such notification are such movements. If the FCMC refuses to allow the investment brokerage firm or its branch to provide investment services in Latvia, then it limits the free movement of capital. This restriction cannot be justified–section 112 of the FIML should require the FCMC to give a formal set of reasons for the refusal and provide the right to review it in the Latvian courts.[68]

Section 113: Latvian companies' investment services within the EEA

An investment brokerage company registered in Latvia that intends to provide cross-border investment services to another Member State, or to found a branch to commence such services in that State, must supply the following information to the FCMC: 1) the State's name, 2) the proposed investment and non-core investment services, and 3) whether or not it is to open a branch, and if so, the personal details of the branch manager, the branch's address, and documentation giving "a fair and true representation" as to its planned activities, investment and non-core investment services, organisational structure and "organisation of work appropriate thereto".[69] The FCMC

> "shall examine the application for the commencement of the provision of investment services and non-core investment services … and inform in writing the supervisory institution of the relevant Member State and the relevant investment brokerage company of the decision thereof".[70]

This information complies with Directive 2004/39/EC, except for Article 32(2)(d), which states that the branch managers' names should be provided to the competent authority; it does not require their birth date, personal identification number, educational record and other details stipulated by the FIML.[71] It is unclear from section 113(5) of the FIML, quoted above, whether the decision taken by the FCMC is not to forward the information to the host Member State's competent authority or to refuse authorisation of investment services in the host State. Only the former interpretation complies with Directive 2004/39/EC–provided that

---

[68] See the subsection '*The requirements for a successful public policy/security derogation*' in section 2.1.3.

[69] ss.113(2)-(4), FIML.

[70] s.113(5), FIML.

[71] ss.113(4), 107(2)(1) and 107(4), FIML.

the FCMC's decision is not made for lack of the superfluous information specified above. Furthermore, section 113 of the FIML does not incorporate Article 32(5) of this Directive, which requires the FCMC to give reasons for refusing to forward the information for opening a branch in the host Member State to the latter's supervisory authority within three months of receiving it.

Although refusing to forward information is not a 'capital movement' in Annex I, establishing a branch and providing cross-border investment services following notification are 'capital movements' in this Annex. Therefore, if the FCMC does not pass the information to the host State's competent authority, then it limits the free movement of capital. This restriction is unjustified without requiring a formal set of reasons for the refusal and the right to review it in the Latvian courts.[72]

Section 140: breach of national law

If the FCMC determines that an investment brokerage company registered in another Member State providing cross-border investment services to Latvia, or providing such services through a Latvian branch, is "carrying out activities" that breach Latvian law: 1) it requests that the company terminates these activities;[73] if this fails, 2) it asks the competent authority of the home Member State to prevent the infringements and to inform it of the measures taken;[74] if this fails, 3) it takes action to prevent such transgressions, including, if necessary, prohibiting the company from providing investment services in Latvia until the contraventions are "rectified", and informs the home State's competent authority of the measures taken.[75] The FCMC may also take action to stop infringements that breach Latvian laws protecting the "public interest".[76]

Sections 140(1)-(3) of the FIML give the FCMC wider authority than Article 62(1) of Directive 2004/39/EC provides for the competent authority of the host Member State. In particular, this authority must have "clear and demonstrable grounds" for believing that the investment firm has breached Latvian law "adopted pursuant to this Directive", and such authority may only "take the appropriate measures needed in order to protect investors and the proper functioning of markets" [Article 62(1)]. Furthermore, section 140(3) does not require the FCMC to inform the

---

[72] See the subsection '*The requirements for a successful public policy/security derogation*' in section 2.1.3.

[73] s.140(1), FIML.

[74] s.140(2), FIML

[75] s.140(3), FIML.

[76] s.140(4), FIML.

European Commission of the measures it takes, as required by Article 62(1). Section 140(4) of the FIML also breaches Directive 2004/39/EC; the latter does not enable the host State's competent authority to act to prevent breaches of national laws protecting the public interest.

Sections 140(1)-(3) of the FIML follow the procedure in Article 30 of Directive 2006/48/EC rather than that in Article 62 of Directive 2004/39/EC. Section 140(4) of the FIML enacts Article 31 of Directive 2006/48/EC, which empowers host Member States to take "appropriate measures" to stop or punish breaches of national law adopted "in the interests of the general good". This Article has no equivalent in Directive 2004/39/EC.

Firms providing investment services are regulated by Directive 2004/39/EC and credit institutions by Directive 2006/48/EC. Article 62 of Directive 2004/39/EC applies to investment firms but not to credit institutions[77]. Since section 140 of the FIML refers to investment brokerage companies rather than to credit institutions, the Latvian government must correct it in order to comply with Directive 2004/39/EC.

Investment services are 'capital movements' in Annex I. If the FCMC prohibits an investment company from providing them, then it limits the free movement of capital. Section 140(4) does not define 'public interest'; hence, this is not a "genuine and sufficiently serious threat to a fundamental interest of society",[78] which is a necessary requirement to satisfy the public policy/security derogation.[79]

Member States may take all necessary measures to prevent transgressions of national law, especially those concerning taxation and "the prudential supervision of financial institutions".[80] These measures must be proportionate, necessary to protect the interests that they are intended to guarantee, and specific, objective and known to the investment firm beforehand.[81] Measures implemented pursuant to section 140 of the FIML do not fulfil these requirements. Therefore, this section breaches Article 56 of the EC Treaty.

5.1.3 Credit Institution Law 1995 (CIL)

Sections 12, 12² and 12³: Latvian credit institutions operating abroad

---

[77] Article 1, Directive 2004/39/EC.

[78] *Eglise de Scientologie and Scientology International* [2000] ECR I-1335.

[79] See the subsection '*The requirements for a successful public policy/security derogation*' in section 2.1.3.

[80] Article 58(1)(b), EC Treaty.

[81] See section 2.1.3.

Latvian credit institutions must obtain a permit from the FCMC to establish a branch in a foreign state.[82] To open a branch in another Member State,[83] a credit institution must provide the FCMC with 1) the name of this State, 2) the branch manager's name and personal identification number and 3) documents providing a "true and fair representation" as to the branch's operation, structure, work organisation and proposed financial services.[84] The FCMC examines this information within 30 days of receiving it, and informs the credit institution and the host State's competent authority "of its decision".[85] Within two months, or on receipt of certification from the host State's authority if earlier, the credit institution can start business in that State.[86]

A credit institution may provide cross-border financial services in another Member State after informing the FCMC of this State's name and of the services that it will supply.[87] The FCMC examines the application, and, within 30 days of its receipt, informs the host Member State's competent authority and the credit institution "of its decision".[88]

Section 12^3 of the CIL complies with Directive 2006/48/EC except for the requirement for the FCMC to send the information to the host State's competent authority within one month rather than to take a decision [Article 28(1)]. Section 12^2 of the CIL breaches this Directive in the following ways: 1) notification must include the address in the host State to obtain documents [Article 25(1)(c)] and the minimum funding requirements [Article 25(3)], 2) the FCMC must give reasons for refusing to forward the information to the host State's competent authority [Article 25(4)], and 3) the applicant credit institution must be granted the right to challenge this refusal in the Latvian courts [Article 25(4)]. It is unclear whether the FCMC's decision under section 12^2(4) of the CIL is not to communicate the information to the host State's competent authority or to

---

82 s.12(1), CIL. 'Credit institution' is defined in note 10. 'Foreign state' in this Law means a country outside the EEA (ss.1(44)-(45), CIL).

83 'Member State' means an EEA country (s.1(44), CIL).

84 ss.12^2(2)-(3), CIL. 'Financial services' in s.1(4) of the CIL resemble the 'list of activities subject to mutual recognition' in Annex I of Directive 2006/48/EC. These are stated in chapter 2 note 84.

85 s.12^2(4), CIL.

86 s.12^2(7), CIL.

87 s.12^3(2), CIL.

88 s.12^3(3), CIL.

deny authorisation of financial services in that State. Only the first interpretation complies with the Directive.[89]

Establishing a branch abroad is a 'capital movement' under Title I(1) of Annex I. Sections 12(1) of the CIL, requiring prior authorisation for such establishment in third countries, and $12^{2}(4)$ of the CIL, empowering the FCMC to prevent it in EEA states, restrict the free movement of capital. Neither is justified because the measures must be specific, objective and known to the credit institution beforehand in order to provide it with legal certainty, and because the FCMC must provide reasons for its decision, which should be challengeable in the Latvian courts.[90]

Providing cross-border financial services is a 'capital movement' in Annex I.[91] If the FCMC limits them by its decision under section $12^{3}(3)$ of the CIL, then it hinders the free movement of capital. This restriction is unjustified because no legal remedy is available to the credit institution. It may also be disproportionate.[92]

Sections 12^{1} and 12^{1111}: EEA credit/financial institutions operating in Latvia

To open a branch in Latvia, a credit institution registered in another Member State must, via that State's supervisory authority, supply the FCMC with 1) proof of its licence, 2) the branch's address and "operations programme", 3) the branch manager's name, 4) capital adequacy indicators for itself and its parent company, 5) information about the "investment guarantee system" in which it participates, 6) written confirmation concerning inspection of its Latvian branches and 7) documents on its operational strategy, financial forecasts, organisational structure, risk management and internal audit policy and procedure, accounting policy, management information system and asset protection regulations.[93]

---

[89] This problem arose for the provision of investment services in the host State under s.113 of the FIML. See the subsection '*Section 113: Latvian companies' investment services within the EEA*' in section 5.1.2.

[90] See the subsection '*The requirements for a successful public policy/security derogation*' in section 2.1.3. Section 12(1) of the CIL may be justified "for serious political reasons and on grounds of urgency" (Article 60(2), EC Treaty). This is unlikely for most third countries.

[91] Financial services are included in Titles III-VI and VIII of the Annex.

[92] See the subsection '*The requirements for a successful public policy/security derogation*' in section 2.1.3.

[93] ss.$12^{1}(1)(1)$, $12^{1}(1)(2)$ and $12^{1}(3)$, CIL.

A financial institution registered in another Member State may provide financial services in Latvia with or without a branch there,[94] provided that 1) the credit institution(s) that control the financial institution have a valid licence, exercise at least 90% of the financial institution's voting rights, ensure the "prudent management" of the financial institution in conformity with their own regulatory requirements, and have published the fact that they are jointly and severally liable for the financial institution's "financial obligations", 2) the latter institution legally provides financial services in the home State and 3) this company's "operations" are "subordinated to" the controlling credit institution(s)' overall supervision, especially in relation to capital adequacy, risky transactions and "participation in other commercial companies".[95] To open a Latvian branch, such a financial institution must also satisfy s.12^1 of the CIL (above) other than point 5).[96]

Section 12^1(1) of the CIL complies with Directive 2006/48/EC. The financial forecasts and accounting policy document required by section 12^1(3) of the CIL are not necessary to satisfy the Directive,[97] which specifies "a programme of operations setting out, inter alia, the types of business envisaged and the structural organisation of the branch" [Article 25(2)(b)], unless they are included within the 'inter alia' clause.[98] Sections 12^{1111}(1)-(4) of the CIL follow Article 24 of the Directive.

Establishment of a branch and cross-border financial services are 'capital movements' in Annex I. Sections 12^1 and 12^{1111}(1) of the CIL contain detailed requirements for an institution registered in another Member State to provide financial services in Latvia, thereby limiting the free movement of capital. This is not justified because such restrictions must be necessary to protect the interests that they are intended to

---

[94] A 'financial institution' is a commercial company established to supply financial services or to acquire the equity shares of other commercial companies (s.1(21), CIL).

[95] s.12^{1111}(1), CIL. 'Participation' in a commercial company means owning rights to its "capital shares" that are used to participate in the company's management, or holding at least 20% of its equity capital or voting stock (s.1(15^1), CIL).

[96] ss.12^{1111}(4)(1) and 12^{1111}(4)(2), CIL. Financial institutions registered in Latvia must satisfy sections 12^{1111}(1) and 12^2 of the CIL (above) to open a branch in another Member State, and must fulfil sections 12^{1111}(1) and 12^3 of the CIL (above) to provide cross-border financial services to another State (ss.12^{1111}(2)-(3), CIL).

[97] See point 7), above in this subsection.

[98] 'Inter alia' means "among other things" (G. McFarlane (1984), *The Layman's Dictionary of English Law,* 145). It is a matter of interpretation how widely this phrase is drawn. It would be helpful for the Community authorities to give Member States a list of information to be included, and another to be excluded, thereby reducing the area of doubt.

guarantee.[99] These interests are not specified in either section. Furthermore, the credit/financial institution does not have access to legal redress in the Latvian courts for an adverse decision of the FCMC.[100] Consequently, sections 12^{1} and $12^{1111}(1)$ of the CIL breach Article 56 of the EC Treaty.

Section 14: issue of licence

The FCMC may refrain from issuing a licence to a new credit institution for several reasons following Article 12 of Directive 2006/48/EC. However, it may refuse authorisation under the CIL if this institution's close links with third persons "may threaten its financial stability".[101] This ground is not permitted by Article 12. Furthermore, section 14 of the CIL does not require the FCMC to give reasons for refusing to issue a licence, in accordance with Article 13 of the Directive.[102]

The FCMC need not issue a licence to a new credit institution if it is a subsidiary of a third country credit/financial institution whose state of registration has lower supervision requirements than "those accepted by Member States on the basis of a consolidated financial report" or whose home state supervisory authority has no agreement with the FCMC for "cooperation and the exchange of information".[103] The establishment of a fully-owned new undertaking is a 'capital movement' in Title I(1) of Annex I. Refusing to issue it with a licence restricts the free movement of capital. Whilst, unlike under the Estonian Credit Institutions Act,[104] the credit institution has legal certainty as to the conditions for it being granted a licence, section 14(1)(7) of the CIL is unjustified because the FCMC is not required to give reasons for refusing to issue a licence, and because there is no appeal against this refusal in the Latvian courts.[105]

---

[99] *Eglise de Scientologie and Scientology International* [2000] ECR I-1335.

[100] See the subsection '*The requirements for a successful public policy/security derogation*' in section 2.1.3.

[101] s.14(1)(2), CIL.

[102] See section 2.4.2.

[103] s.14(1)(7), CIL. This subsection complies with Article 12(3) of Directive 2006/48/EC.

[104] The Estonian Financial Supervision Authority has considerable discretion under s.21 of the Estonian Credit Institutions Act 1999 to decide whether or not to authorise foreign credit institutions to establish a branch or subsidiary in Estonia. See the subsection '*Section 21: authorisation of foreign credit institutions in Estonia*' in section 3.1.4.

[105] See the subsection '*The requirements for a successful public policy/security derogation*' in section 2.1.3.

Section 27: withdrawal of licence

Section 27(1) of the CIL provides eight grounds for the FCMC to withdraw a credit institution's licence, all of which comply with Article 17(1) of Directive 2006/48/EC, either explicitly or as "one of the other cases where national law provides for withdrawal of authorisation" [Article 17(1)(e)]. Section 27(3) of the CIL permits an appeal against a decision of the FCMC to cancel a licence, but does not require the FCMC to give reasons for the revocation as specified by Article 17(2) of the Directive.

Since licence withdrawal is not a 'capital movement' in Annex I, section 27 of the CIL does not breach Article 56 of the EC Treaty. Nevertheless, such cancellation restricts the free movement of capital because it limits cross-border financial services.

Section 108^1: infringement of Latvian law

If the FCMC determines that a credit institution registered in another Member State, which provides financial services to Latvia directly or through a local branch, "performs operations" that contravene "the laws of Latvia": 1) it requests that the credit institution terminates these operations;[106] if they are not discontinued, 2) it tells the home State's supervisory authority about the infringements and asks the latter to inform it of the actions taken;[107] if the transgressions continue, 3) it takes "measures so that such violations are rectified", and informs the home State's competent authority.[108]

The FCMC may also "perform ... activities in order to rectify" and penalize infringements that contradict Latvian laws "safeguarding the interests of society".[109] It may "implement measures" in a crisis to "protect the interests of depositors, investors, and other recipients" of a credit institution's services, informing the European Commission and the home State's supervisory authority of the actions taken.[110]

Sections 108^1(1)-(3), 108^1(4) and 108^1(6) of the CIL follow the procedure in Articles 30, 31 and 33 of Directive 2006/48/EC respectively. However, the Directive is breached in the following ways. Firstly, measures pursuant to Articles 30 and 31 must be "properly justified and communicated" to the credit institution, and "subject to a right of appeal" in the courts of the State in which they were adopted [Article 32]. These

[106] s.108^1(1), CIL.
[107] s.108^1(2), CIL.
[108] s.108^1(3), CIL.
[109] s.108^1(4), CIL.
[110] s.108^1(6), CIL.

requirements are absent from section 108^1 of the CIL. Secondly, sections 108^1(1)-(3), in referring to violations of "the laws of Latvia",[111] are broader than Article 30, which concerns non-compliance with national rules enacted "pursuant to the provisions of this Directive involving powers of the host Member State's competent authorities" [Article 30(1)].[112] Thirdly, measures adopted under Article 31 must be "appropriate"; section 108^1(4) of the CIL does not incorporate this qualification.[113]

Financial services are 'capital movements' in Annex I. The FCMC may reduce the supply of these services by taking action against credit institutions' infringements of national law, thereby limiting the free movement of capital. For this restriction to be justified for public policy or security, there must be a "genuine and sufficiently serious threat to a fundamental interest of society",[114] such as to a minimum supply of petroleum products at all times.[115] Sections 108^1(1)-(4) do not specify a fundamental interest, but section 108^1(6) introduces one: the protection of depositors' and investors' interests in a crisis.[116] However, the FCMC's power under this section to "implement measures" does not provide credit institutions with legal certainty–the measures must be specific, objective and known to these institutions beforehand.[117]

Measures taken to stop transgressions of national law concerning "the prudential supervision of financial institutions",[118] must also observe the requirements of legal certainty. Since section 108^1 of the CIL does not state specific, objective measures, it is an unjustified restriction on the free movement of capital. It therefore contravenes Article 56 of the EC Treaty.

---

[111] See above in this subsection.

[112] Linguistic precision in the transposition of a Directive is necessary to prevent national cases being brought that are misaligned with the Directive's purpose. If, for instance, the foreign credit institution breaches Latvian tax law, a literal interpretation of s.108^1 of the CIL may empower the FCMC to act under this section, especially as "performs operations" (see above in this subsection) is not defined.

[113] See above in this subsection. The phrase "safeguarding the interests of society" in s.108^1(4) of the CIL is similar to "adopted in the interests of the general good" in Article 31 of Directive 2006/48/EC, and therefore should refer to the same national laws.

[114] *Eglise de Scientologie and Scientology International* [2000] ECR I-1335.

[115] *Campus Oil and Others* [1984] ECR 2727.

[116] See above in this subsection.

[117] See the subsection '*The requirements for a successful public policy/security derogation*' in section 2.1.3.

[118] Article 58(1)(b), EC Treaty.

5.1.4 2002-08-15 Regulations on the Issue of Credit Institution and Credit Union Operating Licences (RICIOL)

A foreign bank must accept four conditions to receive a licence to open a Latvian branch, two of which give discretion to the FCMC:[119] 1) the home country's supervisory authority "ensures appropriate, complete effective supervision" complying with the Basel Committee's Core Principles for Effective Banking Supervision;[120] 2) this supervisory authority and the FCMC have agreed a cross-border banking cooperation contract, or regulations in the home country apply "appropriate standards conforming with international standards" for establishing a foreign bank branch there.[121] A Latvian bank wishing to found a branch abroad must submit extensive documentation to the FCMC in order for the latter to grant it a permit.[122]

Establishing a branch is a 'capital movement' under Title I(1) of Annex I. The licensing conditions restrict the free movement of capital, since the foreign branch requirements are more extensive than those required to found a domestic branch. To be justified, the conditions must provide the applicant credit institution with legal certainty i.e. be specific, objective and known to it beforehand.[123] Whilst this is true for opening a branch abroad, it is not so for establishing a Latvian branch because the RICIOL provides no guidance as to what the FCMC considers to be "appropriate" supervision or standards.[124] In both cases, the Regulation neither requires the FCMC to give reasons for refusing a permit, nor

---

[119] The RICIOL does not define 'foreign'. It means 'non-EEA' in the CIL; see note 82.

[120] Paragraph 4.1.1, RICIOL. The revised version of the 25 principles is published at http://www.bis.org/publ/bcbs129.pdf.

[121] Paragraph 4.1.3, RICIOL.

[122] Paragraphs 2, 5.1 and 5.3, RICIOL. Neither the RICIOL nor the CIL define 'abroad'. If this term includes EEA countries, s.12^2 of the CIL (see section 5.1.3) takes precedence over Paragraph 5 of the RICIOL (ss.15(2) and 15(6), Administrative Procedure Law 2002).

[123] See the subsection '*The requirements for a successful public policy/security derogation*' in section 2.1.3.

[124] This is analogous to the FCMC's discretion in deciding supervision "of equal value" in section 64(2)(1) of the LIC. See the subsection '*Sections 62 to 65: investment types*' in section 5.1.1.

provides an appeal against a refusal in the Latvian courts.[125] Paragraphs 4 and 5 of the RICIOL therefore breach Article 56 of the EC Treaty.

5.1.5 Law on Insurance Companies and Supervision Thereof 1998 (LICST)

Article 7: third country insurance services

An "insurance company" or a "branch of a non-Member State insurer" may provide the insurance services specified in its licence from the FCMC,[126] or "intermediary services" to another insurer or to a reinsurer,[127] or perform "entrepreneurial activity" connected to insurance.[128] It may neither issue debt securities nor take loans, other than loans agreed in advance with the FCMC that are to "ensure timely payment of insurance indemnities".[129]

Capital transfers in respect of insurance contracts are 'capital movements' in Title X of Annex I. Article 7(1) of the LICST restricts the free movement of capital because it does not permit third country insurers to provide cross-border insurance services to Latvia. This is only justifiable "for serious political reasons and on grounds of urgency" or to protect Latvia's security in association with making or trading "arms, munitions or war material".[130] These are unlikely possibilities for most third countries.

The issue of bonds and the taking of loans are 'capital movements' under Titles IIIB and VIII of Annex I respectively. Article 7(4) of the LICST does not restrict the free movement of capital because it defines a funding characteristic of Latvian insurance firms, with Latvian and third

---

[125] See the subsection '*The requirements for a successful public policy/security derogation*' in section 2.1.3.

[126] Article 7(1)(1), LICST. An 'insurance company' is a "joint stock company" or "mutual cooperative insurance society" that is entitled to provide insurance in accordance with the LICST (Article 1(3)(b), LICST). Neither the Commercial Law 2000 nor the insurance legislation define these enterprises. 'Insurance' is risk transfer of potential loss from the insured to the insurer (Article 1(1), LICST). A 'branch of a non-Member State insurer' is a branch "established and registered" in Latvia of a company registered in a country outside the EEA with the right to provide insurance there (Articles 1(12) and 1(14)-(15), LICST).

[127] Article 7(1)(2), LICST. The insurance laws do not define 'intermediate services'.

[128] Article 7(1)(3), LICST. The Commercial Law 2000 does not define 'entrepreneurial activity'.

[129] Article 7(4), LICST.

[130] Articles 60(2) and 296(1)(b), EC Treaty.

country entities being treated similarly. Deterring foreign investors, as in *Commission v Spain*,[131] is insufficient to render this rule restrictive of free capital movement because insurance premiums provide most of the firm's resources.

Article 8^{11111}: outsourcing

The FCMC prohibits an insurance company or a branch of a third country insurer from arranging a "planned outsource service" with an "outsource service provider",[132] if 1) the insurance firm breaches the LICST,[133] 2) the outsourcing may affect the policyholder's legal position or impede the firm's management in its legal obligations,[134] 3) the outsourcing restricts or prevents the FCMC from performing its legal functions,[135] or 4) the outsource contract is illegal and does not provide a "true and fair view" of cooperation between the insurance firm and the outsource provider, or of the amount and quality of the outsource service required.[136] The FCMC may request that an insurance company or a non-Member State insurer's branch "immediately terminate" the outsource contract if it "has detected that" any of the above circumstances,[137] or three others concerning inadequate supervision, poor risk management and deficient provision of outsourcing services respectively,[138] has occurred.

Although the outsourcing arrangement is not a 'capital movement', if the services resulting from it involve cross-border transfers, they are 'capital flows' in Title X of Annex I. This may or may not hinder the free movement of capital. The claim in favour is that the principle in *Commission v France*,[139] *Commission v Spain*,[140] and *Commission v United Kingdom*,[141] that the national restriction inhibits share purchase and therefore discourages investors from other Member States,[142] can be

[131] [2003] ECR I-4581. See the subsection '*Commission v Spain*' in section 2.1.2.

[132] To 'outsource services' means to "delegate the performance of activities" (Article $8^{3}(1)$, LICST). An 'outsource service provider' is a person who agrees in writing with an insurance company or a non-Member State insurer to provide "external services" (Article 1(39), LICST).

[133] Article $8^{11111}(1)(1)$, LICST.

[134] Articles $8^{11111}(1)(2)$ and $8^{11111}(1)(3)$, LICST.

[135] Article $8^{11111}(1)(4)$, LICST.

[136] Article $8^{11111}(1)(5)$, LICST.

[137] Article $8^{11111}(4)(4)$, LICST.

[138] Articles $8^{11111}(4)(1)$, $8^{11111}(4)(2)$ and $8^{11111}(4)(3)$, LICST.

[139] [2002] ECR I-4781.

[140] [2003] ECR I-4581.

[141] [2003] ECR I-4641.

[142] See section 2.1.2.

extended to the outsourcing restriction dissuading third country insurers from providing insurance services in Latvia. The argument against the outsourcing restrictions limiting free movement of capital is that, whilst they may discourage non-EEA insurance firms from providing insurance services in Latvia, they do not affect those registered in EEA countries from doing so.

The EU needs to clarify two points .[143] 1) Do the arguments applying to capital flows to and from other Member States apply to flows to and from third countries? If the latter can legally be restricted more than the former, Community Law should make this clear.[144] 2) Are insurance services to be treated similarly to investments in shares? In the absence of EU case law on such services, it is consistent that they should be so treated.[145]

---

[143] Until relevant cases are brought before the ECJ, the European Commission could publish an Interpretative Communication or an Opinion that addresses these issues.

[144] In *Skatteverket v A* [2007] ECR I-11531, the first reported case on the movement of capital between Member States and third countries, the ECJ stated that the taxation by a Member State of economic activities with cross-border elements within the European Community is "not always comparable" to similar activities between Member States and third countries because of the extent of legal integration between Member States [Paragraph 37]. Indeed, a Member State may be able to justify a restriction on the movement of capital to or from third countries under conditions in which it would be an unacceptable limitation on capital movements between Member States. In this case, the ECJ held that a Member State was not required to offer a tax advantage in a situation in which it depended upon satisfying requirements, compliance with which can only be verified by obtaining information from the competent authority of a third country, and in which it "proves impossible to obtain such information from that country" because it is not contractually obliged to provide it [Paragraph 63]. 'Proves impossible' is a high standard; nonetheless, this case allows a higher level of restrictions to be legally applied to capital movements to and from third countries than to cross-border capital flows within the EU. Further cases may define the precise extent of this difference.

[145] Mr. Christopher Vajda QC stated at the United Kingdom Association for European Law conference on 28 April 2007, that the free movement of capital cases fall into two groups: the 'golden shares' cases, discussed in sections 2.1.2 and 2.1.3, and the direct taxation cases, presented in section 2.3. There are also real property cases, discussed in section 2.1.4, which follow the same principles as the 'golden shares' cases. Whilst these principles have general applicability to the free movement of capital, there are legal issues not yet resolved that require new cases with particular facts. A national insurance rule treating the home country and third countries similarly is one such case.

Article 10: licensing of a third country insurer

A branch of a non-Member State insurer must obtain a licence from the FCMC to "launch operations" in Latvia.[146] The branch may only provide the classes of insurance services stated in the licence.[147] Requirements include agreeing to abide by Latvian law and FCMC regulations in branch accounting,[148] satisfying a minimum solvency margin,[149] and reaching a cooperation and exchange of information agreement with the home country's insurance supervision authority.[150] The insurer must submit extensive documentation in support of its licence application, including a three year plan,[151] a description of the internal control system, its policies and its procedures,[152] and annual reports for the previous three years.[153] The FCMC may not issue the licence if the insurance is "not economically substantiated",[154] the planned operations breach national law,[155] the home country's laws restrict FCMC supervision,[156] and/or the branch's structure inhibits this supervision.[157]

Establishing a branch is a 'capital movement' under Title I(1) of Annex I. If the FCMC refuses to issue a licence for the branch to provide insurance services in Latvia, it breaches the free movement of capital. The extensive licensing requirements provide the third country insurer with legal certainty, although the FCMC has discretion as to whether or not to grant a licence. This discretion is reduced if, for instance, 'economically substantiated' is divided into minimum sales figures for each class of insurance. Refusing to grant a licence may be disproportionate, and the refusal should be accompanied by reasons and subject to appeal in the Latvian courts.[158] Unless it can be justified "for serious political reasons and on grounds of urgency" or to protect Latvia's security in connection

---

[146] Article 10(1), LICST.
[147] Ibid.
[148] Article 10(2)(1)(c), LICST.
[149] Article 10(2)(1)(f), LICST.
[150] Article 10(2), LICST.
[151] Article 10(3)(6), LICST.
[152] Article 10(3)(7), LICST.
[153] Article 10(3)(8), LICST.
[154] Article 10(6)(1), LICST.
[155] Article 10(6)(3), LICST.
[156] Article 10(6)(4), LICST.
[157] Article 10(6)(7), LICST.
[158] See the subsection '*The requirements for a successful public policy/security derogation*' in section 2.1.3.

with arms' production or trading,[159] Article 10 of the LICST contravenes Article 56 of the EC Treaty.

Articles 11, 11¹ and 11³: Latvian companies providing insurance services abroad

A Latvian insurance firm intending to establish a branch in another EEA country must notify the FCMC,[160] with the following information appended: 1) the country's name,[161] 2) the branch's address, "organisational structure", proposed services and three year operational plan,[162] and 3) "information concerning" the branch manager.[163] The FCMC communicates this information to the host state's insurance supervisory authority within three months of receiving it all.[164] The FCMC may not forward the information if, amongst other things, the branch's structure "does not allow" it to be supervised in accordance with Latvian law,[165] or "deficiencies detected by the Financial and Capital Market Commission have not been eliminated within the term specified by the Financial and Capital Market Commission".[166]

Article 11 of the LICST differs from Article 10 of Directive 73/239/EEC as follows:[167] 1) it requires information about the branch manager rather than the authorised agent's name [Article 10(2)(d)]; 2) it neither requires the FCMC to give reasons for refusing to communicate the information to the host state's competent authority, nor provides a right of appeal against this refusal in the Latvian courts [Article 10(3)], and 3) the "deficiencies detected" reason in Article 11(3¹)(5) of the LICST for the FCMC to refuse to forward the information is absent from the Directive.

Opening a branch is a 'capital movement' in Annex I. If the FCMC refuses to communicate the information concerning branch foundation to the host state's competent authority, then it potentially restricts the free movement of capital. This is unjustified because the FCMC has discretion, especially under Article 11(3¹)(5) of the LICST,[168] as to

[159] Articles 60(2) and 296(1)(b), EC Treaty.
[160] Article 11(1), LICST.
[161] Article 11(2)(1), LICST.
[162] Articles 11(2)(2) and 11(2)(3), LICST.
[163] Article 11(2)(4), LICST.
[164] Article 11(3), LICST.
[165] Article 11(3¹)(2), LICST.
[166] Article 11(3¹)(5), LICST.
[167] This Article of Directive 73/239/EC is described in section 2.4.3.
[168] See above in this subsection.

whether or not to forward such information. Therefore the refusal to forward it does not observe the requirements of legal certainty. Furthermore, the refusal need neither be accompanied by reasons, nor be actionable in the Latvian courts.[169]

A Latvian insurance company must be authorised by the FCMC to open a branch in a non-EEA country.[170] The information required for authorisation is similar to that for notification in Article 11 of the LICST.[171] The FCMC may refuse authorisation if 1) the branch's structure "does not allow" it to be supervised,[172] 2) the third country's laws limit FCMC supervision,[173] 3) the FCMC has not made a cooperation and information exchange agreement with the host state's insurance supervision authority,[174] or "deficiencies detected by the [FCMC] have not been eliminated within the term specified by the [FCMC]".[175]

Establishment of a branch is a 'capital movement' in Annex I. If the FCMC refuses to authorise the branch's foundation, then it restricts the free movement of capital. It has discretion in granting such authorisation, especially under Article 11¹(4)(8) of the LICST;[176] hence, the grounds for refusing it do not provide the insurance company with legal certainty.[177] Unless justified "for serious political reasons and on grounds of urgency" or to protect Latvia's security in association with arms' production or trade,[178] Article 11¹ of the LICST breaches Article 56 of the EC Treaty.

A Latvian firm supplying cross-border insurance services to another EEA country must notify the FCMC,[179] informing it of that state's name and the "risks insured".[180] Within 30 days of receiving this information, the FCMC must communicate to the host state's competent authority: i) proof that the firm complies with "the required solvency margin

---

[169] See the subsection '*The requirements for a successful public policy/security derogation*' in section 2.1.3.

[170] Article 11¹(1), LICST.

[171] Article 11¹(2) LICST replicates Article 11(2) LICST (see above) with minor exceptions.

[172] Article 11¹(4)(3), LICST.

[173] Article 11¹(4)(5), LICST.

[174] Article 11¹(4)(6), LICST.

[175] Article 11¹(4)(8), LICST.

[176] See above in this subsection.

[177] *Eglise de Scientologie and Scientology International* [2000] ECR I-1335; *Commission v France* [2002] ECR I-4781. See section 2.1.3.

[178] Articles 60(2) and 296(1)(b), EC Treaty.

[179] Article 11³(1), LICST.

[180] Article 11³(2), LICST. This complies with Article 14 of Directive 88/357/EEC. See section 2.4.3.

requirements",[181] ii) the classes of insurance that the firm is permitted to provide,[182] and iii) the "risks to be insured".[183] The FCMC may refuse to forward such information if 1) documents supplied "contain false or incomplete information",[184] 2) the insurance company is implementing a financial improvement plan,[185] or 3) "deficiencies detected by the [FCMC] have not been eliminated within the term specified by the [FCMC]".[186] The FCMC must give reasons for this refusal.[187]

There are three differences between Article 11^3 of the LICST and Directive 88/357/EEC.[188] Firstly, the FCMC must communicate the "nature of the risks" to the host state's competent authority [Article 16(1)(c)] rather than the risks.[189] Secondly, the Directive provides no grounds for the FCMC to refuse to forward the information. Thirdly, this refusal must be challengeable in the home country's courts [Article 16(2)]; Article 11^3 of the LICST gives no such right of appeal.

The forwarding of information is not a 'capital movement' in Annex I. If the FCMC refuses to communicate such information to the host state's competent authority, however, it potentially restricts the free movement of cross-border insurance services, which are 'capital movements' under Title X of Annex I. Such restriction is unjustified because the "deficiencies detected" reason for refusing to communicate the information in Article $11^3(4^1)(3)$ of the LICST does not provide the insurance company with legal certainty, and because there is no right of appeal against this refusal in the Latvian courts.[190]

Articles 16 to 19: licence cancellation/suspension

The FCMC may cancel the licence of a Latvian insurance firm or of a branch of a non-EEA country insurer for several reasons including non-provision of insurance for 12 months initially or 6 months subsequently,[191] breach of FCMC instructions, licence conditions, commercial laws and

---

[181] Article $11^3(4)(1)$, LICST. These are stated in Articles 16-17 of Directive 73/239/EEC.
[182] Article $11^3(4)(2)$, LICST.
[183] Article $11^3(4)(3)$, LICST.
[184] Article $11^3(4^1)(1)$, LICST.
[185] Article $11^3(4^1)(2)$, LICST.
[186] Article $11^3(4^1)(3)$, LICST.
[187] Article $11^3(5)$, LICST.
[188] See section 2.4.3.
[189] See point iii), above in this subsection.
[190] See the subsection '*The requirements for a successful public policy/security derogation*' in section 2.1.3.
[191] Articles 16(1)(1) and 16(1)(2), LICST.

regulations,[192] licence renouncement,[193] insolvency,[194] or liquidation.[195] Alternatively, the FCMC may "suspend the validity of the licence" for up to 6 months for the above reasons.[196] It must provide information about the cancellation/suspension to the foreign country's supervision authority.[197] The insurance company or branch may appeal against the decision to cancel or suspend the licence within one month.[198]

Licence cancellation/suspension is not a 'capital movement' in Annex I. It can be argued that cancellation/suspension restricts the free movement of capital because it stops cross-border insurance services, which are 'capital movements' in Title X of Annex I. However, Articles 16 and 17 of the LICST do not discriminate between Latvian and third country insurance companies. Consequently, these provisions may or may not limit the free movement of capital, as discussed above for Article 8[11111] of the LICST.

Articles 41 to 43: technical provisions

Assets acceptable as cover for technical provisions must be situated in the EEA if "insurance objects" connected to insured risks are located there.[199] Such assets must be in Latvia for branches of third country insurers.[200] Assets must be situated in an EEA or OECD country.[201] There are investment percentage limitations on individual assets and on asset categories; up to 10% of technical provisions may be assigned to one mortgage loan and no more than 25% of such provisions to all mortgage loans, for instance.[202]

---

[192] Articles 16(1)(3) and 16(1)(4), LICST.
[193] Article 16(1)(5), LICST.
[194] Article 16(1)(7), LICST.
[195] Article 16(1)(10), LICST.
[196] Articles 17(1)-(2), LICST.
[197] Article 16(2), LICST.
[198] Article 19(2), LICST.
[199] Article 41(3), LICST. 'Technical provisions' are an insurance firm's contingent liabilities, calculated in accordance with insurance contracts and "reinsurance accepted" (Article 1(9), LICST). Acceptable assets include debt and equity securities, investment certificates, mortgage loans, land and buildings, deposits with credit institutions and insurance policyholders' debts from direct insurance (Article 42(1), LICST). 'Insurance objects' are a person's life, health, physical condition and civil liability, and "valuable property or interests", as befits the type of insurance (s.1(7), Law on Insurance Contracts).
[200] Article 41(4), LICST.
[201] Article 42(2), LICST.
[202] Article 43(1)(6), LICST.

Investment in assets abroad is a 'capital movement' in Annex I. Articles 41 and 42 of the LICST restrict the free movement of capital because they favour investments in Latvia, the EEA, OECD states and other countries, in that order.[203] The investment percentage limitations are non-discriminatory, and would only limit the free movement of capital if the principle in *Commission v Spain* applies,[204] namely that despite affecting residents and non-residents equally, the limitations deter investment from other Member States' nationals.[205]

Articles 41 and 42 of the LICST are not justified for public policy or security because there is no "genuine and sufficiently serious threat to a fundamental interest of society",[206] such as to the supply of petroleum products at all times.[207] These provisions breach Article 56 of the EC Treaty, unless enacted "for serious political reasons and on grounds of urgency".[208]

Articles 99 and 99^1: contravention of Latvian law

The FCMC may request a "branch of a Member State insurer",[209] or a "Member State insurer" providing cross-border services to Latvia,[210] to terminate its infringements of Latvian law, and must notify the insurer and the home State's competent authority of "decisions taken".[211] If the FCMC finds that such an insurer or branch "performs activities" breaking

[203] Articles 41(3)-(4) of the LICST are practical. Assets should be matched against liabilities in amount, duration and location, thereby reducing interest rate and foreign exchange risks. The free movement of capital principle permits other choices, however.

[204] [2003] ECR I-4581.

[205] See section 2.1.2. It is an extension of EU law to apply this principle to third countries. See the discussion of Article 8^{11111} LICST in the subsection '*Article 8^{11111}: outsourcing*', above in section 5.1.5.

[206] *Eglise de Scientologie and Scientology International* [2000] ECR I-1335.

[207] *Campus Oil and Others* [1984] ECR 2727. See the subsection '*The requirements for a successful public policy/security derogation*' in section 2.1.3.

[208] Article 60(2), EC Treaty. This is consistent with the treatment of investment limitations in the LIC–see the subsection '*Section 66: investment limitations*' in section 5.1.1.

[209] A 'branch of a Member State insurer' is a branch "established and registered" in Latvia of an insurer registered in an EEA country that is entitled to provide insurance there (Articles 1(11)-(12) and 1(14), LICST).

[210] A 'Member State insurer' is an insurer registered in an EEA country with the right to provide insurance there (Articles 1(11)-(12), LICST).

[211] Articles 99(3)-(4), LICST.

national law: 1) it requests that the insurer stops these activities;[212] if this fails, 2) it notifies the home Member State's insurance supervision authority thereof;[213] if these activities continue, 3) it takes "measures preventing such violations" and informs the home State's competent authority.[214] The FCMC may also act to prevent breaches of Latvian laws protecting "public interests", notifying the insurer or branch and the home State's authority of the measures taken.[215]

Articles 99(3), 99(4) and $99^1(4)$ of the LICST are permitted by Directive 92/49/EEC, which permits Member States "to penalize infringements within their territories" [Article 40(7)]. Articles $99^1(1)$-(3) of the LICST follow the procedure in Articles 40(3)-(5) of the Directive. However, the host State's competent authority must take "*appropriate* measures to prevent or penalize such infringements", including preventing the insurance firm "from *continuing to conclude new insurance contracts within its territory*" [Article 40(5)].[216] Article $99^1(3)$ of the LICST lacks both of the emphasised elements. The Directive's use of "appropriate" indicates that measures taken should be proportionate to the infringement's gravity. The national legislation must include this concept to transpose the Directive satisfactorily. The LICST does not adopt Article 40(9) of Directive 92/49/EEC, which requires the FCMC's measures to be "properly reasoned and communicated to the undertaking concerned", although Articles 99(3), 99(4) and $99^1(4)$ of the LICST fulfil the communication requirement.

Insurance services are 'capital movements' in Title X of Annex I. If the FCMC stops an insurance company or branch from providing these services, then it restricts the free movement of capital. Although Member States may adopt "all requisite measures" to prevent breaches of national law, especially those affecting taxation and "the prudential supervision of financial institutions",[217] such measures must be proportionate, necessary to protect the relevant interests, and provide legal certainty to the insurer.[218] Actions taken under Articles 99 and 99^1 of the LICST do not

[212] Article $99^1(1)$, LICST.
[213] Article $99^1(2)$, LICST.
[214] Article $99^1(3)$, LICST.
[215] Article $99^1(4)$, LICST.
[216] Emphasis mine.
[217] Article 58(1)(b), EC Treaty.
[218] See the subsection '*The requirements for a successful public policy/security derogation*' in section 2.1.3.

fulfil these requirements. These provisions therefore contravene Article 56 of the EC Treaty.[219]

5.1.6 Activities of Insurance and Reinsurance Intermediaries Law 2005 (AIRIL)

'Insurance mediation' includes preparing documents for, explaining the rules of and the rights and duties in, performing activities for entering into, and signing and administration of, an insurance contract.[220] These activities are performed by 'insurance intermediaries', who may be insurance brokers, agents or tied agents.[221]

Insurance mediation is a 'capital movement' in Title X of Annex I for two reasons. Firstly, one activity for entering into an insurance contract is paying the insurance premium, which is in Title X. Secondly, the other components of insurance mediation are "operations necessary for the purpose of capital movements",[222] which qualify as 'capital movements'.

Sections 8 to 11: registration of insurance and reinsurance intermediaries (hereafter 'intermediaries')

The FCMC enters Latvian commercial companies and self-employed persons in the Enterprise Register's commercial register, and self-employed persons listed with the State Revenue Service, into the intermediaries' register.[223] This gives them the right to provide insurance and reinsurance mediation (hereafter 'mediation') in "other Member States".[224] The FCMC also puts Latvian branches of non-Member State intermediaries into this register.[225]

---

[219] This reasoning is consistent with the 'breach of national law' provisions in the FIML and the CIL. See the subsection '*Section 140: breach of national law*' in section 5.1.2 and the subsection '*Section 108¹: infringement of Latvian law*' in section 5.1.3.

[220] s.1(1), AIRIL. 'Reinsurance mediation' is defined the same, but with 'reinsurance' substituted for 'insurance' (s.1(2), AIRIL).

[221] s.1(3), AIRIL. 'Reinsurance intermediaries' perform reinsurance mediation (s.1(4), AIRIL).

[222] Annex I.

[223] ss.8(1)(1) and 8(1)(2), AIRIL.

[224] s.8(2), AIRIL. The AIRIL does not define 'Member State'. Article 1(12) LICST equates it with an EEA country.

[225] s.8(1)(3), AIRIL.

The FCMC requires extensive information and documentation in order to register an intermediary,[226] and may refuse to do so if 1) documents are missing or include false or incomplete information,[227] 2) the procedures submitted to the FCMC, such as for protecting the "information system",[228] breach the law,[229] or 3) the intermediary's "responsible person" does not meet the requirements of the AIRIL.[230] The FCMC may cancel an entry in the intermediaries' register for one of the reasons above,[231] or because the intermediary has practised mediation for one year or less,[232] contravened the AIRIL,[233] violated money laundering laws,[234] or breached a Member State's rules "protecting public interests" and the "general good".[235] There is a right of appeal against a cancellation.[236]

These rules comply with Directive 2002/92/EC, except that sanctions should be "properly justified and communicated to the intermediary" and subject to a right of appeal [Article 8(5)], the latter being unavailable if the FCMC refuses to register an intermediary.[237] Refusal to register potentially restricts, and registration cancellation limits, insurance mediation, which is a 'capital movement' in Annex I.[238] Since Latvian intermediaries and branches of non-EEA state insurers are treated the same, the free movement of capital is only restricted if the principle in *Commission v Spain* is extended to third countries and to insurance mediation.[239]

Sections 32 and 34: refusal to forward information

A Latvian intermediary wishing to establish a branch in another Member State must notify the FCMC,[240] providing it with that State's

---

226 ss.9(1) and 10(1), AIRIL.
227 s.11(1)(1), AIRIL.
228 s.10(1)(8), AIRIL.
229 s.11(1)(2), AIRIL.
230 s.11(1)(3), AIRIL.
231 s.11(2)(1), AIRIL.
232 s.11(2)(2), AIRIL.
233 s.11(2)(3), AIRIL.
234 s.11(2)(4), AIRIL.
235 s.11(2)(5), AIRIL.
236 s.11(4), AIRIL.
237 Directive 2002/92/EC only applies if the Latvian intermediary, or branch of a non-EEA state intermediary, pursues insurance mediation in an EEA country.
238 See above in section 5.1.6.
239 [2003] ECR I-4581. See the subsection '*Article 8[11111]: outsourcing*' in section 5.1.5.
240 s.32(1), AIRIL.

name,[241] a description of the planned services,[242] the branch's address,[243] "information regarding" the branch's manager,[244] and the name, address, telephone number and e-mail address of the insurance company on whose behalf the intermediary intends to act.[245] The branch manager must be at least 21 years old and of "good repute", with a tertiary education, the "knowledge necessary" for practising mediation, the "necessary" market experience and no international criminal record.[246] The FCMC must send the information to the host Member State's competent authority within 30 days, and inform the intermediary that it has done so.[247] It need not do so if the branch's manager does not fulfil the above criteria, or if the intermediary is financially unstable or breaches the AIRIL, and must provide the intermediary with reasons for the refusal.[248]

A Latvian intermediary wishing to provide cross-border insurance mediation to another Member State must notify the FCMC, and include "information regarding" that State and the contact details of the insurance company in whose cause the intermediary will act.[249] Communicating the information to the host State's competent authority follows the process described in the previous paragraph, but without the first ground for refusal.[250]

The information needed for branch foundation in, but not for cross-border mediation to, another Member State exceeds that demanded by Directive 2002/92/EC. The Directive only requires the intermediary to "inform the competent authorities of the home Member State" [Article 6(1)].[251] In addition, Directive 2002/92/EC requires a decision to refuse to forward information to the host State's competent authority to be subject to an appeal in the Latvian courts, because this decision involves "restrictions on the activities of an insurance or reinsurance intermediary" [Article 8(5)].

Although refusing to forward information is not a 'capital movement' in Annex I, branch establishment and cross-border insurance mediation are

---

[241] s.32(2)(1), AIRIL.
[242] s.32(2)(2), AIRIL.
[243] s.32(2)(3), AIRIL.
[244] s.32(2)(4), AIRIL.
[245] s.32(2)(5), AIRIL.
[246] ss.32(3) and 17(4), AIRIL.
[247] s.32(4), AIRIL.
[248] s.32(5), AIRIL.
[249] s.34(1), AIRIL.
[250] ss.32(2)-(3), AIRIL.
[251] See section 2.4.4.

'capital movements' in Titles I(1) and X of the Annex respectively. Such a refusal restricts the free movement of capital if the intermediary is opening a branch in the host State, and potentially limits capital movement if the intermediary is to provide cross-border mediation to that State. The grounds for refusal are unjustified because they may be disproportionate, do not all provide legal certainty to the intermediary–for instance, there are no specific, objective criteria on which the FCMC decides that an intermediary is financially unstable, and are not accompanied by a right of appeal in the Latvian courts.[252] Sections 32 and 34 of the AIRIL therefore breach Article 56 of the EC Treaty.

Section 39: violation of national law

If the FCMC ascertains that a branch of a Member State intermediary, or a such an intermediary providing cross-border mediation to Latvia "carries out activities" contravening national law: 1) it requests that the insurer terminates these activities;[253] if this fails, 2) it notifies the home Member State's competent authority thereof;[254] if the activities continue, 3) it takes "measures to prevent such violations" and notifies the home State's competent authority.[255] The FCMC may also act to stop infringements of Latvian laws defending "public interests (general good)", informing the branch or intermediary and the home State's authority of the measures taken.[256]

Section 39 of the AIRIL reflects Article 99¹ of the LICST,[257] but with 'intermediary' and 'mediation' substituted for 'insurer' and 'insurance' respectively. Consequently, sections 39(1)-(3) of the AIRIL follow Articles 40(3)-(5) of Directive 92/49/EEC. Although Directive 2002/92/EC does not prescribe a 'breach of national law' procedure, it requires Member States to provide "*appropriate* sanctions" if an intermediary breaks national laws "*adopted pursuant to this Directive*"

---

[252] See the subsection '*The requirements for a successful public policy/security derogation*' in section 2.1.3.

[253] s.39(1), AIRIL.

[254] s.39(2), AIRIL.

[255] s.39(3), AIRIL.

[256] s.39(4), AIRIL.

[257] See the subsection '*Articles 99 and 99¹: contravention of Latvian law*' in section 5.1.5.

[Article 8(3)].[258] Sections 39(1)-(3) of the AIRIL lack the emphasised elements.[259]

Section 39(4) of the AIRIL does not transpose the following emphasised terms in Directive 2002/92/EC: the host Member State may "take *appropriate* measures to prevent or penalise irregularities" that breach national law "adopted in the interest of the general good", including "*the possibility of preventing*" *offending intermediaries from "initiating any further activities" there* [Article 8(4)].[260] Furthermore, section 39 of the AIRIL neither requires measures to be "properly reasoned and communicated" to the intermediary, nor to be subject to a right of appeal in the national courts [Article 8(5)].

Insurance mediation is a 'capital movement' in Title X of Annex I. If the FCMC prevents a branch or intermediary from providing mediation, then it hinders the free movement of capital. The justification for Member States to take all necessary measures to prevent violations of national law, especially those concerning taxation and "the prudential supervision of financial institutions",[261] is inapplicable because section 39 of the AIRIL states no specific, objective measures that provide the intermediary with legal certainty, and because the remedies that the FCMC chooses may be disproportionate and may not be necessary to protect the interests they are intended to guarantee.[262] Consequently, section 39 of the AIRIL breaches Article 56 of the EC Treaty.

5.1.7 Law on Private Pension Funds (LPPF)

Pension plan assets may be invested in 1) securities issued or guaranteed by state or local governments of EEA countries,[263] or of OECD states with an investment grade long-term country credit rating,[264] 2) securities issued or guaranteed by international financial organisations to which one or more EEA countries belong,[265] 3) capital securities, or commercial companies' debt securities, officially listed on a stock

---

258 Emphasis mine.

259 The comments on "appropriate" in the subsection '*Articles 99 and 99¹: contravention of Latvian law*' in section 5.1.5 apply here.

260 Emphasis mine.

261 Article 58(1)(b), EC Treaty.

262 See the subsection '*The requirements for a successful public policy/security derogation*' in section 2.1.3.

263 s.23(3)(1), LPPF.

264 s.23(3)(2), LPPF.

265 s.23(3)(3), LPPF.

exchange in one of these EEA/OECD states,[266] or to be so listed within a year of initial subscription,[267] 4) term deposits of a credit institution licensed in an EEA country to provide financial services there,[268] 5) open-ended investment funds registered in one of the above EEA/OECD states,[269] 6) immovable property registered in an EEA country,[270] or 7) "derivative financial instruments".[271] There are individual and collective investment percentage limitations, such as 10% and 15% maximum of the pension fund assets in one immovable property and all such property respectively.[272]

Investment in foreign assets is a 'capital movement' in Annex I. Section 23(3) of the LPPF favours investments in the EEA, OECD states with investment grade long-term credit ratings and other countries, in this order. It therefore restricts the free movement of capital. The investment percentage limitations in section 23(4) of the LPPF are non-discriminatory. They therefore do not limit the free movement of capital, unless the rule in *Commission v Spain* is extended to investments in third countries.[273]

Section 23(3) of the LPPF can only be justified "for serious political reasons and on grounds of urgency" or to protect Latvia's security in relation to "the production of or trade in arms, munitions and war material".[274] Both of these grounds are unlikely for pensions. This section therefore breaches Article 56 of the EC Treaty. The pension plan assets investment restrictions can be applied in the pension fund prospectus and regulations without restricting the free movement of capital.

5.1.8 Comparison with Estonia and Poland

Estonian Investment Funds Act (EIFA), Polish Investment Funds Act (PIFA) and Latvian Law on Investment Companies (LLIC): investment funds

266 ss.23(3)(4) and 23(3)(5), LPPF.
267 s.23(3)(6), LPPF.
268 s.23(3)(7), LPPF. 'Credit institution' is defined in note 10.
269 ss.23(3)(8), LPPF and 21(2), LIC.
270 s.23(3)(9), LPPF.
271 s.23(3)(10), LPPF. 'Derivative financial instruments' are defined in note 29.
272 s.23(4)(6), LPPF.
273 [2003] ECR I-4581. See the discussion of Article 8^{11111} of the LICST in section 5.1.5.
274 Articles 60(2) and 296(1)(b), EC Treaty.

Both the PIFA and the LLIC classify 'investment funds' as open-end or closed-end,[275] and apply to each an upper limit on the percentage of fund assets that can be invested in different categories.[276] The EIFA neither distinguishes between fund types, nor restricts investments in particular asset categories.[277]

Foreign fund units must be released into public circulation in Estonia and Latvia, but not in Poland, by an investment firm or credit institution which is, or whose branch is, registered there.[278] A foreign investment company is exempt from this requirement in Estonia if it has a branch there to organise the transfer of its fund units.[279] This is not so for Latvia. Consequently, the Latvian rule restricts the free movement of capital more than the Estonian law.

With minor differences, all three countries require at least 90% of fund assets to be invested in EEA or OECD states.[280] The Polish provision applies only to open-end funds; closed-end funds have different restrictions.[281] Closed-end funds in Latvia can disapply this rule if the prospectus provides different limitations.[282] Both Poland and Latvia permit (open-end) funds to invest in third countries if the supervisory authority approves and if certain other conditions are satisfied.[283] By contrast, Estonia limits such investment to the countries listed in Regulation No.73 of the Minister of Finance.[284] Hence, whilst Estonian, Polish and Latvian laws for investing fund assets restrict the free movement of capital, the Estonian rules limit such movement more than those of Latvia and Poland.

Estonian Securities Market Act (ESMA), Polish Public Offer (PPOA) and Trading in Financial Instruments Acts (PTFIA), and Latvian Financial Instrument Market Law (LFIML): investment services

None of the above laws provide for cross-border investment services between non-EEA countries and Estonia, Poland and Latvia, in either

---

[275] Article 14(1)(3), PIFA; s.21, LLIC.
[276] Articles 93 and 145, PIFA; s.66, LLIC.
[277] See section 3.1.1.
[278] s.229(1), EIFA; s.60(1), LLIC, which refers only to open-end funds.
[279] s.229(2), EIFA.
[280] For Estonia and Poland, see section 4.1.7; s.66(13), LLIC.
[281] See section 4.1.1.
[282] s.66(14), LLIC.
[283] See sections 4.1.1 and 5.1.1.
[284] See section 3.1.2.

direction. There is consequently no movement of capital in respect of these services.

Estonian investment firms require the FSA's permission to establish a branch in a third country.[285] The conditions for such permission restrict the free movement of capital.[286] Neither the PTFIA nor the LFIML enable a national investment company to found a branch outside the EEA.[287] This limits outward capital movement more than the Estonian rules do.

Third country investment companies require authorisation from the financial authority to establish a branch in Estonia or Poland.[288] The LFIML does not provide for these firms to open a Latvian branch.[289] This restricts inward capital movement more than the Estonian and Polish provisions do.

Estonian, Polish and Latvian companies can provide investment services to other Member States, directly or through a branch, without requiring further authorisation from the host State.[290] Whilst the Polish conditions do not restrict the free movement of capital,[291] the Latvian rules restrict cross-border capital movement less than the Estonian provisions because the latter give the FSA discretion as to whether or not to forward information to the host State's competent authority about the proposed supply of such services there.[292]

Firms licensed in other Member States to supply investment services there may provide these services, directly or via a branch, to Estonia, Poland and Latvia using this permit.[293] The Polish conditions do not limit the free movement of capital.[294] The Estonian provisions hinder free capital movement more than the Latvian conditions because the former are

---

[285] s.59(1), ESMA.

[286] See section 3.1.3.

[287] See sections 4.1.3 and 5.1.2.

[288] s.66(1), ESMA; Article 115(1), PTFIA. The PTFIA refers to 'brokerage activity', which is defined in note 36 of chapter 4 and is similar to the 'list of investment services and activities and financial instruments' in Annex I to Directive 2004/39/EC, which are listed in note 82 of chapter 2. Article 115(1) of the PTFIA excludes non-member countries of the OECD or World Trade Organization (WTO), but this is insignificant as the latter has 151 members (World Trade Organization, 17 November 2007).

[289] See section 5.1.2.

[290] ss.64(1) and 65(1)-(2), ESMA; Article 104(1), PTFIA; ss.113(2)-(4), LFIML.

[291] See section 4.1.3.

[292] See sections 3.1.3 and 5.1.2.

[293] ss.69(1) and 70(2), ESMA; Article 117(1), PTFIA; ss.112(2) and 112(4), LFIML.

[294] See section 4.1.3.

vague and provide the FSA with discretion as to whether or not to permit the provision of investment services to Estonia.[295]

The 'breach of national law' provisions of all three countries limit the free movement of capital. However, the Estonian and Latvian rules restrict such movement more than the Polish approach because 1) the PPOA provides the FSC with graded remedies for legal breach of securities' issue legislation,[296] which are unavailable in the ESMA and the LFIML; and 2) the PTFIA empowers the FSC to protect the public interest by suspending a foreign investment company's activities for up to a month if it breaches national law,[297] before taking further measures,[298] whereas the Estonian and Latvian supervisory authorities may "apply measures provided for in legislation" to protect the public interest,[299] and "carry[] out activities to prevent infringements [of national law] protecting the public interest",[300] respectively. These powers are discretionary and broad.

Estonian Credit Institutions Act (ECIA), Polish Banking Law (PBL), and Latvian Credit Institution Law (LCIL) and Regulations on the Issue of Credit Institution and Credit Union Operating Licences (LRICIOL): credit institutions

None of the above laws provide for cross-border services to the home state by credit institutions registered in a third country. Consequently, there is no capital movement relating to these services. Estonian credit institutions may provide cross-border services to non-EEA states on various conditions,[301] whilst the PBL and the LCIL do not enable Polish and Latvian credit institutions to supply such services to third countries. Hence, the Estonian rules partly limit, and the Polish and Latvian provisions fully restrict, the movement of capital associated with outbound cross-border services to states outside the EEA.

[295] See sections 3.1.3 and 5.1.2.
[296] The remedies are publication of the contravention, suspension for ten days of a public offer or securities' admission to a regulated market, and prohibition of such offer or admission (Articles 16-17, PPOA).
[297] Article 169(7), PTFIA.
[298] These measures are a suspension "not exceeding six months", a prohibition and/or a fine (Article 169(3), PTFIA).
[299] s.236^{1}(6), ESMA.
[300] s.140(4), LFIML.
[301] These conditions are in s.20^{1111}(5) of the ECIA, and are stated in the subsection '*Section 20^{1111}: cross-border services in Contracting States and third countries*' in section 3.1.4.

All three Member States require a credit institution to be authorised by their financial supervision authority in order for it to establish a branch in a third country.[302] The information that must accompany the application differs in Estonia and Poland, but is more extensive for Poland.[303] A Latvian bank must submit many documents to register with the FCMC.[304] However, once so registered, it only needs to provide the latter with the branch's by-law,[305] and the branch director's curriculum vitae, including his/her identity number and date of birth, and a copy of his/her passport.[306] Section 20(4) of the ECIA contains grounds for the FSA to refuse authorisation.[307] The PBL has no corresponding provision. The FCMC "shall … take a decision" to grant or refuse a permit;[308] the LRICIOL does not state the criteria on which this decision is based. Whilst all three countries' rules limit the free movement of capital, the Polish position is the most restrictive, followed by Latvia then Estonia. This is due to the lack of guidance for applicant credit institutions and to the information needed for them to apply to open a branch abroad.

A credit institution registered in a third country requires a permit from the FSA/FSC/FCMC to found an Estonian/Polish/Latvian branch.[309] In all three Member States, the licence application must be accompanied by considerable documentation.[310] Section 21(5) of the ECIA and Paragraph

---

302 s.20(1), ECIA; Article 39(1), PBL; s.12(1), LCIL.

303 The Estonian application must include a branch "action plan" and data on the branch's director, and must describe the proposed activities and organisational structure (s.20(1), ECIA). The required Polish documentation includes a "justification" for opening the branch and the foreign country's laws on the issue of permits, the taxation of banks, foreign exchange and banking supervision (Articles 39(4) and 39(3)(3), PBL).

304 See Paragraph 2 LRICIOL, which is not discussed here.

305 Paragraph 5.3.2, LRICIOL.

306 Paragraph 5.3.3, LRICIOL.

307 See section 3.1.4.

308 Paragraph 6.4, LRICIOL.

309 s.21(2), ECIA; Article 40(1), PBL; Paragraph 1.2.1, LRICIOL.

310 The Estonian application must contain the information specified for Estonia in note 303, plus further documentation, such as certificates confirming the credit institution's existence and the branch director's authority (s.21(2), ECIA; ss.386(2)(1) and 386(2)(3), Estonian Commercial Code). The Polish application must include the planned banking operations and branch funds, details concerning the proposed director and deputy director of the branch, the branch's regulations, and a guarantee from the credit institution to satisfy third party claims against the branch (Articles 40(2)-(3), PBL). The required Latvian documentation includes a detailed account of the branch's proposed activities, in particular operational and market research plans, financial forecasts for the next 3 years, the internal control

4.1 of the LRICIOL give reasons for the FSA and FCMC respectively to deny permission; the Latvian grounds for such denial are more specific than those of Estonia.[311] In Poland, the credit institution must satisfy further conditions to receive a permit, such as the branch being "adequately prepared" to commence activity,[312] and have "appropriate conditions" for storing cash.[313]

Whilst all three countries' rules partially hinder the free movement of capital, Poland limits this movement more than Latvia and Estonia because it combines demanding application requirements with little guidance on the FSC's grounds for decision. Latvia requests more information than Estonia in order to establish a branch of a foreign bank in the home Member State, but provides greater legal certainty to applicants on what satisfies the financial authority to grant a licence for such foundation. It is therefore reasonable to conclude that Estonia and Latvia equally restrict the free movement of capital in this context.

Estonian, Polish and Latvian credit institutions can supply services to another Member State, directly or through a branch, without needing its authorisation.[314] The documentation requirements are similar in all three countries in order to implement Directive 2006/48/EC.[315] The ECIA and the PBL provide discretionary grounds on which the FSA and FSC can refuse to forward information to the competent authority of the host State concerning a credit institution's application to provide services there.[316] These grounds apply to both branch and cross-border services from an Estonian credit institution,[317] but only to Polish services through a branch;[318] the PBL makes no comment on FSC decisions relating to cross-border services.

In Latvia, the FCMC informs the host State's competent authority and the credit institution "of its decision" within 30 days of receiving the

and management information systems, the organisational structure, risk management and accounting policies, asset and information system protection guidelines, and procedures to identify suspicious financial transactions (Paragraphs 4.2-4.4, LRICIOL).

311 See sections 3.1.4 and 5.1.4.

312 Articles 40(6) and 36(3)(1), PBL.

313 Articles 40(6) and 36(3)(3), PBL.

314 ss.20^{1}(1) and 20^{1111}(7), ECIA; Articles 48a and 48b, PBL; ss.12^{2}(2) and 12^{3}(2), LCIL.

315 ss. 12^{2} and 12^{3} LCIL breach this Directive: see section 5.1.3.

316 See section 3.1.4. The Polish requirements in Article 48d(1) of the PBL are similar to the Estonian provisions.

317 ss.20^{3} and 20^{1111}(5), ECIA.

318 Articles 48c(1) and 48d(1), PBL.

latter's application to open a branch in, or provide cross-border services to, that State.[319] The LCIL does not indicate on what grounds this decision is taken. Whilst all three countries' rules limit the free movement of capital, the Latvian provisions restrict this movement more than those of Estonia and Poland because they provide no guidance to national credit institutions on whether the FCMC will accept an application to provide services to other Member States.

Credit institutions authorised to supply services in other Member States may provide such services to Estonia and Poland, directly or via a branch, and to Latvia through a branch, without requiring permission from these countries.[320] The LCIL does not consider cross-border services to Latvia by a credit institution registered in another Member State. This is a serious omission, most probably mistaken, which must be rectified to comply with the EC Treaty and with Article 28 of Directive 2006/48/EC.[321]

The Polish provisions follow Directive 2006/48/EC,[322] and are less restrictive to the free movement of capital than those of Estonia and Latvia.[323] The Estonian rules are of particular concern; this is due to the discretion conferred on the FSA to determine the requirements under which credit institutions from another Member State establish a branch in,[324] or provide cross-border services to,[325] Estonia.

The Estonian, Polish and Latvian rules, empowering the national supervision authority to take measures against a credit institution registered in the EEA that contravenes national law, are in breach of Article 56 of the EC Treaty.[326] It is stated in section 4.1.7 that the Estonian rules restrict the free movement of capital more than the Polish provisions, because the former are less proportionate and specific than the latter, and do not provide a right of appeal against the authority's decisions. The Latvian position is similar to that of Estonia. Section 108^{1}

---

319 See section 5.1.3.

320 ss.21^{1111}(1) and 21^{11111}(1), ECIA; Articles 48i and 48j, PBL; s.12^{1}(1), LCIL.

321 Article 28 of Directive 2006/48/EC is stated in section 2.4.2. Barriers to the free movement of services between nationals of different Member States are prohibited (Article 49, EC Treaty). The lack of a suitable national provision renders the position of credit institutions from other Member States wishing to provide cross-border services to Latvia unclear and, consequently, restricts free movement.

322 See section 4.1.4.

323 See sections 3.1.4 and 5.1.3.

324 s.21^{1111}(2), ECIA.

325 s.21^{11111}(3), ECIA.

326 See sections 3.1.4, 4.1.4 and 5.1.3.

of the LCIL provides no appeal against the FCMC's decision to rectify violations, and authorises the FCMC to "take measures",[327] "perform[] activities",[328] or "implement measures",[329] without any indication as to what the possible actions are.

Estonian Insurance Activities Act (EIAA), Polish Insurance Activity Act (PIAA), and Latvian Law on Insurance Companies and Supervision Thereof (LLICST): insurance services

None of these laws provide for cross-border insurance services between the home state and countries outside the EEA, in either direction. Consequently, there is no capital movement associated with these services.

An Estonian or Latvian insurance company may open a branch in a third country, provided that it has been authorised to do so by the national supervision authority.[330] This authority may refuse authorisation on several grounds that are neither specific nor objective, thus denying legal certainty to the applicant insurance firm.[331] The PIAA does not enable a Polish insurance company to establish such a branch. The Estonian and Latvian rules substantially restrict, and the Polish position prevents, the free movement of capital in connection with providing insurance services to a third country through a branch.

Insurance undertakings registered in a third country require a permit from the FSA, FSC and FCMC respectively to found a branch in Estonia, Poland or Latvia.[332] The Estonian, and Latvian, financial authority may refuse to issue the licence on several grounds, some of which bestow discretion on it and therefore do not provide the applicant insurance firm with legal certainty.[333] The precise, plentiful conditions that must be satisfied to establish a Polish branch make such establishment more difficult than opening a branch in Estonia and Latvia.[334] The Polish rules therefore restrict the free movement of capital more than the Estonian and Latvian provisions.[335]

Insurance companies registered in all three countries may supply insurance services to other EEA states, directly or via a branch, without

---

[327] s.108^{1}(3), LCIL.
[328] s.108^{1}(4), LCIL.
[329] s.108^{1}(6), LCIL.
[330] s.31(1), EIAA; Article 11^{1}(1), LLICST.
[331] See sections 3.1.5 and 5.1.5.
[332] s.43(1), EIAA; Articles 104(3), 128(1) and 2(2), PIAA; Article 10(1), LLICST.
[333] See sections 3.1.5 and 5.1.5.
[334] See section 4.1.5.
[335] This point was reasoned similarly in section 4.1.7.

needing further authorisation from the host state.[336] The Estonian, Polish and Latvian laws provide discretionary scope for the national supervision authority to refuse to communicate information to the host state's competent authority, both for establishing a branch in, and for providing cross-border services to, that country.[337] Latvian insurance firms are least able to mitigate the risk of refusal, because the FCMC may refuse to forward their information if "deficiencies detected" by it persist beyond a time it states.[338] All three countries' rules hinder the free movement of capital, but the Latvian provisions restrict it more than those of Estonia and Poland.

The 'breach of national law' provisions of all three Member States limit the free movement of capital.[339] There is little difference between them, since all transpose Article 40 of Directive 92/49/EEC, with some deviations.[340] The EIAA empowers the FSA to issue a precept to prevent violations of Estonian law.[341] This feature is not contained in the Polish and Latvian legislation, but is unlikely to affect the measures taken in response to the discovery of a contravention of national law. The FCMC will immediately take measures to prevent infringements of Latvian laws "protecting public interests".[342] Such actions may impede cross-border capital flows, but do not make the Latvian laws substantially more restrictive to the free movement of capital than the Estonian and Polish rules.

---

336 ss.35(1) and 38(1), EIAA; Articles 127(1) and 2(2), PIAA; Articles 11(1) and $11^3(1)$, LLICST.

337 See sections 4.1.5 and 5.1.5. The Estonian FSA need not forward information for founding a branch in, or providing cross-border services to, another EEA country if the insurance company's financial and/or organisational resources are "insufficient" to provide the insurance services described in the business plan (ss.36(2) and 39(2), EIAA), or if these services, branch foundation or plan implementation "may damage the interests of" the insured, the insurance company's "financial position" or "the reliability of its activities" (ss.36(4) and 39(3), EIAA).

338 Articles $11(3^1)(5)$ and $11^3(4^1)(8)$, LLICST.

339 See sections 3.1.5, 4.1.5 and 5.1.5.

340 Ibid.

341 ss.172(1)-(2) and 180(6), EIAA.

342 Article $99^1(4)$, LLICST.

EIAA, Polish Insurance Mediation Act (PIMA), and Latvian Activities of Insurance and Reinsurance Intermediaries Law (LAIRIL): insurance mediation

None of these laws provide for cross-border insurance mediation between the home state and third countries, in either direction.[343] Hence, there is no movement of capital connected with these services.

An Estonian insurance intermediary requires an authorisation from the FSA to open a branch in a country outside the EEA.[344] The FSA has wide powers to refuse to grant, and to revoke, a permit.[345] Neither the PIMA nor the LAIRIL provide for the establishment of a branch in a third country. Thus, the Estonian rules substantially limit the movement of capital relating to the provision of insurance mediation to non-EEA states, whilst the Polish and Latvian positions do not allow such movement.

A third country insurance intermediary must be licensed by the FSA to found a branch in Estonia.[346] The FSA has discretion to refuse to grant, and to revoke, an authorisation.[347] The PIMA does not enable an insurance intermediary registered outside the EU to open a Polish branch. A Latvian branch of a third country intermediary may provide insurance mediation in Latvia once registered in the Latvian list of insurance and reinsurance intermediaries,[348] but there are several grounds on which the FCMC may refuse to enter the branch on the list, and also to cancel its entry.[349] The Polish position does not permit the movement of capital in respect of inbound insurance mediation from third countries. The Estonian and Latvian provisions substantially restrict such movement.

Estonian, Polish and Latvian intermediaries may provide insurance mediation to other Member States,[350] directly or via a branch, without needing permission from the host State.[351] The Estonian and Polish provisions for providing such mediation do not restrict the free movement

---

[343] The Estonian legislation explicitly excludes cross-border mediation to and from countries outside the EEA (ss.151(5) and 160(5), EIAA).
[344] s.152(1), EIAA.
[345] See section 3.1.5.
[346] s.161(1), EIAA.
[347] See section 3.1.5.
[348] s.8(1)(3), LAIRIL.
[349] See section 5.1.6.
[350] 'Member State' means 'EEA country' for Estonia (s.18(1)(14), EIAA) and Latvia (see note 224), and 'EU Member State' for Poland (Article 17(1), PIMA).
[351] ss.156(1) and 158(1), EIAA; Articles 17(1)-(2) and 32(1)-(2), PIMA; ss.32(1) and 34(1), LAIRIL.

of capital.[352] The LAIRIL requires considerable documentation, especially to establish a branch, and gives broad terms on which the FCMC may refuse to forward this information to the host State's competent authority.[353] The Latvian provisions therefore restrict cross-border capital movement.

Intermediaries registered in another Member State to supply insurance mediation there may use this authorisation to provide these services to Estonia, Poland and Latvia, directly or through a branch.[354] All three countries specify minimal notification requirements.[355] These provisions do not restrict the free movement of capital.

The Estonian and Latvian 'breach of national law' rules limit the free movement of capital to a similar extent as they transpose Articles 40(3)-(5) of Directive 92/49/EEC.[356] The PIMA omits such rules. It only contains penal provisions for providing insurance mediation without authorisation,[357] and for inaccurately presenting as an insurance agent, insurance broker or reinsurance broker.[358] The Polish position does not restrict the free movement of capital.

Comment

The comparison yields the following observations.

1. The national legislation permits a greater degree of cross-border capital movement between Member States than between these States and third countries.[359] This is contrary to Article 56(1) of the EC Treaty which, subject to the derogations,[360] requires *all*

---

352 Both countries require the intermediary to provide minimal information requirements to its financial supervision authority (ss.156(1)-(2) and 158(1)-(2), EIAA; see section 4.1.6).

353 See section 5.1.6.

354 ss.165(1) and 166(1), EIAA; Articles 16(1) and 31(1), PIMA; ss.33 and 36, LAIRIL.

355 ss.165(1)-(2) and 166(2)-(3), EIAA; see section 4.1.6; ss.33 and 35, LAIRIL.

356 See sections 3.1.5 and 5.1.6. This legislation should follow Article 8 of Directive 2002/92/EC, which empowers Member States to take "appropriate" sanctions or measures in four different circumstances. These measures should be "properly justified" and imparted to the (re)insurance intermediary, and subject to a right of appeal in the national courts [Article 8(5)].

357 Article 47, PIMA.

358 Article 48, PIMA.

359 Much of the law discussed in chapters 3, 4, and 5 concerns the EEA: i.e. it applies to Iceland, Liechtenstein and Norway as well as to the Member States of the EU.

360 See section 2.1.3, especially its first paragraph.

restrictions on capital movement "between Member States and *between Member States and third countries*" to be *prohibited*.[361] The difference may be due to the following factors. a) Estonia's, Poland's and Latvia's main trading partners are Member States.[362] This induces their governments to reduce barriers to cross-border capital flows within the EU. b) Countries acceding to EU Membership must implement the financial regulation Directives as part of the acquis communautaire.[363] Although these Directives address the free movement of services and the freedom of establishment, they also facilitate cross-border capital movement between Member States.[364]

2. All three Member States have made legislative omissions. None have transposed Article 8 of Directive 2002/92/EC.[365] The PIMA does not consider insurance mediation between Poland and third countries. The LCIL ignores cross-border services to Latvia from another Member State's credit institution.[366] The Polish, Latvian, and most of the Estonian, laws discussed in this section omit cross-border services to and from third countries.
3. Some Polish and Latvian provisions include detailed requirements. The Estonian rules are less specific and more ordered than those of the other two Member States, but tend to confer discretion on the FSA in deciding whether or not cross-border services (directly or through a branch) are to be permitted.[367]

[361] Emphasis mine.

[362] A greater proportion of the sales of validation study questionnaire respondents are to other EEA states than to third countries; see section 7.2.1.

[363] Section 1.3.1 considers implementation of the acquis communautaire.

[364] Some provisions in the Directives conflict with Article 56 of the EC Treaty. This problem is discussed in section 8.2.4.

[365] See note 356.

[366] See the subsection '*Estonian Credit Institutions Act (ECIA), Polish Banking Law (PBL), and Latvian Credit Institution Law (LCIL) and Regulations on the Issue of Credit Institution and Credit Union Operating Licences (LRICIOL): credit institutions*', above in this section.

[367] A similar point is made in section 4.1.7.

5.2 Other Financial Laws

5.2.1 Law on State Funded Pensions 2000 (LSFP)

Pension scheme funds may be invested in 1) securities or money market instruments issued and guaranteed by state or local governments of EEA countries, by state governments of OECD states with an investment grade long-term country credit rating, by local governments of OECD states, and by international financial organisations to which at least one EEA country belongs,[368] 2) capital securities, or commercial companies' debt securities, officially listed, or to be so listed within a year of initial subscription, on a stock exchange in an EEA country or OECD state, provided, in the latter instance, that the exchange belongs to the International Stock Exchange Federation,[369] 3) a credit institution licensed in an EEA country to provide financial services there,[370] 4) open-ended investment funds registered in an EEA state,[371] or 5) "derivative financial instruments" whose counterparty is a credit institution licensed in an EEA country, and which are officially listed on a stock exchange described in point 2) above.[372] Most of the investment percentage limitations are at the individual level; for instance, deposits in one credit institution, and deposits plus financial instruments in such an institution, may not exceed 10% and 15% of the investment plan assets respectively.[373]

Foreign investment is a 'capital movement' in Annex I. Section 12(1) of the LSFP permits investments in EEA and OECD states, but not in other countries. It therefore limits the free movement of capital between Latvia and third countries, and can only be justified "for serious political reasons and on grounds of urgency" or to protect Latvian security in connection with the manufacture of or trade in armaments.[374] Since these grounds are unlikely for pensions, section 12(1) of the LSFP contravenes Article 56 of the EC Treaty.

---

368 ss.12(1)(1) and 12(1)(2)(a), LSFP. 'Transferable securities' and 'money market instruments' are defined in note 17. The local government securities and money market instruments must satisfy the conditions in point 2) of the text (ss.12(1)(2)(b) and 12(1)(3), LSFP).

369 s.12(1)(3), LSFP.

370 s.12(1)(4), LSFP.

371 ss.12(1)(5), LSFP and 21(2), LIC.

372 s.12(1)(6), LSFP. 'Derivative financial instruments' are defined in note 29.

373 ss.12(2)(5) and 12(2)(10), LSFP.

374 Articles 60(2) and 296(1)(b), EC Treaty.

The investment percentage limitations in sections 12(2)-(3) of the LSFP are non- discriminatory. Therefore, they do not restrict the free movement of capital, unless the rule in *Commission v Spain* is extended to investments in third countries.[375]

5.3 Taxation

The Law on Personal Income Tax (LPIT) and the Law on Enterprise Income Tax (LEIT) contain provisions restricting the free movement of capital, although the LPIT's supplementary Regulation does not.[376] Residents are taxed on worldwide income,[377] and non-residents on Latvian income.[378]

5.3.1 Law on Personal Income Tax 1993

Section 9: non-taxable income

Dividends paid to residents from companies registered in a Member State are exempt from personal income tax, unless the undertaking does not pay enterprise income tax.[379] Dividends from foreign and domestic undertakings that do not pay enterprise income tax are charged to personal income tax.[380] Income from mortgage bonds, and from deposits in savings and loans associations and credit institutions registered in a Member State, is not subject to personal income tax.[381]

Dividends, deposits and mortgage bonds are 'capital movements' in Annex I. Sections 9(1)(2) and 9(1)(3) of the LPIT treat enterprises registered a Member State more favourably than those registered in third countries by exempting the recipients of dividends and deposit interest from the former, but not the latter, from paying personal income tax (on condition that EU dividend-paying companies pay enterprise income tax). The third country organisations are in an objectively comparable situation

---

[375] [2003] ECR I-4581. See the discussion of Article 8^{11111} of the LICST in section 5.1.5.

[376] Cabinet Regulation No.793: Procedures for the Application of the Norms of the Law On Personal Income Tax (2006).

[377] ss.2(1), LPIT and 3(1), LEIT.

[378] ss.2(2), LPIT and 3(4), LEIT.

[379] See section 5.3.2 for enterprise income tax.

[380] s.9(1)(2), LPIT.

[381] s.9(1)(3), LPIT.

to Community institutions.[382] Consequently, the above provisions restrict the free movement of capital and, as none of the overriding reasons in the general interest apply,[383] breach Article 56 of the EC Treaty.

Section 10: tax deductions

Payments into private pension funds and to insurance companies under life assurance contracts, which are registered in a Member State, are deducted from annual taxable income, provided that these sums do not exceed 10% of a person's taxable income.[384] Pension fund contributions and insurance premiums are 'capital movements' in Annex I. Sections 10(1)(5) and 10(1)(6) of the LPIT offer tax relief to residents investing in Community private pension funds and insurance companies respectively, but not to residents investing in such organisations in third countries, even though these enterprises are objectively comparable. The rules therefore limit the free movement of capital and, as there are no applicable reasons in the general interest,[385] contravene Article 56 of the EC Treaty.

Sections 12 and 13: tax reliefs

The annual non-taxable minimum amount only applies to Latvian residents, and to residents of another Member State that have acquired more than 75% of their total income in the taxation year in Latvia.[386] These persons are the sole possible recipients of tax relief for the maintenance of dependent relatives and for legally "disabled or politically repressed" individuals.[387]

Income to non-residents is a 'capital movement' in Annex I.[388] Although the national rules can legitimately limit tax reliefs to residents

---

[382] See section 2.3.1, especially *Lenz* [2004] ECR I-7063. The situation differs from that in *Blanckaert* [2005] ECR I-7685 in that there is discrimination against companies from third countries after considering their enterprise income tax status (see section 2.3.2).

[383] These are the need to safeguard the tax system's cohesion, the fight against tax avoidance and the effectiveness of fiscal supervision. See section 2.3.

[384] ss.10(1)(5) and 10(1)(6), LPIT.

[385] See note 383.

[386] s.12(2), LPIT.

[387] ss.13(1)(1), 13(1)(4) and 13(4), LPIT.

[388] This is a simplification of the true position. Income from employment is not expressly included in Annex I. It may fall under Title XIIIE 'Transfers of the moneys required for the provision of services' or Title XIIIF 'Miscellaneous', because the nomenclature is "not exhaustive" (*Trummer and Mayer* [1999] ECR I-1661). In section 2.1.1, it is stated that the Annex's definition of capital movements is "wide", and a number of items that are within the definition are listed. Income to non-residents should include at least one of these capital flows.

and to non-residents with the majority of their income in Latvia,[389] sections 12 and 13 of the LPIT discriminate between residents of a Member State and residents of third countries that have earned more than three-quarters of their annual income in Latvia. These groups are in objectively comparable situations, both being non-Latvians that acquire most of their income in Latvia. The above provisions restrict the free movement of capital because they treat such situations differently. They violate Article 56 of the EC Treaty because none of the overriding reasons in the general interest apply.[390]

5.3.2 Law on Enterprise Income Tax 1995

Enterprise income tax is charged on "economic activity",[391] which is paid work.[392] It is charged at 15% to 'residents', which are profit-making domestic enterprises,[393] and at various rates to 'non-residents'.[394]

Section 3(4): non-residents and exemptions

Dividend payments, payments for management and consultancy services and interest payments between "affiliated undertakings or persons" made by non-residents are taxed at 10%.[395] Payments for intellectual property are taxed at 5%,[396] except for copyright (15%).[397]

---

[389] Article 58(1)(a), EC Treaty; *D.* [2005] ECR I-5821, reported in section 2.3.2. Sections 12 and 13 of the LPIT were modified since Latvia acceded to the EU in May 2004, so the Declaration on Article 73D of the Treaty Establishing the European Community (1992) applies: see section 2.3. The judgment in *D.* does not consider the Declaration's effect, even though it is relevant.

[390] See note 383.

[391] s.2(1)(1), LEIT. Non-residents pay enterprise income tax on income "from economic activity or related activity" (s.3(4), LEIT). The LEIT does not define 'related activity'.

[392] s.1(19), LEIT.

[393] s.2, LEIT. There are a few exceptions, such as private pension funds (s.2(2)(5), LEIT).

[394] Non-residents are "foreign commercial companies, natural persons and other persons" (s.2(1)(2), LEIT). The LEIT does not define 'other persons'. Furthermore, natural persons do not pay enterprise income tax (s.2(2)(1), LEIT). 'Non-residents' in section 5.3.2 therefore means non-Latvian profit-making organisations.

[395] ss.3(4)(1), 3(4)(2) and 3(4)(3), LEIT. "Affiliated undertakings" are companies or co-operative societies that are parent and subsidiary, at least 20% share ownership associates, or both at least 50% owned by a legal person or by a natural person and up to nine of his/her relatives (s.1(3), LEIT). "A person affiliated with

Dividend and interest payments, and payments for intellectual property, are exempt from enterprise income tax when paid to companies in another Member State under certain circumstances.[398] For instance, dividends are exempt if the recipient EU-registered company owns 10% or more of the share capital and voting rights for at least two years,[399] although the recipient must present a bank guarantee of 10% of the proposed dividend to the State Revenue Service.[400]

Dividend and interest payments, and payments for services and for intellectual property, are 'capital movements' in Annex I. As section 3 of the LEIT treats non-residents at least as well as residents, it does not limit the free movement of capital by discriminating against the former.[401] However, the enterprise income tax exemptions do not apply to payments to companies registered in third countries, which are in an objectively comparable situation to recipient companies in Member States. Section 3(4) of the LEIT therefore restricts the free movement of capital to third countries and, as none of the overriding reasons in the general interest apply,[402] breaches Article 56 of the EC Treaty.

Section 11: dividends receivable

Residents' taxable income is reduced by the 'dividends receivable' figure in the profit and loss account.[403] It is increased by dividends receivable from non-residents,[404] except if the dividends are paid by 1) a non-resident that owns at least 25% of the recipient's shares and voting rights, and which is not located in a low-tax or no-tax country,[405] or 2) a company resident in a Member State, at least 10% of whose shares and voting rights are owned by the recipient.[406]

---

an undertaking" is a legal person, or a natural person and his/her relatives, who owns up to 50% of a company's or co-operative society's shares, or who has "decisive influence" over such an organisation (s.1(5), LEIT).

[396] s.3(4)(4)(b), LEIT.

[397] s.3(4)(4)(a), LEIT.

[398] ss.3(4)(1), 3(4)(2) and 3(4)(4), LEIT.

[399] s.3(4)(1), LEIT.

[400] s.3(4¹), LEIT.

[401] See section 2.3.1, especially *Kerckhaert and Morres* [2006] ECR I-10967.

[402] See note 383.

[403] s.11(1), LEIT.

[404] s.11(2), LEIT.

[405] s.11(3), LEIT.

[406] s.11(4), LEIT. This exception also applies to dividend recipients that are non-resident permanent representative offices (s.11(5), LEIT).

Cross-border dividends payments are 'capital movements' in Annex I. Section 11 of the LEIT follows *Verkooijen*,[407] *Manninen*,[408] and *Meilicke and Others* in prescribing a tax credit for dividends received from resident companies but not for those received from non-resident enterprises.[409] But it differs from these cases in allowing the tax credit for dividends received from two categories of non-residents. The discrimination is therefore against non-resident companies that fall outside these categories. These are 1) all companies resident in low-tax territories, 2) enterprises registered in third countries that own less than 25% of the dividend recipient's shares and/or voting rights, 3) EU-registered companies that own less that 25% of the recipient's shares and/or voting rights and that are less than 10% owned by the recipient. Since these companies are in an objectively comparable situation with resident and non-resident dividend payers whose dividend receives a tax credit,[410] section 11 of the LEIT restricts the free movement of capital. Since none of the overriding reasons in the general interest apply,[411] this provision violates Article 56 of the EC Treaty.

5.3.3 Comparison with Estonia and Poland

In all three Member States, residents are taxed on their worldwide income, whilst non-residents only pay tax on income arising from Estonia/Poland/Latvia.[412]

Estonian Income Tax Act (EITA), Polish Natural Persons' Income Tax Act (PNPITA) and Latvian Law on Personal Income Tax (LLPIT)

Estonian rules relating to the transfer of real property and the receipt of some benefits such as gifts, donations and lottery prizes, discriminate against non-resident taxpayers.[413] Latvian residents, and residents of other Member States that have received more than 75% of their annual income in Latvia, are entitled to the annual tax and maintenance allowances, but

---

407 [2000] ECR I-4071.
408 [2004] ECR I-7477.
409 [2007] ECR I-1835. See section 2.3.1.
410 See section 2.3.1, especially *Lenz* [2004] ECR I-7063 and *Manninen* [2004] ECR I-7477.
411 See note 383.
412 ss.6(1) and 6(3), EITA; Articles 3(1) and 3(2a), PNPITA, and Articles 3(1)-(2), PLPITA; ss.2(1)-(2), LLPIT, and ss.3(1) and 3(4), LLEIT.
413 See section 3.3.1.

residents of third countries are not so entitled.[414] The PNPITA contains no equivalent provisions. The Estonian laws restrict the free movement of capital to Member States and third countries, whilst the Latvian provisions limit capital movement to the latter. The Polish position does not hinder cross-border capital flows.

The foreign and domestic tax on income from abroad to residents sum to the Estonian/Polish income tax rate as a minimum; any excess foreign income tax is non-refundable.[415] This discriminates against residents receiving such income from countries withholding income tax at greater than the Estonian/Polish tax rate.[416] The LLPIT does not consider the coordination of foreign and domestic income tax on income to Latvian residents from abroad. However, section 9(1) of this Act discriminates against companies from third countries paying such income.[417] The Estonian and Polish provisions equally restrict the free movement of capital. The Latvian rules limit this movement to a similar extent, but the impediment is to capital flows from third countries, independent of their income tax rates.

EITA, Polish Legal Persons' Income Tax Act (PLPITA) and Latvian Law on Enterprise Income Tax (LLEIT)

Income tax withheld at source on dividends from non-resident companies is deductible from the national tax assessment in all three Member States,[418] but only for 75% subsidiaries and 25% associates that are third country dividend payers to Polish and Latvian residents respectively,[419] and for 10% associates that are EU-resident dividend providers to Polish and Latvian residents.[420] The Polish rules restrict the free movement of capital more than the Latvian provisions. The Estonian position does not limit cross-border capital movement.[421]

---

[414] See section 5.3.1.

[415] ss.45(2)-(3), EITA; Articles 30b(5a) and 30c(4), PNPITA.

[416] See sections 3.3.1 and 4.3.1. This comparative point is made in section 4.3.3.

[417] See section 5.3.1.

[418] The foreign income tax is only deductible from the Estonian tax assessment to the extent that it is mandatory (s.54(5), EITA).

[419] The 25% associates must not be in low-tax or no-tax countries (s.11(3), LLEIT).

[420] See sections 3.3.1, 4.3.2 and 5.3.2. The direction of ownership is from dividend receiver to dividend payer, except for the 25% associates (Articles 20(2)-(3), PLPITA; ss.11(3)-(4), LLEIT).

[421] This extends the approach in section 4.3.3.

5.4 Property

The transitional provisions permit Latvia to retain its legislation concerning the acquisition of arable land and forests until 1st May 2011.[422] This legislation enables only Latvian citizens and organisations to acquire land in these areas.[423]

5.4.1 Law on Privatization of Land in Rural Areas 1992 (LPLRA)

Non-Latvians may not acquire land in the Latvian border region,[424] natural preserves,[425] the protected zones of the Baltic Sea and the Gulf of Riga and of reservoirs and watercourses,[426] agricultural and forest areas other than in accordance with town planning,[427] and mineral deposit regions of national importance.[428]

5.4.2 Law on Land Reform in the Cities of the Republic of Latvia 1991 (LLRCRL)

Land may be acquired by EU citizens,[429] state and local governments and government enterprises,[430] Latvian companies (subject to ownership limitations),[431] religious organisations registered in Latvia in July 1940,[432]

---

[422] See section 2.5.3. These provisions are transposed in s.28 of the LPLRA and in s.34 of the LLRCRL, without breach of Appendix VIII of the Act of Accession to the European Communities 2003.

[423] Agricultural land in Latvia may be acquired by Latvian citizens, state and municipal governments and government enterprises, companies registered in the Latvian Commercial Register (subject to ownership restrictions), religious organisations, farms and individual/family enterprises entered in the Commercial Register that are owned by Latvian citizens, and universities of state and local governments (s.28, LPLRA).

[424] s.29(1), LPLRA.

[425] s.29(2), LPLRA.

[426] ss.29(3)-(4), LPLRA.

[427] s.29(5), LPLRA.

[428] s.29(6), LPLRA. Section 29 of the LPLRA applies to persons not listed in note 423 (s.28, LPLRA).

[429] s.20(1)(1), LLRCRL.

[430] s.20(1)(2), LLRCRL.

[431] s.20(1)(3), LLRCRL.

[432] s.20(1)(4), LLRCRL.

and government institutions of higher education.[433] Other persons who wish to acquire land must apply to the city or county council in whose territory the land is situated, giving objectives for its use.[434] The council's head authorises the purchase within 20 days, provided that it does not contradict the legally valid "master plan of the city" and observes the following land ownership restrictions.[435] The 'other persons' referred to above may not acquire land in Latvian border zones,[436] the protected areas of the Baltic Sea, the Gulf of Riga, reservoirs and watercourses,[437] and agricultural and forest regions except in compliance with town planning,[438] other than if the land is to be inherited.[439]

5.4.3 The Free Port of Riga Law 2000 (FPRL)

Government land within the "territory of the Free Port" may not be transferred.[440] Land within the Free Port belonging to natural or legal persons may only be alienated for the government's benefit.[441]

5.4.4 The Free Port of Ventspils Law 1996 (FPVL)

State land in the territory of the Free Port may not be transferred.[442] Land owned by natural or legal persons within the Free Port may only be alienated in accordance with the procedures in the Law on Ports,[443] which include encumbrance with easements provided in The Civil Law by the port authority and alienation as prescribed by the Law on Enforced Alienation of Immovable Property for State and Public Needs.[444]

---

[433] s.20(1)(5), LLRCRL.
[434] ss.20(2) and 22(1), LLRCRL.
[435] s.22(2), LLRCRL.
[436] s.21(2)(1), LLRCRL.
[437] s.21(2)(2), LLRCRL.
[438] s.21(2)(3), LLRCRL.
[439] s.21(3), LLRCRL.
[440] s.4(1), FPRL. 'Territory of the Free Port' means Latvian land corresponding to the Free Port of Riga's borders, as decided by the Cabinet (s.1(1), FPRL).
[441] s.4(3), FPRL.
[442] s.4(1), FPVL.
[443] s.4(3), FPVL.
[444] s.4(7), Law on Ports. Alienation of property procedure is in the Civil Law, but there is no mention of easements.

5.4.5 Comment

Investments in real estate on national territory by non-residents are 'capital movements' in Title IIA of Annex I. Section 29 of the LPLRA and section 20 of the LLRCRL hinder the free movement of capital because they discriminate against non-Latvian and third country citizens respectively. These land acquisition restrictions are unjustified because they do not specify an objective in the public interest that is pursued in a non-discriminatory way.[445] They therefore contravene Article 56 of the EC Treaty.

Section 29 of the LPLRA and section 20 of the LLRCRL are inconsistent. The former prevents non-Latvians from acquiring land in the specified areas, whilst the latter prohibits persons from third countries from obtaining such land. Two of these areas in section 29 of the LPLRA–natural preserves and mineral deposit regions–are absent from section 20 of the LLRCRL. Furthermore, neither section excludes agricultural and forest land acquisitions in accordance with town planning, which contradicts section 28 of the LPLRA.[446] Section 29 of the LPLRA is in breach of Articles 39, 43 and 49 of the EC Treaty, following the Court's judgment in *Commission v Hellenic Republic*.[447]

Neither section 4 of the FPRL nor section 4 of the FPVL discriminate between Latvian and foreign persons. However, these provisions limit the free movement of capital because they discourage investors from other Member States from acquiring property in the Free Port territories.[448] The restrictions do not specify a public interest objective and are disproportionate.[449] They are therefore unjustified, and breach Article 56 of the EC Treaty.[450]

---

[445] See section 2.1.4. The 'town planning' and 'master plan of the city' phrases are not specific enough to amount to an objective in the public interest, such as "maintaining … a permanent population and an economic activity independent of the tourist sector in certain regions" (*Konle v Austria* [1999] ECR I-3099).

[446] See note 423.

[447] [1989] ECR 1461. This case, discussed in the subsection '*Real property laws*' in section 8.2.3, concerns a Presidential Decree that favours Greek nationals in the acquisition of immovable property in the border regions of Greece.

[448] See section 2.1.2, especially *Commission v Spain* [2003] ECR I-4581.

[449] See section 2.1.4.

[450] Although there is a transitional measure concerning arable land and forests (see section 2.5.3), this does not apply to the Free Port territories.

5.4.6 Comparison with Estonia and Poland

Estonia's property legislation does not restrict the free movement of capital.[451] Persons from third countries must obtain an authorisation to acquire land in Poland and Latvia.[452] The conditions required for permission to be granted are more extensive in Poland than in Latvia.[453] Consequently, the Polish provisions limit the free movement of capital from third countries more than those of Latvia. Since the authorisation requirements do not apply to EEA/EU citizens wishing to acquire Polish/Latvian property,[454] these countries do not restrict the free movement of capital from other Member States.[455]

5.4.7 Conclusions

The Latvian law concerning cross-border capital flows is extensive. Its comprehensive coverage is a remarkable achievement for a Member State that had just four years to implement the acquis communautaire.[456] However, the clarity needs to be improved. There are omissions, such as rules on cross-border payments and on the treatment of double taxation in Latvia and other countries inside and outside the Community.

One recurring area of concern is the discrimination against the residents of states outside the EEA. The free movement of capital and payments to and from third countries is an equally important part of Article 56 of the EC Treaty to such free movement between Member States. Countries that have recently acceded to the EU may not have had the time or resources to consider the fundamental freedoms as they affect relations with countries outside the Community. This should be rectified to prevent the risk of the EU becoming a closed-barrier trade bloc.

In chapter 6, a legal index is constructed to measure the restrictions to cross-border capital flows identified and compared in chapters 3-5.

---

[451] See section 3.4.1.
[452] Articles 1(1) and 8(2), PAIPFPA; ss.20(2) and 22(1), LLRCRL.
[453] See sections 4.4.1 and 5.4.2.
[454] Article 8(2), PAIPFPA; s.20(1)(1), LLRCRL.
[455] The ambiguity in the Latvian position is discussed in section 5.4.5.
[456] See the introduction to this chapter.

CHAPTER SIX

THE LEGAL INDEX

Indices are used in regression analysis to measure mutually exclusive gradations of qualitative variables. An index also shows to what extent elements of a group display one or more attributes. The information it gives is succinct and useful. However, construction of an index may involve simplification and/or subjectivity.[1]

The legal index measures the degree to which Estonian, Polish and Latvian laws restrict the free movement of capital. The scale involves only four categories in order to preserve accuracy in the transition from qualitative to quantitative data. Section 6.1 calculates the index for the three Member States. Section 6.2 considers its limitations, and comments on its construction in the light of the European Bank for Reconstruction and Development's (EBRD's) indices.[2]

6.1 Calculating the Legal Index

As stated in section 1.4, the following scale is applied to each comparison:

0 = national law allows cross-border capital movement;
1 = national law imposes minor restrictions on cross-border capital movement;
2 = national law places major restrictions on cross-border capital movement;
3 = national law prevents cross-border capital movement.

For each country, the scores are added, and the total is divided by the number of national rules compared to obtain a value for its legal index. Comparisons in table 6.1 correspond to the written order in chapter 5.

---

[1] Ethnicity indices, for instance, show both these qualities. If the scale starts 1 = White British, 2 = White Irish, 3 = Other White, then I would classify myself as 1, although I also have some of 2 and a little of 3 in my background. Section 6.2.1 discusses index subjectivity.

[2] These are contained in the EBRD's Transition reports.

Table 6-1: Construction of the legal index for Estonia, Poland and Latvia

Comparison number	Section and subtitle	Paragraph number	Restricts inflows (I) or outflows (O)	Affects intra-EEA flows (EEA) or flows to/from third countries (TC)	Rank for Estonian rule	Rank for Polish rule	Rank for Latvian rule
1	5.1.8 Investment funds	2	I	EEA	1	0	2
2				TC	1	0	2
3		3	O	TC	2	1	1
4	5.1.8 Investment services	1	I	TC	3	3	3
5			O	TC	3	3	3
6		2	O	TC	2	3	3
7		3	I	TC	2	2	3
8		4	O	EEA	2	0	1
9		5	I	EEA	2	0	1
10		6	I	EEA	2	1	2
11	5.1.8 Credit institutions	1	I	TC	3	3	3
12			O	TC	2	3	3
13		2	O	TC	1	2	1
14		3-4	I	TC	1	2	1
15		5-6	O	EEA	1	1	2
16		7-8	I	EEA	2	1	2
17		9	I	EEA	2	1	2
18	5.1.8 Insurance services	1	I	TC	3	3	3
19			O	TC	3	3	3
20		2	O	TC	2	3	2

21		3	I	TC	1	2	1
22		4	O	EEA	1	1	2
23		5	I	EEA	1	1	1
24	5.1.8 Insurance mediation	1	I	TC	3	3	3
25			O	TC	3	3	3
26		2	O	TC	2	3	3
27		3	I	TC	2	3	2
28		4	O	EEA	0	0	2
29		5	I	EEA	0	0	0
30		6	I	EEA	1	0	1
31	5.3.3	1	O	EEA	1	0	0
32				TC	1	0	1
33		2	I	EEA	1	1	0
34				TC	1	1	2
35		3	I	EEA	0	1	1
36				TC	0	2	1
37	5.4.6	1	I	EEA	0	0	0
38				TC	0	2	1
Total (a)					**58**	**58**	**67**
Number of comparisons (b)					38	38	38
Legal index (a/b)					**1.53**	**1.53**	**1.76**

The legal index is greater for Latvia than for Estonia and Poland, which indicates that the Latvian laws restrict cross-border capital movement more than those of the latter countries. Table 6.2 investigates sources of difference between these Member States through classifications into 1) capital inflows and capital outflows, 2) capital flows within the

EEA and between EEA states and third countries, and 3) capital flows relating to each area of national law.

Table 6-2: Calculation of subsidiary legal indices

Classification basis	Common characteristic	Total Estonian restrictions (c)	Total Polish restrictions (d)	Total Latvian restrictions (e)	No. of comparisons (f)	Legal index		
						Estonia (c/f)	Poland (d/f)	Latvia (e/f)
Direction of capital flows	Restricts inflows (I)	32	32	37	23	1.39	1.39	1.61
	Restricts outflows (O)	26	26	30	15	1.73	1.73	2.00
Location of capital flows	Intra-EEA (EEA)	17	8	19	16	1.06	0.50	1.19
	To/from third countries (TC)	41	50	48	22	1.86	2.27	2.18
National law topic	Investment funds	4	1	5	3	1.33	0.33	1.67
	Investment services	16	12	16	7	2.29	1.71	2.29
	Credit institutions	12	13	14	7	1.71	1.86	2.00
	Insurance services	11	13	12	6	1.83	2.17	2.00
	Insurance mediation	11	12	14	7	1.57	1.71	2.00
	Taxation	4	5	5	6	0.67	0.83	0.83
	Property	0	2	1	2	0.00	1.00	0.50

Direction of capital flows

Capital outflows are more restricted than capital inflows. Furthermore, Latvian laws limit inflows and outflows more than the Estonian and Polish rules do. The low scale values for insurance mediation, taxation and property are material to the smaller legal indices for capital inflows, because more of these values relate to inflows than to outflows. For the other categories, inflows are not substantially more restricted than outflows.[3]

Location of capital flows

Capital flows within the EEA are less restricted than capital movements between EEA states and third countries. The difference is largest for Poland, which has a legal index of 0.5 for intra-EEA flows and of 2.3 for movements to/from third countries. The higher scale values for non-EEA countries are more pronounced for investment services, credit institutions, insurance services and insurance mediation than for the other categories.[4] This is because 1) the financial regulation Directives stipulate removal of most barriers to cross-border capital movements within the EU, and 2) Estonia, Poland and Latvia require authorisation by the national financial services authority and further conditions for branch establishment there by a third country institution, and also for branch foundation by a domestic company in the foreign state; furthermore, cross-border services to/from third countries may be prohibited, and are often not considered by national law.[5]

National law topic

The legal rules relating to investment services, credit institutions, insurance services and insurance mediation limit cross-border capital flows more than those in the other categories. The main contributory factor to the high legal indices for the former is the restriction of capital flows between EEA states and third countries.[6]

The Latvian index is equal to or higher than the Estonian index for all seven categories, confirming that Latvia has more legal restrictions to cross-border capital flows than Estonia. The Polish index is the lowest for investment funds and the highest for insurance services and property, and is equal highest with Latvia for taxation.

---

[3] See table 6.1.

[4] Ibid.

[5] See section 5.1.8.

[6] In table 6.1, comparisons 4-7, 11-14, 18-21 and 24-27 yield 30, 12, 6 and 0 scale values of 3, 2, 1 and 0 respectively.

Legal indices of 2.29 for Estonian and Latvian investment services, and of 2.16 for Polish insurance services, are caused by scale values of 2 or 3, especially in relation to capital movements between these states and third countries. Values of 2 for intra-EEA flows contribute to the Estonian index of 2.29.[7]

6.2 Comment

6.2.1 Limitations of the legal index

The index enables a clear comparison to be made between the three countries' national legal restrictions to cross-border capital movement on several dimensions. It has the following drawbacks, however.

1. *Subjectivity*. The legal index's scale has only four points.[8] In most cases it is clear into which category the national provisions should be placed.[9] However, it is difficult to determine the boundary between 1 (minor restrictions) and 2 (major restrictions). Furthermore, the categories are broad, which allows variation within each one. Consider comparisons 8 and 9 in table 6.1. An analysis of the national legislation shows that the Estonian rules are the most restrictive to the free movement of capital. These rules are allocated to 2 (major restrictions), with the Latvian provisions being classified as 1 (minor restrictions). It requires further investigation and information to ascertain whether these Estonian rules limit cross-border capital movement more or less than other laws classified as 2 (major restrictions).

   Dr. Siems criticises the legal indices of Dr. Raphael La Porta and his colleagues for subjectivity.[10] However, Siems indicates that numerical methods reduce complexity, which raises the practical role of comparative law.[11] Subjectivity is an unavoidable problem in converting qualitative inputs to quantitative data, which must be balanced against the gain in clarity from information simplification.

---

[7] See table 6.1.

[8] The EBRD indices discussed below have five points, one a benchmark.

[9] As the number of points in the index scale is increased, the accuracy of assigning information to each class falls.

[10] See the subsection '*Siems' critique*' in Appendix F.

[11] Ibid.

2. *Accuracy.* As the number of comparisons increases, the index becomes more representative of the true position concerning legal restrictions to cross-border capital movements for each Member State. Thirty eight observations are enough to provide a satisfactory value.

   The calculation of subsidiary legal indices, as in table 6.2, enables a meaningful discussion of the data. However, the smaller the number of comparisons for each subsidiary index, the less accurate is the estimate. Whilst most of the subsidiary indices have sufficient data points to be a reasonable estimate of the 'true' value, the indices for investment funds and property are unreliable.[12] This does not substantially affect the analysis.

3. *Omitted factors.* National legal provisions in chapters 3, 4 or 5 that have no equivalent in the other countries' rules are omitted because there is no basis on which to compare them.[13] Whilst such treatment renders the free movement of capital comparison incomplete, most laws discussed in these chapters are included in the comparison. The essential information in the legal analysis is preserved in table 6.1.

These limitations reduce, but do not eliminate, the connection between the degree of cross-border capital movement that the national laws permit and the legal index. In chapter 7, the index and its subsidiary indices are considered to be representative of legal barriers to such capital flows.

6.2.2 Index calibration

The World Bank and the EBRD have constructed indices of reform for transition countries.[14] Campos and Horváth (2006) state grounds on which these indices fall short of an objective standard, and propose alternative

[12] The legal index of 0.00 for Estonian property law is reliable because there are no such rules that restrict the free movement of capital. See section 3.4.1.

[13] For example, Article 214 of the PIAA has no equivalent in Estonian and Latvian law. This Act empowers the FSC to restrict the number of permits issued to third country insurance companies wishing to provide insurance services in Poland. See section the subsection '*Article 214: limiting permits to third country insurance firms*' in section 4.1.5.

[14] 'Transition' is "the progression from a command economy to an open-market economy" (EBRD, *Transition report 1994*, 4). The EBRD classifies Estonia, Poland and Latvia as transition countries.

reform indices.[15] Their comments are discussed with reference to the legal index calculated in section 6.1.

The EBRD indices have a discrete scale from 1 to 4+, which represent broad categories. For instance, the 'price liberalisation' index has the following divisions.

1 Most prices controlled by the government.
2 Some price liberalisation with price controls for most product categories.
3 Significant price liberalisation with some state price regulation.
4 Comprehensive price liberalisation with a few administered prices.
4+ Price controls similar to advanced industrial countries; price controls only on housing, transport and natural monopolies.[16]

For all eight general transition indicators, the 4+ category is a benchmark against "advanced industrial economies".[17]

Campos and Horváth state five reasons why these indices are unsatisfactory.[18]

i.) One cannot identify the precise underlying variables.
ii.) There is no explanation of how these variables are converted to reform scores.
iii.) The variables include both policy inputs and outcomes.[19] An index constructed from inputs only is more accurate.
iv.) Sometimes the reform score is changed without a shift in the underlying data.
v.) The scale is not continuous, and the benchmark against advanced industrial economies is imprecise because these countries vary in the implementation of reforms.

These authors build three 'objective' reform indices, which avoid the above difficulties. For example, their 'internal liberalisation' index is constructed from three underlying variables,[20] one a reform outcome that

[15] *CEPR Discussion Papers*, No.5673.
[16] EBRD, *Transition report 2007*, 210.
[17] Ibid., 210-211.
[18] (2006), *CEPR Discussion Papers*, No.5673, 3-4 and 9-10.
[19] The EBRD's external liberalisation index includes both tariff levels (input) and trade openness (outcome), for instance (ibid., 3 and 10).
[20] These are the number of products in the 15-good EBRD basket whose prices are regulated, the share of regulated prices in the Consumer Price Index (CPI), and a dummy variable for wage regulation (ibid., 12).

is omitted from one of two calculations of the index,[21] which are converted to reform scores using a method used by Lora (1997).[22] This method sums for all underlying variables the difference in a variable's value from its maximum value as a percentage of the gap between this variable's maximum and minimum values.[23] The 'Lora transformation' does not require benchmarking because the reference point is in the sample; it is "the maximum reform index observed across our sample of countries in the respective time window".[24]

Campos and Horváth replicate four studies that measure the effect of reform on economic growth, replacing the EBRD/World Bank reform indices with their own.[25] The significant and insignificant variables are, with a few exceptions, the same in the original and in the replicated research. The correlation coefficients between each new reform index and the equivalent EBRD index are 0.52, 0.79 and 0.66 for internal liberalisation, external liberalisation and privatisation, respectively.[26] Good replication is consistent with the strong, positive correlation.

There is greater flexibility in calibrating the legal index calculated in section 6.1 than in assessing reform indices using the Campos and Horváth criteria, because the former is not a reform index. The criteria are nonetheless applicable in whole or in part to all indices.

1. *Identification of the precise underlying variables.* The only variable is the degree to which the Estonian, Polish and Latvian laws restrict the cross-border movement of capital.
2. *Conversion of the variable to index scores.* This is performed in two stages. Stage 1 is the comparison of the national rules in chapter 5.[27] Each comparison states the three countries' positions, and concludes with a sentence on which Member State's rules restrict the free movement of capital the most. Stage 2 is the translation of this concluding sentence to a number on the legal index scale.[28]

---

[21] The second variable is a reform outcome because it is a function of the share of unregulated prices in the CPI: the number of goods (prices) in the economy is not controlled by the government's internal liberalisation policies (ibid., 16).
[22] *Inter-American Development Bank Working Papers*, No.348, 15-16.
[23] Campos and Horváth (2006), *CEPR Discussion Papers*, No.5673, 14-15.
[24] Ibid., 15.
[25] Ibid., 33-37 and 51-52.
[26] Ibid., 19 and 21-22.
[27] See sections 5.1.8, 5.3.3 and 5.4.6 for financial regulation, tax and property respectively.
[28] See table 6.1.

3. *Exclusion of variables measuring outcomes from the index.* The legal index contains no such variables.
4. *Consistency of the index score with the underlying data over time.* The legal index is calculated at one moment only. Therefore, consistency of time-related changes with the underlying data does not arise.
5. *Index with a continuous scale and precise benchmarking.* The legal index is calculated to two decimal points, which gives a sufficient degree of accuracy without superfluity.[29] The benchmark is a national legal rule that does not restrict the free movement of capital. This is precise, and is attained by some domestic provisions.[30]

The legal index therefore satisfies four of the five Campos and Horváth criteria. The other criterion, time-related consistency of the index score with the data it is constructed from, does not apply.

Campos and Horváth do not explain why they provide these specific criticisms. A reasoned discussion as to what constitutes a good index would be helpful. Nonetheless, their criteria identify attributes that reasonable indices should display. For instance, if the underlying variables for an index include measures of outcomes, then the index will be biased if there is a correlation between any such outcome variable and the item that the index is intended to represent. The authors are therefore correct in stating that an index built only from inputs is more accurate than one containing both inputs and outcomes.

6.2.3 Conclusions

The legal index and its subsidiary indices calculated in section 6.1 contain the essential information concerning the domestic restrictions to the free movement of capital. Whilst the previous three chapters assess the degree to which the national rules on capital movement comply with the EU legislation on the free movement of capital, described in chapter 2, the comparisons in chapter 4 and, especially, in chapter 5 apply the information contained therein to the restriction of cross-border capital flows. Most limitations to such movement contravene the European legislation. Consequently, construction of the index in chapter 6 is

[29] See table 6.2.

[30] For instance, the Estonian property laws do not limit the free movement of capital (see section 3.4.1), which translates to a legal index value of 0.00 in table 6.2.

performed pursuant to the legal analysis in the preceding chapters whilst keeping good alignment in the progress of the research.

Chapter 7 investigates the effect of the legal index on the cross-border capital flows of Estonia, Poland and Latvia. It also reports on a validation study in which companies in the sectors most affected by the national legislation are asked to comment on the results from the research.

CHAPTER SEVEN

THE IMPACT OF LEGISLATION ON CAPITAL FLOWS

> "Capital flows to developing countries may be classified into four broad categories: private portfolio flows ...; commercial bank lending from developed to developing countries; FDI [foreign direct investment], whereby a firm largely owned by residents in a developed country acquires or expands a factory or subsidiary firm located in a developing country; and OF [official flows], representing loans from international agencies".[1]

These categories broadly correspond to the classes of foreign investment in the Financial Account stated in the IMF Balance of Payments Manual,[2] which are direct, portfolio and other investment,[3] financial derivatives and reserve assets. Since Estonia,[4] Poland,[5] and Latvia[6] follow the methodology therein to construct their balance of payments statistics, these figures are comparable for the three Member States. Consequently, they are the main source of data used to compare the legal index on restrictions to the free movement of capital with cross-border capital flows.

The economic data are from the World Bank, the Bank for International Settlements, Eurostat, and the Central Banks, National Statistical Offices and Financial Supervision Authorities of Estonia, Poland and Latvia. Since these data are publicly available on-line, the

[1] Sarno and Taylor (1999), *Journal of Development Economics*, 59, 341.

[2] (1993), 5th edition.

[3] 'Other investment' comprises loans, trade credits, deposits, currency and miscellaneous other items (ibid, 95).

[4] E-mail communication from the Bank of Estonia to me, 14 April 2008.

[5] E-mail communication from the National Bank of Poland to me, 18 April 2008.

[6] E-mail communication from the Bank of Latvia to me, 11 April 2008.

specific sources are not referenced.[7] Tables of published figures are included only to illustrate particular points.

Section 7.1.1 puts the legal index and subsidiary indices on a time basis according to the date of implementation of the relevant law. The index (section 7.1.2) and sub-indices (sections 7.1.3, 7.1.4 and 7.1.5) are compared with cross-border capital flows over time, and comments are made (section 7.1.6). Section 7.2 reports the results from the validation study and discusses them in the light of the research findings.

7.1 Comparing the Legal Index with Cross-Border Capital Flows

7.1.1 Constructing timelines for the legal index using implementation dates

The legal index scale is from 0 (national law allows cross-border capital movement) to 3 (national law prevents cross-border capital movement).[8] The following assumptions are made concerning implementation dates.

1. There was no cross-border capital movement before the implementation date of each provision.[9] The legal index prior to the implementation date therefore takes the value of 3.
2. If there is no national law provision on a comparison of legal restrictions to the cross-border movement of capital, then the situation will be deemed to take effect on the implementation date of the relevant Act or Regulation.
3. If a provision has more than one implementation date, then it will be deemed to take effect on the date following 31st March 1998 (Estonia and Poland) or 29th February 2000 (Latvia).[10]

---

[7] All data are presented in Euros. Conversion from national currencies to Euros is performed at the average exchange rate for the relevant trimester (quarterly data) or year (annual data)–source: Eurostat.

[8] Values 1 and 2 of the index scale represent minor and major legal restrictions to cross-border capital flows respectively. See section 6.1.

[9] This is not strictly true. In the banking sector, for instance, there were small capital movements into Poland, Estonia and Latvia before 1998 (Dąbrowska and Gruszczyński (2002), *22nd NBP Conference: Session 1*, 5-6; Havrylchyk and Jurzyk (2006), *BOFIT Discussion Papers*, No.5, 11-12). Nonetheless, the assumption is sufficiently true to undertake the analysis.

The legal index and subsidiary indices are recorded on a yearly basis from 1997-2007, to correspond with annual data on cross-border capital flows. Since quarterly data on such flows are extensively used, these indices are also presented on a trimestrial basis from the first quarter of 1998 to the fourth quarter of 2007.[11]

Figure 7.1 shows the legal index's path over time for Estonia, Poland and Latvia, using the quarterly data.[12] The legal restrictions to cross-border capital flows are lowered most rapidly in quarter I of 2004 (Poland) and quarter I of 2005 (Estonia), with Latvia showing an earlier and more gradual implementation of legislation conducive to cross-border capital movement.

Implementation of current legislation occurred most frequently shortly before and soon after May 2004, when all three countries joined the EU. This would indicate a late but substantial introduction of the Internal Market, if progress on the free movement of capital is similar to that for the other fundamental freedoms.[13] As the index remains over 1.5, there are still substantial national legal barriers to cross-border capital movement.

---

[10] These dates relate to the start of the accession talks for EU Membership (see chapter 5, note 2). After this, national laws are passed with a view to compliance with the acquis communautaire (see sections 1.1 and 1.3.1).

[11] The data tables are available on request.

[12] Figures A.1-A.11 in Appendix A show the quarterly movements of the subsidiary legal indices from 1998-2007.

[13] See section 1.2.3.

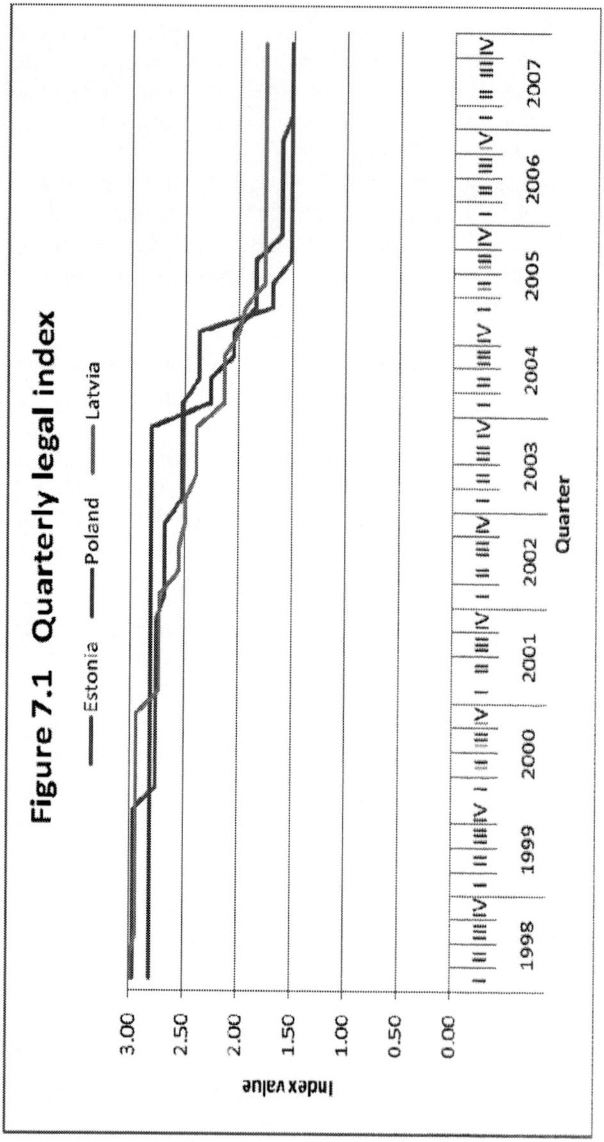

Figure 7.1 Quarterly legal index

7.1.2 The overall position: total cross-border capital flows

The total international investment position for each of Estonia, Poland and Latvia,[14] together with the sum of its capital inflows and outflows for direct, portfolio and other investment and financial derivatives,[15] is plotted against that country's annual legal index (see figures 7.2-7.4).[16] In figures 7.5-7.7,[17] the yearly change in each Member State's total cross-border capital flows and their components are compared with its legal index.[18]

In all three countries, total cross-border capital flows rise as the legal index falls. The greatest incremental increase in such movements occurs in 2005-2007, when the index is under 1.8.

For Estonia, gross capital movements increase substantially after 2003. This occurs during and after the main decrease in the legal index. The Polish total capital flows remain constant in 2002-2003, and then rise substantially as the index falls. In Latvia, other investment is the main component of increasing gross capital flows in 2005-2007, when the index is at its lowest level. Unlike in Poland and Estonia, direct and portfolio investment are not substantial contributors to rising cross-border capital movements.

---

[14] Financial assets plus financial liabilities. Reserve assets are controlled by the State and are therefore excluded.

[15] Financial derivatives data for Estonia's international investment position are unavailable for 1999.

[16] Figure 7.3 excludes 2007 because neither annual nor quarter IV data on Poland's international investment position are available for that year. In figure 7.4, data for 2007 are those provided for quarter IV of that year because no separate annual amounts are given. Data are provided in lats and converted to Euros (see note 7).

[17] Figure 7.5 lacks portfolio investment flows for 1999-2003 and financial derivatives flows, as only net data are available. Figure 7.6 lacks financial derivatives flows, as only net data are available. The annual gross capital flows for these categories cannot be calculated because the inflows and outflows data for the year are not provided. In figure 7.7, data for 2007 are the sum of quarters I-IV of that year because no separate annual amounts are given. Data are provided in lats and converted to Euros (see note 7).

[18] An increase/(decrease) in cross-border flows in either direction is a positive/(negative) value on the primary vertical axis. Annual data are used to provide the general picture of how each Member State's legal index relates to its total cross-border capital flows. Sections 7.1.3-7.1.5 use quarterly data on capital movements, where available.

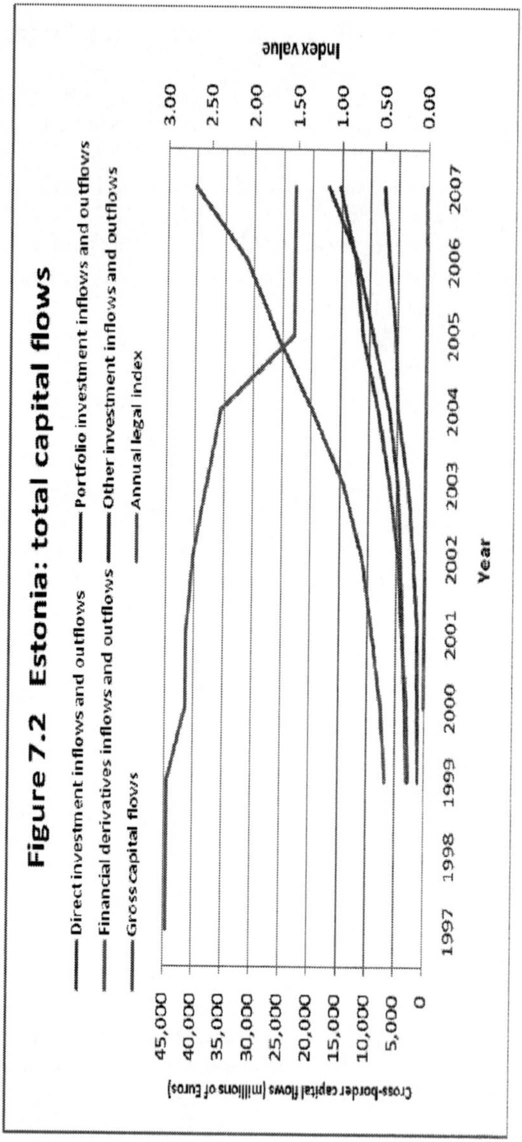

Figure 7.2 Estonia: total capital flows

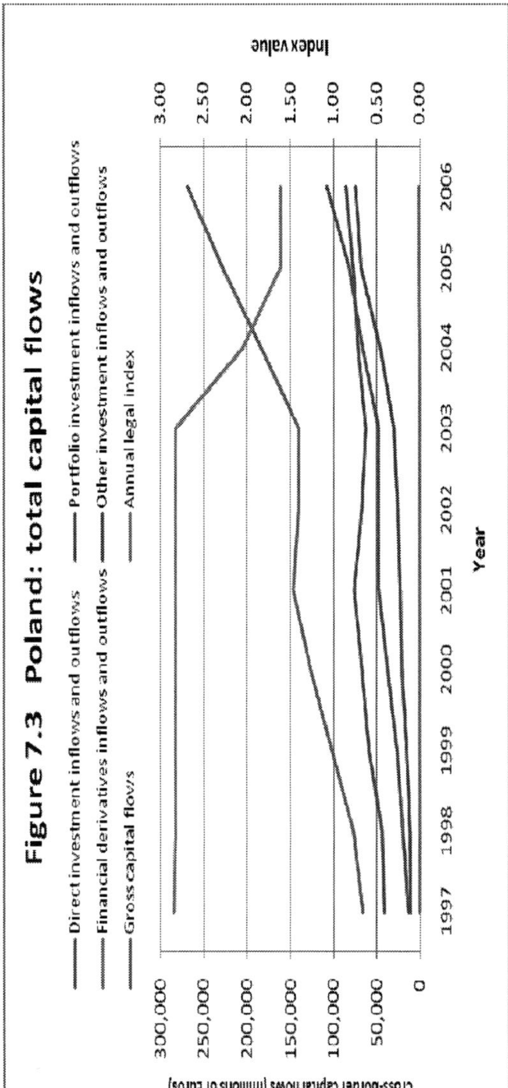

Figure 7.3 Poland: total capital flows

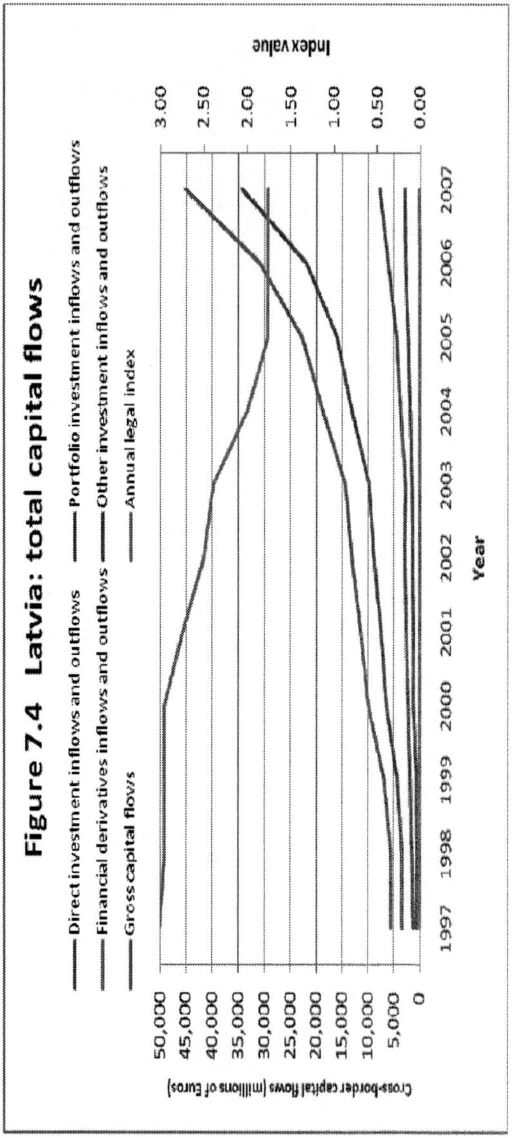
Figure 7.4 Latvia: total capital flows
Direct investment inflows and outflows
Portfolio investment inflows and outflows
Financial derivatives inflows and outflows
Other investment inflows and outflows
Gross capital flows
Annual legal index
Cross-border capital flows (millions of Euros)
50,000
45,000
40,000
35,000
30,000
25,000
20,000
15,000
10,000
5,000
0
Index value
3.00
2.50
2.00
1.50
1.00
0.50
0.00
1997
1998
1999
2000
2001
2002
2003
2004
2005
2006
2007
Year

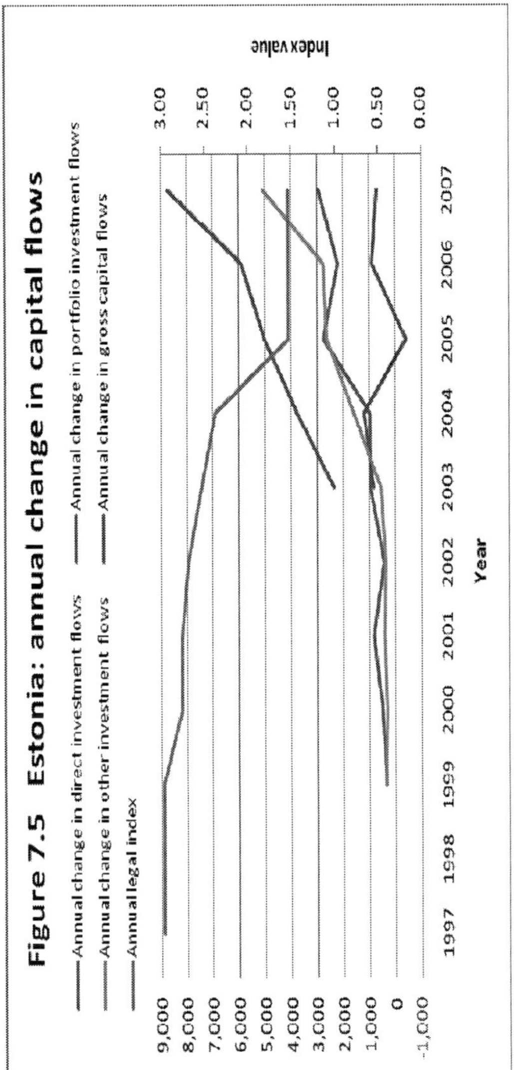

Figure 7.5 Estonia: annual change in capital flows

For all three Member States, the greatest cross-border capital movements occur when the legal index is at or near its lowest value. In Estonia and Poland, direct, portfolio and other investment all contribute substantially to gross capital flows. In Latvia, however, other investment is the main component of these flows.

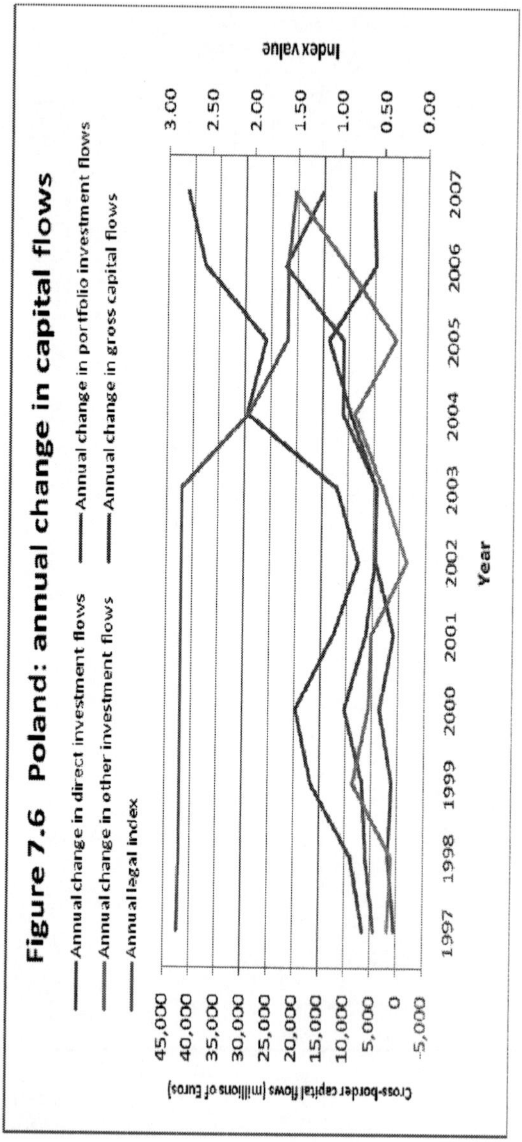

Figure 7.6 Poland: annual change in capital flows

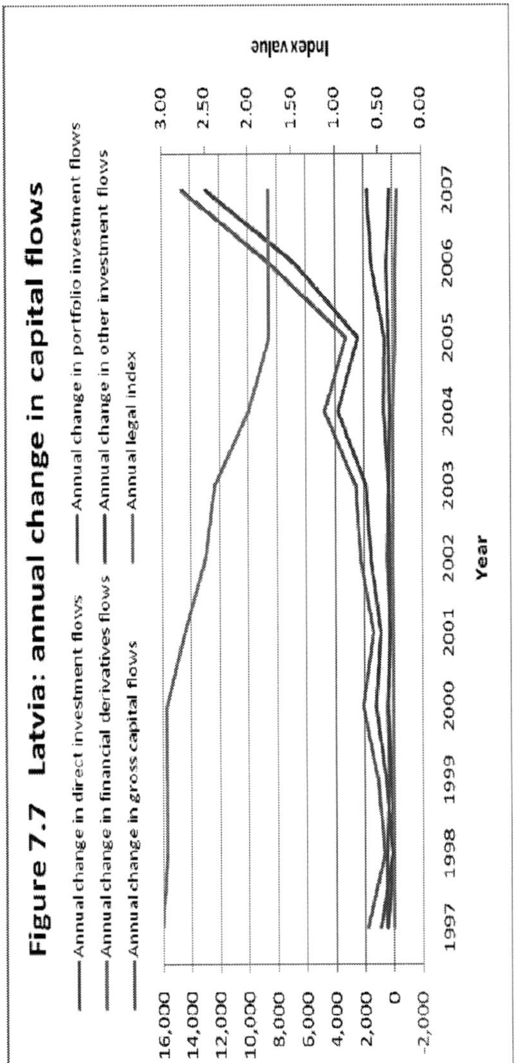

Figure 7.7 Latvia: annual change in capital flows

The small cross-border capital movements before 2004 coincide with high index values; it is possible that legal barriers may have reduced the volume of such flows. The large Polish flows in 1999-2000, when the index is 2.82, are inconsistent with this interpretation. However, the other data points for all three countries are compatible with it. Section 7.1.3 considers the effect of legal restrictions to capital inflows and outflows separately.

7.1.3 Subdivision 1: capital inflows and outflows

A capital inflow accompanies an increase in foreign liabilities and a decrease in cross-border assets. A capital outflow corresponds to a fall in the former and a rise in the latter. Balance of payments statistics present changes in financial assets and liabilities, rather than capital inflows and outflows. In the data presented below, capital inflows have mainly arisen from rises in liabilities, and outflows from increases in assets. Therefore, the legal sub-index for capital inflows is plotted with changes in liabilities (figures 7.8-7.10) and the subsidiary index for capital outflows with changes in assets (figures 7.11-7.13).[19]

For all three Member States, capital inflows increase with a fall in sub-index D:I. For Estonia and Poland, much of the rise occurs whilst the legal index is falling. For Latvia, inflows rise once the index is at its lowest level.

In figure 7.8 (Estonia), the outflow corresponding to a reduction in portfolio investment liabilities in quarter II of 2005 is surprising. It follows a reduction in sub-index D:O (figure 7.11). Hence, a lowering of legal barriers to capital outflows may have enabled this capital movement to occur.

[19] Figures 7.8 and 7.11 lack portfolio investment flows for 1999-2003 and financial derivative flows, and figures 7.9 and 7.12 omit the latter, as only net data are available. Data for figures 7.10 and 7.13 are provided in lats and converted to Euros (see note 7).

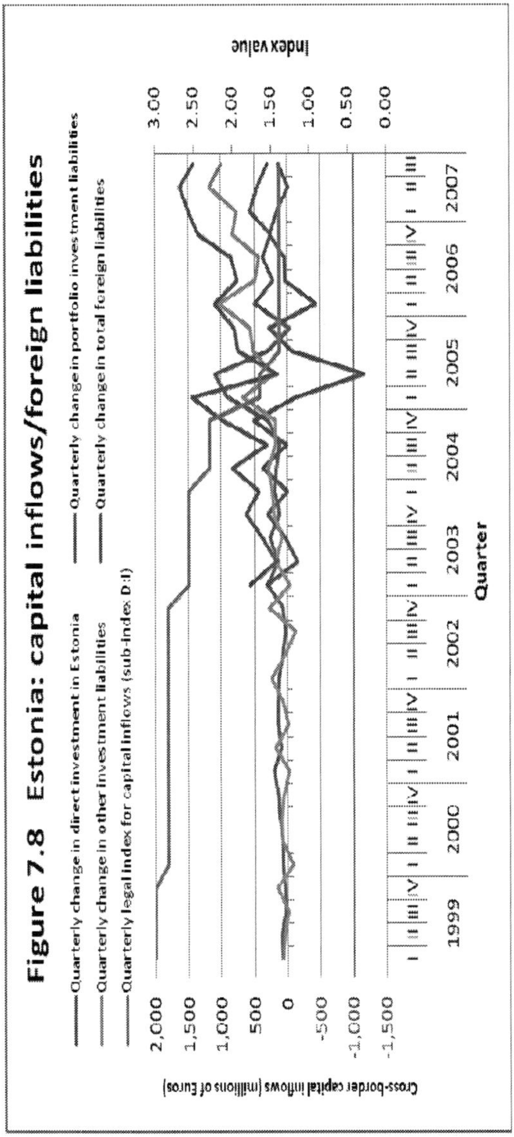
Figure 7.8 Estonia: capital inflows/foreign liabilities
Quarterly change in direct investment in Estonia
Quarterly change in other investment liabilities
Quarterly legal index for capital inflows (sub-index D:I)
Quarterly change in portfolio investment liabilities
Quarterly change in total foreign liabilities
Cross-border capital inflows (millions of Euros)
Index value
Quarter
1999
2000
2001
2002
2003
2004
2005
2006
2007

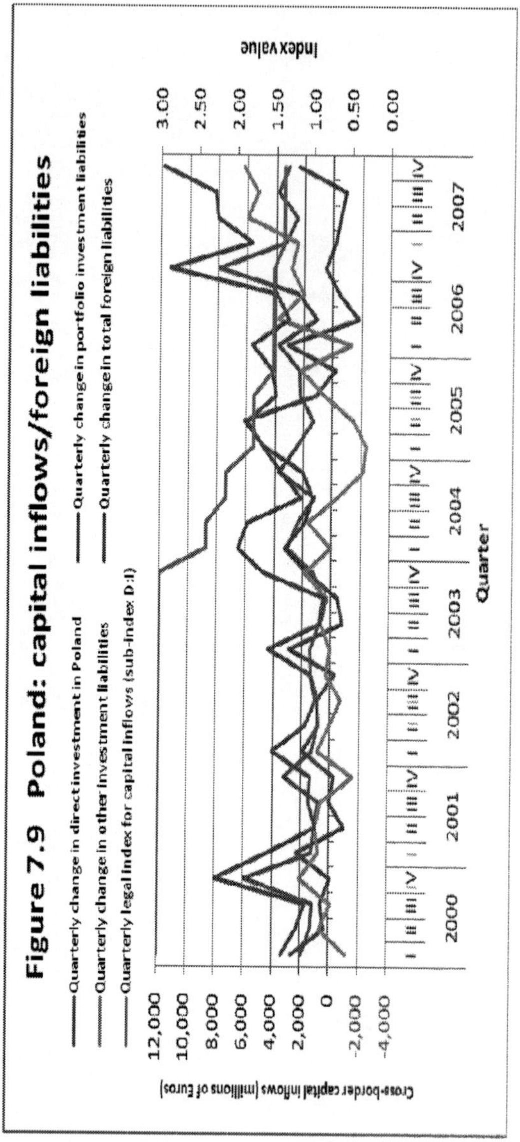
Figure 7.9 Poland: capital inflows/foreign liabilities
Quarterly change in direct investment in Poland
Quarterly change in portfolio investment liabilities
Quarterly change in other investment liabilities
Quarterly change in total foreign liabilities
Quarterly legal index for capital inflows (sub-index D:I)
Cross-border capital inflows (millions of Euros)
Index value
Quarter
12,000
10,000
8,000
6,000
4,000
2,000
0
-2,000
-4,000
3.00
2.50
2.00
1.50
1.00
0.50
0.00
2000
2001
2002
2003
2004
2005
2006
2007

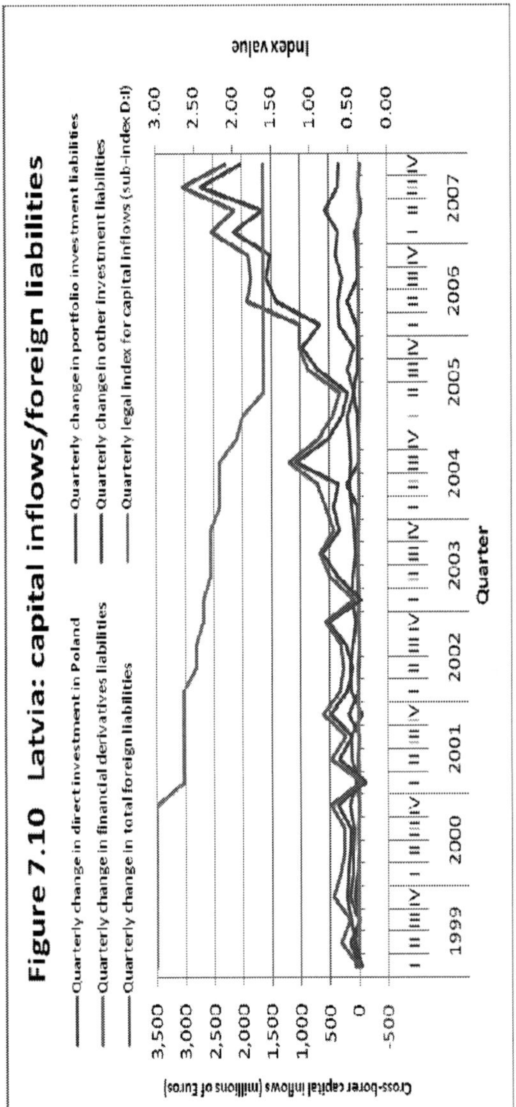

Figure 7.10 Latvia: capital inflows/foreign liabilities

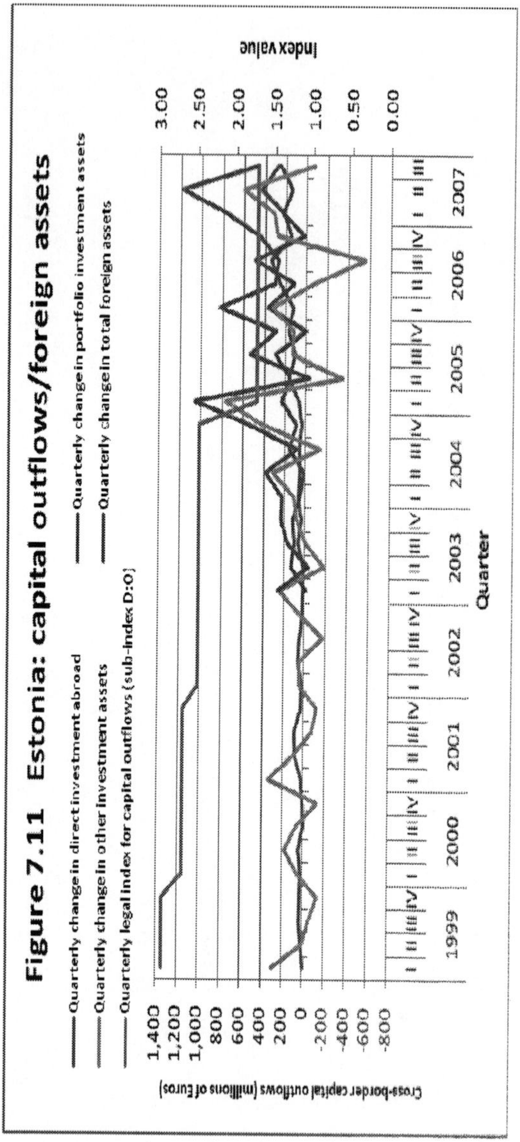

Figure 7.11 Estonia: capital outflows/foreign assets

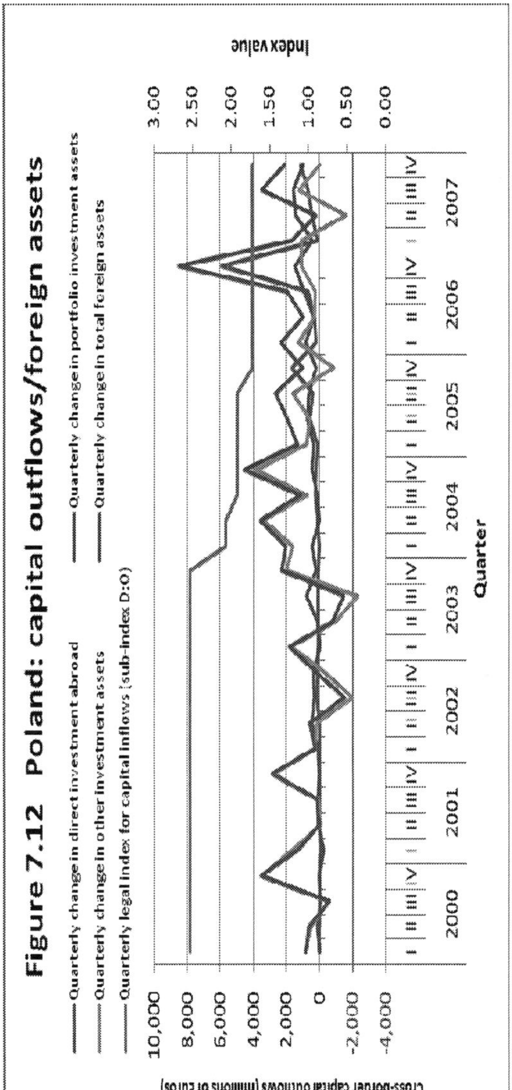

Figure 7.12 Poland: capital outflows/foreign assets

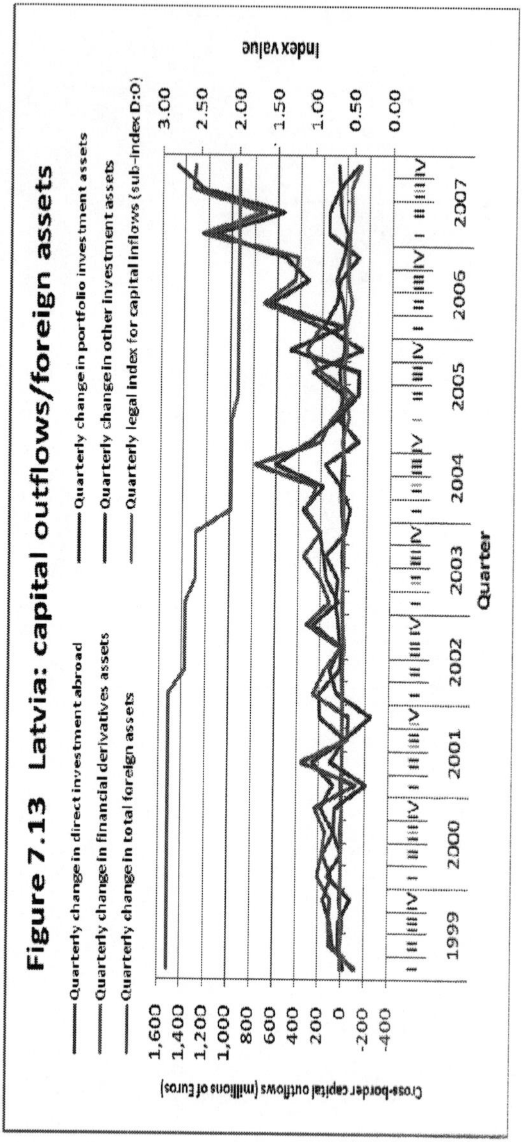

Figure 7.13 Latvia: capital outflows/foreign assets

In all cases, capital outflows increase during the fall in sub-index D:O and are highest when this index is at its ebb. Flows relating to other investment assets are particularly volatile. In general, a fall in subsidiary indices D:I and D:O respectively correlate with a rise in capital inflows and outflows respectively.

7.1.4 Subdivision 2: capital flows within the EEA or to/from third countries

Geographical records are available for FDI, portfolio investment and other investment for Estonia, for FDI and in total for Poland, and for FDI only for Latvia.[20] The graphs in this section show each country's periodic investment position and capital flow changes relative to EU and EEA Member States (figures 7.14-7.23), and to countries outside the EEA (figures 7.24-7.33).[21] Missing records tend to concern capital flows of small or negligible size,[22] and therefore do not substantially affect aggregate values.

Capital flows between EU/EEA Member States

Figures 7.14 and 7.15 show that FDI in Estonia from other EU/EEA countries increases most steeply during the main reduction in subsidiary index L:EEA. Both inbound and outbound FDI are at their maximum in 2007, when the sub-index is at its lowest level. There is an inverse relationship between the volume of FDI flows and the index.

In figures 7.16 and 7.17,[23] portfolio investment in other EU/EEA countries from Estonia increases from 2003 to 2007, although at only a slightly greater rate after the major fall in sub-index L:EEA than before this event. Inbound portfolio investment rises until quarter I of 2005, but falls sharply in quarter II of that year and again in quarter I of 2006, before recovering to the level of 2004 quarter IV. Both these decreases occur after the subsidiary legal index has substantially reduced.

Neither of these graphs reflects the expected negative correlation between the legal sub-index and capital flows. However, the large fall in inward portfolio investment in quarter II of 2005 may be an exceptional

[20] Quarterly data are presented for Estonia. With one exception, Polish and Latvian geographical items are annual only.

[21] Data showing Poland's international investment position on a geographical basis are unavailable.

[22] For instance, Bulgarian FDI inflows to Estonia are unavailable prior to 2004.

[23] 'EEA countries' in figures 7.16-7.19 excludes Liechtenstein.

item with a specific cause. For instance, investors may have switched from portfolio to direct investment, since FDI in Estonia from other EEA countries is at its highest level in 2005 quarter II (see graph 7.15).

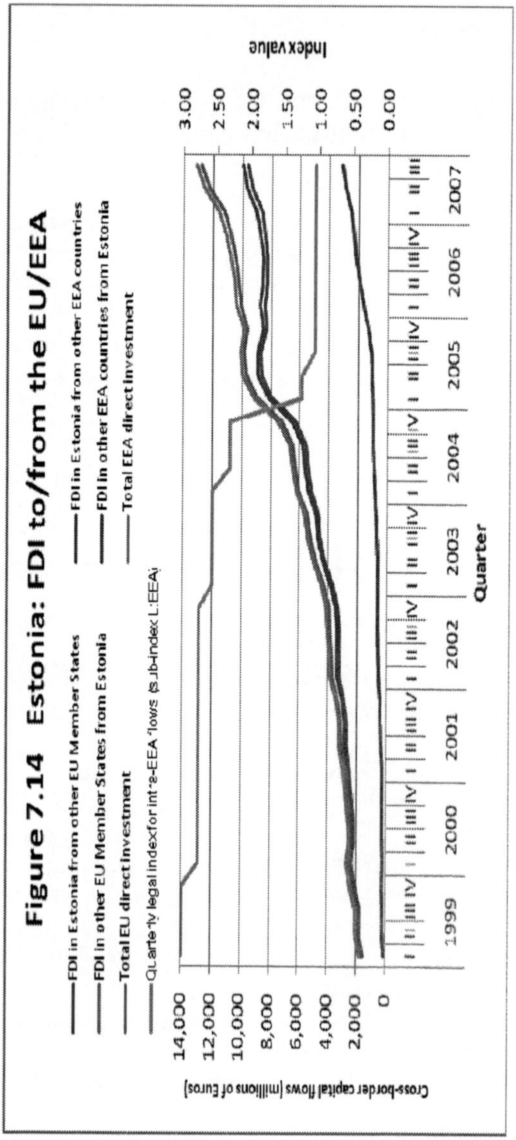

Figure 7.14 Estonia: FDI to/from the EU/EEA

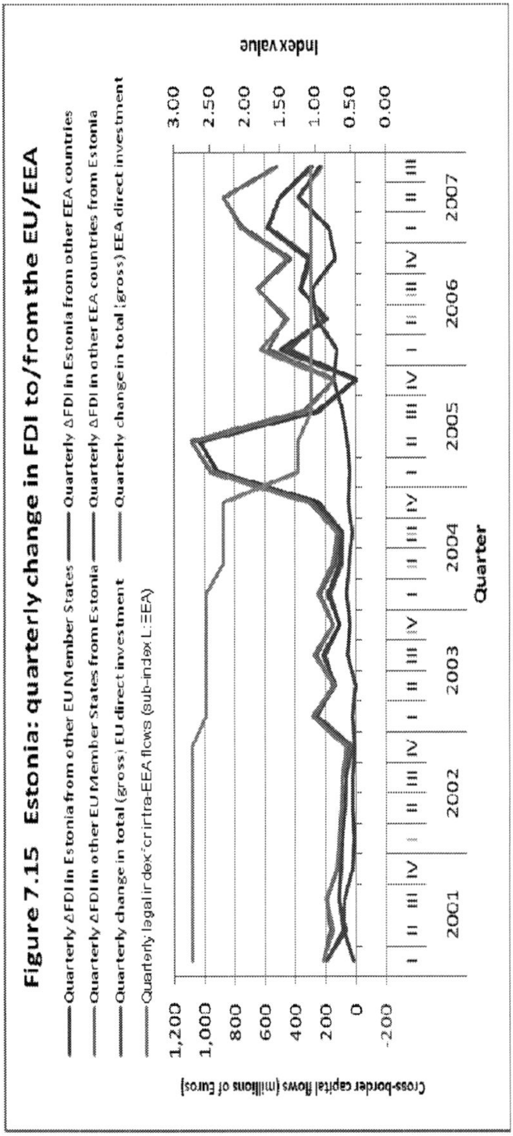

Figure 7.15 Estonia: quarterly change in FDI to/from the EU/EEA

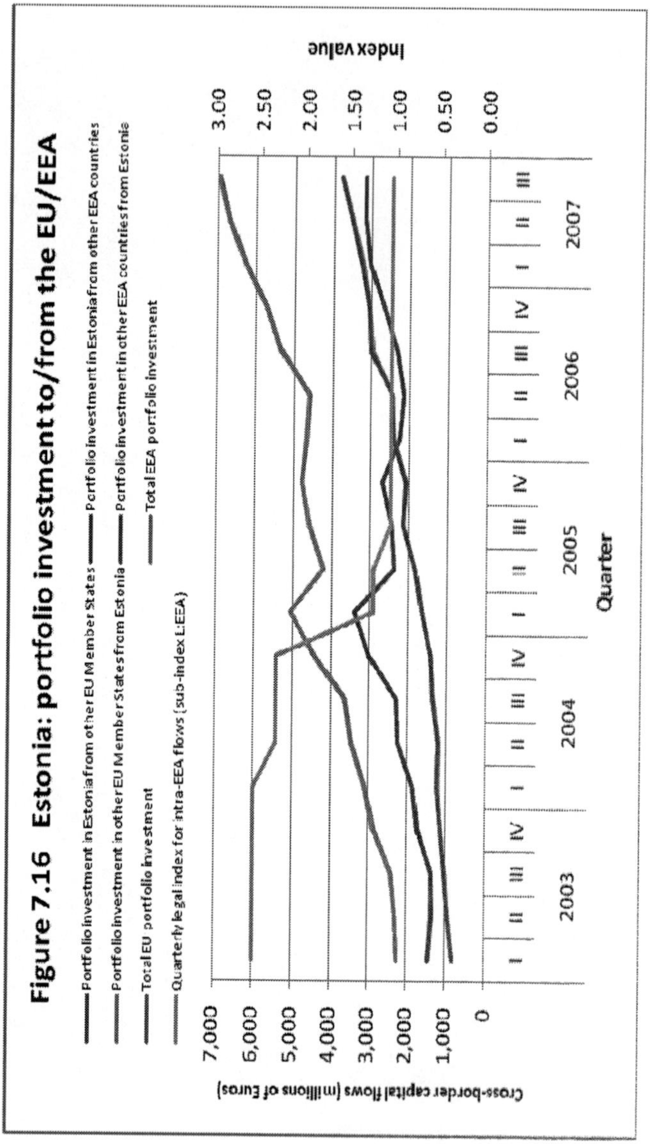

Figure 7.16 Estonia: portfolio investment to/from the EU/EEA

Figure 7.17 Estonia: quarterly change in portfolio investment to/from the EU/EEA

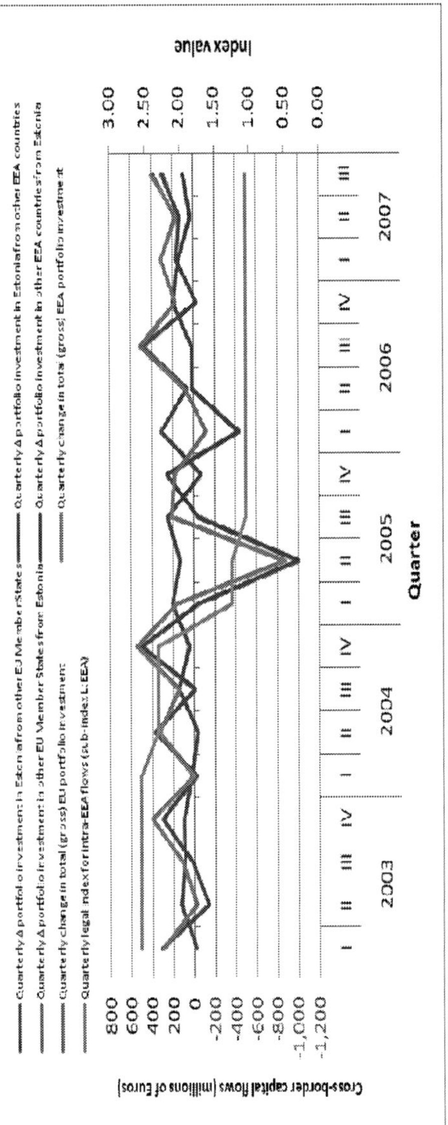

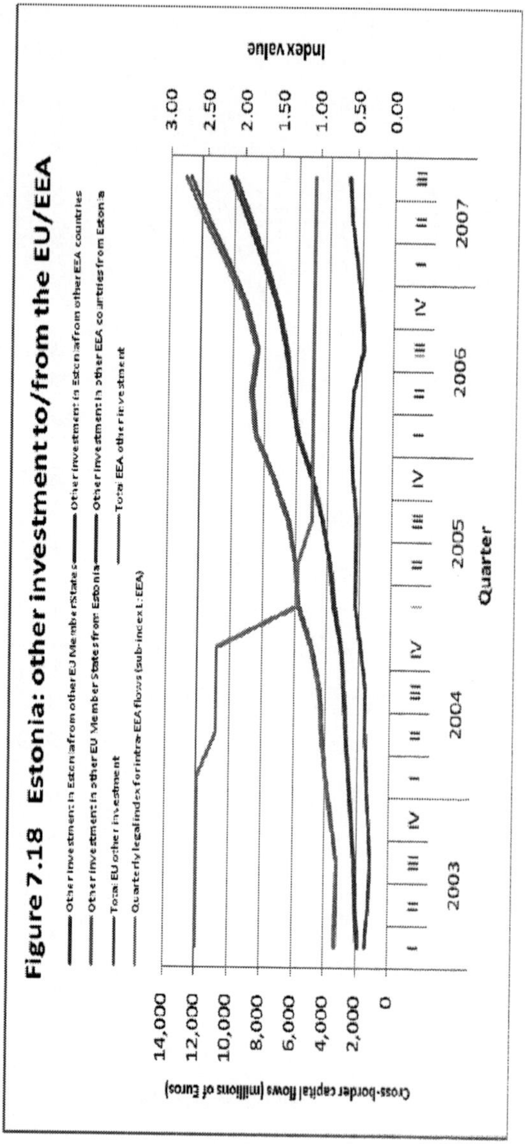

Figure 7.18 Estonia: other investment to/from the EU/EEA

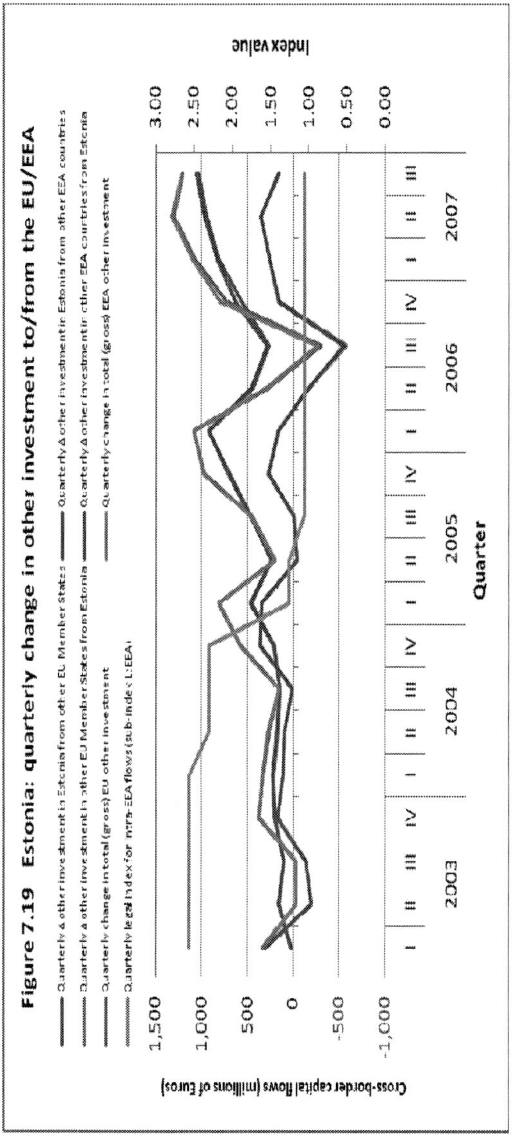

Figure 7.19 Estonia: quarterly change in other investment to/from the EU/EEA

Figures 7.18 and 7.19 show that other investment in Estonia from elsewhere in the EU/EEA rises after the major reduction in sub-index L:EEA.[24] Outbound other investment increases only slightly between 2003 and 2007, with reversals in 2003 and 2006. Subsidiary index L:EEA is inversely related to capital inflows but is independent of outflows.

For Estonia, therefore, subsidiary legal index L:EEA is inversely related to FDI and to inbound other investment, but is independent of portfolio investment and outbound other investment. The correlation between FDI inflows and L:EEA is particularly strong. However, the high FDI inflows after the fall in the index may be partly due to substitution of inbound FDI for incoming portfolio investment.

Figures 7.20 and 7.21 display the relationship of subsidiary index L:EEA to capital flows between Poland and other Member States. The former graph shows that capital flows stated in the Financial Account increase after the substantial fall in sub-index L:EEA, and rise further following the second large reduction in the index.[25] Poland's L:EEA index decreases to 0.5 in quarter I of 2007. Henceforth there is almost free movement of capital between Poland and other EEA states, which is reflected in high values for both capital inflows and outflows.

Figure 7.21 shows that inbound and outbound FDI rise in 2006, after sub-index L:EEA has fallen.[26] A low L:EEA level is associated with large and rising FDI flows. There is less FDI volatility for Poland than for Estonia.[27] However, the Polish annual data do not display capital movements as precisely as the Estonian quarterly information does–the former may be smoothing much of the variation.

[24] See note 23.

[25] The Financial Account comprises direct, portfolio and other investment, and financial derivatives. Reserve assets are excluded (see note 14).

[26] In figure 7.21, 'other EU Member States' excludes Bulgaria and Romania.

[27] See figure 7.15.

Figure 7.20 Poland: quarterly change in financial account flows (excluding reserve assets) to/from the EU

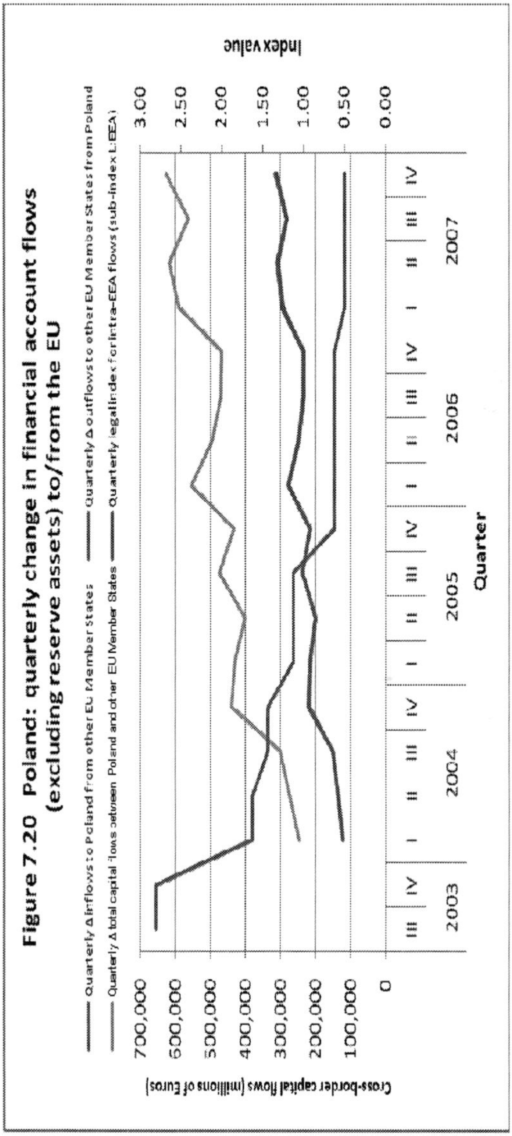

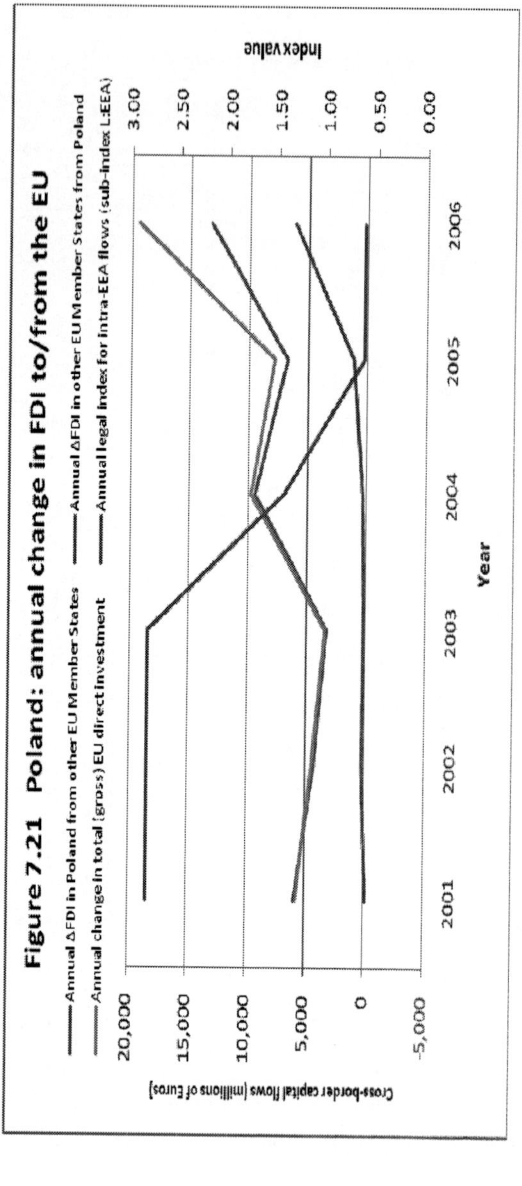

Figure 7.21 Poland: annual change in FDI to/from the EU

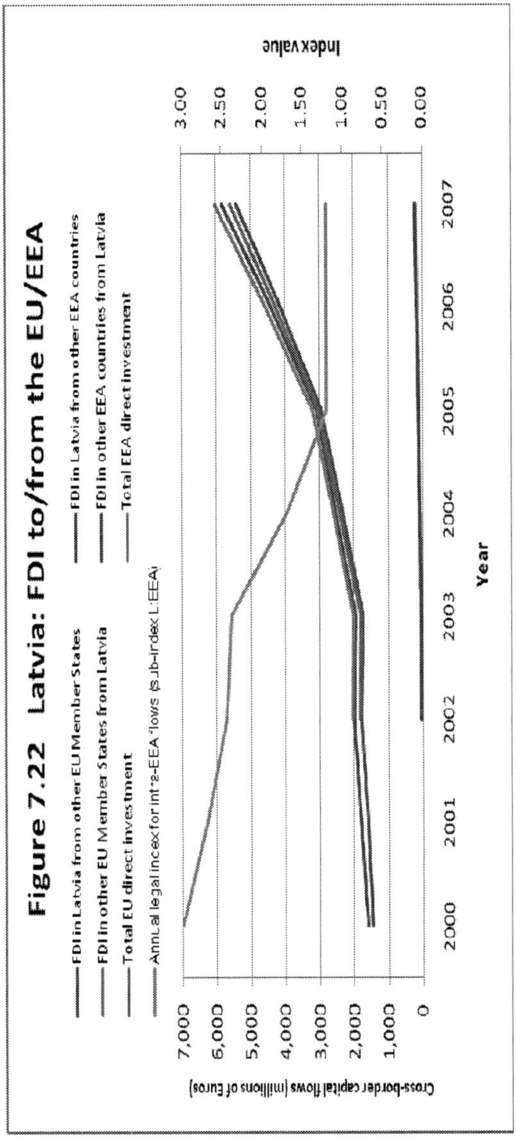

Figure 7.22 Latvia: FDI to/from the EU/EEA

Figures 7.22 and 7.23 show how sub-index L:EEA for Latvia relates to FDI between this country and other EU/EEA Member States.[28] As expected, there is a strong inverse correlation between this index and inbound direct investment. However, outward FDI only rises slighty during and after the reduction in L:EEA. One possible cause of this trend may be lack of availability of funds to invest abroad: until 2006, Latvia had the lowest GDP per capita of the three countries studied.[29]

For all three countries, capital inflows from other EEA states tend to rise during and after cross-border restrictions to the movement of capital are lowered. The greatest exception, considered above, is the large capital outflow in quarter II of 2005 for inward portfolio investment to Estonia.

Outward FDI flows to EEA states tend to increase as the legal restrictions to them are reduced, but less for Latvia than for Estonia or Poland. It is clear, when comparing figures 7.14 and 7.15 with graphs 7.22 and 7.23 respectively, that FDI outflows are higher for Estonia than for Latvia, even though the latter has a greater population than the former. A possible reason for the Latvian position is given above in this subsection.

Porfolio and other investment outflows from Estonia to other EEA countries tend to increase with time,[30] but are volatile.[31] These flows appear to be unaffected by the reduction of legal barriers to cross-border capital movement. It is uncertain whether or not these observations apply outside Estonia, due to the absence of comparable data for Poland and Latvia.

---

[28] 'EEA countries' in figures 7.22 and 7.23 includes Liechtenstein for capital inflows, but not for outflows. Data are provided in lats and converted to Euros (see note 7). Data for 2007 are those provided for quarter IV of that year for the direct investment position (figure 7.22), and are the sum of quarters I to IV of that year for the annual change in FDI (figure 7.23) because no separate annual figures are given.

[29] See figures 7.57, 7.62 and 7.67 for the GDP per capita of Estonia, Poland and Latvia respectively. Latvian GDP per capita overtakes Polish GDP per capita in early 2006, but remains below the Estonian level.

[30] See figures 7.16 and 7.18.

[31] See figures 7.17 and 7.19.

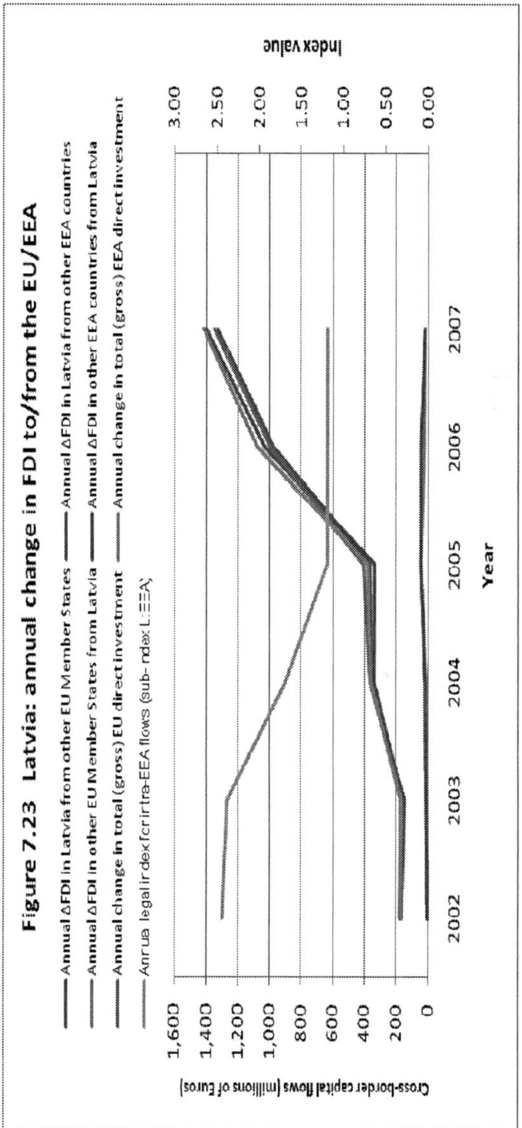

Figure 7.23 Latvia: annual change in FDI to/from the EU/EEA

It is clear from chapters 3-5 that, whilst most of the laws considered distinguish between third countries and EEA states,[32] a minority contrast the former with EU Member States.[33] This would be problematical to the analysis in section 7.1.4 if there were substantial differences between EU and EEA capital movements. It is clear from figures 7.14-7.19 and 7.22-7.23 that, for Estonia and Latvia at least,[34] the discrepancy between these flows is always small and often negligible.

One objection is that the omission of Liechtenstein from some of these graphs may materially reduce this discrepancy, given its prominence as a financial centre. An inspection of the Liechtenstein data used to construct the FDI graphs shows that such significant reduction is unlikely. 1) FDI in Liechtenstein from Estonia is negligible.[35] 2) FDI in Estonia and Latvia from Liechtenstein decreases over the period considered.[36] 3) Total FDI inflows to Estonia and Latvia from Liechtenstein are always smaller than those from Norway over this period and, by 2007, are lower than those from Iceland. For direct investment, therefore, Liechtenstein is numerically insignificant and constitutes a minority of the difference between EU and EEA capital flows.

Capital flows to/from countries outside the EEA (third countries)

Inspection of figures 7.14-7.23 in comparison with 7.24-7.33 shows that subsidiary index L:TC falls less than sub-index L:EEA, especially for Poland.[37] This difference reflects the observation from section 5.1.8 that national law allows greater cross-border capital movement within the EEA than between EEA states and third countries.[38]

A similar inspection of these graphs reveals that capital inflows to Estonia, Poland and Latvia from other EEA states are larger than those from third countries. Capital outflows from Estonia and Poland to such EEA states are more than those to third countries, but outbound FDI from Latvia to its EEA co-signatories is lower than that to third countries.[39]

---

[32] For instance, Estonian provisions consistently refer to 'Contracting States', which means Contracting Parties to the EEA Agreement (see section 3.1).

[33] See, for instance, the provisions of the PIMA (section 4.1.6).

[34] The Polish geographical data are not sufficiently detailed to construct EEA graphs.

[35] Data on Latvian FDI to Liechtenstein are unavailable.

[36] 1999-2007 for Estonia; 2000-2007 for Latvia.

[37] This index differential is noted in section 6.1.

[38] In this section, for Poland only, 'third countries' means those that are not EU Member States.

[39] As stated above, Latvian geographical data are only available for FDI.

There follows individual study of the graphs with a view to a possible link between high legal cross-border capital restrictions and small capital flows.

Figures 7.24 and 7.25 show that FDI outflows from Estonia to third countries are inversely related to subsidiary index L:TC. However, inbound FDI falls after L:TC has reached its minimum. The greatest increase in trimestrial capital movements is in quarter II of 2005, which immediately follows the largest fall in the sub-index.

Figures 7.26 and 7.27 reveal that outward portfolio investment is negatively correlated with sub-index L:TC. There is no association between L:TC and portfolio investment inflows. A comparison of figures 7.25 and 7.27 shows that the reduction in these inflows in early 2005 is not fully compensated for by greater inward FDI. Therefore, investment switching does not substantially explain these lower inflows.

An inspection of figures 7.17 and 7.27 shows that the inbound portfolio investment to Estonia falls in quarter II of 2005, regardless of source, but that the magnitude of the drop in such investment from third countries is much smaller than that from EEA states. Investors from non-EEA countries may have withdrawn their shares and loans when they observed similar behaviour from European investors. Alternatively, poor news about the Estonian economy announced in this quarter may have triggered the fund withdrawal. These events occur in the trimester following substantial reduction in legal barriers to capital flows, but it is unlikely that the latter were a causative factor.

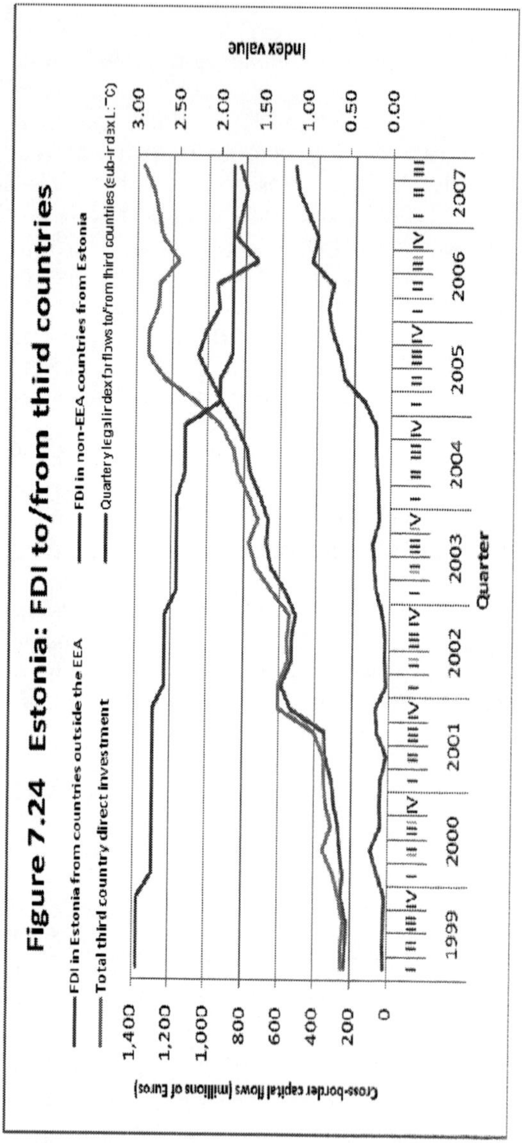
Figure 7.24 Estonia: FDI to/from third countries
FDI in Estonia from countries outside the EEA
FDI in non-EEA countries from Estonia
Total third country direct investment
Quarterly legal index for flows to/from third countries (sub-index L:TC)
Cross-border capital flows (millions of Euros)
1,400
1,200
1,000
800
600
400
200
0
Index value
3.00
2.50
2.00
1.50
1.00
0.50
0.00
1999
2000
2001
2002
2003
2004
2005
2006
2007
Quarter

Figure 7.25 Estonia: quarterly change in FDI to/from third countries

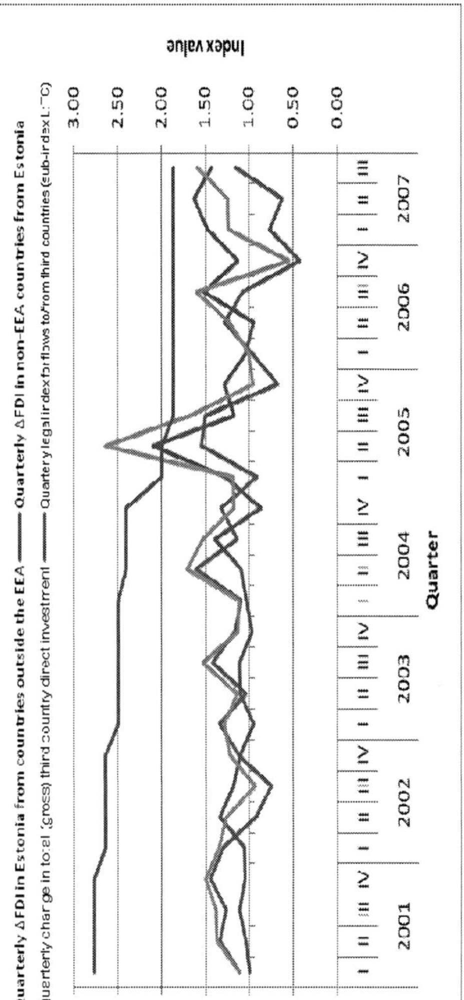

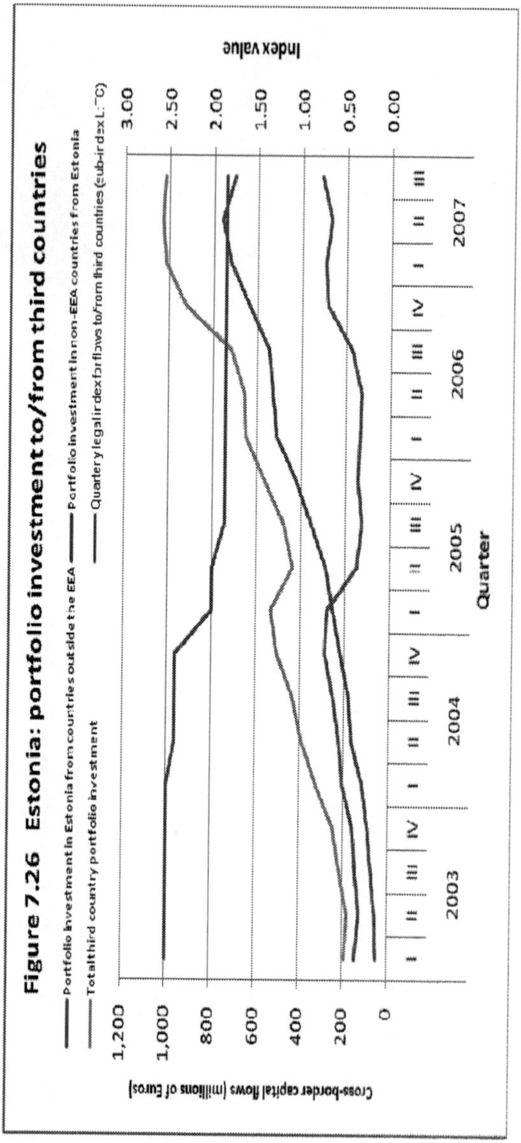

Figure 7.26 Estonia: portfolio investment to/from third countries

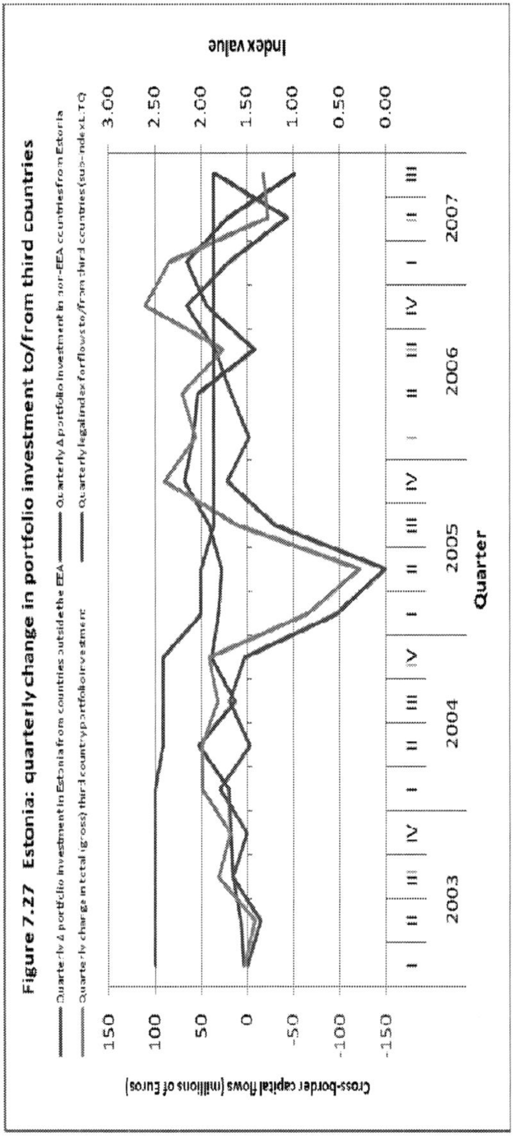

Figure 7.27 Estonia: quarterly change in portfolio investment to/from third countries

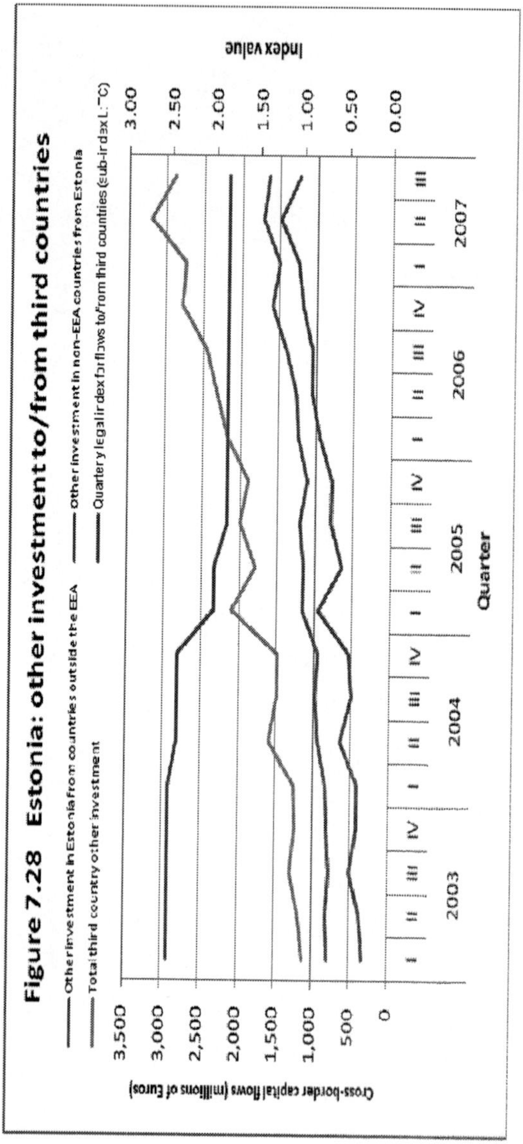

Figure 7.28 Estonia: other investment to/from third countries

Figure 7.28 shows that both inbound and outbound other investment rise over time as sub-index L:TC falls. However, as figure 7.29 illustrates, the flows are volatile. The inverse relationship between L:TC and other investment is tenuous.

Hence, for Estonia there is negative correlation between legal sub-index L:TC and outward investment flows. There is weak inverse association between L:TC and inward investment, other than inbound portfolio investment. This contrasts with the strong inverse relationship between subsidiary index L:EEA and inbound (non-portfolio) investment noted above. The tenuous relationship between L:TC and inflows may be because this index only falls a small amount, so legal restrictions to cross-border capital movement between Estonia and third countries remain high. It may also be because there are other significant factors that affect capital movements to/from third countries.[40]

[40] Other factors affecting capital flows are discussed in section 7.1.6.

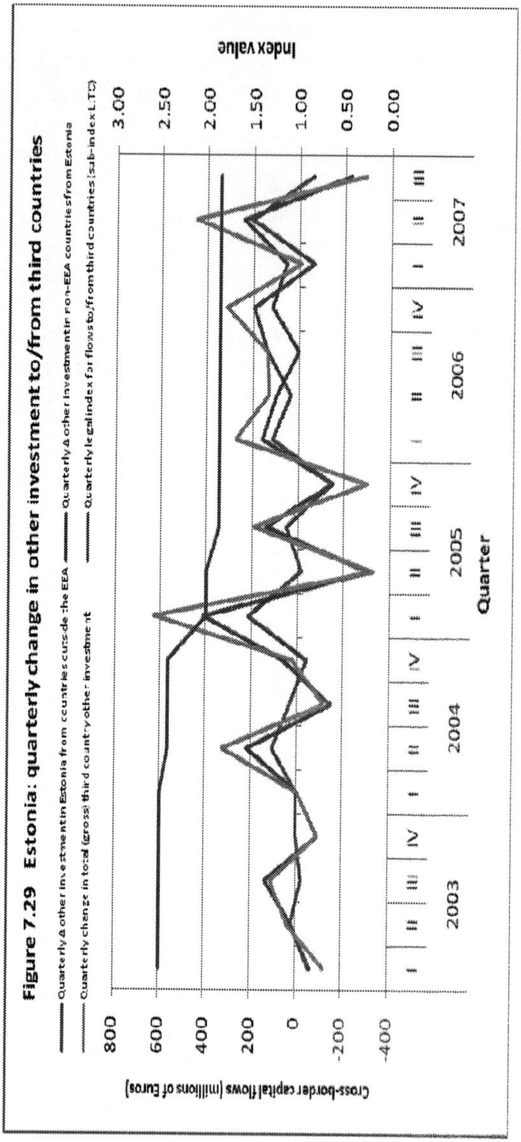

Figure 7.29 Estonia: quarterly change in other investment to/from third countries

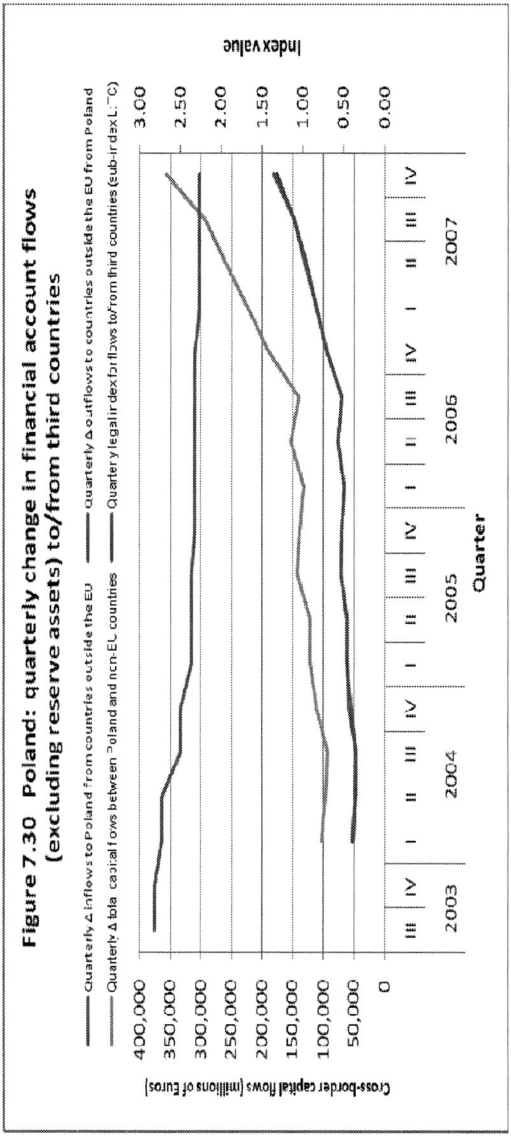

Figure 7.30 Poland: quarterly change in financial account flows (excluding reserve assets) to/from third countries

In figure 7.30, quarterly capital flows from the Financial Account rise only slightly until quarter III of 2006, then increase substantially.[41] Polish subsidiary index L:TC is high throughout the period shown, but falls in small steps. There is weak negative correlation between L:TC and cross-border capital flows. Figure 7.31 shows that both inward and outward FDI rise as sub-index L:TC falls.[42]

There are substantial cross-border capital flows between Poland and third countries, especially in 2007. This is despite the high value of legal sub-index L:TC. Capital movements may be taking place in areas with permissive legal rules. Alternatively, or additionally, the assumptions for construction of the legal index may be inaccurate and/or insensitive.[43]

Figures 7.32 and 7.33 illustrate how Latvian subsidiary index L:TC relates to FDI between this state and third countries.[44] As L:TC falls, FDI inflows and outflows both rise. Outward FDI is much smaller than inward FDI, but in 2007 the former is increasing almost as much as the latter. As stated above for Latvia's investment in other EEA states, the low level of FDI outflows may be due to a shortage of funds to invest abroad.

---

[41] The constituent components of the Financial Account are stated in note 25.

[42] 'EU' in figure 7.31 excludes Bulgaria and Romania.

[43] See the subsection '2. *Source of possible overestimation of legal subsidiary index L:TC*' in section 7.1.6.

[44] Data for figures 7.32 and 7.33 are provided in lats and converted to Euros (see note 7). Data for 2007 are those provided for quarter IV of that year for the direct investment position (figure 7.32), and are the sum of quarters I to IV of that year for the annual change in FDI (figure 7.33) because no separate annual figures are given.

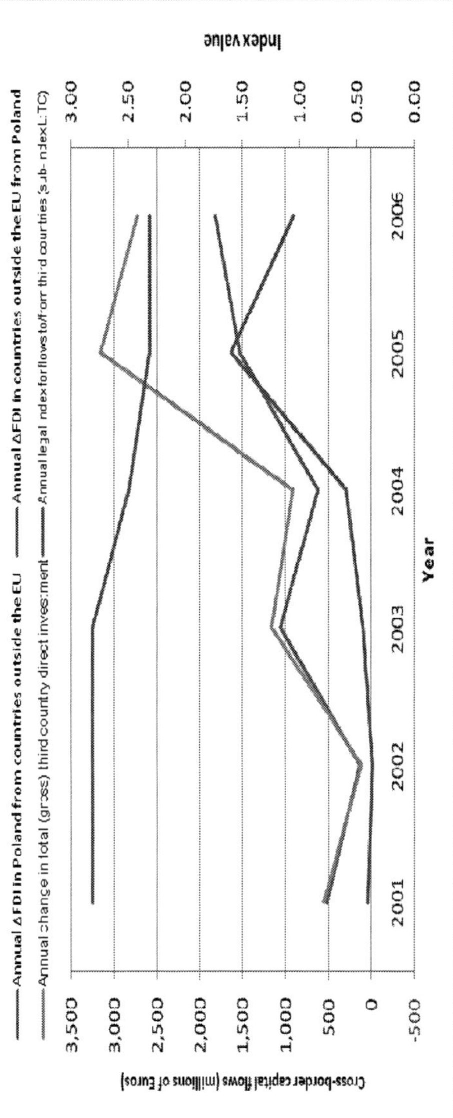

Figure 7.31 Poland: annual change in FDI to/from third countries

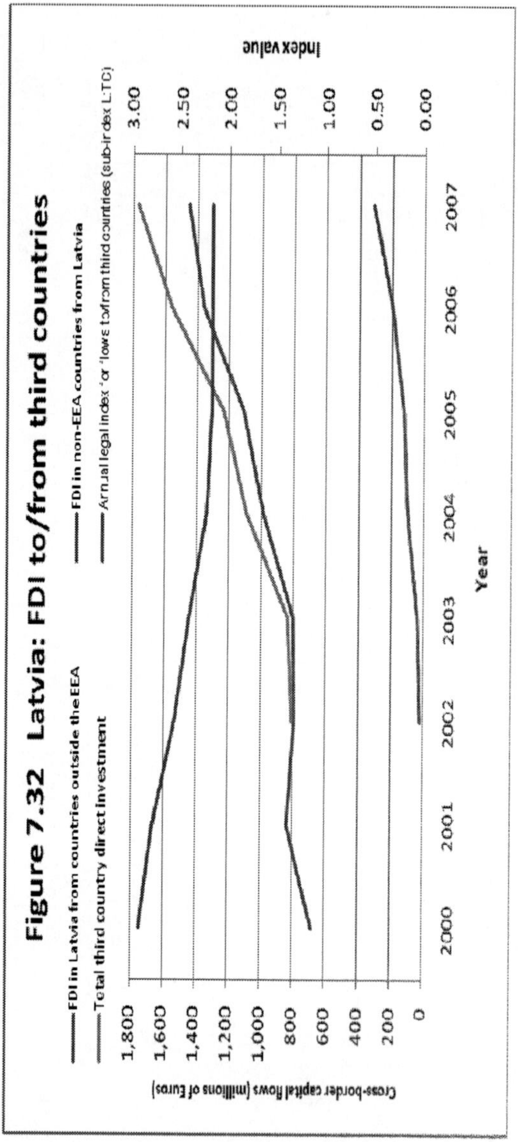

Figure 7.32 Latvia: FDI to/from third countries
FDI in Latvia from countries outside the EEA
FDI in non-EEA countries from Latvia
Total third country direct investment
Annual legal index for flows to/from third countries (sub-index LTC)
Cross-border capital flows (millions of Euros)
1,800
1,600
1,400
1,200
1,000
800
600
400
200
0
2000
2001
2002
2003
2004
2005
2006
2007
Year
Index value
3.00
2.50
2.00
1.50
1.00
0.50
0.00

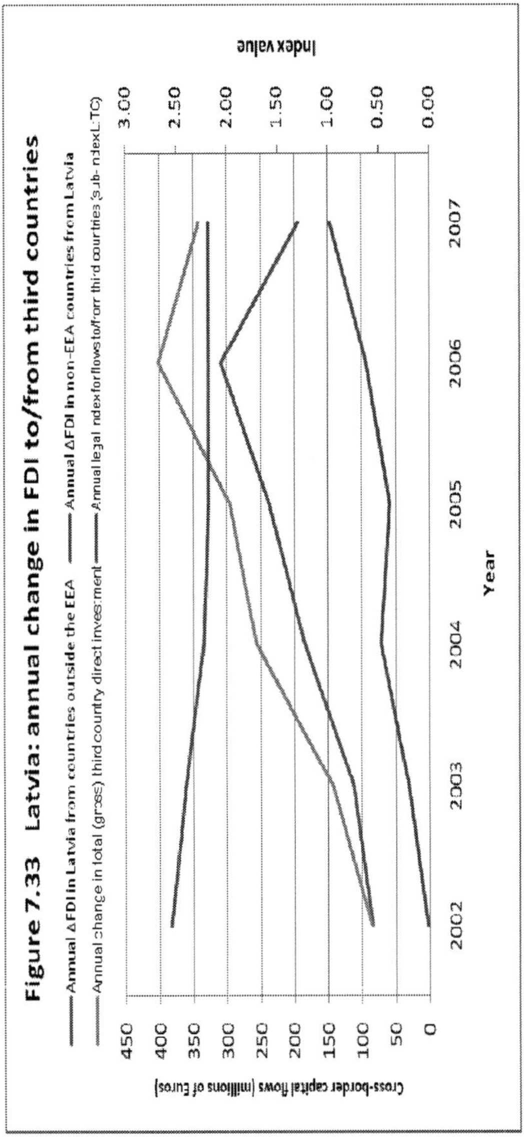

In general, legal sub-index L:TC is inversely related to cross-border capital movements to/from third countries. However, the connection is weak for some Estonian and Polish flows.

Comment

From the graphs in this section, it can be argued that substantial legal restrictions to the free movement of capital–represented by a high index value–are associated with small cross-border flows, and few restrictions (shown by a low index score) with large flows. Firstly, as already noted, the numerical amounts of the capital movements between EU/EEA Member States are larger than those to/from third countries. Secondly, there is a clear inverse relationship between subsidiary index L:EEA, which falls considerably (especially for Poland), and the substantial, increasing capital inflows. This contrasts with the weak negative correlation between sub-index L:TC and inflows.

This claim is countered by the fact that capital movements to third countries tend to increase even though L:TC drops only slightly. As stated above, these flows may be permitted by laws recently passed that allow cross-border capital movements. But L:TC may be overestimated. If L:TC is consistently in excess of its 'true' value by 0.5, for instance, then it might be stated incorrectly that high legal index values are unassociated with small cross-border capital flows.

There is therefore not enough information to conclude either that high/(low) index values are related to small/(large) capital flows, or that they are not so connected. The assumptions underlying the index will be discussed in section 7.1.6 in order to clarify how to progress.

7.1.5 Subdivision 3: capital flows to/from the relevant industrial sectors

In this section, the cross-border capital flows data are divided into the relevant sectors: investment funds, investment services, credit institutions, insurance services (including insurance mediation) and real property, and are compared with the corresponding subsidiary legal index. As noted in section 6.2.1, the sectoral sub-indices are constructed from fewer cross-country comparisons than the indices already used. This compromises the accuracy and reliability of the former, but most of these have six or seven data points; these are enough to produce a reasonable estimate of the 'true' value.[45] As a consequence, however, the comments made in this section are tentative and to be considered carefully.

The only appropriate data about investment funds and investment services concern the growth of foreign companies supplying domestic

[45] The number of comparisons used in calculating the subsidiary legal indices is shown in table 6.2.

residents. There are no relevant Polish records. Balance of payments information is used for credit institutions, insurance services and real estate. Estonia and Latvia use the 'Statistical Classification of Economic Activities in the European Community NACE Revision 1.1' (2002) in defining 'financial intermediation' and 'real estate, renting and business activities'.[46] These definitions are broader than the industrial sectors,[47] but include the relevant capital flows.

In addition, the exports and imports of 'financial services' and 'insurance services' in the Current Account are used as capital flows data for credit institution and insurance services sectors respectively. The definitions of these terms in the IMF Balance of Payments Manual correspond to the sectors.[48]

Since 'financial intermediation' includes services by credit institutions, insurance services and insurance mediation,[49] the relevant graphs (figures 7.38-7.40 and 7.43) plot legal sub-indexes for all three activities. As 'insurance services' include insurance agents' commissions,[50] figures 7.44-7.46 show the indices for both insurance services and insurance mediation.

---

[46] A later version of this classification is NACE Revision 2 (2006).

[47] 'Financial intermediation' includes the receipt and redistribution of funds by both monetary and non-monetary institutions, insurance and pension funding, and activities ancillary to the above (such as asset management, the supervision of financial markets and insurance agency). 'Real estate, renting and business activities' include the buying, selling and letting of property, the renting of machinery and equipment and of personal and household goods, and various business activities including computer-related services and advertising (Eurostat, NACE Revision 1.1 (2002)).

[48] 'Financial services' comprise financial intermediation and auxiliary services between residents and non-residents. The former include financial leasing, brokerage, credit and underwriting services, foreign exchange transactions and arrangements for hedging instruments. The latter include security custody and financial market operational and regulatory services. 'Insurance services' comprise services provided by resident(/non-resident) insurance companies to non-residents(/residents) for freight, life, non-life and other direct insurance and for reinsurance (IMF Balance of Payments Manual (1993), 5th edition, 39). 'Insurance services' also include "agent commissions related to insurance transactions" (ibid., 66).

[49] See note 47.

[50] See note 48.

Investment funds

Figures 7.34 and 7.35 show the investment in foreign funds made by Estonian and Latvian residents respectively.[51] In both Member States, investment rises after legal sub-index S:InvF has fallen, although Estonian debt fund investments are unaffected by this decrease.

The capital flows are larger for investments in foreign funds by Estonian residents than those by Latvian residents. This may be because Latvians tend to have fewer funds to invest abroad than Estonians,[52] the range of securities considered in an investment portfolio is narrower for Latvia than for Estonia,[53] and/or the legal restrictions to cross-border capital movement, as measured by sub-index S:InvF, are greater for Latvia than for Estonia.

---

[51] Data for figure 7.34 are provided in kroons and converted to Euros (see note 7). Data for figure 7.35 are provided in lats and converted to Euros (see note 7). The date for 2007 are omitted because additional items are included in the securities portfolio for that year: time deposits with, and claims on demand to, credit institutions, plus land and buildings. The securities portfolio for 2000-2006 inclusive includes only debt securities, equity, derivatives and investment fund investment certificates.

[52] See the subsection '*Capital flows between EU/EEA Member States*' in section 7.1.4.

[53] The Estonian Financial Supervision Authority (EFSA) does not define 'debt funds' and 'equity funds' for these data sets. For Latvia, see note 51.

Figure 7.34 Estonia: investment in foreign funds

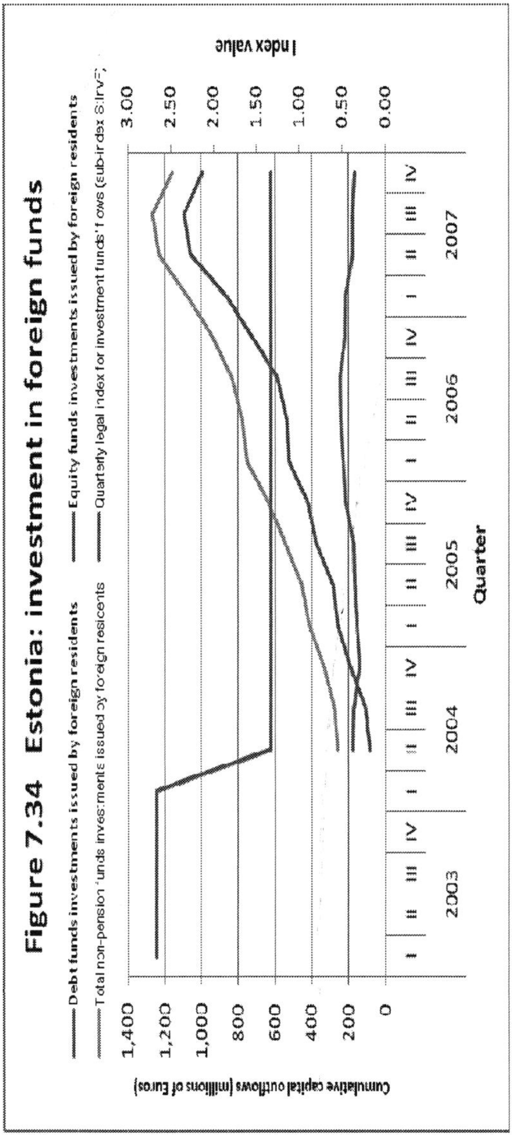

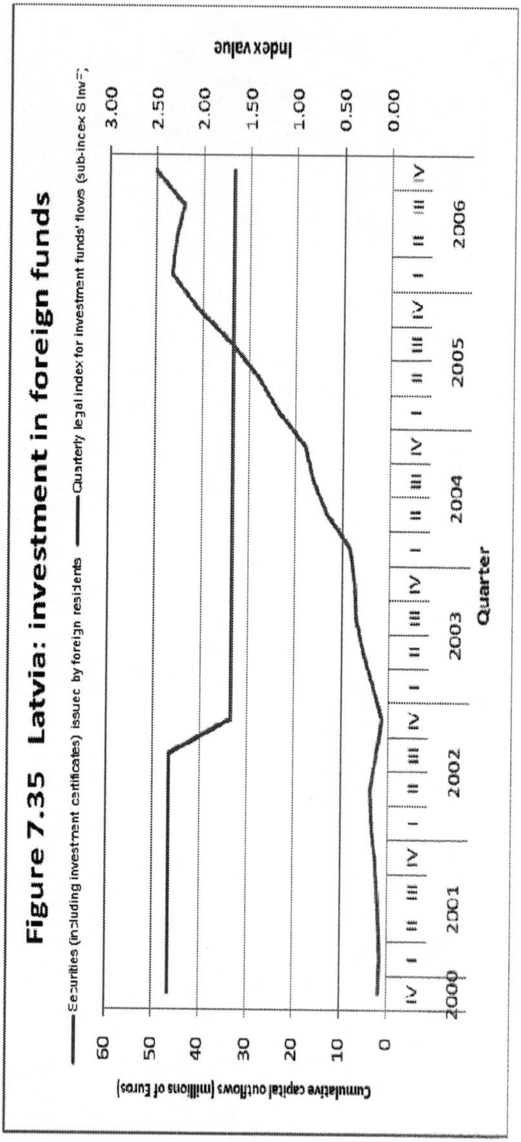
Figure 7.35 Latvia: investment in foreign funds
Securities (including investment certificates) issued by foreign residents
Quarterly legal index for investment funds' flows (sub-index S InvF)
Cumulative capital outflows (millions of Euros)
Index value
Quarter

Investment services

Figure 7.36 shows that investment services from foreign providers rise substantially after quarter II of 2005,[54] one trimester after subsidiary index S:InsS has fallen. Although the sub-index remains high, its decrease in 2005 quarter I may be permitting the additional cross-border capital flows shown on the graph.

Credit institutions

Figure 7.37 shows that cross-border capital movements relating to Estonian imports and exports of financial services rise substantially after legal sub-index S:CI has fallen to its minimum. There is a strong inverse relationship between these flows and this subsidiary index.

Figures 7.38, 7.39 and 7.40 display Estonian cross-border investment flows for financial intermediation. Sub-indices S:CI, S:InsS and S:InsM fall in quarter I of 2005. The large peak and trough for quarter II of 2005 in figures 7.38 and 7.39 correspond to those in figures 7.15 and 7.17 respectively, and may be due to foreign investors switching from portfolio investment to FDI.[55]

[54] The Estonian FSA publishes data on the custodian service of investment firms. However, the flows are small for non-resident firms, other than one outlying datum which exceeds the next largest value by one hundredfold.

[55] This explanation was proposed in section 7.1.4. It is strengthened by the fact that these large capital movements concern financial intermediation, and therefore may involve investments in the Estonian economy by foreign financial institutions.

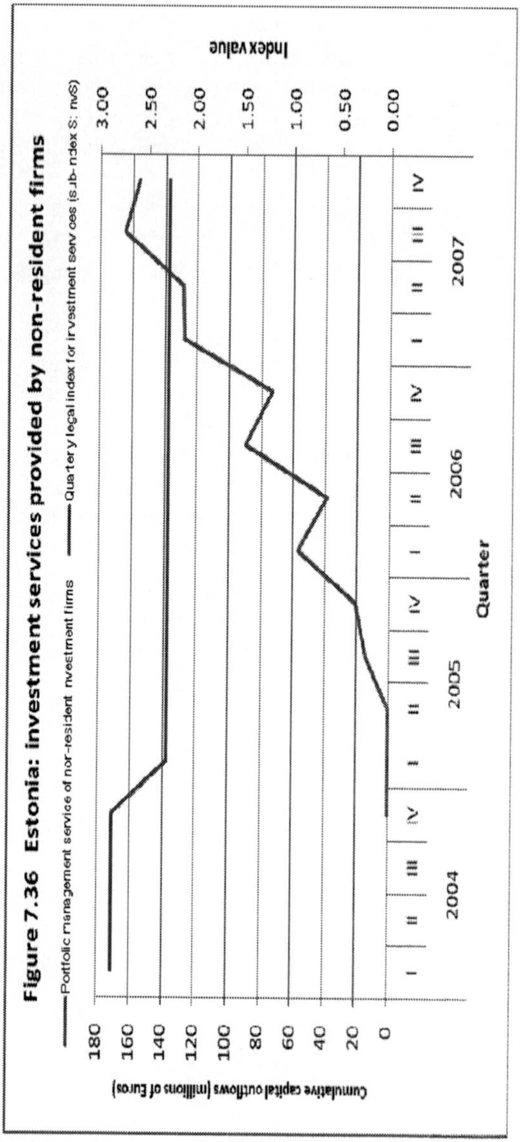

Figure 7.36 Estonia: investment services provided by non-resident firms

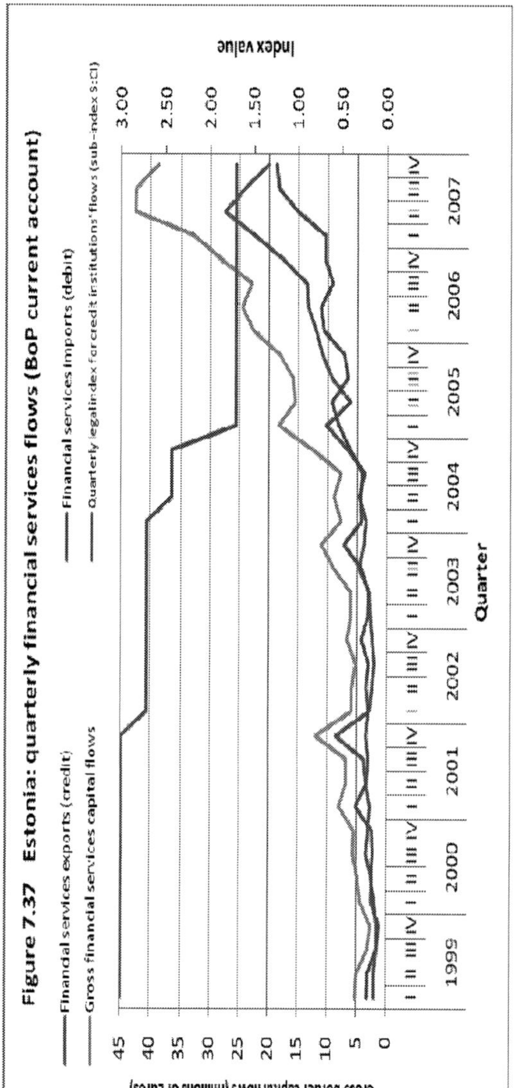

Figure 7.37 Estonia: quarterly financial services flows (BoP current account)

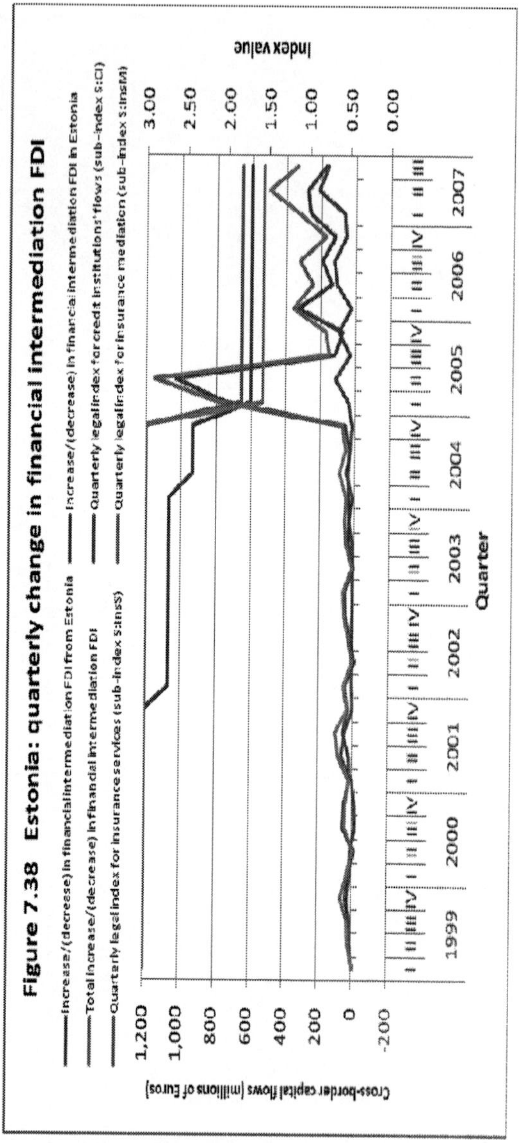

Figure 7.38 Estonia: quarterly change in financial intermediation FDI

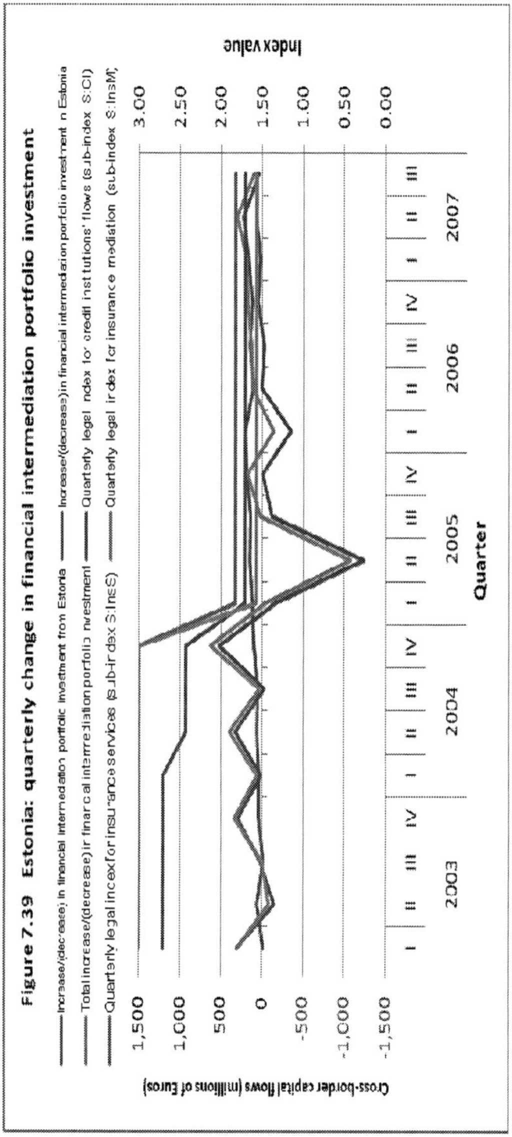

Figure 7.39 Estonia: quarterly change in financial intermediation portfolio investment

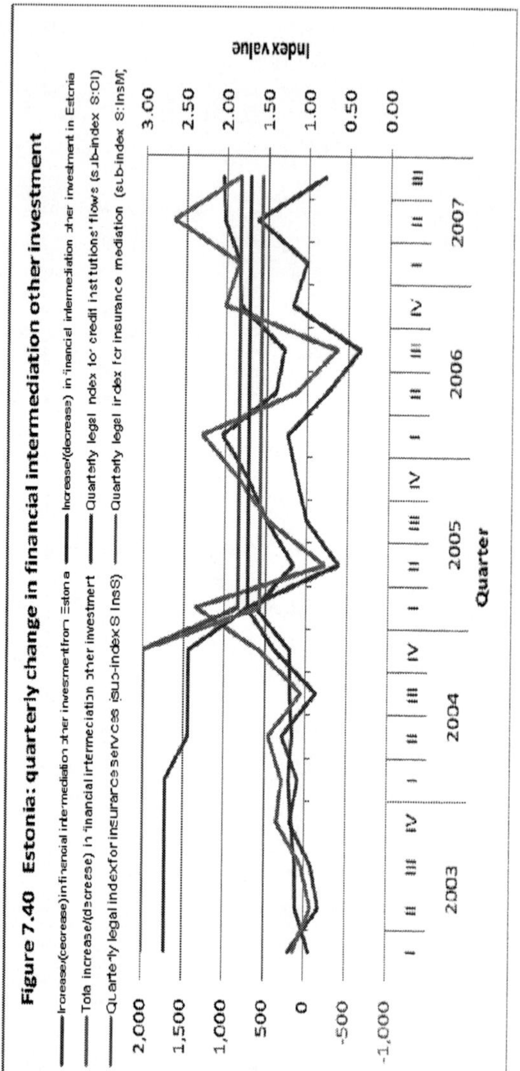

Figure 7.40 Estonia: quarterly change in financial intermediation other investment

Figure 7.38 shows that financial intermediation FDI inflows and outflows are higher following the fall in the sub-indices than before this event. There is no correlation between portfolio investment and these indexes (figure 7.39). Inward other investment rises after S:CI, S:InsS and S:InsM decrease, but outward other investment becomes more volatile (figure 7.40). Overall, financial intermediation flows to Estonia, and to a lesser extent from Estonia, tend to rise after the legal sub-indices for its constituent sectors fall.

Figure 7.41 shows that capital movements corresponding to Polish exports and imports of financial services increase slightly after the reduction in subsidiary index S:CI. The outlying value in quarter IV of 2001 is difficult to explain. Nonetheless, the inverse relationship between S:CI and gross flows is clear.

In figure 7.42,[56] Latvian financial services' exports and, to a much lesser extent, financial services' imports, are inversely correlated with legal sub-index S:CI. It is surprising that the level of exports exceeds that of imports. However, as table 7.1 shows,[57] this is not mistaken.

[56] Data for figures 7.42 and 7.43 are provided in lats and converted to Euros (see note 7).

[57] Title and ownership of the data in table 7.1 remain with the Bank of Latvia. The emphasis in the table is mine. Data are in thousands of lats. Differences between table 7.1 and figure 7.42 are due to changes in the lat-Euro exchange rate.

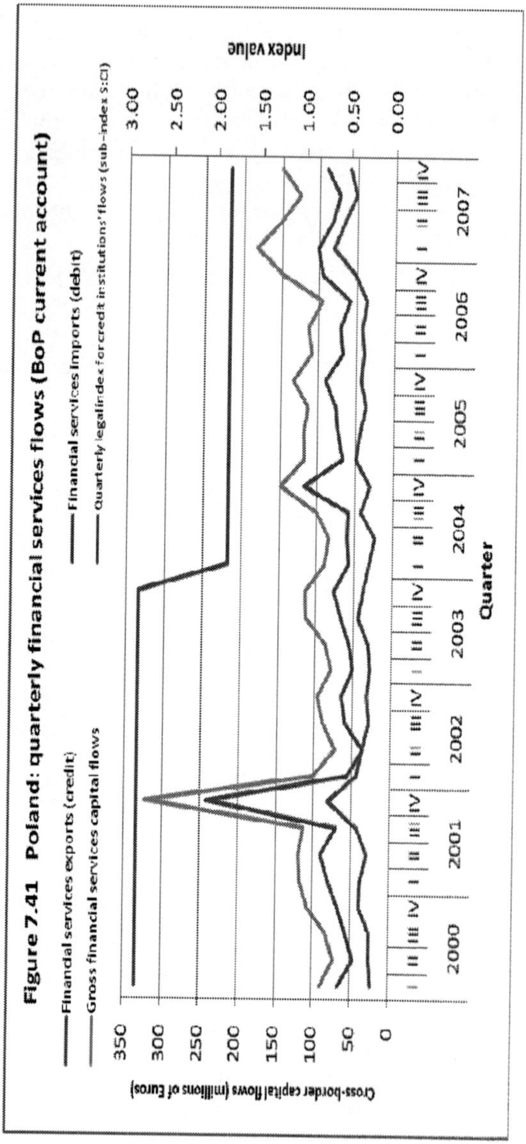

Figure 7.41 Poland: quarterly financial services flows (BoP current account)

Table 7.1: Extract from Latvia's annual balance of payments 2001-2007.

2001	2002	2003	2004	2005	2006	2007	Components
183 294	190 497	223 017	281 166	342 397	418 188	595 538	**Other services (credit)**
14 531	15 510	20 846	28 367	34 671	45 806	41 526	Communication services
8 408	4 071	17 816	25 375	7 933	13 647	30 593	Construction services
7 866	6 618	5 770	6 220	5 987	5 793	8 487	Insurance services
27 185	**35 559**	**52 751**	**61 875**	**73 072**	**100 138**	**136 126**	**Financial services**
13 759	15 330	18 667	23 462	30 770	40 660	50 501	Computer and information services
1 571	2 073	2 508	4 332	5 553	6 309	6 324	Royalties and licence fees
98 194	100 038	92 210	115 023	165 214	185 571	297 507	Other bussiness services
457	534	1 956	1 494	2 971	3 646	4 791	Personal, cultural and recreational services
11 322	10 764	10 493	15 019	16 226	16 618	19 683	Government services, n.i.e.
x	x	x	2 503	4 922	5 312	6 827	of which EU reimbursement for cost of collecting
							traditional own resources
- 151 177	- 147 075	- 171 090	- 208 992	- 268 008	- 355 238	- 502 829	**Other services (debit)**

- 5 991	- 8 832	- 12 278	- 25 194	- 32 942	- 45 428	- 54 196	Communication services
- 10 502	- 6 266	- 9 628	- 10 013	- 6 857	- 23 049	- 79 032	Construction services
- 26 520	- 22 882	- 29 108	- 21 593	- 15 603	- 14 898	- 27 058	Insurance services
- 14 320	**- 14 460**	**- 14 061**	**- 14 858**	**- 17 267**	**- 16 499**	**- 27 601**	**Financial services**
- 9 858	- 10 350	- 12 883	- 14 998	- 29 237	- 35 063	- 44 728	Computer and information services
- 4 577	- 3 983	- 5 839	- 7 786	- 8 243	- 11 058	- 20 126	Royalties and licence fees
- 70 665	- 71 469	- 76 439	- 99 250	- 141 470	- 190 979	- 227 402	Other bussiness services
- 3 045	- 2 924	- 3 998	- 7 931	- 7 587	- 8 161	- 10 547	Personal, cultural and recreational services
- 5 698	- 5 908	- 6 857	- 7 369	- 8 802	- 10 102	- 12 139	Government services, n.i.e.

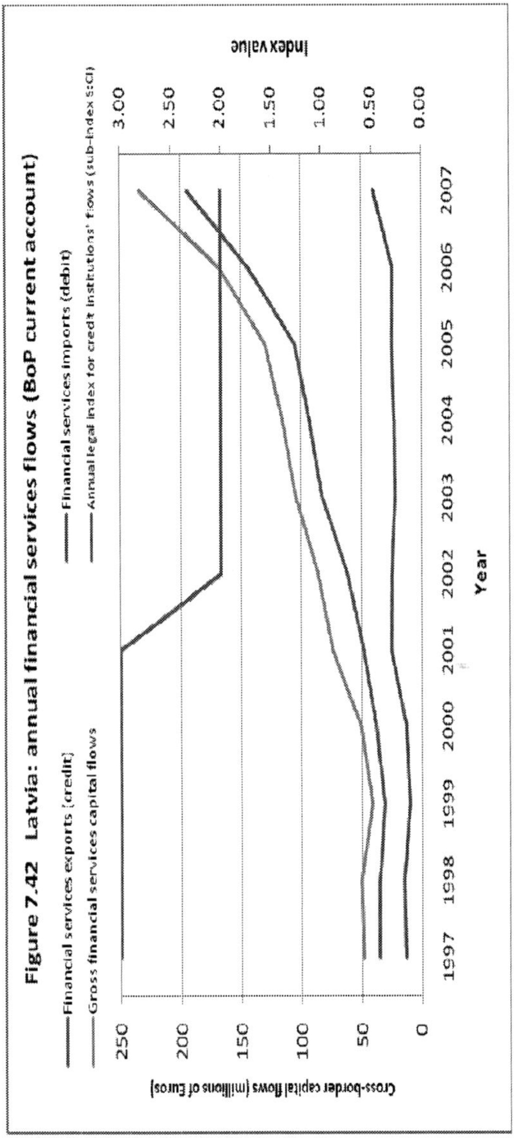

Figure 7.42 Latvia: annual financial services flows (BoP current account)

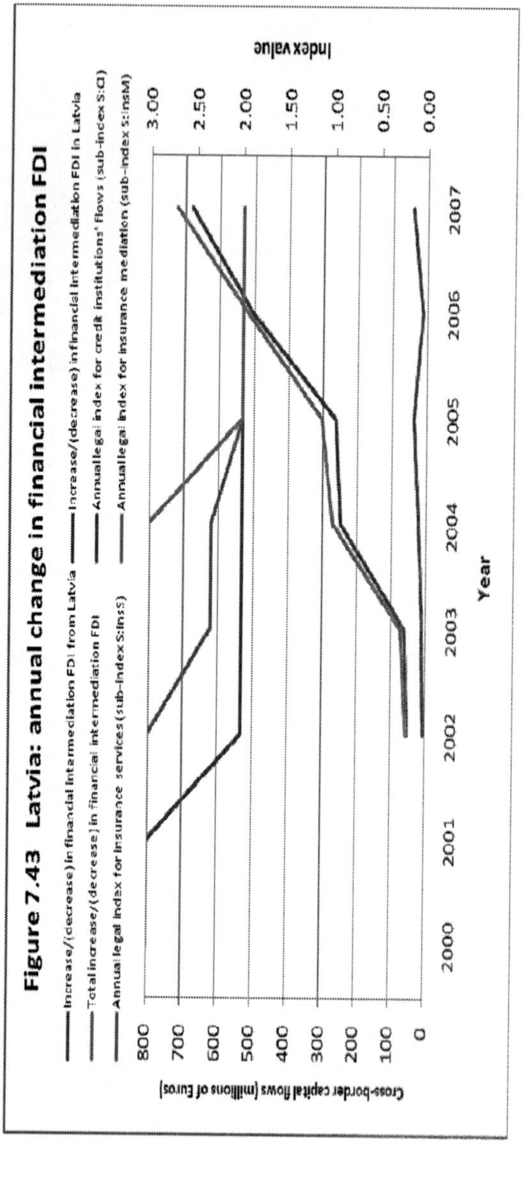
Figure 7.43 Latvia: annual change in financial intermediation FDI
Increase/(decrease) in financial intermediation FDI from Latvia
Increase/(decrease) in financial intermediation FDI in Latvia
Total increase/(decrease) in financial intermediation FDI
Annual legal index for credit institutions' flows (sub-index S:CI)
Annual legal index for insurance services (sub-index S:InsS)
Annual legal index for insurance mediation (sub-index S:InsM)
Cross-border capital flows (millions of Euros)
Index value
Year
800
700
600
500
400
300
200
100
0
3.00
2.50
2.00
1.50
1.00
0.50
0.00
2000
2001
2002
2003
2004
2005
2006
2007

Figure 7.43 shows that FDI inflows concerning financial intermediation increase as legal sub-indices S:InsS and S:InsM are falling, and rise at a greater rate after the indexes have reduced.[58] By contrast, there is only weak negative correlation between the indexes and outward financial intermediation FDI.

In general, subsidiary legal index S:CI is inversely related to cross-border capital movements for financial services, and sub-indices S:CI, S:InsS and S:InsM are negatively associated with financial intermediation investment flows, especially those of FDI. These indexes correlate more strongly with investment inflows than with investment outflows. The removal of legal restrictions to cross-border capital movements in the financial services, insurance services and insurance mediation sectors in Estonia, Poland and Latvia may be permitting greater capital flows, especially inflows, to occur. Insurance services and insurance mediation are further considered below.

Insurance services (including insurance mediation)

Figures 7.44, 7.45 and 7.46 show imports and exports of insurance services for Estonia, Poland and Latvia, respectively.[59] For Estonia and Latvia, the decrease in legal sub-indices S:InsS and S:InsM do not affect insurance services capital movements in either direction, although there is an increase in Latvian insurance service imports in 2007. In Poland, the fall in the subsidiary indexes in quarter I of 2004 is followed by smaller capital flows, especially relating to exports of insurance services.

[58] In figure 7.43, the data for 2007 are the sum of quarters I to IV of that year for the annual change in FDI because no separate yearly figures are given.

[59] Data for figure 7.46 are provided in lats and converted to Euros (see note 7).

Figure 7.44 Estonia: quarterly insurance services flows (BoP current account)

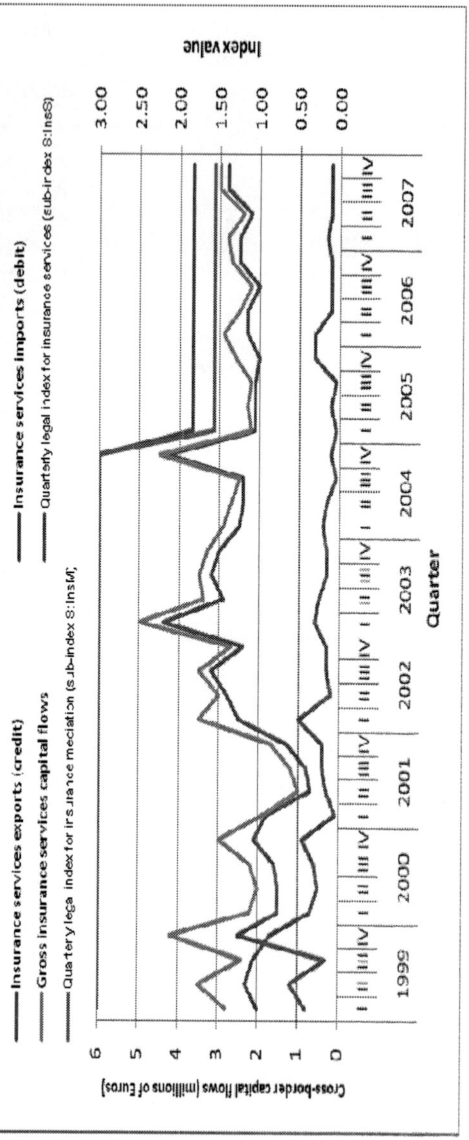

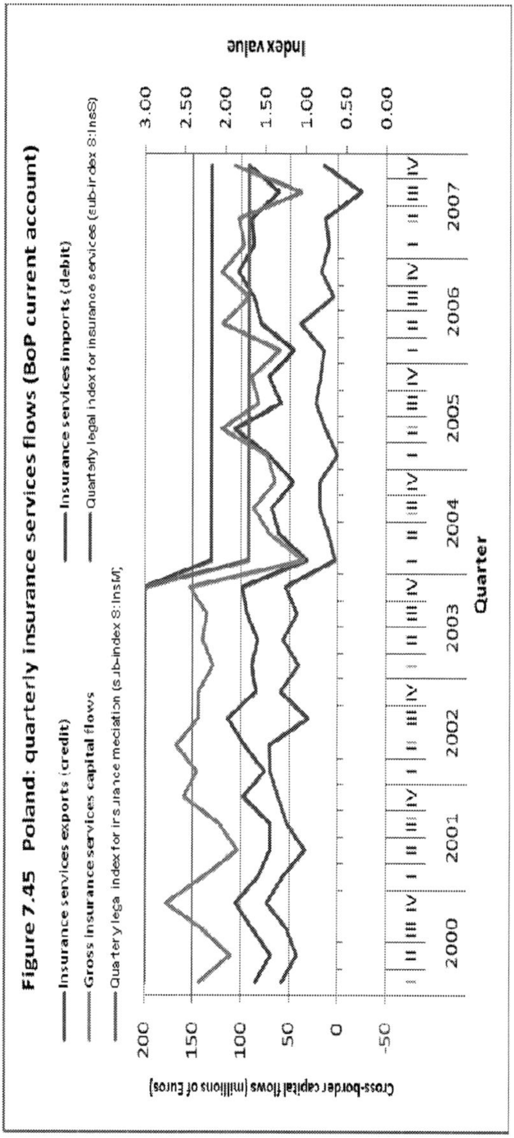

Figure 7.45 Poland: quarterly insurance services flows (BoP current account)

Figure 7.46 Latvia: annual insurance services flows (BoP current account)

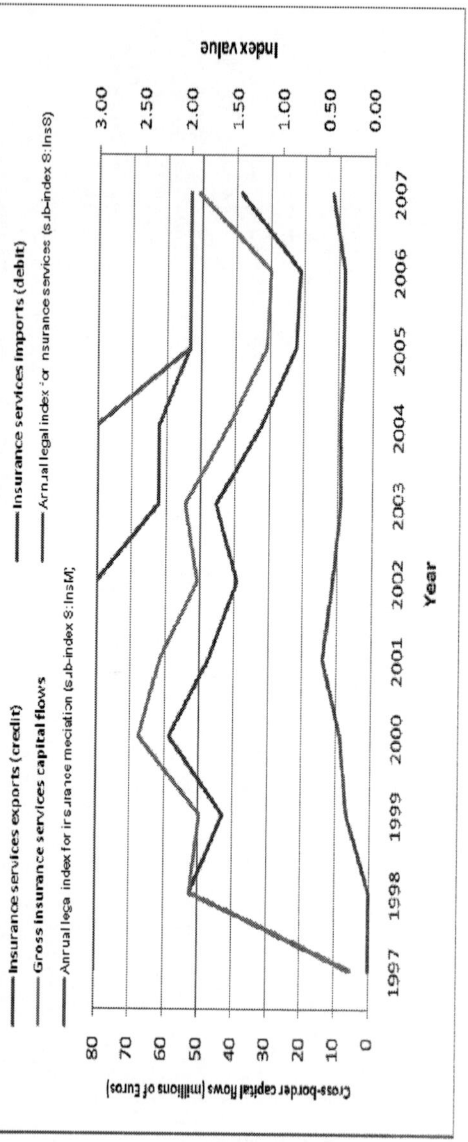

In the insurance services and insurance mediation sectors, therefore, cross-border capital movements are unaffected by the removal of legal restrictions, as represented by legal sub-indices S:InsS and S:InsM. An explanation is that most provision of these services occur within each Member State–i.e. the free movement of capital across national borders is not an issue for the majority of Estonian, Polish and Latvian insurance companies, agents and brokers, so cross-border capital flows do not increase as the legal barriers fall.[60]

If, as suggested above, most insurance services and insurance mediation are provided between residents, then one would expect cross-border capital movements relating to these services to be small relative to those in the financial sector. Comparison of figures 7.37 and 7.44 (Estonia), 7.41 and 7.45 (Poland), plus 7.42 and 7.46 (Latvia) show that this is true for Estonia, for Latvian exports and for Polish exports from 2004. This is a persuasive but inconclusive result.

Further comparison of 7.37 with 7.44 and of 7.42 with 7.46 shows that, for Estonia and Latvia, cross-border capital flows relating to financial services tend to increase after subsidiary index S:CI falls, whilst capital movements associated with insurance services are not significantly affected by changes in S:InsS and S:InsM. It is therefore proposed that the rise in cross-border financial intermediation investment flows following a fall in sub-indices S:CI, S:InsS and S:InsM (see figures 7.38, 7.40 and 7.43) relates more to the decrease in S:CI than to the reduction in S:InsS and S:InsM. In short, the credit institution/financial services sector may in practice be more affected by legal restrictions to the free movement of capital across national borders than the insurance services and insurance mediation sectors. Section 7.2.2 explores this issue further.

Real property

Figures 7.47, 7.48 and 7.49 show, for Estonia, the quarterly change in FDI, portfolio investment and other investment flows respectively for real estate, renting and business activities (henceforth ‘real estate and renting’).[61] Figure 7.50 shows, for Latvia, the trimestrial change in FDI for these services. As capital movements relating to the cross-border real property are only a part of these investment flows, their comparison with subsidiary legal index S:L cannot yield firm conclusions.

In figure 7.47, real estate and renting FDI inflows and outflows increase after the fall in sub-index S:L, and the FDI inflows become more volatile. The inward FDI plot may indicate that the removal of strict cross-border restrictions on the acquisition of Estonian real property in March 2003 facilitates capital inflows.[62]

---

[60] See section 7.2.2 for comment on this matter.

[61] These terms are defined in note 47.

[62] See chapter 3 note 174.

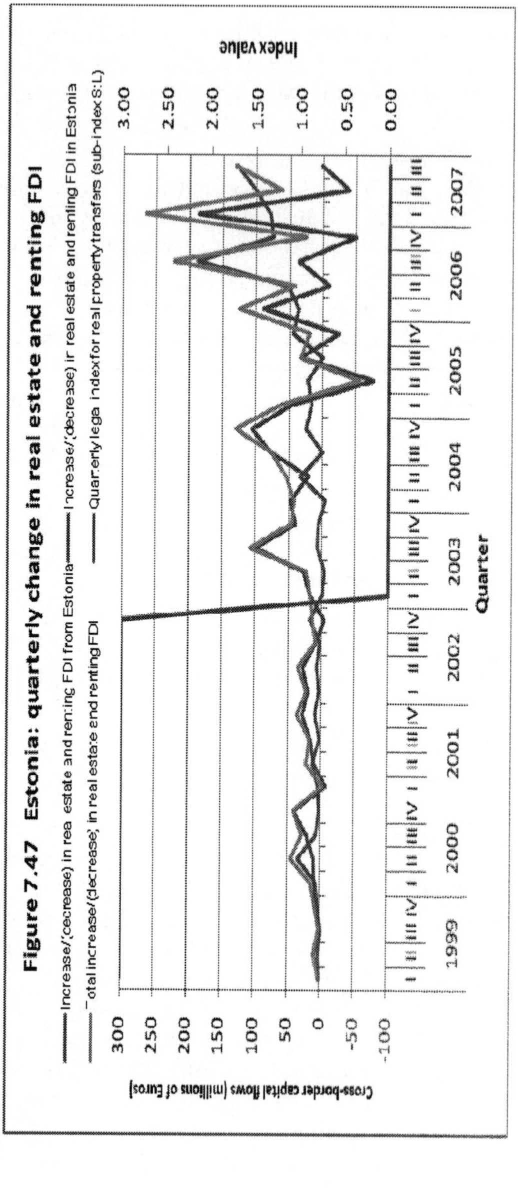

Figure 7.47 Estonia: quarterly change in real estate and renting FDI

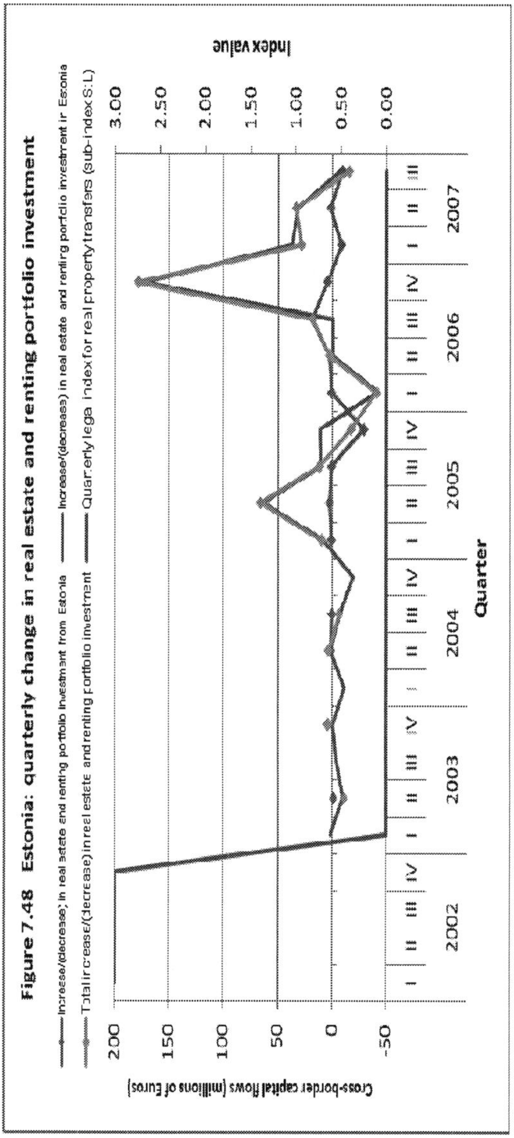

Figure 7.48 Estonia: quarterly change in real estate and renting portfolio investment

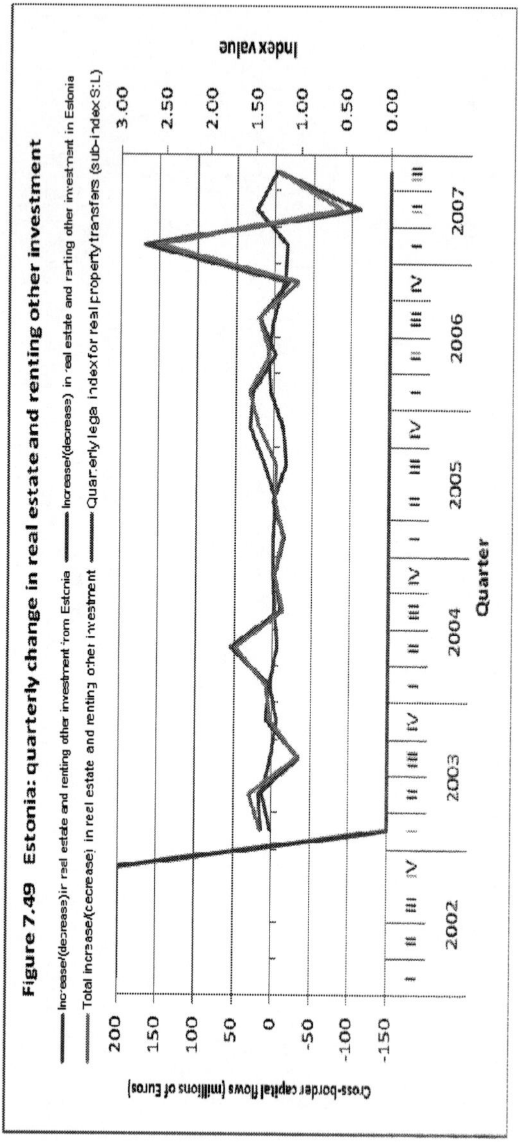

Figure 7.49 Estonia: quarterly change in real estate and renting other investment

Estonian portfolio investment and other investment flows for real estate and renting appear to be unaffected by the fall in subsidiary index S:L.[63] Inward portfolio investment rises sharply in quarter IV of 2006, and then falls to previous levels. Outward other investment increases substantially in quarter I of 2007, becoming negative in the next quarter, and then returning to zero. Although these large swings are difficult to explain, the absence of Estonian legal restrictions to cross-border capital movement relating to real property (shown by the value of sub-index S:L) allows them if they involve cross-border acquisition of such property.

In figure 7.50,[64] the decline in Latvian subsidiary index S:L in 2004 is followed by a small fall in inward real estate and renting FDI, then a large rise and another reduction in these flows. Outward real estate and renting FDI is unaffected by the decrease in sub-index S:L.

Conclusions

In general, an inverse relationship is found between legal sub-indices S:InvF, SInvS, S:CI and the cross-border capital flows relating to the relevant sectors: investment funds, investment services and credit institutions respectively. Subsidiary indices S:InsS and S:InsM are independent of cross-border capital movements in the insurance services and insurance mediation sectors; an explanation is proposed above for this unexpected result.

In Estonia, sub-index S:L is negatively related to real estate and renting FDI, but unconnected with portfolio and other investment. In Latvia, sub-index S:L and inward real estate and renting FDI are negatively correlated, but the outward FDI flows are unaffected by this index. Section 7.1.6 comments on issues raised by the comparisons made between the legal index and cross-border capital flows.

---

[63] The phrase 'appear to be' is used because portfolio and direct investment data prior to the decline in sub-index S:L are absent.

[64] Data for figure 7.50 are provided in lats and converted to Euros (see note 7); the data for 2007 are the sum of quarters I to IV of that year for the annual change in FDI because no separate yearly figures are given.

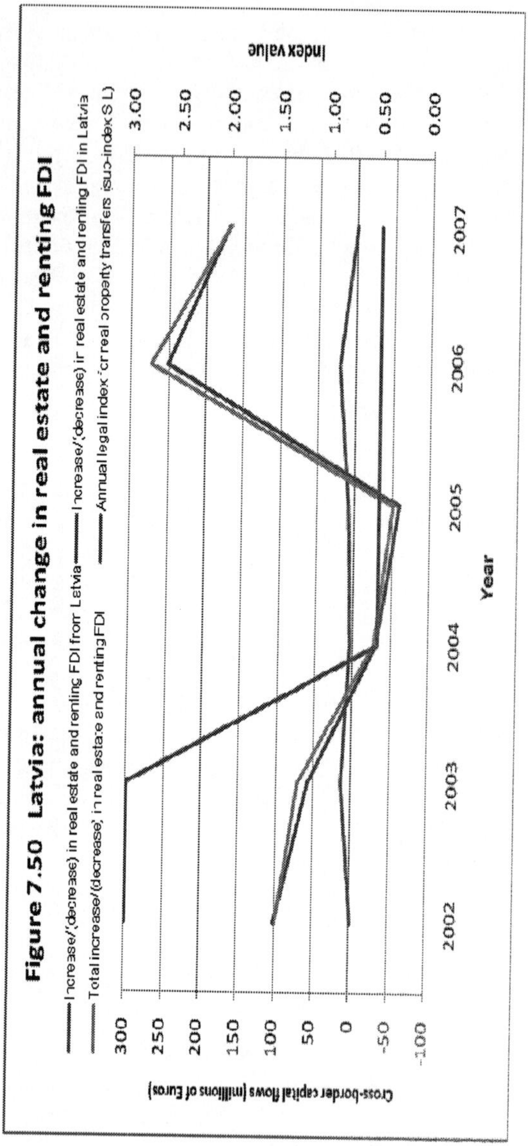

Figure 7.50 Latvia: annual change in real estate and renting FDI

7.1.6 Comment

The following concerns arise from the analysis above. 1) Data from different statistical sources may be inconsistent. 2) In section 7.1.4, it was suggested that overestimation of the legal subsidiary index for capital flows to/from third countries (L:TC) may be responsible for the observed result that such flows tend to increase even though L:TC does not substantially decline.[65] The assumptions made in calculating the legal index may have caused L:TC to have been overestimated. 3) Section 1.4 establishes that there are several non-legal factors that affect cross-border capital flows. The current section addresses these concerns.

1. Statistical data inconsistency

Inconsistency of data representing the same phenomenon but from different sources may arise for several reasons, including the use of non-identical input records, varying definitions of terms and different exchange rates. The greater is the magnitude of these inconsistencies, the less robust are the observations that are made from the data.

The degree of 'acceptable' inconsistency depends upon the use to which the data are put. In the comparisons made in this chapter, a high degree of inconsistency–several percentage points–would not substantially alter the conclusions drawn. This is because *the general trend over time in the magnitude of capital flows and their quarterly/annual changes* is the object to be compared with the legal index and its subsidiary indices.

It may be informative to consider an example of data describing the same cross-border capital movements but from different sources, *given the low sensitivity level for consistency that would be acceptable in this comparative analysis.* Consistent data, i.e. those of identical or similar value, are sufficiently robust to enable valid interpretation to be made. Highly inconsistent plots of capital flows, by contrast, render questionable any conclusions made.

The following two graphs are constructed from data available from more than one source. Both figure 7.51 and 7.52 show the annual change in FDI between Latvia and other Member States (excluding Bulgaria and Romania).[66] The respective sources of the data are the Bank of Latvia (1)

[65] Sub-index L:TC falls to 1.86, 2.27 and 2.18 by quarter IV of 2007 for Estonia, Poland and Latvia respectively.

[66] Figure 7.51 uses the same data as the EU plots in figure 7.23. The latter differs from the former by including Bulgaria and Romania as 'other EU Member States'. Figure 7.51 omits these two countries in order to represent the same capital flows as Figure 7.52.

and Eurostat (2). Although the two graphs cover different but overlapping time periods, they are very similar.

As table B.1 shows,[67] the information for figure 7.51 is obtained by summation of the individual country FDI flows in lats, followed by translation into Euros at the average annual exchange rate.[68] By contrast, data for table B.2 are integers in Euros.[69] Despite the differences in presentation of the data in the two tables, the values of the FDI inflows are almost identical, and those of the FDI outflows are sufficiently similar for the trend to be recognised in the graphs below.

Tests of data robustness should involve different inputs. Further testing is omitted because there is little duplication of data sources. Most, though not all, of the data used in sections 7.1.2-7.1.5 are extracted from the quarterly balance of payments and international investment position information available from the national banks. Much of this information is unavailable from the national statistical offices or from international data sources: the former tend to refer to the national banks and the latter tend to publish annual balance of payments data, which may be incomplete and/or in summary form.[70] Furthermore, as Estonia, Poland and Latvia construct their international accounts in accordance with the methodology provided in the IMF Balance of Payments Manual,[71] these records are comparable with each other as well as with the legal index on restrictions to cross-border capital movements.

Hence, the input data on cross-border capital flows are mostly available only from the national banks. The small amount of information used that is produced by more than one source is sufficiently similar to enable robust conclusions to be drawn from its comparison with the legal index and sub-indices, given the high threshold for consistency in this analysis.

---

[67] See Appendix B.

[68] See note 7.

[69] See Appendix B.

[70] For instance, the annual current account balance, FDI and external debt are items that are published by international data sources. Country and sector classifications of cross-border capital flows, especially on a quarterly basis, are only available (if at all) from national statistical sources.

[71] See the introduction to chapter 7.

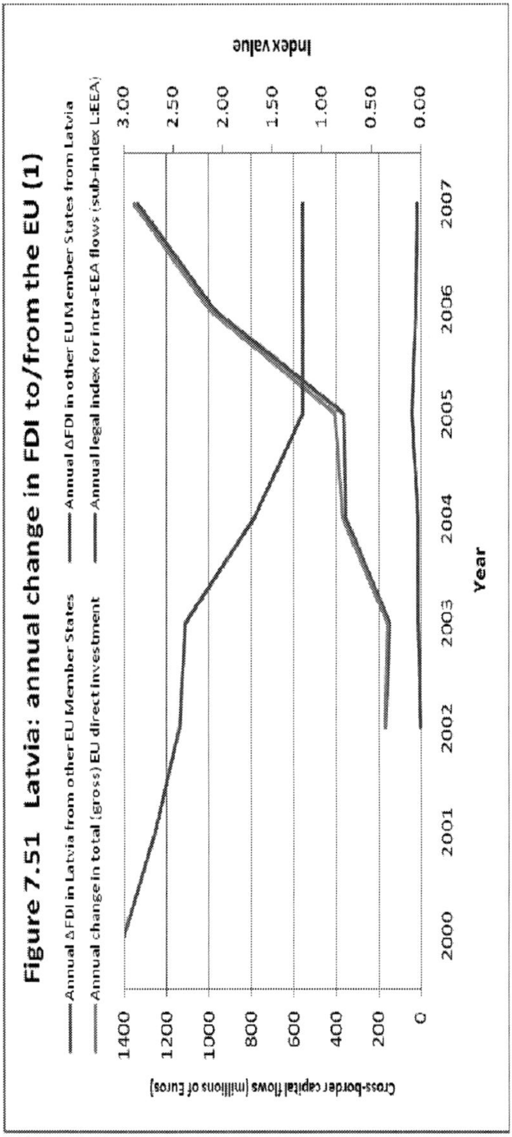

Figure 7.51 Latvia: annual change in FDI to/from the EU (1)

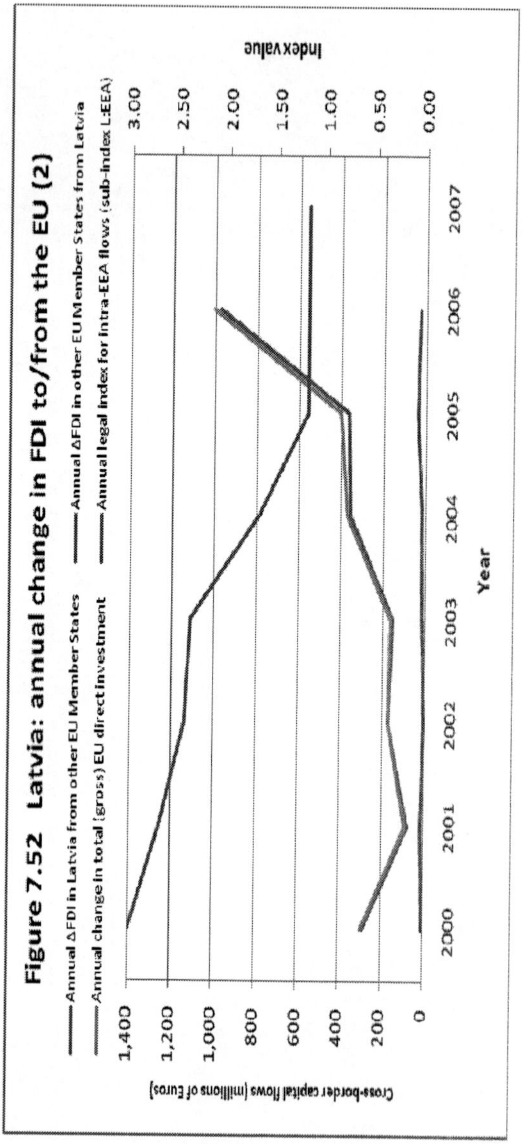

Figure 7.52 Latvia: annual change in FDI to/from the EU (2)

2. Source of possible overestimation of legal subsidiary index L:TC

There are three points in the legal index construction process at which assumptions are made. These are 1) the functional comparison of national rules, which requires subjective judgment of which legal provisions of similar or identical application most and least restrict the free movement of capital, based on their compliance with EU law;[72] 2) the allocation of a number on the legal index scale to the comparative results, followed by calculation of the index and its sub-indices;[73] 3) the construction of timelines for the index using the implementation dates of the relevant legal provisions.[74]

Assumptions that may cause overestimation of L:TC at each point are as follows.

Point 1): the assumption that, in the absence of legal provisions, capital movement is prohibited because these flows are not officially provided for. Lack of national legal provisions for services to/from third countries is common, affecting at least one of the three Member States studied in 12 out of 22 comparisons involving capital movements to/from third countries.[75] By contrast, there are few legislative omissions in the intra-EEA comparisons. One instance is the absence of a national provision for cross-border services to Latvia by a credit institution registered in another Member State.[76]

Point 2): the allocation of legally absent provisions for services to/from third countries to the maximum on the legal index scale, on the implied assumption that the new Member States are likely to provide services to and, accept services from, other Member States within the framework of

[72] See sections 4.1.7, 4.3.3, 4.4.2, 5.1.8, 5.3.3 and 5.4.6. The input material for these sections is the content of chapters 3-5, whose inputs are the EU free movement of capital laws (chapter 2) and the national laws. Section 1.3.2 describes the comparative methodology used.

[73] See sections 6.1 and 6.2.1. The calculation of the index is by arithmetic average, which assumes that all cross-country comparisons carry equal weight: i.e. they involve the same volume of capital flows in the absence of legal restrictions. Subsequent analysis in section 7.1.5 has shown this assumption to be false: i.e. cross-border capital flows are higher in the financial services sector than in the insurance services and insurance mediation sectors.

[74] See section 7.1.1.

[75] These are comparisons 4, 5, 6, 7, 11, 12, 18, 19, 20, 25, 26 and 27 in table 6.1. Such legislative omission is particularly common for the provision of cross-border services to/from third countries: see section 5.1.8.

[76] See section 5.1.8.

the Internal Market and, in particular, the financial regulation Directives,[77] in preference to countries outside the EEA–which lack this framework. Point 3): none; these assumptions apply equally to intra-EEA capital movement restrictions and to such restrictions between the EEA and third countries.

It is difficult to assess how much overestimation of subsidiary index L:TC the specified assumptions have caused. A reasonable position would be some but not much. There is some overestimation because figures 7.24-7.33 show increasing capital flows. There is not much overestimation because the comparison of intra-EEA flows (figures 7.14-7.23) with capital movements to/from third countries (figures 7.24-7.33) shows that the former are greater and tend to increase more than the latter, at least in absolute terms.[78]

Clarification of this issue strengthens the argument made in section 7.1.4 that high/(low) index values tend to be associated with small/(large) capital flows. However, this is a weaker claim than that the former cause the latter. Before any issues of causation can be considered, other factors affecting cross-border capital flows must be discussed.

3. Non-legal factors affecting cross-border capital flows

Section 1.4 and Appendix E consider factors affecting cross-border capital flows. Since some of these are difficult to define and measure, international diversification and cross-border mergers and acquisitions for instance, this review considers the determinants specified in the 'Economic Indicators' section of Appendix E, other than transaction costs.[79] These are the real interest rate,[80] the volatility of nominal interest rates,[81] the inflation rate,[82] the exchange rate against the Euro,[83] and

[77] The Internal Market and the financial regulation Directives are discussed in section 1.2.3 and 2.4 respectively.

[78] See section 7.1.4.

[79] These determinants, except for exchange rates, are represented by the World Bank's World Development Indicators, defined in notes 80-82 and 85-86. Transaction costs are omitted because 1) they are difficult to define, and 2) they vary according to the type of capital flows, and according to the countries and enterprises involved.

[80] This is the lending interest rate (see note 81) adjusted for inflation by the GDP deflator (GDP in current prices / GDP in constant prices, measured in local currency).

[81] The lending interest rate is the bank rate on loans to creditworthy customers. The deposit interest rate is that paid by commercial banks for demand, savings or time deposits. Both interest rates are represented in figures 7.53, 7.58 and 7.63.

[82] This is the annual growth rate of the GDP deflator (see note 80).

against a basket of currencies,[84] and the net barter terms of trade.[85] GDP per capita is included as a control variable.[86]

These factors are plotted against the quarterly change in total foreign liabilities and in total foreign assets respectively,[87] in figures 7.53-7.57 for Estonia, 7.58-7.62 for Poland and 7.63-7.67 for Latvia, together with the net change in capital flows.[88] Comments are made on the graphs.

Estonia

Figure 7.53 shows that the real interest rate is variable, declining, and negative in 2006. The lending interest rate falls in 1999 and 2000, and then reduces slowly. The deposit rate falls gently and then stabilises at 2-3%. The interest rate spread declines with time. The inflation rate decreases from 9%, but returns to over 6%. The kroon/Euro exchange rate is fixed (figure 7.54), whilst Estonia's NEER is rising at a slower rate than that of the Eurozone (figure 7.55). Estonia's net barter terms of trade increases until 2002, and then declines to below the 2000 level (figure 7.56). GDP per capita rises from 1999, even in constant prices (figure 7.57).

---

[83] The average quarterly exchange rate is used (source: Eurostat).

[84] The Bank for International Settlements Nominal Effective Exchange Rate (NEER) is used: the broad index, available at http://www.bis.org/statistics/eer/index.htm. This was chosen for its combination of a double-weighting for exports (the weight includes a term for direct export competition and one for third-market export competition) and its range and balance of countries for Estonian/Polish/Latvian trade–24/(26) from within the EU/(EEA) and 25 third countries (Klau and Fung, *BIS Quarterly Review*, March 2006, 53 and 64). The index is monthly, but March, June, September and December values are plotted in figures 7.55, 7.60 and 7.65.

[85] This is the percentage ratio of the export price index to the import price index relative to 2000 (= 100%).

[86] Two measures of GDP/capita are plotted in figures 7.57, 7.62 and 7.67–Purchasing Power Parity (PPP) GDP in current international dollars, and PPP GDP in constant 2005 international dollars. An international dollar has equal buying power over GDP as a US dollar has in the USA. GDP is converted to international dollars using PPP rates.

[87] These capital flows are compared with legal sub-indices D:I and D:O in figures 7.8-7.13. See section 7.1.3.

[88] Figures 7.53-7.57 lack portfolio investment flows for 1999-2003 and financial derivative flows, and figures 7.58-7.62 omit the latter, as only net data are available. Data for figures 7.63-7.67 are provided in lats and converted to Euros (see note 7).

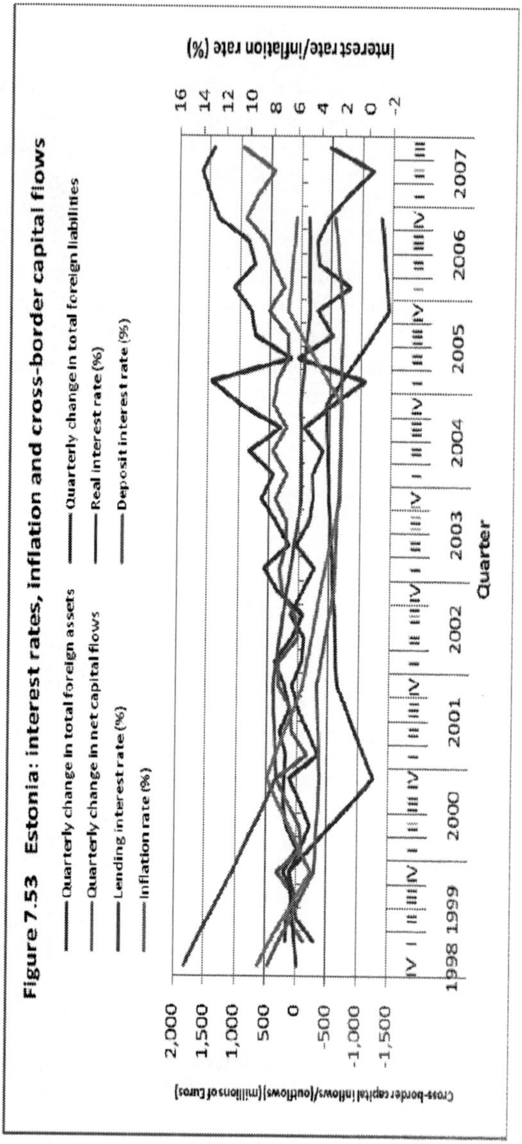

Figure 7.53 Estonia: interest rates, inflation and cross-border capital flows

Figure 7.54 Estonia: kroon/Euro exchange rate and cross-border capital flows

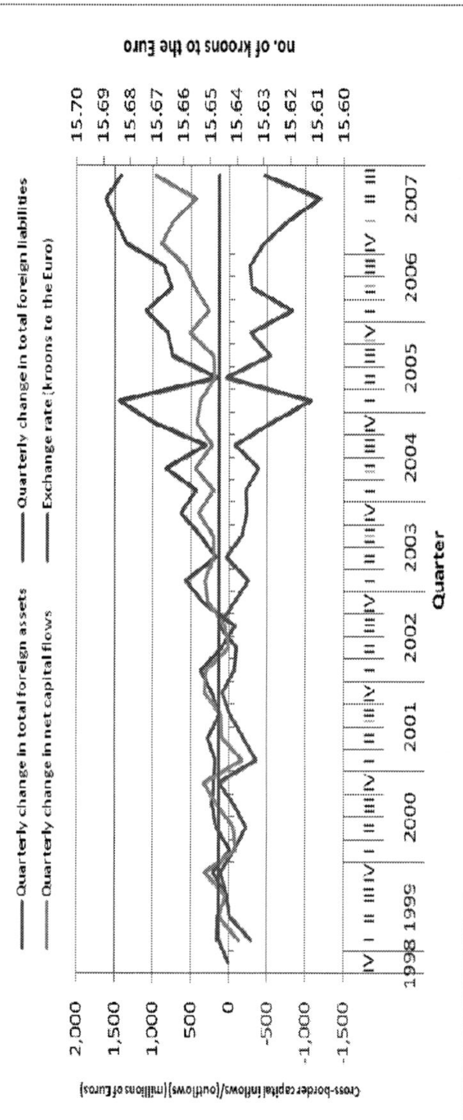

Figure 7.55 Estonia: NEER and cross-border capital flows

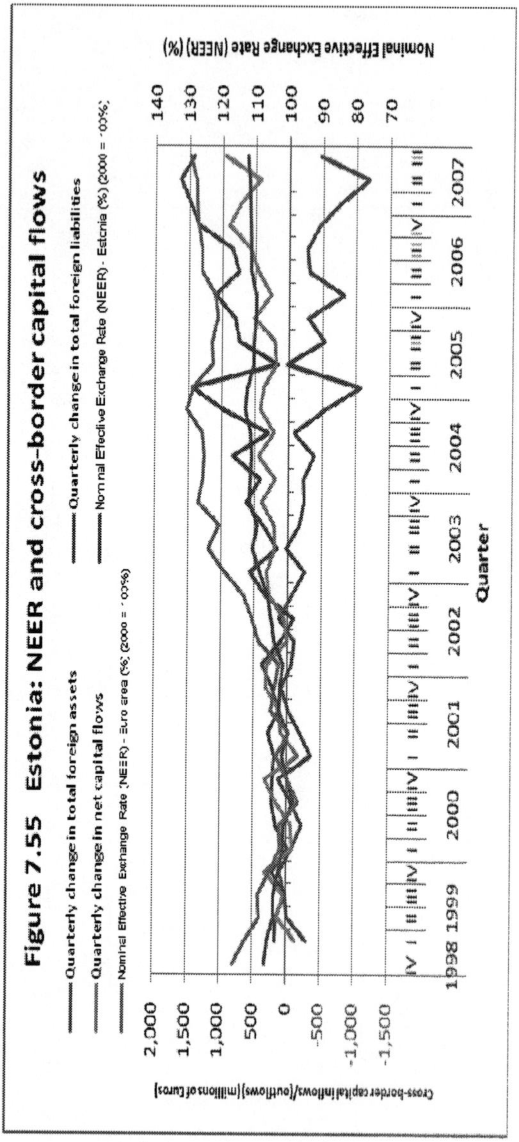

Estonia is a healthy, open economy with increasing capital flows, especially inflows, stable interest rates, a low interest rate spread and rising GDP per capita. The fixed exchange rate and rising NEER encourage investment, especially from the Eurozone, with the pegging of the kroon to the Euro saving foreign exchange transaction costs. However, the volatile, low real interest rate, the variable inflation rate, and the falling terms of trade reduce capital inflows. Inward investment could be increased further by a lower, stable inflation rate and a steady, positive real interest rate.

Figures 7.2 and 7.5 show that the largest decline in Estonia's legal index is in quarter I of 2005, with increasing but variable capital flows from this time. The combination of the low, falling inflation rate, the level, positive real exchange rate, high terms of trade and stable exchange rates from 2002-2004 should induce considerable inward investment during this period. As figures 7.53-7.57 show, however, capital inflows increase more from 2005-2007, once the legal index has fallen, than from 2002-2004. This fact, together with the less favourable conditions for foreign investment in the latter period–negative real interest rates, rising inflation and falling terms of trade, indicates that the reduction of legal barriers to cross-border capital movements may contribute to the rise in inflows. This is confirmed by the profile of subsidiary legal index D:I for capital inflows (figure 7.8).

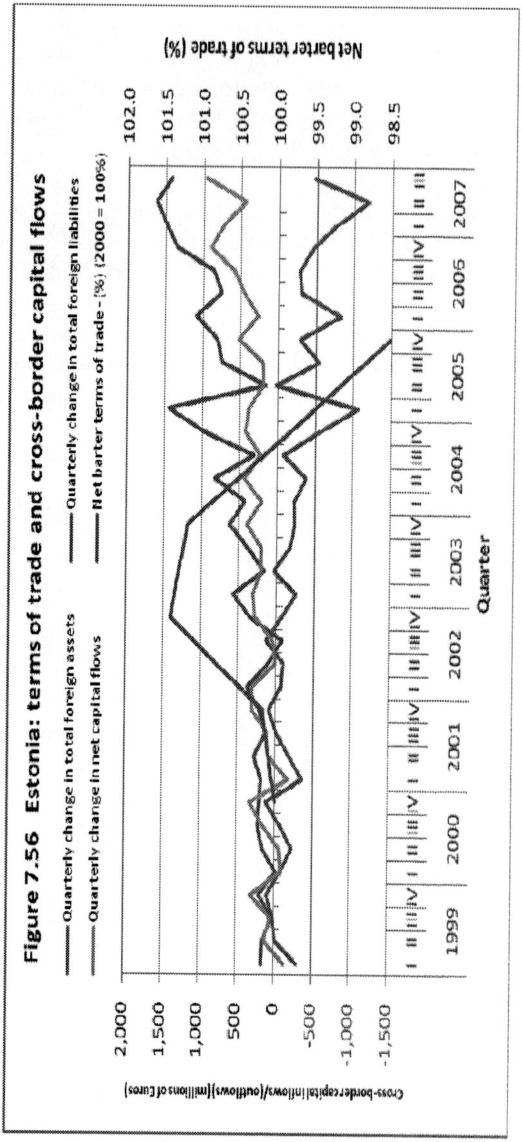

Figure 7.56 Estonia: terms of trade and cross-border capital flows

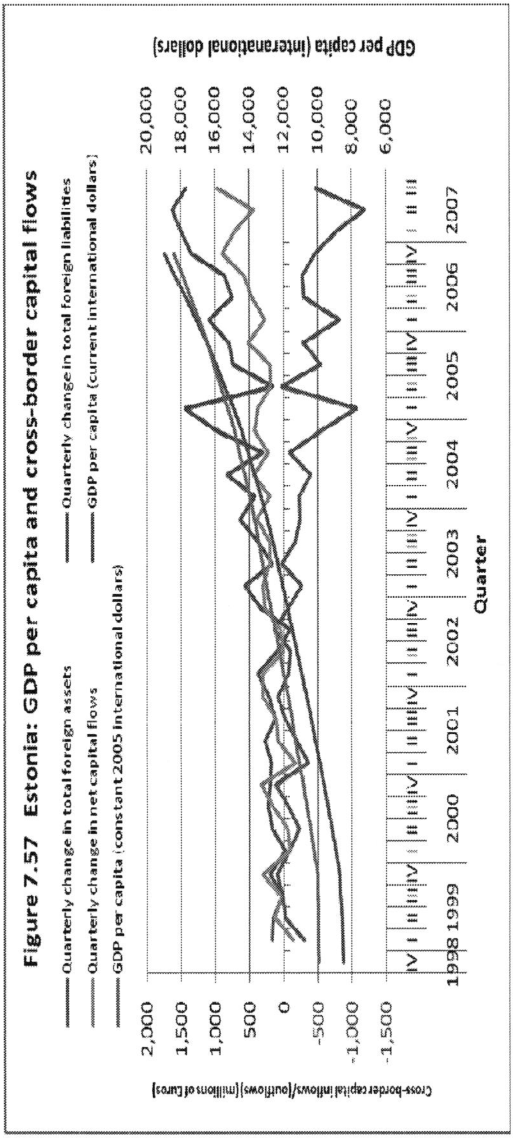
Figure 7.57 Estonia: GDP per capita and cross-border capital flows
Quarterly change in total foreign assets
Quarterly change in total foreign liabilities
Quarterly change in net capital flows
GDP per capita (current international dollars)
GDP per capita (constant 2005 international dollars)
Cross-border capital inflows/(outflows) (millions of Euros)
GDP per capita (international dollars)
Quarter

Poland

In figure 7.58, the real interest rate is positive. It declines from 14% in 2001, settling at 4% in 2005. Interest rates are high in 1999-2001, but then fall and subsequently stabilise with a large spread of 4%. Inflation decreases from 7% to (almost) 0% over three years, and then rises to 4% and falls to 1%. The zloty weakens against the Euro from 1999-2001, and then strengthens by 50% over three years, subsequently returning to 2001 levels by late 2007 (figure 7.59). Poland's NEER moves in the opposite direction to the zloty/Euro exchange rate, declining to 90% of its December 2000 value in early 2004, and then rising to more than 120% of that value (figure 7.60). The net barter terms of trade are volatile, but improve considerably over five years (figure 7.61). Like Estonia, GDP per capita increases from 1999, even in constant prices, but the rise is gentler, with Estonian GDP per capita overtaking Polish GDP per capita in quarter IV of 2001.

The determinants of capital flows in 2001-2003 are mainly conducive to rising capital inflows and falling outflows: an inflation rate declining to low levels, a high (but falling) real interest rate, decreasing nominal interest rates, a rising zloty/Euro exchange rate and improving (but variable) terms of trade. Only the high volatility of the interest rates and the falling NEER over this period are contra-indicators. However, figures 7.58-7.62 show that, although outward investment is small over this period as expected, inward foreign investment is also low during these three years. This contrasts with 2004-2007, during which capital outflows and, especially, inflows increase. Like 2001-2003, this latter period is favourable to capital inflows, with a positive real interest rate, stable nominal interest rates, a low inflation rate, a rising NEER and positive terms of trade (although the zloty/Euro exchange rate is falling).

Figure 7.6 shows that Poland's index for legal restrictions to cross-border capital movements falls during 2004 and 2005. A comparison of figure 7.9 with figure 7.12 shows that subsidiary legal index D:I for barriers to capital inflows falls to a greater extent than sub-index D:O for legal impediments to outflows. The timing of the reduction in both subsidiary indices is compatible with the substantial rise in outward investment and, in particular, inward investment, during 2006-2007. It is possible that the favourable economic climate to capital inflows, described above, is unable to induce substantial inward investment until the legal restrictions to such inflows, represented by sub-index D:I, are reduced. Similarly, although the economic conditions in Poland are less favourable to capital outflows during 2001-2007 than to inflows, the fall in sub-index D:O may be material to the larger outward capital movements from 2004.

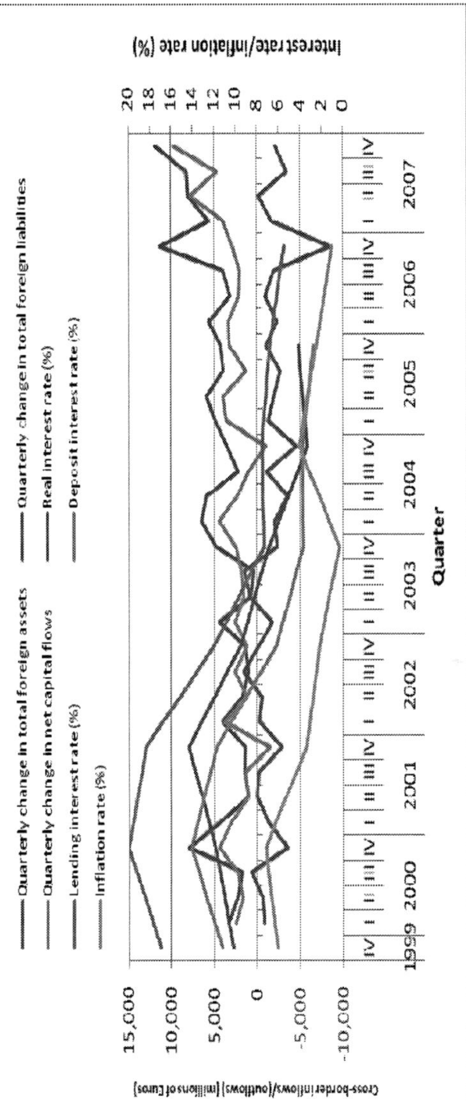

Figure 7.58 Poland: interest rates, inflation and cross-border capital flows

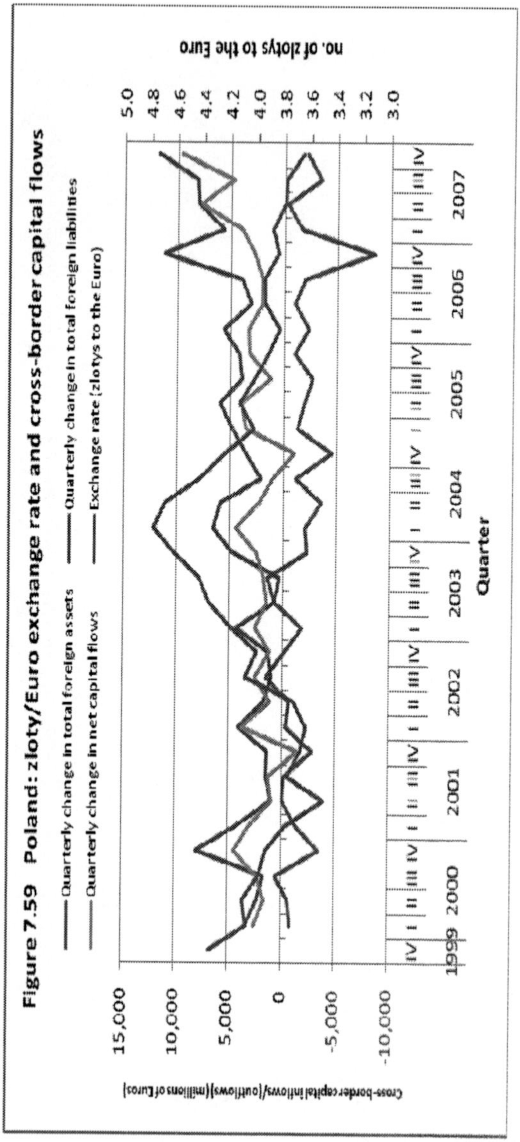

Figure 7.59 Poland: zloty/Euro exchange rate and cross-border capital flows

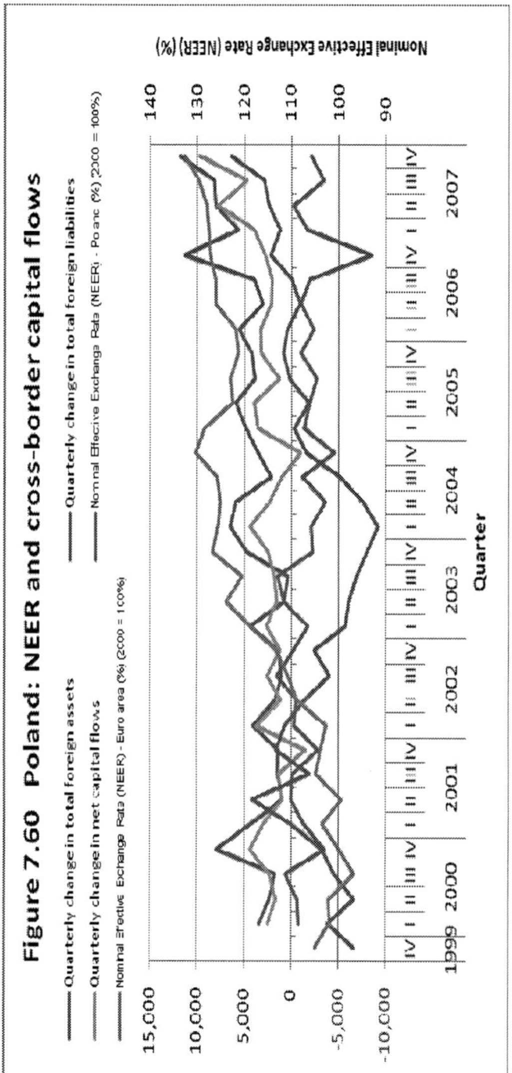

Figure 7.60 Poland: NEER and cross-border capital flows

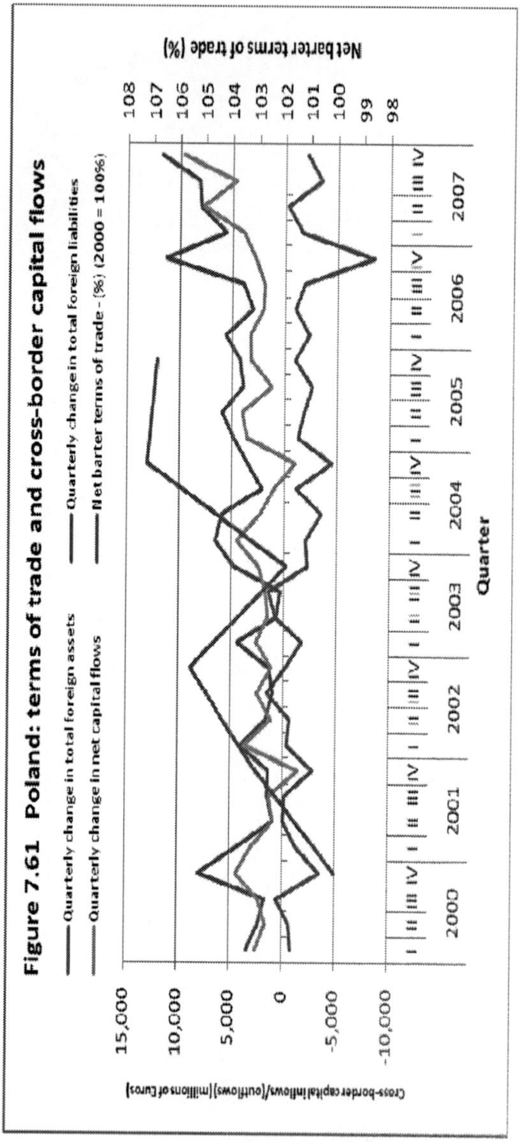

Figure 7.61 Poland: terms of trade and cross-border capital flows

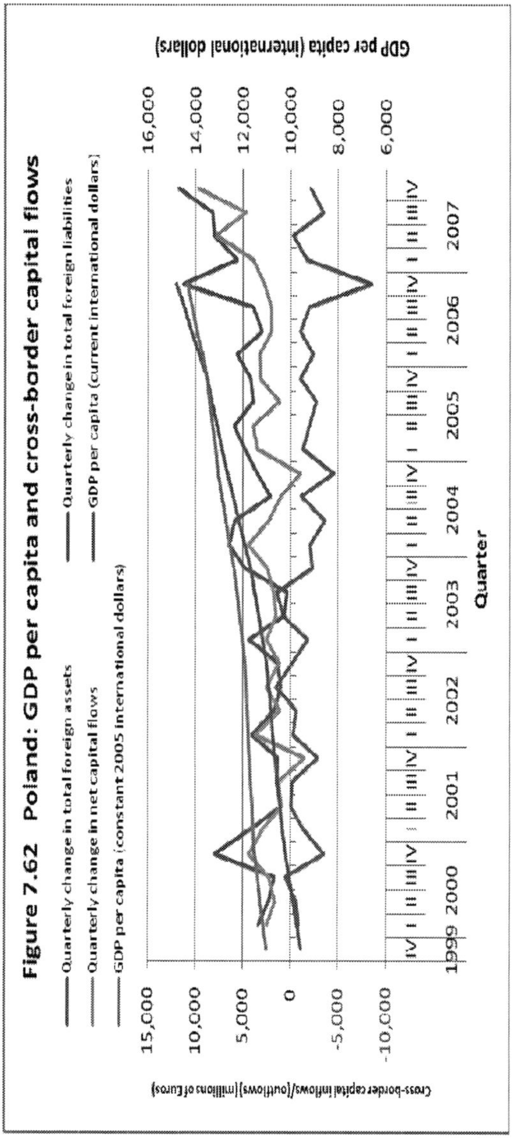
Figure 7.62 Poland: GDP per capita and cross-border capital flows
Quarterly change in total foreign assets
Quarterly change in total foreign liabilities
Quarterly change in net capital flows
GDP per capita (current international dollars)
GDP per capita (constant 2005 international dollars)
Cross-border capital inflows/(outflows) (millions of Euros)
15,000
10,000
5,000
0
-5,000
-10,000
GDP per capita (international dollars)
16,000
14,000
12,000
10,000
8,000
6,000
1999
2000
2001
2002
2003
2004
2005
2006
2007
Quarter

Latvia

Figure 7.63 shows that Latvia's real inflation rate is high from 1998-2001, then falls to -4% in 2005, and remains negative in 2006. The lending interest rate declines from 14% to 7% from 1998-2006, whilst the deposit interest rate decreases gently, causing the interest rate differential to reduce from 9% to 4%. The inflation rate is stable and low until 2003, but then rises to 11% over the next three years. The lat loses 15% of its value against the Euro from 1998-2000, then gains 25% over the next four years, which it subsequently maintains (figure 7.64). The NEER rises until 2000, declines from early 2002 until 2005, and then retains 84% of its December 2000 value (figure 7.65). Latvia's net barter terms of trade rise to 130% of their 2000 value in 2004, and then reduce slightly (figure 7.66). Latvian GDP per capita rises throughout the period, overtaking Polish GDP per capita in early 2006 but remaining below that of Estonia (figure 7.67).

The Latvian economy is growing rapidly, especially since 2004. The actual output may be greater than the potential output, leading to a rise in inflation and a consequent fall in the real interest rate, given that nominal interest rates are stable.[89] The rising capital inflows in 2006-2007 may be contributing to this economic growth, although outflows also increase in these years. Nonetheless, the inflation rate and real interest rate trends are not conducive to stable investments, and may be responsible for some of the capital outflows.[90]

[89] The approximate relationship is (1 + nominal interest rate(%/100%)) = (1 + real interest rate(%/100%)) * (1 + expected inflation rate(%/100%). Since both the real interest rate and the inflation rate are calculated using the GDP deflator (see notes 80 and 82), this relationship holds for these statistics.

[90] As stated in section 7.1.4, low GDP per capita may have inhibited Latvian investment abroad. However, rapid GDP per capita rises from 2004 may have made more funds available for such investment.

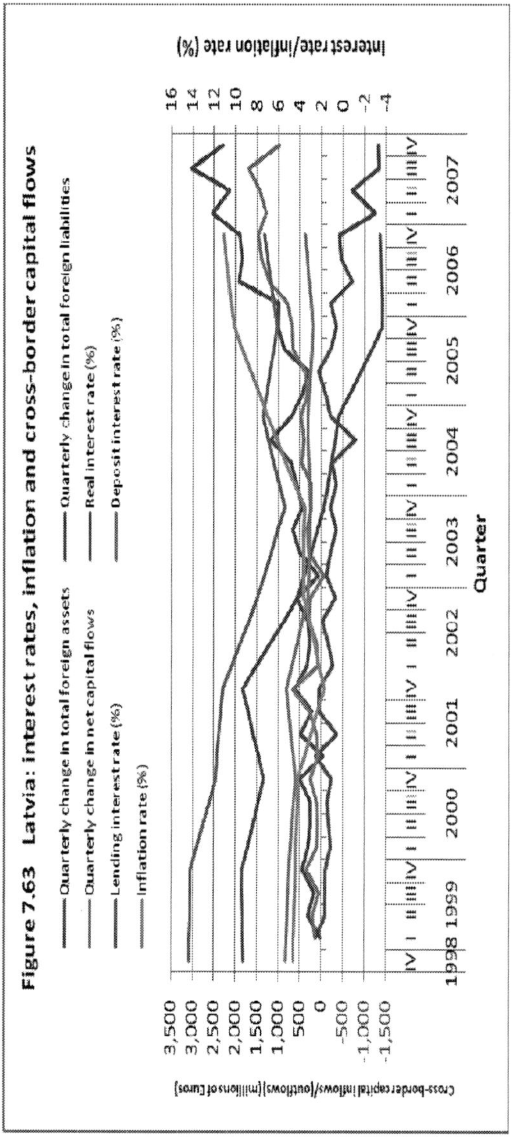

Figure 7.63 Latvia: interest rates, inflation and cross-border capital flows

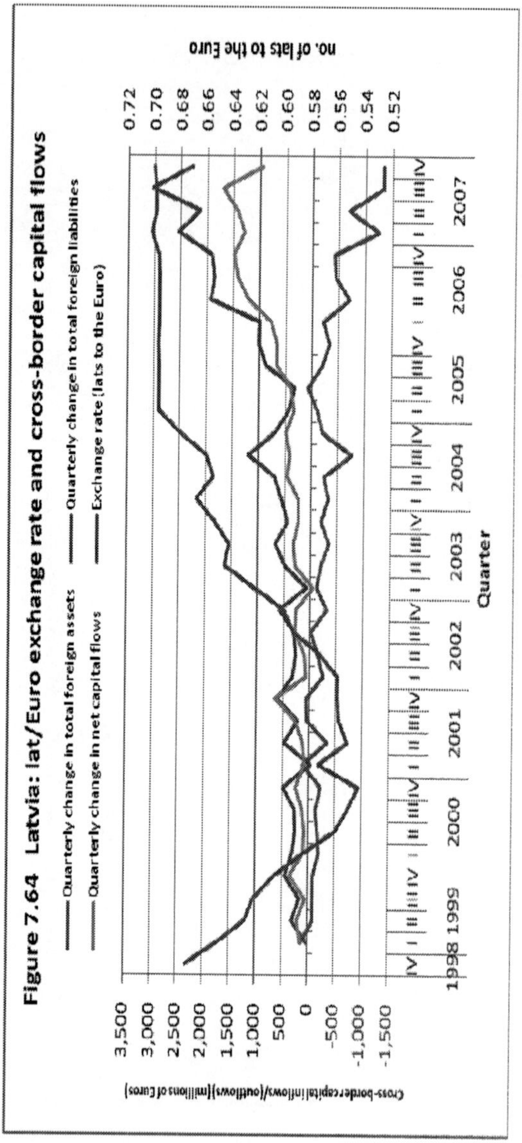

Figure 7.64 Latvia: lat/Euro exchange rate and cross-border capital flows

Figure 7.65 Latvia: NEER and cross-border capital flows

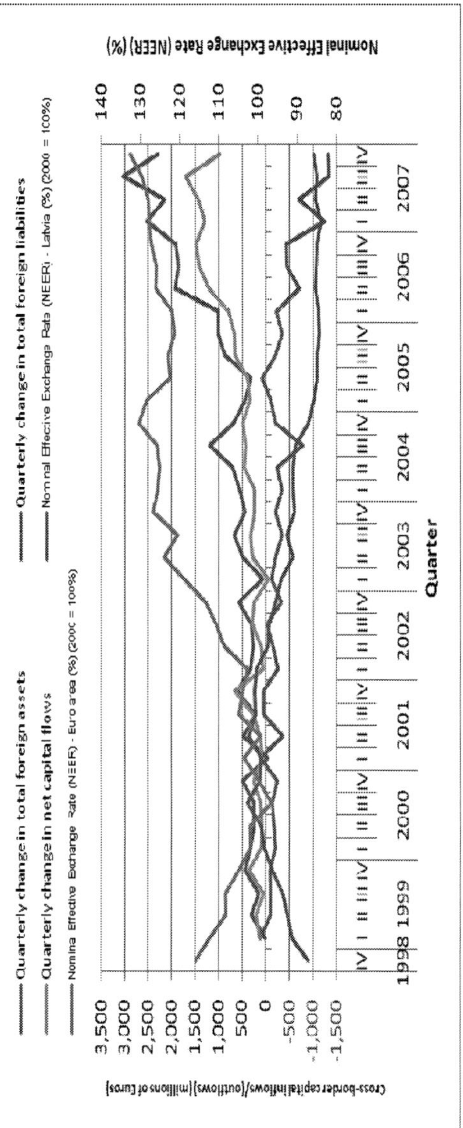

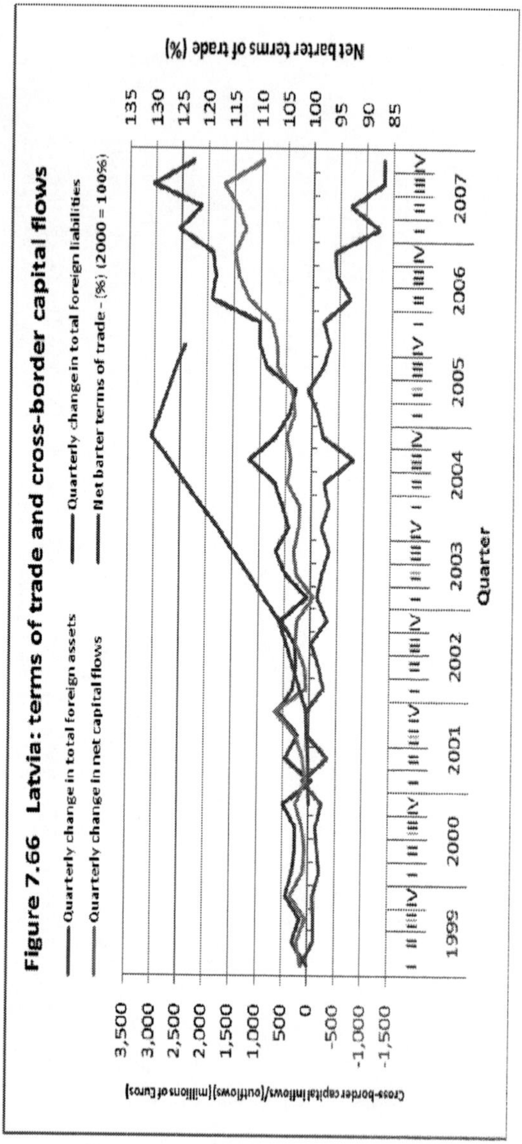

Figure 7.66 Latvia: terms of trade and cross-border capital flows

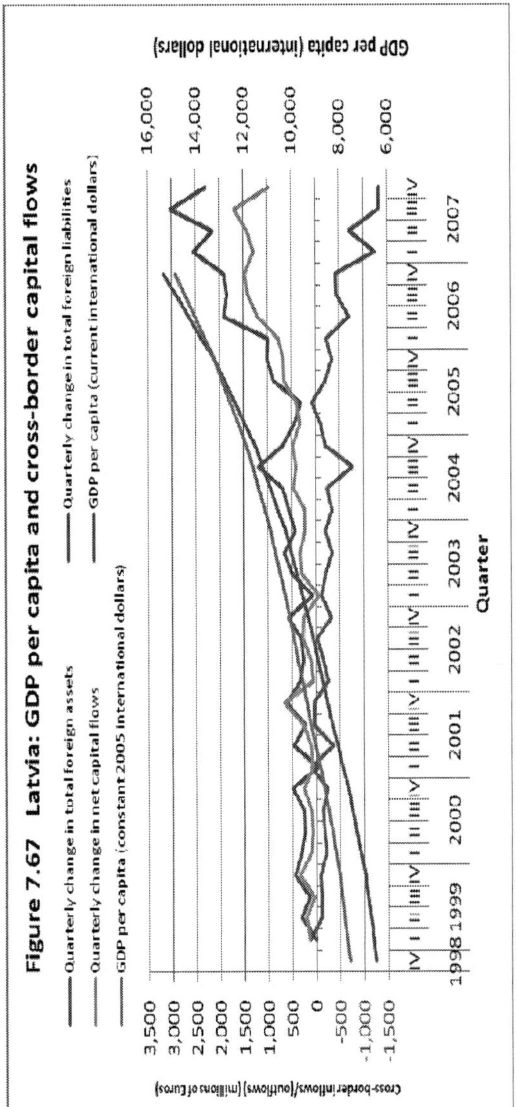

Figure 7.67 Latvia: GDP per capita and cross-border capital flows

The improving net barter terms of trade from 2001-2004 and the rising lat/Euro exchange rate over this period, followed by exchange rate stability, may induce capital inflows. However, the falling real interest rate and NEER, and the rising inflation rate, do not encourage such inward investment. It is surprising that inward capital movements are increasing rapidly in 2006 and 2007, given the level of inflation and real interest rates.

Figure 7.4 shows that the Latvian legal index decreases gradually from 2000-2005. A comparison of figure 7.10 with 7.13 reveals that subsidiary index D:I falls more than sub-index D:O, indicating that legal barriers to inward capital movements are reduced more than those to outward flows. Both these indices are at their lowest in 2006-2007, when cross-border capital flows are increasing.

Legal barriers may be responsible for preventing greater inward investment before 2004, when the economic conditions in Latvia were favourable: low, stable inflation rates, a positive real interest rate and a rising lat/Euro exchange rate. However, legal restrictions are unlikely to have inhibited capital outflows substantially, because the economic circumstances became favourable to such movements from 2004 onwards for the above reasons–at which point those restrictions were being removed. Such removal may have facilitated the rising outward investment in 2006 and 2007.

4. Conclusion

Section 7.1 has compared the legal index and its subsidiary indices, measuring restrictions to cross-border capital movements, with capital flows data for Estonia, Poland and Latvia. To a large extent, the indices are inversely related to the corresponding flows, as expected. The final part of the analysis has considered three issues complementary to it: statistical data inconsistency, possible causes of overestimation of subsidiary index L:TC, and non-legal determinants of cross-border capital flows. The next step is to examine the views of organisations in the sectors most affected by the legal restrictions, in their response to the validation study questionnaire.

7.2 Validation Study Report

7.2.1 Results

The 38 validation study questionnaires returned are analysed by industrial sector.[91] These sectors are investment fund management companies, investment services providers, credit institutions, insurance services providers, insurance intermediaries and real property companies. The categories correspond to the classification in sections 6.1 and 7.1.5.

15 executives state that the free movement of capital is an issue for their business. 23 directors hold the opposite view. Only investment service providers and credit institutions give a majority of affirmative answers.

9 directors agree that national law in his/her business sector causes a significant restriction on cross-border capital flows. The other 29 executives disagree. The latter category includes more organisations from every sector than the former group.

Executives from Estonia, Poland and Latvia say that national law does not significantly restrict cross-border capital flows, enabling freedom to borrow, lend and invest outside state borders. Two replies state that international taxation is a problem; one specifies this in relation to cross-border mergers. Two responses in different sectors refer to limitations imposed by the national authorities. One insurance company mentions investment restrictions, and a property company identifies limitations on funds transferred between Poland and third countries. One bank states that barriers to cross-border capital flows have been significantly reduced due to increased cooperation among regulators, multijurisdictional agreements such as for underwriting shares and loans, and harmonisation of the regulatory framework.

Steps suggested for business-specific improvements in cross-border capital movements include 1) harmonisation of national laws and/or a supranational regulatory framework (4 replies, 3 of these from insurance

---

[91] See section 1.5.1 for methodological issues relating to the study, and for the profile of returns. The questionnaire and covering letter sent to organisations in each sector are in Appendix C. The replies from the two major bank headquarters are classified as results from credit institutions. One of these did not provide a sales profile, and one investment fund management company did not specify its sales to other EEA countries, so questions 10 and 11 received 37 and 36 replies respectively. Questions 4 and 5 were not put to property companies because such organisations are not affected by the EU financial regulation Directives (see note 92); consequently, there were 36 replies to these questions.

firms), 2) EU/third country cooperation agreements on the free movement of capital, especially with Russia and Ukraine (2 replies, both from Latvia), 3) taxation simplification and/or harmonisation (2 replies), and five single responses.

10 executives state that the EU's regulatory framework strongly encourages them to provide services to other EEA countries.[92] There are organisations from all sectors in this category,[93] and 3 of the 4 investment services providers. 14 respondents find the regulatory framework mildly encouraging to provide cross-border services within the EEA, including 7 of the 11 credit institutions. 11 directors state that the framework neither encourages nor dissuades them from supplying such services, and 1 executive is mildly dissuaded by it. This is a positive cross-sector endorsement of the EU's single passport regime for the free movement of services.[94]

7 respondents, at least one from each sector,[95] are strongly encouraged by the EU's regulatory framework to establish branches in other EEA states; 10 are mildly encouraged, including 7 of the credit institutions. 17 executives are neither encouraged nor dissuaded from founding such branches, including 7 of the 11 insurance service providers. 2 directors are mildly dissuaded by the framework from establishing branches in other EEA countries. This response indicates approval of the EU's single passport regime for the freedom of establishment,[96] but with less enthusiasm than for the free movement of services (credit institutions excepted).

26 and 22 respectively of the 38 respondents are neither encouraged nor dissuaded by national law from providing cross-border services to, and from establishing branches in, other EEA states. 8 and 10 respectively are encouraged, and 4 and 6 respectively are dissuaded, from supplying such services and from opening such branches. Although these results show that respondents are, in general, indifferent to the effect of national law on the free movement of services and the freedom of establishment within the

---

[92] This framework includes Directives 2004/39/EC for investment firms, 2006/48/EC for credit institutions, 73/239/EEC, 88/357/EEC and 92/49/EEC for non-life insurance undertakings, 2002/83/EC for life assurance companies and 2002/92/EC for insurance intermediaries. See section 2.4.

[93] This excludes property companies. See note 91.

[94] See section 2.4.

[95] See note 93.

[96] See section 2.4.

EEA, credit institutions are more positive–especially to the effect of national provisions on the founding of branches in other EEA countries.[97]

1 respondent is strongly encouraged, 19 are neither encouraged nor dissuaded and 5 are strongly dissuaded by national law from providing cross-border services to, and from establishing branches in, countries outside the EEA. 4 and 3 respectively are mildly encouraged, and 9 and 10 respectively are mildly dissuaded, from supplying such services and from opening such branches. These results show that, with few exceptions, respondents are either indifferent to the effect of national law on the free movement of services to, and freedom of establishment in, third countries, or are discouraged by these provisions. Executives from insurance service providers and from investment fund management companies tend to reply more negatively than respondents from the other sectors.

30 out of 37 organisations derive less than 10% of their sales from non-EEA states,[98] including all of the investment service providers, insurance service providers and insurance intermediaries. No company makes more than 50% of its sales in or from third countries.

18 out of 36 enterprises earn less than 10% of their turnover from other EEA states.[99] All sectors are represented in this category in similar proportions, ranging from 2 out of 5 investment fund management companies to 6 from 11 insurance service providers. The 10%-20%, 30%-40%, 50%-60% and >70% categories contain 5, 3, 4, and 6 respondents respectively; the other divisions comprise none. Four sectors are represented in the last category. Insurance intermediaries rely strongly on domestic revenues: all four companies make more than 70% of their sales from the country of residence.

In the further comments section, two respondents refer to their business as being part of a large, international group; one of these specifies that the views expressed are those of the national unit. Two credit institutions and one investment fund management company mention other factors that affect the provision of cross-border services and the establishment of foreign branches. These are 1) the size and growth rate of a particular economy, 2) the fact that some Polish banks are controlled by foreign credit institutions means that these institutions and their investors influence capital flows, and 3) national laws in other Member

---

[97] The profile of credit institutions for the effect of national law on branch establishment in other EEA states is: strongly encourage 2, mildly encourage 4, neither encourage nor dissuade 4, mildly dissuade 1, strongly dissuade 0.

[98] The reason for the receipt of only 37 replies is explained in note 91.

[99] The reason for the receipt of only 36 replies is explained in note 91.

States discourage the provision of investment services to those countries: specific areas mentioned are employment, marketing and taxation.

In general, the respondent executives state that national law does not significantly restrict cross-border capital flows in their business sector. They are favourable to the EU's regulatory framework, both for the free movement of services and the freedom of establishment. They are neither encouraged nor dissuaded by national law to provide cross-border services to, and to establish branches in, other EEA states. However, several respondents are dissuaded by domestic law from supplying services to, and from opening branches in third countries.

The sales percentages reflect this information. Most organisations derive less than 10% of their turnover from countries outside the EEA, including all the companies in the investment services, insurance services and insurance mediation sectors. Half of the respondent enterprises make less than 10% of their sales in or from other EEA states; however, more than one quarter of such respondents derive more than 50% of their sales from those countries.

7.2.2 Comment

The picture portrayed by the organisations is, at first glance, one favourable to cross-border capital movement, close to that of Article 56(1) of the EC Treaty.[100] In particular, the majority of the respondent executives state that national law does not significantly limit cross-border capital flows in the sector in which their business is placed, and most of them are indifferent to the effect of national law on the free movement of services and the freedom of establishment within the EEA.

However, some of the doubts expressed, especially for the supply of services to third countries, endorse the main observation from the legal analysis, which is that the national legislation allows more capital movement between Member States than between these States and third countries.[101] Furthermore, the variety of the executives' opinions on the effect of national law on the free movement of services and the freedom of establishment, both within the EEA and to third countries, is compatible with the findings in chapters 3-5 that there are a number of national restrictions to the free movement of capital to and from Estonia, Poland and Latvia, particularly in relation to countries outside the EEA.

---

[100] See section 2.1.

[101] See the subsection '*Comment*' in section 5.1.8.

A minority of the executives are unfamiliar with the specific national legal rules about which they are asked. The clearest cases are sections 29(5) and 151(5) of the EIAA.[102] Section 29(5) states: "Estonian insurance undertakings shall not engage in cross-border insurance activities in third countries." Section 151(1) reads: "Estonia shall not engage in cross-border mediation in a third country."

Question 8 asks Estonian insurance service providers/insurance intermediaries: 'To what extent does national law encourage or dissuade you from providing insurance services/mediation to countries outside the EEA?', to which the informed answer is 'strongly dissuade' for those insurance entities wishing to provide their services to such countries. Of the 5 Estonian insurance companies, 2 give that reply and the other 3 select 'neither encourage nor dissuade'. The 3 Estonian insurance intermediaries choose 'strongly dissuade', 'mildly dissuade' and 'strongly encourage'. Only 3 of these 8 organisations appear to be familiar with the relevant national legal provision.[103] The other 5 may not have considered the issue of supplying insurance services/mediation to third countries.[104]

A related issue is that of non-reply to the questionnaire. The overall response rate is 7.2%. This comprises 5.3% for the first batch of English questionnaires and 9.2% for the second set of Estonian, Polish and Latvian questionnaires.[105] This is excellent for a group of organisations whose respondent executive, in 23 instances from 38, did not consider the free movement of capital an issue for his/her business.[106]

Nonetheless, the questionnaire recipients in the lowest response sectors–insurance intermediaries and real property companies–may have been so adamant about the insignificance and/or irrelevance of cross-border capital movements that the cost of answering the questionnaire exceeded the benefit. Insurance intermediaries may have considered the

---

[102] See the subsections '*Chapter 2 Division 2: activities of Estonian insurance undertakings abroad*' and '*Chapter 10 Division 6: Estonian intermediaries in foreign countries*', respectively, in section 3.1.5. Section 1.3.1 uses s.29(5) of the EIAA as its methodological example because this provision is unequivocal.

[103] The 3 insurance firms that select 'neither encourage nor dissuade' may be aware of section 29(5) of the EIAA, whilst having no intention of providing cross-border insurance services to states outside the EEA.

[104] None of these enterprises have breached either section 29(5) or section 151(5) of the EIAA. All of them report 0%-10% sales arising from outside the EEA. Difficulty in understanding the English questionnaire is not the reason for the unexpected responses: 7 of the 8 executives completed the Estonian questionnaire.

[105] Section 1.5.1 considers the spread of the questionnaire returns.

[106] See section 7.2.1.

questionnaire irrelevant because they have no international business;[107] three of the four who replied were all directors of Estonian insurance brokerage firms–the larger type of intermediary from the smallest of the three Member States,[108] each such firm with a majority of domestic sales.[109] The directors of real property companies may have found the questionnaire insignificant because, as legal subsidiary index S:L shows,[110] there are few legal restrictions to cross-border capital movements in this sector.

Section 7.1.5 proposes that the unresponsiveness of cross-border capital movements to the fall in the subsidiary legal index in the insurance services and insurance mediation sectors may be due to companies in these sectors having mainly domestic business,[111] and that the increase in financial intermediation investment flows following a decrease in sub-indices S:CI, S:InsS and S:InsM relates more to the fall in S:CI than in the reduction in the latter indices.[112] Whilst all of the insurance service providers and insurance intermediaries derive less than 10% of their sales from third countries, 2 of the 10 credit institutions make more than 30% of their sales from that source.[113] Furthermore, while 7 of the 11 insurance service providers and all of the insurance intermediaries make less than 20% of their turnover from other EEA states, only 6 out of 10 credit institutions derive less than 20% of their sales from those countries.

These figures indicate that credit institutions tend to make a greater proportion of foreign sales than insurance service providers, and a much larger percentage of such sales than insurance intermediaries. This supports the above proposition concerning S:CI, S:InsS and S:InsM because the removal of the legal barriers to cross-border capital movements enables the flows associated with foreign sales to take place–these flows being proportionately larger for banks than for insurance traders. However, whilst it is true that insurance intermediaries have mostly domestic business, some insurance companies provide a substantial quantity of insurance services to other EEA states. One would therefore

[107] In section 7.1.5, the lack of insurance service and insurance mediation provision to foreigners is proposed as a reason for cross-border capital flows being unaffected by the removal of legal barriers in these sectors.
[108] Insurance agents are the smaller class of insurance intermediary.
[109] See section 7.2.1.
[110] See table 6.2 and/or figure A.11 (in Appendix A).
[111] See figures 7.44-7.46.
[112] See figures 7.38, 7.40 and 7.43.
[113] There are 11 respondent credit institutions, but one has not provided its sales profile (see note 91).

expect a rise in cross-border capital flows after legal sub-index S:InsS has fallen.

Other possible explanations for the unexpected unresponsiveness of capital flows to the reduction in S:InsS in figures 7.44-7.46 are 1) the respondent insurance service providers are not typical of the population of insurance service providers from Estonia, Poland and Latvia in that they proportionately make more sales to other EEA states than the rest of that population do; 2) there is a time lag between the decrease in legal restrictions to cross-border capital movements in the insurance services sector and the expected rise in insurance services–this is consistent with figure 7.46 (Latvia) and with insurance services exports in figure 7.44 (Estonia); 3) there are non-legal sector-specific factors preventing cross-border capital flows from increasing in the insurance services sector after the legal restrictions have been removed.

In addition, the 2007 value of sub-index S:InsS is high for Estonia (1.83) and Latvia (2.00), and is the highest amongst all of the Polish sectors (2.17).[114] As figure A.8 shows, this subsidiary index has not fallen greatly either in absolute terms or in comparison with the other sectoral subsidiary indices.[115] It is therefore proposed that, especially for Poland, cross-border capital flows in the insurance services sector have not risen in response to the removal of legal barriers because substantial restrictions remain in place.

In summary, the responses to the validation study questionnaire confirm the main results from the research in chapters 3, 4 and 5, which are that there are national legal restrictions to the free movement of capital to/from Estonia, Poland and Latvia, especially in relation to countries outside the EEA. Many of the respondent executives do not consider the free movement of capital across national borders an issue for their business, and most of them state that domestic law in the industrial sector in which their organisation is placed does not cause a significant restriction to cross-border capital flows. Nonetheless, there is a full range of responses to the four questions investigating the effect of national law on the provision of services to foreigners, which peaks in the 'neither encourage or dissuade' category but shows substantial negative skew to the 'mildly/strongly dissuade' classes for the supply of services to third countries. An example from Estonian law shows that a small number of replies are unreliable.

---

[114] See table 6.2.

[115] See figures A.5-A.11 (in Appendix A).

7.2.3 Conclusions

The analysis presented in this chapter establishes an inverse relationship between the legal index, representing national legislative and regulatory restrictions to cross-border capital movements, and the capital flows between Estonia/Poland/Latvia and other countries. This relationship holds for inflows and outflows,[116] for intra-EEA capital movements and flows to/from third countries,[117] and for the business sectors other than insurance services and insurance mediation.[118] An explanation for the insurance services/mediation anomaly is given in the light of the validation survey results.[119]

Section 7.1.6 considers non-legal determinants of cross-border capital flows for Estonia, Poland and Latvia. For all three Member States, legal barriers may have restricted cross-border capital flows. This is particularly evident for inward investment because economic conditions are favourable to such flows in the years preceding the lowering of legal restrictions, yet rising capital inflows follow the removal of these limits.

Section 7.1.6 also addresses the concern raised in section 7.1.4 that capital movements to third countries increase even though the subsidiary index measuring legal restrictions to such flows, L:TC, does not fall greatly. It identifies assumptions that may have caused L:TC to be overestimated. The problem, encountered in chapters 3, 4, and 5 and identified as a general research result in section 5.1.8, is that Estonia, Poland and Latvia have made legislative omissions, especially in relation to third countries.

The low sales figures of validation study survey respondents to countries outside the EEA,[120] their varied but predominantly negative response to the contribution of national law to the provision of services to these states,[121] and comments made by Latvian executives on the need for cooperation agreements between the EU and other countries on the free movement of capital,[122] indicate that there is a considerable area of uncertainty concerning the regulation of capital movements between Estonia/Poland/Latvia and third countries. The eminent jurist Professor H.L.A. Hart states

---

116 See section 7.1.3.
117 See section 7.1.4.
118 See section 7.1.5.
119 See section 7.2.2.
120 See section 7.2.1.
121 See section 7.2.2.
122 See section 7.2.1.

> "[A]t the margin of rules and in the fields left open by the theory of precedents, the courts perform a rule-producing function which administrative bodies perform centrally in the elaboration of variable standards".[123]

Cases considering the movement of capital to and from third countries would put national courts to a stiff production test.

This chapter completes the investigation as to the impact of Estonian, Polish and Latvian law on the free movement of capital. There remains the need to ascertain what the research has achieved and to assess how it may be developed. Chapter 8 makes conclusions and suggestions for further study.

[123] H.L.A. Hart (1961), *The Concept of Law,* 132.

CHAPTER EIGHT

SUGGESTIONS FOR REFORM AND FOR RESEARCH

> "Lateral thinking is concerned with changing patterns. Instead of taking a pattern and then developing it as is done in vertical thinking, lateral thinking tries to restructure the pattern by putting things together in a different way. Because the sequence of arrival of information in a self-maximising system has so powerful an influence on the way it is arranged some sort of restructuring of patterns is necessary in order to make the best use of the information imprisoned within them." [1]

Chapters 2-7 follow a sequential process, from the discovery of EU law on the free movement of capital through to comparison of national legal restrictions to such movement with cross-border flows. This is vertical thinking as described above. By contrast, chapter 8 employs lateral thinking.

Section 8.1 describes the position reached by the research. This summary restructures the earlier conclusions because it describes them from the perspective of completed practical work. It is an input to sections 8.3 and 8.4, which consider possible future directions for legal and economic studies respectively. These sections also involve restructuring of the information in the book, extending and adapting it in ways that may be feasible in terms of time and resources.

Section 8.2 converts the legal observations made in chapters 3, 4 and 5 to suggestions for reform. Section 8.5 comments on issues raised in the previous sections of chapter 8.

8.1 What Point has been Reached?

For Estonia, Poland and Latvia, there are several national legal provisions that breach Article 56 of the EC Treaty, which prohibits limitations on the movement of capital and on payments between Member

[1] E. De Bono (1977), *Lateral Thinking*, 48.

States and also between such States and third countries. A substantial number of these laws concern similar flows for each of these countries. This enables a functional cross-country comparison of national restrictions to cross-border capital movement to be made.[2]

Estonian law tends to be prescriptive, giving the Estonian FSA considerable discretion in making decisions relating to the provision of services in Estonia by non-Estonians, and in other countries by Estonians. This feature of the Estonian financial regulatory laws renders these Acts similar to one another in presentation and, to an extent, in content.

By contrast, Polish and Latvian legislation and regulations tend to be descriptive, with many detailed and differing provisions both in form and in content. Consequently, these laws are often difficult to understand and assess as to their impact on cross-border capital movement. These legal drafting patterns work through into the length of the chapters, with that on Latvia being the longest,[3] and the Estonian chapter the shortest but one.[4]

There are more legal restrictions to the movement of capital between EEA states and third countries than there are between countries within the EEA. Two explanations for this observation are proposed in section 5.1.8, namely 1) the main trading partners of Estonia, Poland and Latvia are Member States, which induces the governments of the former to reduce restrictions to cross-border capital flows within the EU, and 2) the national legislation transposing the financial regulation Directives facilitates capital movement between Member States.

The results to the validation study verify that the three countries studied trade more extensively with other EEA states than with third countries.[5] However, it is likely, given the short time between the start of negotiations for EU Membership and the date of accession to the Community,[6] that the lower level of restriction to cross-border capital movements within the EEA than between Estonia/Poland/Latvia and third countries is due to the adoption of the financial regulation Directives and

---

[2] Sections 4.1.7, 4.3.3 and 4.4.2 compare Estonian and Polish financial services, taxation and real property laws respectively. Sections 5.1.8, 5.3.3 and 5.4.6 compare Estonian, Polish and Latvian laws over these respective subjects.

[3] Chapter 5 has the highest word count, but chapter 7 extends to more pages than chapter 5.

[4] The length and content of sections 8.2.1, 8.2.2 and 8.2.3 also reflect the prescriptive/descriptive of the national laws (as indicated in the introduction to section 8.2).

[5] See section 7.2.1.

[6] This period is approximately 6 years for Estonia and Poland, and 4 years for Latvia; see the introduction to chapter 5, especially note 2.

transitional measures on the purchase of real estate rather than to Community-mindedness on the part of national Trade Departments.[7]

A cautionary note is the observation made in section 5.1.8 and re-emphasised in section 7.1.4, that there are many legal omissions concerning capital movements between the three Member States studied and third countries, especially with respect to cross-border services. Nonetheless, the national laws that are in place for the regulation of such movements between these States and third countries tend to be more restrictive of the free movement of capital than the domestic rules that govern cross-border flows within the EU.

The functional comparison of Estonian, Polish and Latvian legal restrictions to the free movement of capital is used to construct a legal index, which is subdivided into subsidiary indices according to the direction and location of capital flows and to the business sectors affected by those restrictions.[8] The index reveals that Estonian and Polish legislation and regulations limit cross-border capital flows to a similar extent, and that Latvian law impedes such flows by a larger margin.[9] The subsidiary indices display much variation within this general result.[10] For instance, Poland has the greatest degree of legal restrictions on cross-border capital movement to and from third countries but the lowest level of legal limitations on such flows within the EEA.

The graphs of the subsidiary legal indices and their corresponding cross-border capital movements show that, in general, there is a strong, positive correlation between the level of restriction to these flows and the flows themselves.[11] In the context of economic determinants of capital flows for Estonia, Poland and Latvia, it is possible, and may be probable, that the national legal restrictions to the free movement of capital adversely affect cross-border flows.[12] It must be stressed, however, that causation can run bidirectionally and that other factors may be involved in the relationship between laws and flows. An econometric analysis may provide further insights into this relationship.[13]

The validation study ascertains the views of executives in the business sectors most affected by the national legal restrictions to the free

[7] See section 2.5.
[8] See section 6.1.
[9] See table 6.1.
[10] See table 6.2.
[11] See section 7.1.
[12] See section 7.1.6.
[13] This is considered further in section 8.4.2.

movement of capital.[14] Whilst these questionnaire respondents tend not to consider the free movement of capital a major issue for their business, their views on these restrictions, in general, coincide with the main results from the substantial analysis, thereby reinforcing the value of the research.[15] In particular, these executives tend to show a neutral response to national legal limitations to cross-border capital movements within the EEA, and a mildly negative response to domestic legal restrictions on flows to and from third countries.[16] All six business sectors are represented in the replies.

Section 8.2 considers suggestions for reform in the Estonian, Polish and Latvian legislation and regulations, in order to improve their compliance with Article 56 of the EC Treaty and/or the financial regulation Directives.

8.2 What Improvements can be Made?

Chapters 3, 4 and 5 show that Estonian, Polish and Latvian legal provisions restrict the free movement of capital and, in mainly minor ways, contravene the financial regulation Directives.[17] Sections 8.2.1, 8.2.2 and 8.2.3 make recommendations as to how these provisions can be modified to comply with Article 56 of the EC Treaty and with the Directives.

Since the Estonian legislation is mainly prescriptive,[18] the offending clauses are similar throughout the Acts regulated by the FSA.[19] Section 8.2.1 therefore offers a selected treatment from these Acts.

By contrast, the descriptive Polish and Latvian legislation requires a comprehensive treatment for the suggestion of reforms, because the form and content of legal provisions are individual across the constituent Acts. This full analysis renders sections 8.2.2 and 8.2.3 lengthy and detailed.

Section 8.2.4 considers whether the financial regulation Directives restrict the free movement of capital, and gives one example. It recommends what should be done over areas of conflict between these

---

[14] See sections 1.5.1 and 7.2.

[15] See section 7.2.2.

[16] Ibid.

[17] These Directives include 2004/39/EC for investment services, 2006/48/EC for credit institutions, 73/239/EEC, 88/357/EEC, 92/49/EEC and 2002/83/EC for insurance services, and 2002/92/EC for insurance mediation. See section 2.4.

[18] See sections 3.4.2 and 8.1.

[19] This is clear from comparing sections 3.1.1, 3.1.3, 3.1.4 and, to a lesser extent, 3.1.5.

Directives and Article 56 of the EC Treaty. Section 8.2.5 comments on the application of EU law on the free movement of capital to the Estonian, Polish and Latvian legislation and regulations.

8.2.1 Reforms to Estonian laws

Acts regulated by the FSA

The FSA should specify the grounds on which it refuses to permit cross-border service provision to or from countries outside the EEA, and/or to found a branch in those states. For instance, in section 40(2) of the Investment Funds Act 2004 (IFA),[20] the FSA's view of the third country's supervisory authority as having "no legal basis" or that it "does not guarantee sufficient supervision" is not specific and objective, and therefore does not provide legal certainty.[21]

Similarly, the power given by section 233 of the IFA to the FSA to refuse to register an offer of foreign fund units if the foreign supervisory authority is unable to cooperate with the FSA should be more clearly explained in this legislation, in order to ensure that the FSA does not discriminate against foreign fund units, acts proportionately and provides legal certainty to the applicant fund.[22] Sections 40 and 233 of the IFA should both require the FSA to give reasons for its refusal, and should provide a right to appeal against it in the Estonian courts.[23]

Sections 297(8) of the IFA and 236¹(8) of the SMA should define 'public interest', because derogations from the free movement of capital must be based on specific, objective criteria known to the parties beforehand. Furthermore, legal redress (i.e. reasons and the right of appeal in the national courts) should be provided for investment firms whose authorisation is revoked or whose activities are prohibited.[24]

---

[20] See the subsection '*Sections 40 and 42: potential capital movements with authorisation problems*' in section 3.1.1.

[21] The requirements for a derogation from Article 56 of the EC Treaty are summarised in the subsection '*The requirements for a successful public policy/security derogation*' in section 2.1.3. These requirements are generally applicable other than the first; see the subsection '*Comment*' in section 2.1.3. The requirements for real property laws are in section 2.1.4 and for taxation provisions are in section 2.3. Section 8.2.5 discusses the validity of this approach.

[22] See the subsection '*The requirements for a successful public policy/security derogation*' in section 2.1.3, and the subsection '*Sections 229 and 233: capital movements without justification*' in section 3.1.1.

[23] See the subsection '*The requirements for a successful public policy/security derogation*' in section 2.1.3.

[24] Ibid.

Regulation No.73 of the Ministry of Finance of 19 November 1997 should be repealed, since the Ministry of Finance has declared that it has become invalid.[25] Section 65(4)(2) of the SMA, which enables the FSA to refuse to forward information to another EEA state if the firm's resources are insufficient to provide cross-border services there, should be repealed because it is not permitted by Article 31 of Directive 2004/39/EC.[26]

Sections 69(3) and 70(3) of the SMA permit the FSA much discretion in determining the conditions for the establishment of a branch and for the provision of cross-border investment services to Estonia.[27] These conditions include "requirements applicable upon provision of investment services",[28] which should be specified in order to provide legal certainty and in order to comply with Articles 7(2), 31(1) and 32(1) of Directive 2004/39/EC.[29] The "other circumstances considered to be necessary by the Supervision Authority"[30] is a broader phrase than that provided by Article 7(2) of the Directive, which requires the investment firm to provide all information that satisfies the authority that the firm has set up "all the necessary arrangements to meet its obligations" provided by the Directive's authorisation chapter.[31] This condition should therefore be modified to conform to Article 7(2).

Section 20^{1111}(5) of the CIA should specify clearly and objectively, in order to provide legal certainty to credit institutions, what it means by an institution's resources being "insufficient" to provide cross-border services in a foreign state, and what amounts to "damage" to client's interests or the institution's financial circumstances or "trustworthiness".[32] Section 20^{1111} of the CIA should require the FSA to provide reasons for, and should provide the right of appeal in the Estonian courts against, its refusal to forward the name and proposed cross-border services of the institution to the foreign supervision authority and also its issuance of a precept to

---

[25] See chapter 3 note 35.

[26] See section 2.4.1 and the subsection '*Sections 64 and 65: forwarding of information by FSA to Contracting State*' in section 3.1.3.

[27] See the subsection '*Sections 69 and 70: investment services in Estonia*' in section 3.1.3.

[28] ss.69(3)(7) and 70(3), SMA.

[29] See the subsection '*The requirements for a successful public policy/security derogation*' in section 2.1.3, and section 2.4.1.

[30] ss.69(3)(8) and 70(3), SMA.

[31] See section 2.4.1.

[32] See the subsection '*Section 20^{1111}: cross-border services in Contracting States and third countries*' in section 3.1.4.

prohibit the institution from forwarding this information, in order to be a justifiable derogation from Article 56 of the EC Treaty.[33]

In section 21 of the CIA, reference to "foreign" credit institution should be changed to "non-EEA Contracting State" in order to confirm that EEA states are excluded. Inclusion of such States leads to a breach of Directive 2006/48/EC.[34]

To comply with Article 56 of the EC Treaty, the IAA should be modified to permit Estonian insurance companies and intermediaries to provide cross-border services/mediation to countries outside the EEA. This involves widening of the term 'cross-border insurance activities' in section 30(1) of the IAA to include those provided to third countries, and a similar broadening of 'cross-border mediation' in section 151(2) of the IAA. Furthermore, the prohibitions of supplying cross-border insurance activities and practising cross-border mediation to third countries in sections 29(5) and 151(5) of the IAA respectively should be repealed.[35]

Article 56 also requires the IAA to allow insurance firms and intermediaries registered in non-EEA countries to provide cross-border services/mediation to Estonia. The terms 'cross-border insurance activities' in section 42(1) of the IAA and 'cross-border mediation' in section 160(2) of the IAA should be widened to include activities/mediation by an insurance company/intermediary registered in a third country. In addition, sections 41(5) and 160(5) of the IAA, which forbid such a company/ intermediary respectively from providing cross-border insurance activities/ practising cross-border mediation in Estonia, should be repealed.[36]

Authorisation from the FSA of branch establishment by insurance undertakings and intermediaries in Estonia, and by Estonian insurance companies and intermediaries in third countries, presents similar problems to those of the IFA, SMA and CIA, i.e. the third country's financial authority "has no legal basis or possibility to cooperate/for cooperation with" the FSA so that the latter cannot supervise the branch sufficiently,[37] and that the insurance companies resources are "insufficient for engaging

---

[33] See the subsection '*The requirements for a successful public policy/security derogation*' in section 2.1.3.

[34] This is explained in chapter 3 note 73.

[35] See the subsections '*Chapter 2 Division 2: activities of Estonian insurance undertakings abroad*' and '*Chapter 10 Division 6: Estonian intermediaries in foreign countries*' in section 3.1.6.

[36] See the subsections '*Chapter 2 Division 3: activities of foreign insurance undertakings in Estonia*' and '*Chapter 10 Division 7: activities of foreign intermediaries in Estonia*' in section 3.1.6.

[37] ss.33(5), 44(2), 154(6) and 163(6) IAA.

in insurance activities/mediation".[38] These phrases should be defined more specifically in order to provide applicant insurance companies/ intermediaries with legal certainty.[39]

Furthermore, sections 33, 44, 154 and 163 of the IAA should require the FSA to give reasons for refusing authorisation, and should provide a right of appeal in the Estonian courts against such a refusal. The decision to withhold authorisation must be proportionate, and must be necessary to protect the interests that it is intended to guarantee; the FSA should specify what these interests are, for example that the insurance activities/mediation are to be provided at a reasonable quality and cost (perhaps specified by secondary legislation).[40] These changes ensure that the authorisation requirements relating to branch foundation are an acceptable derogation from Article 56 of the EC Treaty.

Section 172(3) of the IAA, which empowers the FSA to issue a precept to counteract situations that endanger an insurance company's or intermediary's activities, insured persons or beneficiaries interests, or the openness of the insurance market,[41] should define these concepts more specifically and objectively in order to offer legal certainty to insurance firms and intermediaries. The IAA should require the FSA to give reasons for issuing a precept, and should provide the right of appeal in the Estonian courts against the decision to issue it.[42]

Section 180 of the IAA, which prescribes a procedure for the breach of Estonian legislation,[43] should transpose paragraph 40(9) of Directive 92/49/EEC, which states that restrictions or penalties on "the conduct of insurance business" must be "properly reasoned". Section 180 should also adopt Article 8(5) of Directive 2002/92/EC, which requires limitations on an insurance intermediary's activities to be "properly justified and communicated" to the intermediary and to be subject to the right of appeal in the courts of the Member State imposing them.[44]

---

[38] ss.33(3), 154(3) and 163(3) IAA. Note also: "the applicant does not have the sufficient facilities or experience to operate as an insurance undertaking with continuity" (s.23(2), IAA).

[39] See the subsection '*The requirements for a successful public policy/security derogation*' in section 2.1.3.

[40] Ibid.

[41] See the subsection '*Sections 172 and 173: precepts*' in section 3.1.5.

[42] See the subsection '*The requirements for a successful public policy/security derogation*' in section 2.1.3.

[43] See the subsection '*Section 180: violation of Estonian legislation*' in section 3.1.5.

[44] Ibid.

Income Tax Act 1999 (ITA)

Under certain conditions,[45] gains from transferring immovable property in Estonia are exempt from income tax for residents but not for non-residents. The situations of residents and non-residents are objectively comparable because both are taxed on income arising in Estonia.[46] None of the defences apply.[47] Therefore, the more favourable treatment of residents than non-residents is a breach of Article 56 of the EC Treaty.[48] The ITA should either make the gains from transferring immovable property in Estonia exempt from income tax for non-residents, or render them subject to income tax for residents.

Sections 20(3), 20(5) and 21(5) of the ITA make certain insurance payments by residents exempt from income tax, whilst non-residents are taxed on these items. Since both residents and non-residents are taxed on their Estonian income, their situations are objectively comparable. None of the defences apply.[49] In order to remedy the breach of Article 56 caused by the more favourable treatment of residents over non-residents,[50] the ITA should either make the insurance payments exempt from income tax for non-residents, or subject to this tax for residents.

If the Estonian tax calculated on income from a foreign country exceeds the income tax paid there, the taxpayer must pay the difference to the Estonian authorities.[51] However, if the former is less than the latter, or if the tax calculated on income from all sources is less than that paid in the foreign state, then the difference is not refunded in Estonia.[52] These are objectively comparable situations with no applicable defences,[53] but Estonian residents are treated differently in each; the discrepancy between them is a "disguised restriction" on the free movement of capital under Article 58(3) of the EC Treaty.[54]

---

45 See chapter 3 note 158.

46 ss.6(1) and 6(3), ITA.

47 These are the need to safeguard the cohesion of the tax system, the fight against tax avoidance and the effectiveness of fiscal supervision: see section 2.3.

48 See the subsection '*Income tax exemptions for residents but not for non-residents*' in section 3.3.1.

49 See note 47.

50 See the subsection '*Income tax exemptions for residents but not for non-residents*' in section 3.3.1.

51 s.45(2), ITA.

52 s.45(3), ITA.

53 See note 47.

54 See the subsection '*Income tax withheld at source by foreign countries (withholding tax)*' in section 3.3.1.

The fairest solution is to equalise the income tax burden between residents receiving foreign income and those acquiring Estonian income. This solution is implemented by modifying section 45(3) of the ITA to state that income tax paid abroad exceeding the Estonian tax assessment on such income is to be refunded by the Estonian tax authorities. The alternative solution is for section 45(2) of the ITA to exempt taxpayers from any excess Estonian income tax due on foreign income taxed at source. Either one of these changes removes the disguised restriction on the movement of capital across borders.[55]

8.2.2 Reforms to Polish laws

Act of 27 May 2004 on Investment Funds (IFA)

The Polish FSC's consent, required by Article 93(2) of the IFA for open-end investment funds to invest in securities and money-market instruments traded on an organised market or purchased in a non-OECD Member country,[56] must be necessary to protect the interests that it is intended to guarantee, and must be based on specific, objective criteria known to the applicants beforehand to provide them with legal certainty.[57] Article 93 IFA should state these interests and criteria, should require the FSC to give reasons for refusing its consent, and should provide a right of appeal in the Polish courts against this refusal, in order to be a justifiable exception to Article 56 of the EC Treaty.

The investment limitations for closed-end investment funds, laid down by Articles 145(6) and 145(8) of the IFA, should be removed because they contravene Article 56 of the EC Treaty.[58] The FSC could make recommendations for such limitations, which could be implemented by the rules of Polish investment funds.

Article 264(6)(3) of the IFA, which permits the FSC to refuse to forward information on a proposed branch or on planned changes to a branch to the financial regulator of the host Member State because the branch managers "do not warrant" that the branch will pursue the proposed investment services,[59] should be repealed because it is not

---

[55] Section 3.3.1 note 169 discusses the logic of this approach.

[56] See the subsection '*Article 93: open-end investment fund*' in section 4.1.1.

[57] See the subsection '*The requirements for a successful public policy/security derogation*' in section 2.1.3.

[58] See the subsection '*Article 145: closed-end investment fund*' in section 4.1.1.

[59] See the subsection '*Articles 264 and 267: investment services in other Member States*' in section 4.1.1.

explicitly permitted by Article 32 of Directive 2004/39/EC.[60] Article 264 of the IFA should specifically and objectively state the criteria for refusing to forward information, require the FSC to give reasons for such refusal (which must be proportionate) and provide a right of appeal in the Polish courts against the decision to refuse, in order for it to be a justified exception from Article 56 of the EC Treaty.[61]

In order to be justifiable under Article 58(1)(b) of the EC Treaty for the "prudential supervision of financial institutions", Article 267 of the IFA, which prohibits investment services in the host Member State for contravention of national law, should provide specific, objective criteria for an action to qualify as a breach, and require reasons to be given for this action to be classified as a violation of the host State's law.[62]

For investment services provided by another Member State to Poland, the standard for the FSC to establish a breach of national law should be increased. Article 62(1) of Directive 2004/39/EC requires the FSC to have "clear and demonstrable grounds" for a violation of national law in relation to the provision of cross-border investment services.[63] Article 273 of the IFA should enact this requirement.

Article 273 of the IFA should require the FSC to give reasons for prohibiting investment services from other Member States, and should provide the right of appeal in the Polish courts against this prohibition, in order for the restriction to free capital movement to be justified under Article 58(1)(b) of the EC Treaty as a measure to prevent infringements of Polish law. Furthermore, to stop this prohibition from being disproportionate, Article 273 of the IFA should provide more guidance to investment firms on what precise behaviour justifies it.[64] This also applies to Articles 169(1)-(3) of the TFIA, which enable the FSC to impose penalties for the breach of Polish law by investment firms from other Member States.[65]

---

[60] See section 2.4.1.

[61] See the subsection '*The requirements for a successful public policy/security derogation*' in section 2.1.3.

[62] Ibid. The decision that restricts the free movement of capital should be subject to review in the national courts (see section 2.1.3, especially *Commission v Belgium* [2002] ECR I-4809). However, a legal provision that empowers review in a Polish court of such a decision by the financial authority of another Member State is controversial, and is likely to be unenforceable.

[63] See the subsection '*Articles 270 and 273: investment services in Poland*' in section 4.1.1.

[64] Ibid.

[65] See the subsection '*Article 169: breach of Polish law*' in section 4.1.3.

Act of 29 July 2005 on Public Offers and the Conditions for Introducing Financial Instruments to the Organised Trading System, and on Public Companies (POA)

Article 19(2) of the POA empowers the FSC to take measures to safeguard investors' interests where the home Member State's financial authority has taken no or ineffective action to prevent breach of the POA, including prohibition of the initiation or completion of a public offer and cancellation of the admission of securities to a regulated market.[66] To be a justified exception to Article 56 of the EC Treaty, the POA should specify objective criteria for the FSC to apply the measures in order to provide the securities' issuer with legal certainty. Furthermore, the POA should require the FSC to give reasons for taking these measures, and should provide the right of appeal in the Polish courts against the decision to apply them.[67]

Act of 29 July 2005 on Trading in Financial Instruments (TFIA)

Article 96 of the TFIA, which requires 20% associates of, or of the parent company of, investment firms, credit institutions and insurance companies authorised to conduct brokerage activity in another EU, OECD or WTO member country to obtain a permit from the FSC in order to practice brokerage activity in Poland,[68] should state that the FSC is to provide reasons for refusing its permission in order to comply with Article 13 of Directive 2006/48/EC.[69] This Article should specify the grounds on which such permission is given so that legal certainty is provided to the applicant; this is one of the requirements for a successful derogation from Article 56 of the EC Treaty.[70]

Article 115(3) of the TFIA requires a legal person that practises brokerage activity in an OECD or WTO member country (outside the EEA) to obtain authorisation from the FSC in order to establish a Polish branch. This Article should provide specific, objective criteria for applicants to satisfy to obtain such authorisation, should require the FSC to give reasons for refusing it, and should provide a right of appeal in the

---

[66] See section 4.1.2.

[67] See the subsection '*The requirements for a successful public policy/security derogation*' in section 2.1.3.

[68] 'Brokerage activity' is defined in chapter 4 note 36.

[69] See the subsection '*Article 96: brokerage activity by foreign subsidiaries in Poland*' in section 4.1.3.

[70] See the subsection '*The requirements for a successful public policy/security derogation*' in section 2.1.3.

Polish courts against the decision to refuse it, in order to be an acceptable restriction on the free movement of capital.[71]

Article 117(5)(2) of the TFIA, which enables the Finance Minister to regulate the provision of cross-border brokerage services to Poland, should be repealed because it contravenes Article 31(1) of Directive 2004/39/EC. Article 31(1) prohibits Member States from imposing additional requirements on investment firms or credit institutions "in respect of matters covered by this Directive", which includes 'investment services and activities' in Annex I of Directive 2004/39/EC–defined similarly to 'brokerage activity' in Article 69(2) of the TFIA.[72]

Article 169(7) of the TFIA, which empowers the FSC to suspend the investment firm's brokerage activity in Poland for up to a month in order to protect the public interest, should define 'public interest' and state specific, objective criteria for preventing suspension in order to provide investment firms with legal certainty.[73]

Act of 29 August 1997: Banking Law (BL)

Articles 39(1) and 40(1) of the BL, which require authorisation from the FSC for a Polish bank to found a bank or branch outside the EU, and for a third country bank to establish a Polish branch,[74] should provide specific, objective criteria upon which authorisation is granted that provide applicant banks with legal certainty, should require the FSC to give reasons for refusing an authorisation, and should provide the right of appeal in the Polish courts against a refusal. These are requirements of a successful derogation to Article 56 of the EC Treaty.[75]

Article 48l(2) of the BL, which empowers the FSC to specify the conditions that a branch of a credit institution registered in another Member State must meet for "public benefit", especially to "protect consumers' interests, ensure safety of economic trading" or prevent legal infringements,[76] should specify these interests more clearly in order to

[71] Ibid.

[72] See chapter 4 note 36.

[73] See the subsection '*Article 169: breach of Polish law*' in section 4.1.3.

[74] See the subsection '*Articles 37 to 48j: authorisation*' in section 4.1.4.

[75] See the subsection '*The requirements for a successful public policy/security derogation*' in section 2.1.3.

[76] See the subsection '*Article 48l and 48ł: banking services in Poland*' in section 4.1.4.

provide applicant credit institutions with legal certainty; this is a requirement to comply with Article 56 of the EC Treaty.[77]

A subsection should be added to Article 63g of the BL to ensure compliance with Article 4 of Directive 97/5/EC, which requires banks, after a cross-border transfer, to give their customers a unique reference number and to inform them of the transfer amount, charges and commission fees and the value date.[78]

Act of 22 May 2003 on Insurance Activity (IAA)

Articles 104-122 of the IAA state rigorous conditions for foreign insurance companies to provide insurance services in Poland.[79] Those provisions that are disproportionate should be repealed; this includes, for instance, Article 122(2) of the BL, which empowers the FSC to liquidate the main branch if it does not "provide insurance benefits" in Poland, or partly or belatedly provides them. Furthermore, as stated in section 4.1.5, the FSC should provide specific, objective criteria that a foreign insurance company must satisfy in order to be granted and to retain a permit, such as the contents of the main branch's business plan to offer particular insurance services. In addition, the IAA should require the FSC to state its reasons for withholding or withdrawing a permit, and provide the foreign insurance firm with the right to appeal in the Polish courts against the decision to withhold or withdraw it. These changes would make Articles 104□122 an acceptable derogation from Article 56 of the EC Treaty.[80]

Article 137(3) of the IAA should be repealed; this measure empowers the FSC to refuse to forward information concerning a Polish insurance undertaking to the financial authority of the Member State to which this company intends to provide cross-border insurance services, if its financial position does not "allow" it to supply these services. Article 16 of Directive 88/357/EEC does not provide this ground for refusing to

[77] See the subsection '*The requirements for a successful public policy/security derogation*' in section 2.1.3.
[78] See section 2.2.1.
[79] See the subsection '*Articles 104 to 122: foreign insurance establishments*' in section 4.1.5. Although a 'foreign insurance establishment' is a non-Polish firm pursuing insurance activity (as defined in chapter 4 note 80), and thus includes insurance undertakings from other Member States, the latter are, in practice, regulated by Articles 128-133 of the IAA. To avoid ambiguity, the definition of 'foreign insurance establishment' in Article 2(1)(16) of the IAA should be narrowed to read 'an establishment outside the European Economic Area that pursues insurance activity'.
[80] See the subsection '*The requirements for a successful public policy/security derogation*' in section 2.1.3.

communicate information. In addition, Article 16(2) of the Directive requires Member States to provide a right of appeal in the national courts against the financial authority's refusal to allow an insurance firm to supply cross-border services to another Member State. The IAA should be amended to include such a right of appeal.

As stated in section 4.1.5, the restriction of cross-border capital movement imposed by the IAA by refusing to forward information to the host Member State's financial authority is unjustified because the grounds specified in the Act provide the FSC with too much discretion. For instance, the FSC may refuse to furnish the information required to establish a branch in another Member State if it finds that the insurance company's financial position "does not permit" such establishment.[81] The IAA should provide specific, objective criteria that accord insurance firms legal certainty, and should supply the right to appeal in the Polish courts against a decision of the FSC to refuse to forward this information to the host Member State's financial authority.[82]

Article 139(1) of the IAA, which transposes the procedure for breach of Polish law prescribed by Article 40 of Directive 92/49/EEC, should be modified to match the requirements of this Directive, in particular 1) limiting the FSC to prohibit insurance activity "*as is strictly necessary*" in Article 139(4) of the IAA,[83] and 2) requiring the FSC's measures to be thoroughly explained and communicated to the insurance company.[84] In addition, to be an acceptable derogation from Article 56 of the EC Treaty, Article 139 of the IAA should state the specific, objective grounds on which the FSC will prohibit insurance activity, require it to give reasons for this prohibition, and provide the injured party with the right of appeal against the prohibition in the national courts.[85]

Act of 22 May 2003 on Insurance Mediation (IMA)

This Act follows the procedure in Article 6(1) of Directive 2002/92/EC for the pursuit of insurance mediation in other Member States.[86] However, the IMA does not include a procedure to be followed when an

---

[81] Article 135(3)(1), IAA.

[82] See the subsection '*The requirements for a successful public policy/security derogation*' in section 2.1.3.

[83] Emphasis mine.

[84] These alterations correspond to the points made in the subsection '*Article 139: breach of Polish law*' in section 4.1.5.

[85] See the subsection '*The requirements for a successful public policy/security derogation*' in section 2.1.3.

[86] See section 2.4.4.

intermediary from another Member State violates Polish law. Article 8(3) of Directive 2002/92/EC requires Member States to apply "appropriate sanctions" if an insurance or reinsurance intermediary contravenes national legal provisions that transpose this Directive. Article 8(4) empowers host Member States to take "appropriate measures" to forestall or to punish breaches of national legal or regulatory provisions enacted "in the interests of the general good". Article 8(5) requires each national financial authority to "properly" justify, and to communicate to the insurance intermediary, measures it takes that penalise or limit the latter's activities, and to provide a right of appeal to the courts of the Member State taking these measures. The IMA should include these provisions from the Directive.

The IMA contains no legal provisions concerning the supply of insurance mediation between Poland and countries outside the EU. To comply with Article 56 of the EC Treaty, the IMA should introduce laws permitting such supply.

Act of 28 February 2004 on Freedom of Economic Activity (FEAA)

The Polish Minister for the Economy can prohibit a foreign entrepreneur from "conducting economic activity" in Poland through a branch or agency for a number of reasons.[87] Since this prohibition restricts the free movement of capital, the grounds on which it is based should be stated as precisely as possible in order to provide the entrepreneur with legal certainty. For instance, the phrase "forfeit the right"[88] to conduct economic activity should be subdivided into causes of forfeiture. Article 91(1) of the FEAA should require the Minister to give reasons for his/her prohibition and provide the right of appeal in the national courts against it, in order to be a justifiable exception to Article 56 of the EC Treaty.[89]

Act of 27 July 2002: Foreign Exchange Law (FEL)

Article 9 of the FEL introduces limitations on cross-border foreign exchange dealings. It states the categories of assets on which these restrictions are placed,[90] but seeks to specify what those limitations are, to

---

[87] See section 4.2.1. 'Foreign entrepreneur' and 'economic activity' are defined in chapter 4 notes 176 and 125 respectively.

[88] Article 91(1)(2), FEAA.

[89] See the subsection '*The requirements for a successful public policy/security derogation*' in section 2.1.3.

[90] See section the subsection '*Articles 9 and 10: limitations on cross-border foreign exchange dealings*' in 4.2.2.

state precisely why in the public interest they are being applied, to require reasons to be given for the limits and to provide an appeal in the national courts against their application. As stated in section 4.2.2, the restriction of so many capital flows to and from third countries is disproportionate.[91] Consequently, some of these limits should be removed.

Article 10 of the FEL should require "special limitations" introduced by the Council of Ministers for ensuring balance of payments equilibrium or for enforcing decisions of international organisations, to be proportionate and necessary to protect the interests specified by the Council. As stated in section 4.2.2, the Council regulations that contain the special measures should provide specific, objective criteria for cross-border flows to avoid restriction, and should give reasons for the limitations and a right of appeal against them in the national courts.[92]

Regulation of the Minister of Finance of 3 September 2002 on General Foreign Exchange Permits

The Regulation should include, in its 'General Provisions' chapter,[93] a right of appeal in the national courts against the decision to refuse to grant a permit.[94] This chapter should also state that Polish officials will give reasons for refusing to issue a permit. These additions would make refusals to issue foreign exchange permits more justifiable restrictions on the free movement of capital.[95]

Act of 26 July 1991 on Natural Persons' Income Tax (NPITA)

Article 30b(5c) of the NPITA offers Polish residents a tax deduction for income on share sales from some Member States but not others, on the condition that these residents have invested more than 40% of their assets in Polish Treasury securities, bonds or notes.[96] This subsection is a breach of Article 12 of the EC Treaty, which forbids discrimination based on nationality. It should therefore either be extended to include income from all Member States, or repealed.

---

[91] There are 15 categories of limitations, more than half of which apply specifically to capital movements to and/or from third countries.

[92] See the subsection '*The requirements for a successful public policy/security derogation*' in section 2.1.3.

[93] Chapter 1.

[94] See section 4.2.3.

[95] See the subsection '*The requirements for a successful public policy/security derogation*' in section 2.1.3.

[96] See the subsection '*Article 30b: residents' tax deductions on income from foreign securities*' in section 4.3.1.

Articles 30b(5a) and 30b(5b) treat Polish residents receiving dividends or interest from foreign countries that is taxed at source at more than 19% (the Polish income tax rate) less favourably than residents receiving investment from Polish companies, thereby restricting the free movement of capital.[97] Two possible solutions are for the Polish tax authority to 1) provide a tax rebate of [foreign income * (foreign tax rate – 19%)] to the former, thus taxing all resident receivers of investment income at 19%; 2) omit taxing all foreign investment income that has been taxed at source, thus leaving non-discriminatory differential tax rates on investment income. The first solution is superior because it minimises tax avoidance in comparison with the second suggestion. Similar reasoning applies to Article 30c of the NPITA, which concerns Polish residents' income from non-agricultural economic activity in Poland and abroad.[98]

Act of 15 February 1992 on Legal Persons' Income Tax (LPITA)

Since Polish companies that receive dividends from domestic associates and subsidiaries are in an objectively comparable situation to Polish companies that receive dividends from foreign associates and subsidiaries,[99] Article 20 of the LPITA should be modified to make foreign tax payable on all dividends received abroad deductible from Polish companies' national tax bill. These dividends should then be taxed at 19%, which is the rate applying to dividends received from Polish corporations.[100]

Act of 24 March 1920 on the Acquisition of Immovable Properties by Foreign Persons (AIPFPA)

Article 1 of the AIPFPA requires a foreign person to obtain a permit from the Minister for Internal Affairs in order to acquire immovable property in Poland. The conditions to obtain the permit discriminate against non-Polish citizens.[101] The requirement for a permit must be based on an objective in the public interest that is pursued in a non-discriminatory way.[102] It is proposed that Articles 1a(1)(2) and 1a(2) of

---

[97] Ibid.

[98] See the subsection '*Article 30c: residents' tax deductions from on foreign non-agricultural income*' in section 4.3.1.

[99] See section 4.3.2.

[100] Article 22(1), LPITA.

[101] See section 4.4.1.

[102] See the '*Comment*' subsection in section 2.1.4.

the AIPFPA, which require the applicant landowner to demonstrate one of several Polish connections,[103] are repealed.

Article 1a(1)(1) of the AIPFPA should be retained; this provision allows the Minister to refuse to issue a permit if the foreign person's immovable property purchase threatens public defence, security, order, health or social policy. However, these objectives in the public interest should be supplemented by additional subsections, which state specific, objective criteria that provide the applicant with legal certainty as to when the Minister will grant or refuse a permit. The AIPFPA should require the Minister to give reasons for refusing to issue a permit, and should provide a right of appeal in the Polish courts against the decision to refuse.[104] It would be helpful if the AIPFPA introduced milder alternatives to refusal of a permit, which could be pursued if non-authorisation is disproportionate, such as the grant of a renewable biennial licence or of a permit subject to annual inspection of the immovable property by the Ministry. Together, these modifications would render the provisions of the AIPFPA acceptable derogations from Article 56 of the EC Treaty.[105]

8.2.3 Reforms to Latvian laws

Law on Investment Companies 1997 (LIC)

Investment certificates of foreign open-ended funds may only be circulated in Latvia by a brokerage company or credit institution registered there.[106] To comply with the free movement of capital, this provision should permit such investment certificates to be so circulated by a Latvian branch of the foreign investment fund management company, thus adopting a similar legal position to that of Estonia.[107]

Documents to be sent by the Latvian distributer of foreign investment certificates to the FCMC should match the requirements of Article 31(2) of Directive 2004/39/EC.[108] Subsections of section 60(2) of the LIC that

---

[103] See section 4.4.1.

[104] These requirements of a successful public policy/security derogation (see section 2.1.3) apply to national real property laws (see section 2.1.4).

[105] An alternative suggestion is made in section 4.4.3 for modifying the AIPFPA in line with EU law on the free movement of capital.

[106] s.60(1), LIC.

[107] See the subsection '*Sections 229 and 233: capital movements without justification*' in section 3.1.1.

[108] Article 31(2) specifies the following information: the name of the host Member State and the "programme of operations" (see section 2.4.1).

specify other items, such as regulations for distributing the investment certificates in Latvia,[109] should be repealed.[110]

Three restrictions on the free movement of capital between Latvia and third countries are stated in section 5.1.1. Sections 62-65 of the LIC should be amended to remove the first two limitations;[111] i.e. investments are to be allowed in money market instruments issued by public institutions of non-EEA, non-OECD states that are not traded on regulated markets, and investment fund resources are to be eligible for deposit with credit institutions in these countries.

Sections 66(1) and 66(11) of the LIC limit the free movement of capital because a lower percentage of fund resources may be invested in a single issuer's financial instruments in third countries than in EEA or OECD states.[112] This discrepancy should be removed by raising the investment limits of the former to the level of the latter i.e. 35% for fund assets in general and 20% for investment in investment certificates of open-end funds in particular.

An alternative suggestion is to replace section 66 of the LIC with a single statement: "Investment limitations, if any, are to be specified by the regulations of each investment fund".[113] These limits are, in this form, a matter for consumer choice rather than a national, legal restriction on the free movement of capital.

Financial Instruments Market Law 2003 (FIML)

Section 112(4) of the FIML should specify the information that the supervisory authority of the home Member State is to communicate to the FCMC when an investment brokerage company registered there wishes to provide cross-border investment services to Latvia.[114] This information must be the same as that specified in Article 31(2) of Directive 2004/39/EC.[115]

---

[109] s.60(2)(6), LIC.

[110] The distributors may choose to send this information to the FCMC, but it should not be legally required. This is because "Member States shall not impose any additional requirements ... in respect of these matters covered by this Directive" (Article 31(1), Directive 2004/39/EC).

[111] The third restriction concerns the FCMC's discretion, and is discussed in the subsection '*Sections 62 to 65: investment types*' in section 5.1.1.

[112] See the subsection '*Section 66: investment limitations*' in section 5.1.1.

[113] This treatment of investment limitations is recommended for Polish investment funds in sections 4.1.1 and 8.2.2, and for Latvian investment funds in section 5.1.1.

[114] The contents of section 112(4) of the FIML are stated in the subsection '*Section 112: EEA companies' investment services in Latvia*' in section 5.1.2.

[115] See section 2.4.1.

As stated in section 5.1.2, the FCMC's refusal to permit an investment brokerage firm from another Member State or its Latvian branch to supply investment services in Latvia restricts the free movement of capital. Consequently, section 112 of the FIML should require the FCMC to give reasons for the refusal, and should provide a right of appeal against it in the Latvian courts. A similar recommendation is made for section 113 of the FIML, should the FCMC refuse to pass information to the financial authority of another Member State to which a Latvian brokerage company wishes to provide investment services.

Section 113 of the FIML should be altered in two respects in order comply with Directive 2004/39/EC. Firstly, Article 32(2)(d) of the Directive only requires the branch managers' names to be communicated to the host State's competent authority. The other details requested by section 113(4) of the FIML should be deleted.[116] Secondly, section 113 should incorporate the requirement of Article 32(5) of Directive 2004/39/EC for the FCMC to give reasons for refusing to forward the information for establishing a branch in the host State to the latter' financial authority.[117]

Section 5.1.2 notes that sections 140(1)-(3) of the FIML, on the contravention of Latvian law by an investment brokerage company registered in another Member State that provides cross-border services to Latvia, follow Article 31 of Directive 2006/48/EC rather that Article 62 of Directive 2004/39/EC. In particular, section 140 should consider the detail of Article 62(1), which empowers the supervisory authority of the host State, when it has "clear and demonstrable grounds" for believing that the foreign investment firm has broken national law "adopted pursuant to this Directive" to refer this information to the home Member State's financial authority. If, despite the measures taken by the latter, or because they are insufficient, the investment firm continues to act in a way "clearly prejudicial to the interests of host Member State investors or the orderly functioning of markets", the host Member State's competent authority "shall take all the appropriate measures needed in order to protect investors and the proper functioning of markets", and shall inform the host State's supervisory authority and the European Commission of these measures.

The Latvian legislators must ensure, in transposing this Article, that in order to satisfy the derogation in Article 58(1)(b) of the EC Treaty, under which Member States may take all measures required to prevent

---

[116] See the subsection '*Section 113: Latvian companies' investment services within the EEA*' in section 5.1.2.

[117] See section 2.4.1.

transgressions of national law and regulations, the principles of a successful derogation are adhered to.[118] Therefore, section 140 of the FIML should specify what the interests of Latvia (i.e. the host Member State) are in this context, and what precisely is meant by the orderly function of markets, in order to provide legal certainty to foreign investment firms. The measures, which are to be stated in the FIML, should be specific and objective, in order to observe the requirements of legal certainty. They should also be necessary to protect that they are intended to guarantee (already specified), and be proportionate i.e. not attainable by less restrictive measures. Finally, section 140 should require the FCMC to give reasons for taking measures, and should provide a right of appeal in the Latvian courts against the decision to prescribe these actions.

These recommendations also apply to section 140(4) of the FIML, which empowers the FCMC to take remedial action against legal violations that protect the "public interest", which is not defined.[119] In addition, this 'public interest', once defined, should be a "genuine and sufficiently serious threat to a fundamental interest of society",[120] which is a requirement to fulfil the public policy/security derogation from Article 56 of the EC Treaty.[121]

Credit Institutions Law 1995 (CIL)

Section 12^2 of the CIL, which requires a Latvian credit institution that wishes to establish a branch in another Member State to provide the FCMC with certain information,[122] contravenes Article 25 of Directive 2006/48/EC. Section 5.1.3 recommends the following insertions into section 12^2 CIL in order to comply with this Article: 1) notification should include the address in the host State from which to obtain documents, the quantity of own funds and the capital requirements, 2) the FCMC should state reasons for refusing to communicate the information to the host State's supervisory authority within three months of receiving it, and 3) the credit institution should be provided with the right to appeal against the refusal, or against a failure to reply, in the Latvian courts. These last two requirements are necessary for 12(1) of the CIL (permission required

[118] See section 2.1.3.
[119] See the subsection '*Section 140: breach of national law*' in section 5.1.2.
[120] *Eglise de Scientologie and Scientology International* [2000] ECR I-1335.
[121] See the subsection '*The requirements for a successful public policy/security derogation*' in section 2.1.3.
[122] See the subsection '*Sections 12, 12^2 and 12^3: Latvian credit institutions operating abroad*' in section 5.1.3.

from the FCMC to establish a branch in a country outside the EEA) and for section 12^3 of the CIL (provision of cross-border services in another Member State) to improve their compliance with the EU free movement of capital rules.[123]

The detailed requirements of 12^1 and $12^{1111}(1)$ of the CIL for a credit or financial institution registered in another Member State to provide financial services to Latvia are an unjustified limitation on the free movement of capital because the restrictive measures must be required to protect the interests that they are intended to guarantee,[124] which are not specified in either section.[125] Sections 12(1) and $12^{1111}(1)$ of the CIL should state these interests. Additionally, they should require the FCMC to give reasons for a decision that the credit/financial institution cannot establish a branch or provide cross-border financial services to Latvia, and should give that institution the right to appeal in the Latvian courts against such a decision.[126]

Article 12 of Directive 2006/48/EC does not permit a Member State's competent authority to authorise a credit institution to start its business if this institution's close links with third parties "may threaten its financial stability".[127] Consequently, this clause in section 14(1)(2) of the CIL, which currently allows such a ground for refusal of authorisation, should be repealed.

A subsection should be added to section 14 of the CIL, which requires the FCMC to give reasons for its decision to refuse to authorise a credit institution in accordance with Article 13 of the Directive.[128] In addition, to be a justified restriction on the free movement of capital, section 14 should grant a right of appeal to credit institutions against any decision of the FCMC to refuse to issue a licence for the provision of financial services in Latvia.[129]

Article 17(2) of Directive 2006/48/EC requires reasons to be given for the withdrawal of authorisation of credit institutions, and requires "those

---

[123] Ibid.
[124] *Eglise de Scientologie and Scientology International* [2000] ECR I-1335.
[125] See the subsection '*Sections 12^1 and 12^{1111}: EEA credit/financial institutions operating in Latvia*' in section 5.1.3.
[126] See the subsection '*The requirements for a successful public policy/security derogation*' in section 2.1.3.
[127] s.14(1)(2), CIL.
[128] See section 2.4.2.
[129] This point is made in section 5.1.3 for s.14(1)(7) CIL, but it applies to all the authorisation provisions of section 14 of the CIL.

censured" and the European Commission to be informed of this.[130] These points should be added to section 27(3) of the CIL.[131]

Section 5.1.3 makes three recommendations that section 108^{1} of the CIL should incorporate in order to comply with Directive 2006/48/EC. Firstly, measures pursuant to Articles 30 and 31 of the Directive, which concern contravention of Latvian law by credit institutions registered in other Member States, should be "properly justified and communicated" to the institution, and "subject to a right of appeal" in the courts of the State that took them [Article 32]. Secondly, the scope of sections 108^{1}(1)□(3) of the CIL should be reduced from "the laws of Latvia"[132] to Latvian laws enacted "pursuant to the provisions of this Directive involving powers of the host Member State's competent authorities" [Article 30(1)].[133] Thirdly, section 108^{1}(4) of the CIL should incorporate the reference to "appropriate" measures in Article 31 of the Directive.

To be a justifiable restriction on the free movement of capital, section 108^{1} should provide specific, objective measures that offer legal certainty to credit institutions, require the FCMC to give reasons for passing a measure, and provide a right of appeal in the Latvian courts against that decision.[134]

2002-08-15 Regulations on the Issue of Credit Institution and Credit Union Operating Licences (RICIOL)

Since the conditions for a foreign bank to establish a Latvian branch restrict the free movement of capital, they should be specific, objective and previously known to that bank in order to provide it with legal certainty. In particular, paragraph 4.1 of the Regulations should state precisely what it means by "appropriate, complete effective supervision"[135] and by "appropriate standards conforming with international standards.[136] In addition, both paragraph 4 and 5 (which

---

[130] See section 2.4.2.

[131] See the subsection '*Section 27: withdrawal of licence*' in section 5.1.3.

[132] s.108(1), CIL.

[133] Linguistic accuracy in the transposition of a Directive is necessary to prevent cases being brought that are misaligned with the Directive's purpose. In chapter 5 note 112, it is argued that a breach of Latvian tax law by a credit institution registered in another Member State may bring this bank within the ambit of section 108^{1} of the CIL.

[134] See the subsection '*The requirements for a successful public policy/security derogation*' in section 2.1.3.

[135] Paragraph 4.1.1, RICIOL.

[136] Paragraph 4.1.3, RICIOL. See section 5.1.4.

considers the conditions for a Latvian bank to establish a branch abroad) should require the FCMC to provide reasons for refusing to issue a licence, and should provide a right of appeal against the refusal in the Latvian courts.[137]

Law on Insurance Companies and Supervision Thereof 1998 (LICST)

Article 7(1) of the LICST should permit third country insurers to provide cross-border insurance services to Latvia. This group should be added to the insurance services providers listed in Article 7(1)(1) of the LICST.[138]

To be a justifiable exception to Article 56 of the EC Treaty, Article 10 of the LICST should require the FCMC to give reasons for refusing to provide a licence to a third country insurer to establish a branch in Latvia. It should also provide a right of appeal in the Latvian courts against the decision to refuse to grant a permit.[139] Although the extensive authorisation requirements offer legal certainty to the issuer, the FCMC retains discretion as to whether to grant a licence. This discretion may be reduced by dividing the 'insurance is "not economically substantiated"'[140] ground for refusal into separate financial targets for each class of insurance, such as minimum sales figures.[141]

Minor modifications are suggested in section 5.1.5 to Articles 11, 11^1 and 11^3 of the LICST on Latvian companies providing insurance services abroad in the light of both Article 56 of the EC Treaty and Directives 73/239/EEC and 88/357/EEC. One particular point is the phrase "deficiencies detected by the [FCMC] have not been eliminated within the terms specified by the [FCMC]",[142] which does not provide legal certainty to Latvian insurance firms, and should be much more clearly specified. All these Articles should state that the FCMC is to give reasons for refusing to issue a permit or to forward information to the host Member State's supervisory authority, and should provide the applicant insurance

---

[137] See the subsection '*The requirements for a successful public policy/security derogation*' in section 2.1.3.

[138] See the subsection '*Article 7: third country insurance services*' in section 5.1.5.

[139] See the subsection '*The requirements for a successful public policy/security derogation*' in section 2.1.3.

[140] Article 10(6)(1), LICST.

[141] See section the subsection '*Article 10: licensing of a third country insurer*' in 5.1.5.

[142] Articles $11(3^1)(5)$, $11^1(4)(8)$ and $11^3(4^1)(3)$, LICST.

company with the right to appeal against the refusal in the Latvian courts.[143]

In section 5.1.5, it is stated that the asset limitations imposed by Articles 41-43 of the LICST as cover for an insurance company's contingent liabilities limit the free movement of capital if the principle in *Commission v Spain* applies,[144] namely that, despite affecting residents and non-residents equally, the restrictions deter investment from the nationals of other Member States.

It is unlikely that asset limitations are a deterrent to insurance companies from other countries from setting up subsidiaries, associates and branches in Latvia, because the main concern of these firms in making the decisions on the presence and size of the Latvian business unit is the depth and spread of the Latvian insurance market.[145] Even though, in practice, these limitations do not substantially restrict the free movement of capital, they should be removed because they are concerned with asset-liability matching,[146] and are therefore a matter for each insurance company and its shareholders rather than for the legislators.[147]

Articles 99¹(1)-(3) of the LICST transpose Articles 40(3)-(5) of Directive 92/49/EEC, which lay down a procedure for the breach of national law by insurance companies established in other Member States and by domestic branches of those organisations. The following amendments are recommended in section 5.1.5, in line with Article 40 of the Directive: 1) Article 99(3) of the LICST should insert the word "appropriate" from Article 40(5) before "measures preventing such violations"; 2) Article 99¹(3) of the LICST should include, as one of these measures, the prevention of the foreign insurance firm "from continuing to conclude new insurance contracts within its territory" [Article 40(5)]; 3)

---

[143] See the subsection '*The requirements for a successful public policy/security derogation*' in section 2.1.3.

[144] [2003] ECR I-4581.

[145] It is established business theory that the strategies for organisational growth are market penetration (current products to current markets), product development (new products to current markets), market development (current products to new markets) and diversification (new products to new markets) (Boyd Jr. and Walker Jr. (1990), *Marketing Management*, 53). As total risk tends to increase from market penetration through to diversification, market development is a promising corporate growth strategy for established EU insurance companies i.e. providing insurance services to new Member States.

[146] See chapter 5 note 203.

[147] This is analogous to the point made about investment limitations; see the subsection '*Law on Investment Companies 1997 (LIC)*', above in section 8.2.3.

Article 99¹ of the LICST should state that measures adopted are "properly reasoned" [Article 40(9)].

Section 5.1.5 concludes that actions taken for the contravention of Latvian law under Articles 99 and 99¹ of the LICST are not justifiable restrictions on the free movement of capital; such measures need to be proportionate, necessary for the protection of the relevant interests, and specific and objective in order to provide insurance companies with legal certainty.[148] Hence, the LICST should state 1) the measures available to the FCMC, 2) the particular situations of breach of Latvian law that could reasonably arise from the provision of insurance services and the interests affected in those circumstances-insurance premium payers, shareholders of the insurance firm, the Latvian government and taxpayers, the government and taxpayers of the home Member State and so on, and 3) which particular measures should apply in each of these situations and why. This is a comprehensive approach, but is helpful in incorporating the principles of EU law concerning exceptions to the free movement of capital stated in sections 2.1.3 and 2.1.4 into the national legislation.

Activities of Insurance and Reinsurance Intermediaries Law 2005 (AIRIL)

Sections 8 to 11 of the AIRIL, which concern the registration of insurance and reinsurance intermediaries,[149] substantially comply with Directive 2002/92/EC. However, section 11 of the AIRIL should require non-registration and registration cancellation to be "properly justified and communicated to the intermediary" and be subject to a right of appeal in the Member State that has taken the non-registration/cancellation decision.[150]

Section 32 of the AIRIL requires a Latvian insurance intermediary that wishes to establish a branch in another Member State to provide the FCMC with information, especially that requested by Directive 2002/92/EC.[151] Since the intermediary only needs to inform "the competent authorities of the home Member State" [Article 6(1)],[152] the AIRIL should only require essential items of information to be provided to

[148] See the subsection '*The requirements for a successful public policy/security derogation*' in section 2.1.3.

[149] See the subsection '*Sections 8 to 11: registration of insurance and reinsurance intermediaries (hereafter 'intermediaries')*' in section 5.1.6.

[150] Section 11(4) of the AIRIL provides a right of appeal against a cancellation.

[151] See the subsection '*Sections 32 and 34: refusal to forward information*' in section 5.1.6.

[152] See section 2.4.4.

the FCMC. Most of the information required by section 32 is essential. The following classification may apply.

Essential information
The name of the host Member State.
A description of the planned services.
The address of the branch.
Communication details of the insurance company on whose behalf the intermediary will act.
The branch manager must be of good repute.
The branch manager has no international criminal record.

Important information
The branch manager has the required knowledge to practise insurance mediation.
The branch manager has the required market experience.

Other information
Information concerning the branch manager.
The branch manager must be at least 21 years.
The branch manager has a tertiary education.

Section 32 of the AIRIL should not require the insurance intermediary to provide the items in 'Other information' to the FCMC. Those facts in 'Important information' are related to whether the prospective branch manager is competent and reliable. Although these items are not essential information, their inclusion would enable the FCMC to identify unsuitable candidates.

To be a justified restriction on the free movement of capital, the grounds given by sections 32 and 34 of the AIRIL should be specified as clearly as possible and be objective, in order to provide the insurance intermediary with legal certainty. For instance, criteria should be provided as to what constitutes financial instability,[153] such as negative cashflow, profit before interest and tax less than twice the interest cover, or at least one loan in default. In addition, these sections of the AIRIL should provide a right of appeal in the Latvian courts against the FCMC's

---

[153] s.32(5), AIRIL. See the subsection '*Sections 32 and 34: refusal to forward information*' in section 5.1.6.

decision to refuse to forward information concerning the insurance intermediary to the host Member State's competent authority.[154]

Section 39 of the AIRIL prescribes a procedure for the violation of Latvian law by an insurance intermediary from another Member State establishing a branch or providing cross-border mediation there.[155] This section requires the following modifications, in order to comply with Directive 2002/92/EC. 1) Sections 39(3) and 39(4) should state that the FCMC is to take "appropriate" measures, in order to comply with Article 8(3) and 8(4) of the Directive respectively. 2) Sections 39(1)-(3) should refer to breach of national law "adapted pursuant to" Directive 2002/92/EC [Article 8(3)]. This is a narrower construction than the present one, which refers to the violation of national law.[156] 3) Section 39(4) should specifically include the sanction of preventing offending insurance intermediaries from "initiating any further activities" in Latvia [Article 8(4)]. 4) Section 39 should require measures taken by the FCMC to be "properly reasoned and communicated" to the intermediary, and should provide a right of appeal against each sanction or restriction in the Latvian courts [Article 8(5)].

To be a justifiable restriction on the free movement of capital, section 39 of the AIRIL should state specific, objective measures that provide legal certainty to the intermediary, and should clearly identify the particular interests that these measures are intended to guarantee.[157] The only interest currently stated in section 39 is "public interests (general good)".[158] This should be subdivided, and those divisions connected with recommended measures, which must be proportionate: i.e. as unrestrictive as possible.[159]

For example, 'public interest' could consist of the interests of investors, creditors, and taxpayers. If the insurance intermediary violates a loan agreement, this is a breach of contract and therefore a contravention

[154] See the subsection '*The requirements for a successful public policy/security derogation*' in section 2.1.3.

[155] See the subsection '*Section 39: violation of national law*' in section 5.1.6.

[156] This modification is required to prevent the contravention of national legal provisions outside the scope of Directive 2002/92/EC from being caught by section 39 of the AIRIL. In note 133, linguistic precision is advised in transposing a Directive in order to adhere to its purpose.

[157] See the subsection '*The requirements for a successful public policy/security derogation*' in section 2.1.3, and the subsection '*Section 39: violation of national law*' in section 5.1.6.

[158] s.39(4), AIRIL.

[159] Section 2.1.3 refers to 'proportionate' measures as those "not attainable by less restrictive measures".

of Latvian law in relation to the 'public interest', subdivision 'creditors'. Appropriate measures from the FCMC may include 1) a warning to the intermediary to regain solvency in order to continue providing insurance mediation in Latvia, 2) an order to the intermediary to direct its operating profits to repayment of the loan for a minimum period, 3) a suspension of the intermediary's Latvian business for a minimum specified time, and 4) a prohibition of such business. To comply with EU law on the free movement of capital, the particular measure taken by the FCMC must correspond to the gravity of the offence against the public interest. In other words, the selected action must be proportionate to the breach of Latvian law.

Law on Private Pension Funds 1997 (LPPF)

Section 23(3) of the LPPF contains investment limitations for pension plan assets that breach Article 56 of the EC Treaty.[160] Two alternative recommendations, of which the second is preferable, are 1) to expand the permissible investments in countries outside the EEA to equal those in EEA states, thus eliminating this section's discrimination against third countries, and 2) to remove the investment limitations; the LPPF could merely state that such restrictions are to be contained in the regulations of the particular pension fund.[161]

Law on State Funded Pensions 2000 (LSFP)

The investment limitations imposed by section 12(1) of the LSFP restrict the free movement of capital because they discriminate against investments in third countries.[162] Since the legislation provides for a single funded pension scheme for all participants in the State funded pension,[163] the transfer of investment restrictions from the LSFP to the pension scheme regulations, as recommended for private pensions,[164] does not remove the contravention of Article 56 of the EC Treaty. Consequently, the investment limitations applied by the LSFP to EEA

---

[160] See section 5.1.7.

[161] This approach is recommended for the investment limitations in the LIC and in the LICST, above in section 8.2.3.

[162] See section 5.2.1.

[163] ss.2-3, LSFP.

[164] See the subsection '*Law on Private Pension Funds 1997 (LPPF)*', above in section 8.2.3. The introduction of consumer choice as to the pension fund means that investment restrictions within the pension scheme's regulations do not restrict the free movement of capital.

states should be extended to countries outside the EEA in order to remove discrimination against third countries.

Law on Personal Income Tax 1993 (LPIT)

Section 9(1) of the LPIT treats companies registered in a Member State more favourably than those registered in a third country by exempting the recipients of dividends and deposit interest from the former, but not the latter, from paying personal income tax.[165] This breach of Article 56 of the EC Treaty is eliminated by extending the exemption to dividends and deposit interest paid by companies registered outside the EU.

Section 10(1) of the LPIT permits payments up to a limit of 10% of taxable income into private pension funds and to life assurance companies to be deducted from annual taxable income, provided that those entities are registered in a Member State.[166] To remove the breach of Article 56 of the EC Treaty due to treating objectively comparable situations differently,[167] the tax deductions should be extended to payments into private pension funds and to life insurance firms registered in countries outside the EU.

The tax reliefs provided by sections 12 and 13 of the LPIT discriminate against residents of third countries relative to residents of the EU, both groups earning more than 75% of their annual income in Latvia.[168] These reliefs should be extended to the latter in order to be compatible with the EU rules on the free movement of capital for taxation issues.[169]

Law on Enterprise Income Tax 1995 (LEIT)

Section 3(4) of the LEIT provides that dividends, interest payments, and payments for intellectual property are exempt from enterprise income tax under certain conditions when paid to companies in another Member State.[170] These exemptions should be extended to similar payments to enterprises registered outside the EU, which are in an objectively comparable situation to recipient organisations in Member States.

Section 11 of the LEIT allows dividends receivable to be tax-deductible for Latvian residents and for certain categories of non-residents.[171] Since the other non-resident companies are in an objectively

---

[165] See the subsection '*Section 9: non-taxable income*' in section 5.3.1.

[166] See the subsection '*Section 10: tax deductions*' in section 5.3.1.

[167] See section 2.3.

[168] See the subsection '*Sections 12 and 13: tax reliefs*' in section 5.3.1.

[169] See section 2.3.

[170] See the subsection '*Section 3(4): non-residents and exemptions*' in section 5.3.2, which gives an example of these conditions.

[171] See the subsection '*Section 11: dividends receivable*' in section 5.3.2.

comparable situation to resident organisations and non-resident enterprises whose dividend receives a tax credit,[172] section 11 should be extended to all non-resident companies.

Real property laws

Section 29 of the LPLRA prohibits non-Latvians from acquiring land in certain areas of Latvia, such as the Latvian border region and natural preserves.[173] This section contravenes EU law, and should therefore be repealed.

In *Commission v Hellenic Republic*,[174] the ECJ held that a Presidential Decree that prohibited foreign natural or legal persons from acquiring immovable property in the border regions of Greece, and an Emergency Law that favoured Greek nationals over those of other Member States in the acquisition of such property, were contrary to Articles 39, 43 and 49 of the EC Treaty.[175] Referring to specific items of Community law, the Court stated that access to housing and property ownership was a natural consequence of the freedom of movement for workers, and that the right to transfer immovable property in another Member State followed from the freedom of establishment. Furthermore, effective exercise of the freedom to provide services required "access to ownership and the use of" such property [paragraph 24]. This judgment demonstrates clearly that, outside the EU's transitional measures on the acquisition of real estate,[176] the fundamental freedoms provided by the EC Treaty require equal rights for residents of all Member States in the transfer of immovable property on Community territories.

Section 20 of the LLRCRL requires local government authorisation for land purchase by residents of third countries, and these persons are prohibited from acquiring land in specified Latvian territories.[177] To be compatible with the EU free movement of capital laws, this section should specify an objective that is pursued in a non-discriminatory way,[178] and the land restrictions should be necessary to protect the interests that they are

---

[172] See section 2.3.

[173] See section 5.4.1.

[174] [1989] ECR 1461.

[175] The ECJ stated that, from the documentation before the Court, approximately 55% of Greek territory appeared to be designated as 'border regions' under the Presidential Decree and Emergency Law.

[176] These transitional measures are stated in sections 2.5.1, 2.5.2 and 2.5.3 for Estonia, Poland and Latvia, respectively.

[177] These territories are stated in section 21 of the LLRCRL; see section 5.4.2.

[178] See the subsection '*Comment*' in section 2.1.4.

intended to guarantee, be proportionate, and be specific and objective in order to observe the requirements of legal certainty. Section 20 should also require that the authorities give reasons for turning down an application for the acquisition of land, and should also provide a right of appeal in the national courts against such a decision.[179]

Since section 4 of the FPRL and section 4 of the FPVL severely restrict the scope of the landowners within the Free Port territories for transferring land,[180] they limit the free movement of capital by discouraging investors from other Member States from acquiring property there.[181] As stated in section 5.4.5, these restrictions do not state an objective in the public interest and are disproportionate.[182] They are therefore unjustified, and contravene Article 56 of the EC Treaty.

To restore the free movement of capital, the Latvian government can either 1) repeal the restrictive provisions or 2) provide precise reasons why the maintenance of the Free Ports is a public interest objective, and explain why strict limits on the transfer of land in the Free Port territories are necessary to achieve this objective. These limits should also be specific and objective in order to provide potential acquirers of land in these territories with legal certainty. The legislation concerning the Free Ports should provide a right of appeal to a party whose application for acquiring land within those territories is rejected, and should require the Port Authorities to give reasons for this rejection.[183]

---

[179] See the subsections '*The requirements for a successful public policy/security derogation*' and '*Comment*' in section 2.1.3.

[180] See sections 5.4.3 and 5.4.4.

[181] This follows the decision in *Commission v Spain* [2003] ECR I-4581, in which the ECJ held that a non-discriminatory legal provision that specified a procedure of government prior approval for decisions concerning the privatisation of Spanish companies restricted the free movement of capital, because it affected the position of share purchasers and therefore deterred nationals from other Member States from investing in the Spanish entities; see section 2.1.2.

[182] See section 2.1.4.

[183] As stated in the '*Comment*' subsection of section 2.1.4, and also in section 8.2.5, the criteria that a national rule on real property that restricts the free movement of capital must satisfy to be a justifiable exception are the same as for the public policy/security derogation (see section 2.1.3), except that, for land issues, there must be an objective in the public interest that is pursued in a non-discriminatory way. This replaces the public policy/security requirement for a genuine and sufficiently serious threat to a fundamental interest of society.

8.2.4 Do the financial regulation Directives restrict the free movement of capital?

Sections 8.2.1, 8.2.2 and 8.2.3 comprise recommendations as to how Estonian, Polish and Latvian laws respectively can be modified to comply with the EU free movement of capital rules and with the financial regulation Directives.[184] The provisions of these Directives, however, do not always comply with such free movement of capital rules. To give an illustration of possible non-compliance, Article 62(1) of Directive 2004/39/EC is discussed below.

Article 62(1) is as follows.

> "Where the competent authority of the host Member State has clear and demonstrable grounds for believing that an investment firm acting within its territory under the freedom to provide services ... or ... that has a branch within its territory is in breach of the obligations arising from the provisions adopted pursuant to this Directive ... it shall refer those findings to the competent authority of the home Member State. If, despite the[se] measures ... or because such measures prove inadequate, the investment firm persists in acting in a manner that is clearly prejudicial to the interests of host Member State investors or the orderly functioning of markets, the competent authority of the host Member State ... shall take all the appropriate measures needed in order to protect investors and the proper functioning of the markets. This shall include the possibility of preventing offending investment firms from initiating any further transactions within their territories ... ."

The method prescribed in section 1.3.2 is applied, as follows.

1. Is there a capital movement?

Directive 2004/39/EC concerns investment services, which include the reception and transmission of orders relating to financial instruments, the execution of orders for clients and on own account, portfolio management, investment advice, underwriting and placement of financial instruments, and the operation of Multilateral Trading Facilities.[185] Since 'financial instruments' include transferable services, money-market instruments and other items that are classified in the nomenclature in Annex I of Directive 88/361/EEC,[186] and since 'capital movements' listed in this nomenclature include "all the operations necessary for the purposes of capital

---

[184] These Directives are listed in note 17, and are discussed in section 2.4.

[185] Section A, Annex I, Directive 2004/39/EC.

[186] These items are listed in section C, Annex I, Directive 2004/39/EC.

movements: conclusion and performance of the transaction and related transfers",[187] the investment services in Directive 2004/39/EC are 'capital movements'.

2. Is there a restriction on the free movement of capital?

This depends upon the interpretation given to Article 62(1) of Directive 2004/39/EC. There is a limitation on the free movement of capital if the legal provision concerned discriminates against residents of other Member States. Article 62(1) applies to investment service providers that are registered in the EU but not in the host Member State. Interpreted literally, this Article discriminates against these companies in comparison with investment service providers registered in the host State.

From a broader perspective, Directive 2004/39/EC applies to all 27 Member States. Any of these countries may be the host State, the particular country qualifying for this description being the one to which the investment services are provided. Therefore, Article 62(1) does not discriminate against any Member State.

If the broader interpretation is accepted, which is the more reasonable one, Article 62(1) may still restrict the free movement of capital. In *Commission v France*,[188] *Commission v Spain*,[189] *Commission v United Kingdom*,[190] and *Commission v Italy*,[191] the ECJ held that the national legal provisions at issue restricted the free movement of capital because they deterred investment from other Member States, even when, as in *Commission v Spain*, those rules were applied equally to residents and non-residents.[192]

Hence, the issue is whether or not Article 62(1) deters investment service providers from other Member States. The answer depends on how the argument is put. For instance, when the Board of Directors of an investment company decides whether to establish a Latvian branch, it is unlikely to consider the possibility of the FCMC applying sanctions under Article 62(1) a major deterrent to proceeding.

Conversely, if, as in the four cases cited above, the ECJ is asked by a national court to rule under Article 234 of the EC Treaty on the compatibility of Article 62(1) of Directive 2004/39/EC (without knowing that it is a provision of EU law) with Article 56 of the Treaty, it may

---

[187] Annex I, Directive 88/361/EEC.
[188] [2002] ECR I-4781.
[189] [2003] ECR I-4581.
[190] [2003] ECR I-4641.
[191] [2005] ECR I-4933.
[192] See section 2.1.2.

conclude that the potential imposition of sanctions by the national financial authority deters the provision of services by investment companies from other Member States, and therefore Article 62(1) restricts the free movement of capital. This latter interpretation is the context in which the question '*Is there a restriction on the free movement of capital?*' is asked. Consequently, its most likely answer is: 'Yes, there is such a restriction.'

3. Is there an acceptable reason for restricting the free movement of capital?

Article 62(1) states two interests that the host Member State's measures are intended to guarantee. These are the protection of investors and the proper functioning of markets. Unfortunately, Directive 2004/39/EC does not specify these interests in practical terms and, with one exception (the prohibition of further transactions by offending investment companies in the host Member State), omits a statement of the measures that either the home or host Member State's competent authority are permitted to apply.

Consequently, those measures may be disproportionate and do not observe the requirements of legal certainty: they must be specific, objective and previously known to the parties (including the specific investment services provider).[193] In addition, whilst Article 62(4) of Directive 2004/39/EC requires the supervisory authority to give reasons for imposing a sanction or restriction,[194] it does not provide a right of appeal in the courts of the Member State taking such a measure against the decision to apply it.[195] Hence, Article 62(1) of Directive 2004/39/EC is an unjustified restriction on the free movement of capital.

In a situation such as this, in which at least one provision of a Directive can reasonably be interpreted as being contrary to the free movement of capital, there are two alternative solutions. Firstly, the EU authorities can uphold Community law on the free movement of capital as it stands, and alter all the provisions in secondary legislation that contravene it. For Article 62(1) of Directive 2004/39/EC, this involves specifying what 'the

[193] See the subsection '*The requirements for a successful public policy/security derogation*' in section 2.1.3.

[194] Article 62(4) states: "Any measure adopted pursuant to paragraphs 1, 2, or 3 involving sanctions or restrictions on the activities of an investment firm or of a regulated market shall be properly justified and communicated to the investment firm or to the regulated market concerned."

[195] See the subsection '*The requirements for a successful public policy/security derogation*' in section 2.1.3.

protection of investors' and 'the proper functioning of markets' mean in specific terms and stating a list of proportionate measures that the national supervisory authority can take, thereby offering legal certainty to investment service providers. It also requires adding to Article 62(4) a right of appeal against each sanction or restriction in the courts of the Member State applying such a measure.

The second solution is to insert the following statement into Chapter 4 of the EC Treaty.[196] 'Article 56 of this Treaty is disapplied in so far as it is contravened by Regulations or Directives adopted by the Council of the European Union and/or the European Parliament, or by legislation of the Member States which, on a strict interpretation, implements these Directives.'

This solution has two advantages over the first alternative. 1) It avoids the need for extensive scrutiny of EU secondary legislation,[197] and for the required process of agreeing modifications to Articles of Regulations and Directives and for enacting the changes. 2) It leaves the national laws and procedures that depend on the EU secondary legislation intact.

However, the second solution necessitates a change to be made to the EC Treaty. This requires another treaty to be agreed between all 27 Member States, which may present divergences of view as to the language of the new clause. Furthermore, even if a suitable legal provision is agreed, one or more Member States may fail to ratify the new treaty. Consequently, this solution may not be feasible. At the very least, there should be prior consensus from the Member States that Article 56 of the EC Treaty should be disapplied in favour of Regulations and Directives with which it conflicts.

There is also the problem of reconciling the second solution with the legal principle that a superior source of law takes precedence over an inferior source. EU law is typical of legal orders in that the primary source of law, the Treaties, gives power to the EU institutions to enact secondary legislation–Regulations, Directives and Decisions. There needs to be a very good reason to restrict the scope of an Article of the EC

---

[196] This is the chapter of the EC Treaty on Capital and Payments. In the Treaty on the Functioning of the European Union, which replaces the EC Treaty, the proposed statement should be inserted into Chapter 4 of Title IV, and should read 'Article 63 of this Treaty is disapplied ...' to reflect the altered numbering of the Treaty provisions.

[197] The insertion of the above statement into the EC Treaty requires no scrutiny. Scrutiny of the national legislation implementing the Directives is required to ensure that its provisions are not of broader application than that which the Directive provides.

Treaty in order to avoid conflict with secondary legislation adopted in accordance with another Article of the same Treaty. In the case of differences between Article 56 of the Treaty and the financial regulation Directives,[198] however, there are the following arguments for considering this alternative.

Firstly, in the case of the financial regulation Directives, national laws implementing the free movement of services and the freedom of establishment are more favourable to the free movement of capital than equivalent national provisions concerning the free movement of services and the freedom of establishment between Member States and third countries.[199] Why change a system that is working well? There is a risk that, if Articles in these Directives are altered for non-compliance with Article 56 of the EC Treaty, the information transfer system for the establishment of branches in, and cross-border services to, other Member States will become non-uniform, bureaucratic, slow and/or unworkable.

The changes recommended to Article 62(1) of Directive 2004/39/EC in the first solution (above) may lead to one or more of these outcomes. The following results may occur, for instance.

Non-uniformity: there may be a different standard between national courts as to whether an appeal against a sanction or restriction is allowed or rejected.

Slowness: the investment services provider may be asked by the host Member State's supervisory authority to provide a detailed record of its provision of services in that country, which the authority then inspects and comments on for legality and for instances of non-observance of investor protection and the proper working of markets.[200]

Secondly, the financial regulation Directives are a practical aid to the implementation of the Internal Market.[201] Whilst recognising the need for supervision of investment, financial and insurance service provision in other Member States, these Directives do not require an organisation to be authorised to provide cross-border services to, or to establish a branch in, another Member State, as long as the competent authority in that firm's

---

[198] Directives 2004/39/EC, 2006/48/EC, 73/239/EEC, 88/357/EEC, 92/49/EEC, 2002/83/EC and 2002/92/EC, discussed in section 2.4.

[199] See the '*Comment*' subsection to section 5.1.8, and also section 8.1.

[200] If changes to financial regulation Directives are made to comply with Article 56 of the EC Treaty, then they should be introduced gradually in order to receive feedback on their effect. This feedback should be used to make further adjustments that minimise both restrictions to cross-border capital movements and undesirable outcomes.

[201] The Internal Market is described in section 1.2.3.

home State has granted it a licence to supply such services there. This facilitates the free movement of services and of capital throughout the EU.

By contrast, Article 56 of the EC Treaty is a statement of principle that prohibits restrictions to the free movement of capital and to payments between Member States and to/from third countries. This principle has exceptions.[202] It is reasonable that a further derogation from Article 56 is permitted in order to enable the maintenance of Directives and their national implementing provisions in instances in which those Directives contravene this principle, especially if such Directives facilitate the operation of the Internal Market.

Thirdly, although the implementation of the free movement of capital between Member States and third countries has not been extensively considered□at least in the laws of Estonia, Poland and Latvia,[203] it may involve the adoption of further Directives. These Directives may restrict the free movement of capital, by requiring conditions for a company registered in a Member State to establish a branch in a country outside the EEA, for instance. Nonetheless, if the net effect of adopting such Directives and transposing them into national legislation is to facilitate the movement of services and of capital between Member States and third countries, then it is of greater importance to implement and maintain the Directives than to alter them for the compliance of specific legal provisions with Article 56 of the EC Treaty.

To summarise, the reasons described above support the addition of a clause to Article 56 of the EC Treaty that requires this Article to be disapplied in so far as it is contravened by Regulations and Directives or by the national legislation implementing these Directives. Whilst this change is simpler than the alternative solution of adapting the provisions of EU secondary legislation that restrict the free movement of capital to comply with, or be justifiable exceptions to, Article 56, it involves the agreement of a new treaty between the 27 Member States, and is contrary to the legal principle of the superiority of primary sources of law over secondary sources.

---

[202] These exceptions are listed in the first paragraph of section 2.1.3.

[203] As stated in section 8.1, there are many legal omissions concerning capital movements between these three Member States and countries outside the EEA, especially in relation to cross-border services.

8.2.5 Comment: the value of the EU/national law comparison

The EU case law for the free movement of capital consists of cases involving public policy, public security and prior authorisation in section 2.1.3, those on real property in section 2.1.4, and the taxation cases in section 2.3. The three-step method in determining whether there is restriction on such movement varies between these types of cases,[204] but the public policy/security and real property case law differ in only one respect: for a national legal provision on real property to be a justifiable restriction on the free movement of capital, there must be an objective in the public interest that is applied in a non-discriminatory way;[205] by contrast, the public policy/security derogation from Article 56 of the EC Treaty requires a genuine and sufficiently serious threat to a fundamental interest of society.[206]

Given this uniformity of approach to the non-taxation cases, it is appropriate to extend the EU rules set out in section 2.1 to all the national legislative and regulatory provisions for Estonia, Poland and Latvia other than those concerning taxation, which follow the case law in section 2.3. The contents of the national laws discussed in chapters 3, 4 and 5 differ from the domestic laws and procedures that are the source of dispute in the EU cases of chapter 2.[207] As the ECJ has neither pronounced judgment on the former nor on the rules of other Member States with similar content for compatibility with Article 56 of the EC Treaty,[208] there is doubt as to whether the extension of the existing EU case law to those legal provisions is an accurate reflection of the view that the Court would take. Nonetheless, it is a reasonable approach to adopt, since the ECJ has consistently applied this case law.

---

[204] In this method, the following questions are asked. Is there a capital movement? Is there a restriction on the free movement of capital? Is there an acceptable reason for restricting the free movement of capital? See the subsection '*The method*' in section 1.3.2.

[205] See section 2.1.4.

[206] See section 2.1.3, especially *Eglise de Scientologie and Scientology International* [2000] ECR I-1335.

[207] There are areas of similarity. For instance, taxation on dividends cases such as *Lenz* [2004] ECR I-7063, *Manninen* [2004] ECR I-7477, and *Kerckhaert and Morres* [2006] ECR I-10967 in section 2.3.1 are directly applicable to Estonian, Polish and Latvian legal provisions involving cross-border dividend payments.

[208] Some of the Estonian, Polish and Latvian laws discussed have similar content to national legal provisions on which the ECJ has already passed judgment, such as those on the taxation of dividends (see note 207).

8.3 Legal Studies: Where to Next?

As stated in section 1.2.3, the free movement of capital is one of the four fundamental freedoms provided by the EC Treaty. Further studies may consider the compliance of Estonian, Polish and Latvian legislation and regulations with EU law on the free movement of goods, persons and services, and with Community Regulations and Directives affecting these freedoms. Since the financial regulation Directives concern the free movement of services, this fundamental freedom would be the appropriate initial extension to the work contained in this book. These studies are valuable because they provide information to the EU institutions and to the governments of the three Member States on the extent to which the fundamental freedoms are safeguarded by Estonian, Polish and Latvian law.

Compliance of the national laws of the other Member States with Article 56 of the EC Treaty is another possible source of further work.[209] A comprehensive comparison of EU and national laws that affect the free movement of capital to and from Hungary, for instance, would enable comparison between legal restrictions to cross-border capital flows for this country and those for Estonia, Poland and Latvia. Smaller scale studies, such as the compliance of Acts regulated by the Slovenian Securities Market Agency with Article 56, may also be worthwhile.

A detailed study of compliance of national law with Article 56 for a particular Member State and/or business sector is another possible line of research. For instance, if the Estonian insurance sector is selected, one could look in depth at the practices in that sector to observe whether cross-border capital movement is being maximised. What do the Estonian providers of insurance services to other countries do? Is it efficient? Does it comply with national law? Does national law restrict the scope of cross-border service provision? Interviews with directors and employees of these companies and with officials at the Estonian FSA may enable a comprehensive scheme of cross-border capital movements in this sector to be constructed, leading to detailed recommendations for practical improvement to the movement of capital.

This approach is valuable because it deepens knowledge acquired from the investigations made as part of the research for the present work. The starting point for compliance with Article 56 in the Estonian insurance sector could be the information contained in section 3.1.5.

---

[209] Article 56 of the EC Treaty has become Article 63 of the Treaty on the Functioning of the European Union. There is no change in the content of this provision.

Another interesting study would be an historical investigation as to how Estonian, Polish and Latvian legislation has developed, especially since the change in the political regimes in Eastern Europe. One could inspect laws likely to affect the free movement of capital from 1985 until the present. This year is an appropriate choice because it was the time that economic reform was started in the Soviet Union under President Gorbacev.[210] The laws identified in this book could be taken as the current position; their predecessors could be identified and, if necessary, translated into English. The study of land laws would be particularly interesting, since these Member States have undergone a substantial land reform process since the early 1990s. This reform will be complete when the EU transitional measures on the purchase of real estate, discussed in section 2.5, are no longer in force.

The discussion in section 8.2.4 yields three additional research options.

1. The Articles of the financial regulation Directives could be analysed for compliance with the EU laws that govern the free movement of capital. Instances of conflict between the EC Treaty and EU secondary legislation need to be investigated in order to maintain the integrity of Community law, which has many users. The free movement of capital is an important and relatively clear area of law in which to pursue this investigation.[211]
2. A feasibility study could be undertaken as to whether it is best on a cost/benefit basis to modify the provisions of Regulations and Directives that conflict with Article 56 of the EC Treaty, to add a clause to the Treaty that disapplies Article 56 to such provisions, or to ignore instances of breach of Article 56 by the EU secondary legislation. There are many interested parties to be consulted, including the Community institutions, the governments of the Member States, and companies that provide cross-border services to, or with branches, subsidiaries and/or associates in, other Member States.
3. The staff of financial supervision authorities and international organisations both in the EEA and in third countries could be interviewed as to the possible scope and content of financial regulation Directives that could be applied exclusively to the

---

[210] From 1985 until 1991, Estonia and Latvia were part of one jurisdiction: the Soviet Union. They have been independent countries with separate legal systems since 1991.

[211] This investigation would compare EU secondary legislation with the Treaty on the Functioning of the European Union, which supersedes the EC Treaty.

provision of services between the EEA and third countries.[212] Since Article 56 applies to capital movements between the EU and third countries, such Directives may improve the free movement of capital in this context.

In addition to these legal studies, there is scope for statistical analysis and for case study research on the relationship between legal barriers to the free movement of capital and cross-border capital flows. Such possibilities are discussed in the next section.

8.4 Econometric Studies: Where to Next?

8.4.1 Econometrics

An econometric analysis that investigates the effect of national legal restrictions to the free movement of capital on cross-border flows assists in determining whether the former causes the latter. The presentation of quarterly data in section 7.1 provides a sufficient number of data points to yield the degrees of freedom necessary for this approach. However, regressions using panel data potentially exhibit all the methodological problems discussed in Appendix F,[213] in which the econometric work of La Porta et al. with legal indices is discussed.

Another difficulty with the proposed econometric work is deciding how many and which determinants of cross-border capital flows to use as explanatory variables in the regressions. A reasonable starting point is to include the economic factors utilised in section 7.1.6, both because they are readily measurable and because they fit well together.[214] Appendix E identifies several further determinants of cross-border flows, which are difficult to define and measure, but could potentially be included in a complex but comprehensive approach to the causation issue identified above. Given the substantial number of subsidiary legal indices calculated

---

[212] The Directives should extend to the provision of services by EEA firms to third countries and by foreign organisations to the EEA. It is better, especially if third country governments and companies are unwilling to accept the legal status of the Directives over this scope of operation, for the content of the Directives to be reflected in EU-third country or EEA-third country agreements, and/or in the legislation of the non-EEA states.

[213] Panel data comprise observations from different countries and time-periods.

[214] These determinants of cross-border capital flows are the real interest rate, the volatility of nominal interest rates, the inflation rate, the exchange rate and the net barter terms of trade.

in section 6.1 and employed in section 7.1 with corresponding capital flows, there is considerable scope for a series of empirical studies.

8.4.2 Case studies

A possible research hypothesis, based on the first paragraph of section 7.2.3, is that there is an inverse relationship between national legislative and regulatory restrictions to cross-border capital movements and the flows to and from Estonia, Poland and Latvia. Two sectors could be selected, credit institutions and insurance service providers for instance, and six institutions could be chosen, one from each country/sector combination.

Several research methods could be used at each company to test and develop the hypothesis. These may include the inspection of data on capital flows at sectoral and company level, the inspection of corporate accounts (especially the geographically-based sales data contained therein), and interviews of employees of the Member State's supervisory authority for the sector, of the company's executives, of employees at the organisation's legal department (for information concerning the legal restrictions to cross-border flows) and at its finance department (for information on international payments and receipts). A report can then be constructed from the results from all the companies, which determines how fully the information gathered supports or refutes the research hypothesis.

The differences between the companies with regard to the research hypothesis should be explained from the existing data, if possible.[215] Additionally or alternatively, these differences could be put to each company's executives in order to discover a consistent and relevant explanation for them. If the differences cannot be satisfactorily explained, then the initial research hypothesis should be modified to incorporate them. This new research hypothesis should be tested by further data collection from the selected companies.

This process may need to be repeated several times before a consistent picture of the relationship between national legal restrictions to cross-border capital movements and the flows to and from the three Member

[215] Section 7.2.2 uses data from the validation study to explain the unexpected unresponsiveness of cross-border capital flows in the insurance services and insurance mediation sectors to the fall in the subsidiary legal indices for insurance services and insurance mediation (see figures 7.44-7.46). This integration of research methods is necessary in case study research in order to explain complex phenomena.

States in the two selected sectors is established. This relationship can be tested for depth by collecting data from other companies in these sectors, and for breadth by putting it as a research hypothesis to companies from other sectors and/or from the same sectors in other Member States. If the case study research is conclusive, then it will produce a robust theory for the relationship.

8.5 Final Remarks

When the research idea was conceived, it was difficult to predict whether this concept would be feasible and what journey the subsequent investigation would take. The core theme was the identification of deviations, if any, of the national laws of the new Eastern European EU Member States from the free movement of capital as specified by Community Law, and the discovery of the impact of these restrictive laws on cross-border capital flows to and from this region. Looking back on the research, it can be cautiously stated that there is a correlation between the national laws restricting the free movement of capital and the cross-border flows, assuming that the three countries studied are typical of the region as a whole.

There is further work to be done, some of which is identified in sections 8.3 and 8.4. The studies suggested there offer exciting new prospects that are worthwhile in terms of time and of benefit over cost.

> "As skimming o'er the spacious plain,
> We look around with joyous eye,
> And view no boundaries but the sky." [216]

---

[216] M. Betham (1795), 'Invitation To JBC' *in* J. Breen *ed.*(1992), *Women Romantic Poets 1785□1832: An Anthology*, 94.

APPENDIX A

LEGAL INDEX GRAPHS

Graphs Showing the Change in the Subsidiary Legal Indices from 1998-2007[1]

[1] Figure 7.1 shows the main legal index for all three Member States from 1998-2007.

Indices concerning the direction of capital flows (D:I and D:O)

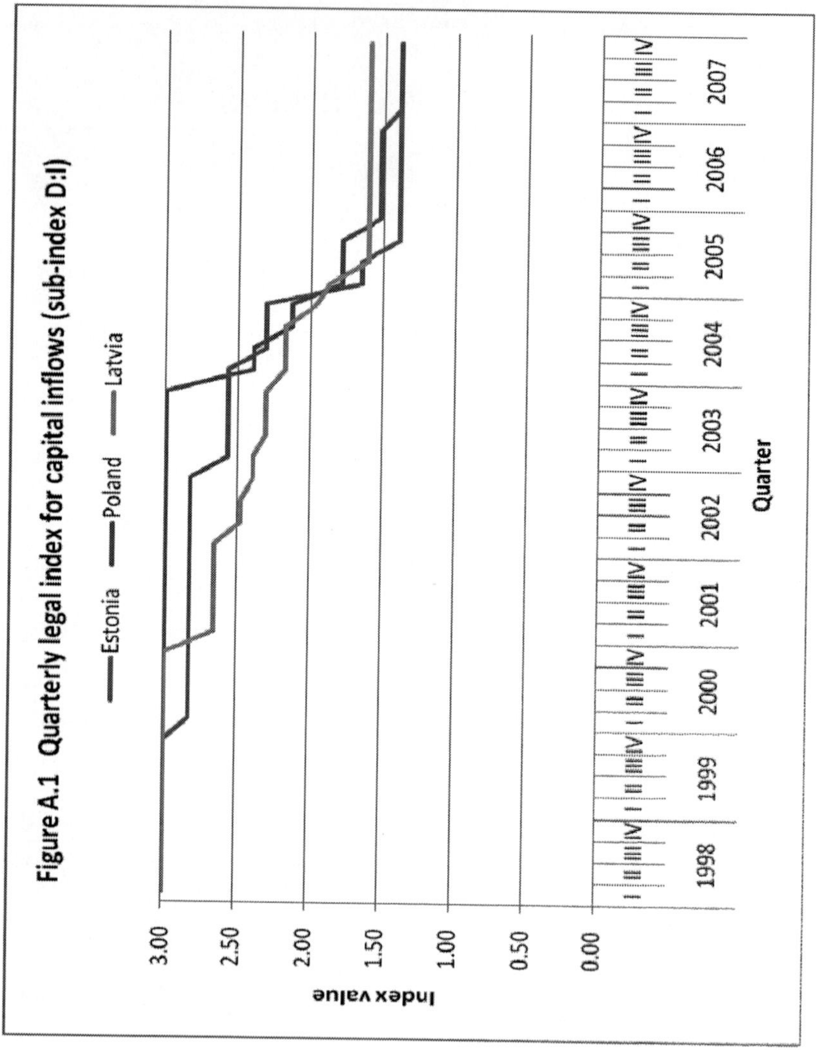

Figure A.1 Quarterly legal index for capital inflows (sub-index D:I)

Figure A.2 Quarterly legal index for capital outflows (sub-index D:O)

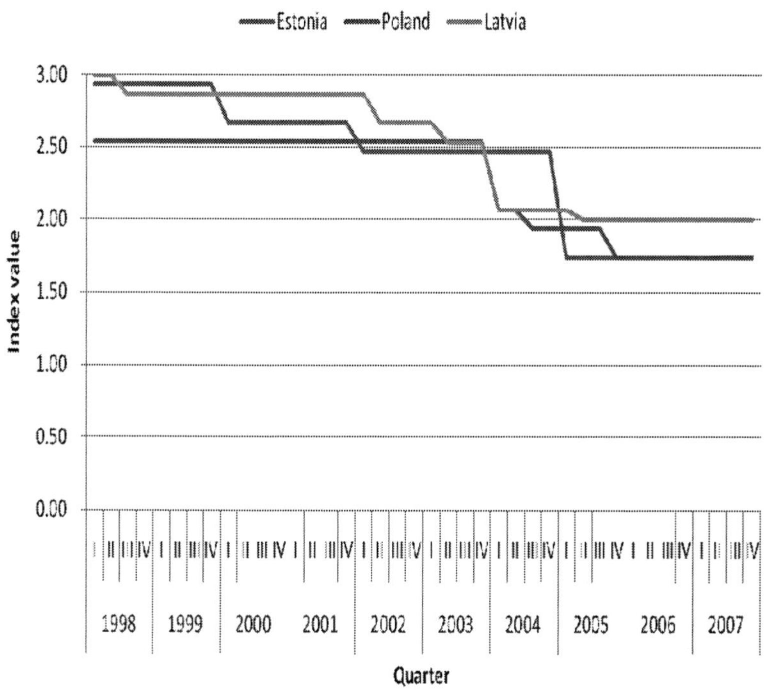

Indices concerning the location of capital flows (L:EEA and L:TC)

Figure A.3 Quarterly legal index for intra-EEA flows (sub-index L:EEA)

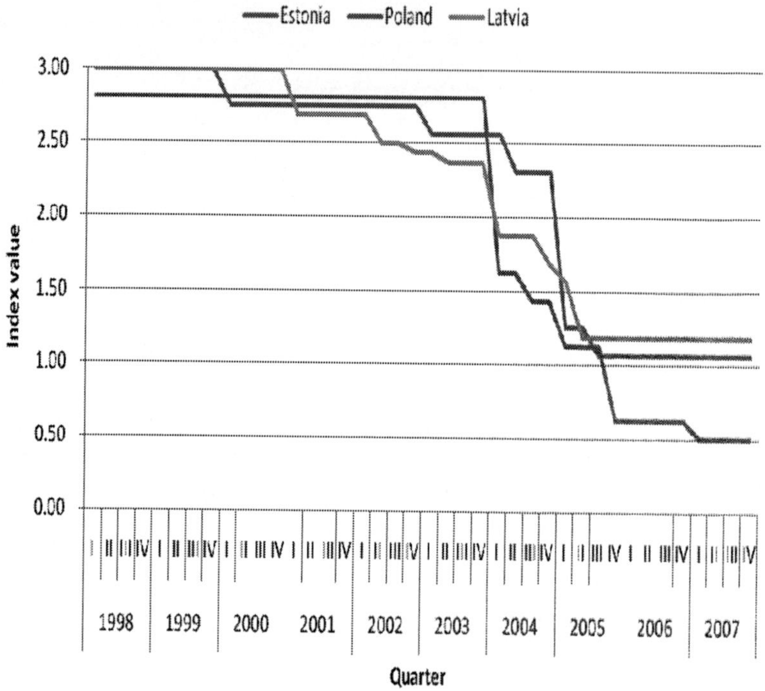

Figure A.4 Quarterly legal index for flows to/from third countries (sub-index L:TC)

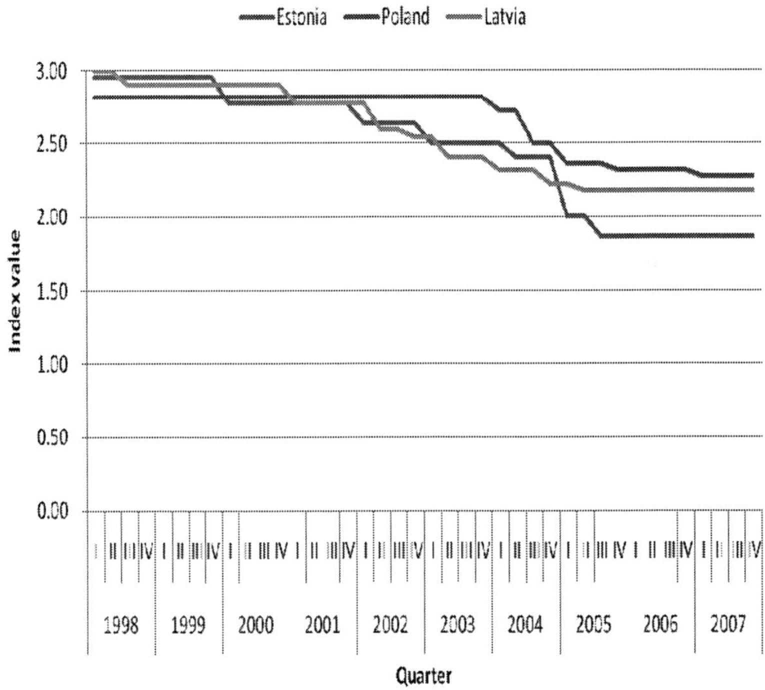

Indices relating to business sectors (S:InvF, SInvS, S:CI, SInsS, S:InsM, S:T and S:L)[2]

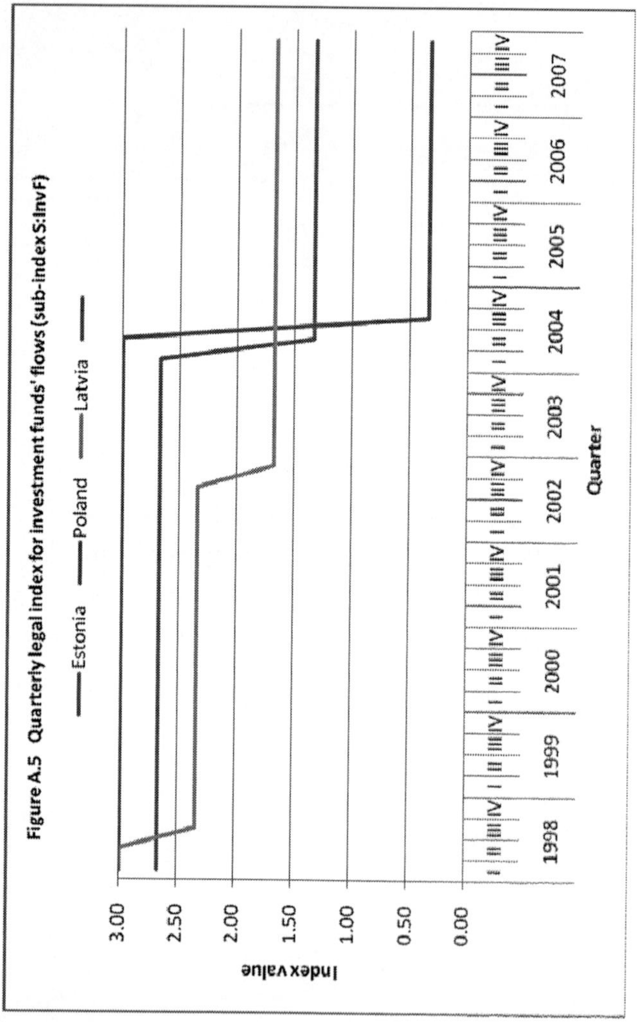

Figure A.5 Quarterly legal index for investment funds' flows (sub-index S:InvF)

[2] Subsidiary legal index S:T measures restrictions to cross-border capital movements concerning taxation. Since international taxation affects organisations with a foreign element from all industrial sectors, this sub-index is not discussed in section 7.1.5. Figure A.10 shows how subsidiary index S:T for Estonia, Poland and Latvia changes with time.

Figure A.6 Quarterly legal index for flows concerning investment services (sub-index S:InvS)

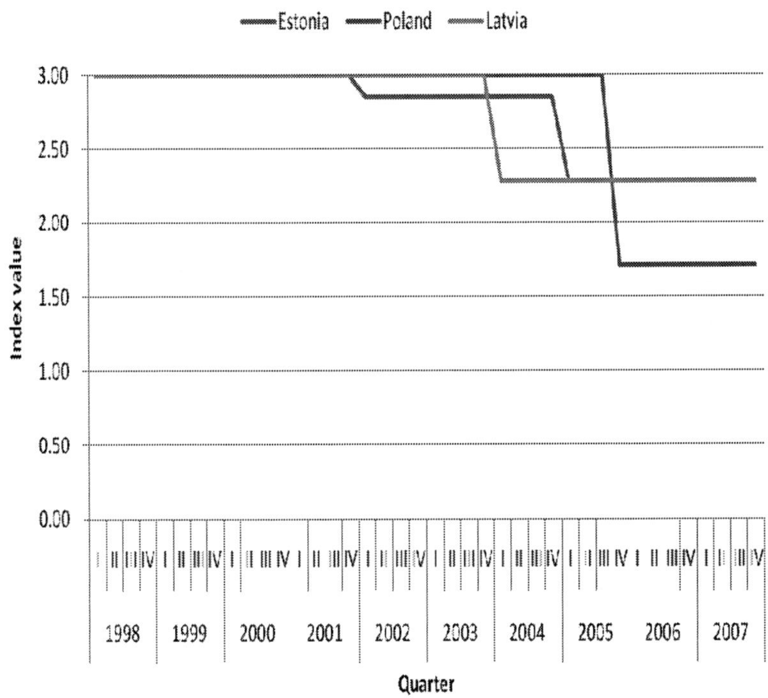

Figure A.7 Quarterly legal index for credit institutions' flows (sub-index S:CI)

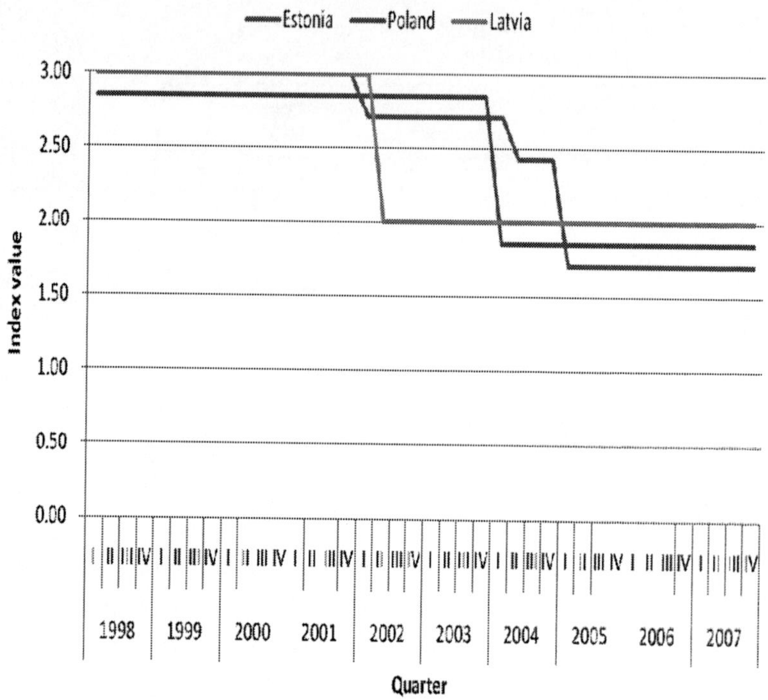

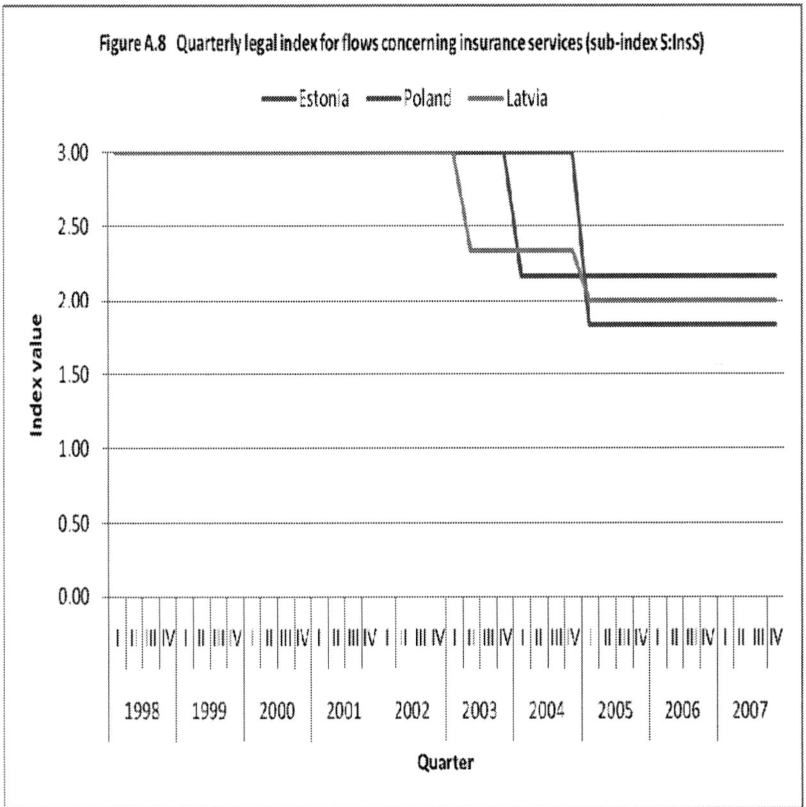
Figure A.8 Quarterly legal index for flows concerning insurance services (sub-index S:InsS)
Estonia
Poland
Latvia
3.00
2.50
2.00
1.50
1.00
0.50
0.00
Index value
1998
1999
2000
2001
2002
2003
2004
2005
2006
2007
Quarter

Figure A.9 Quarterly legal index for flows concerning insurance mediation (sub-index S:InsM)

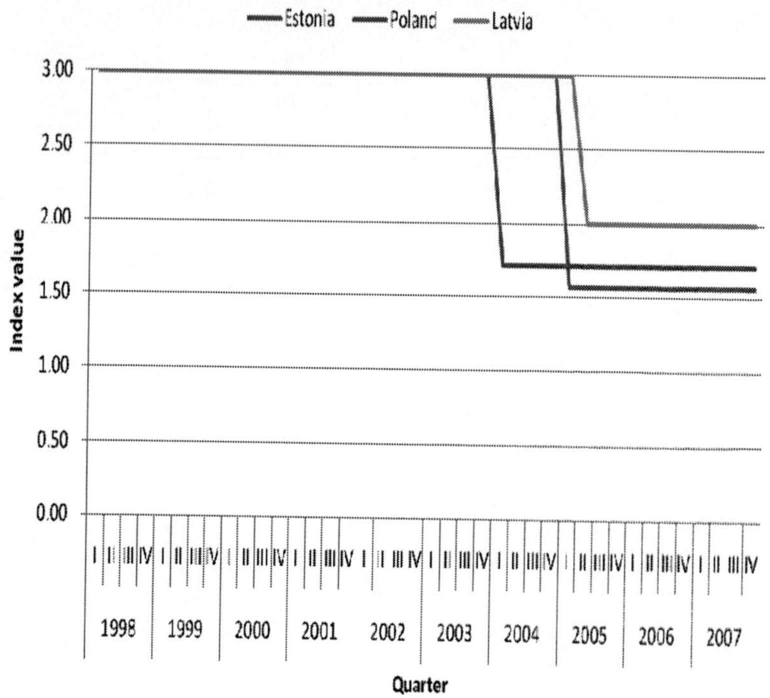

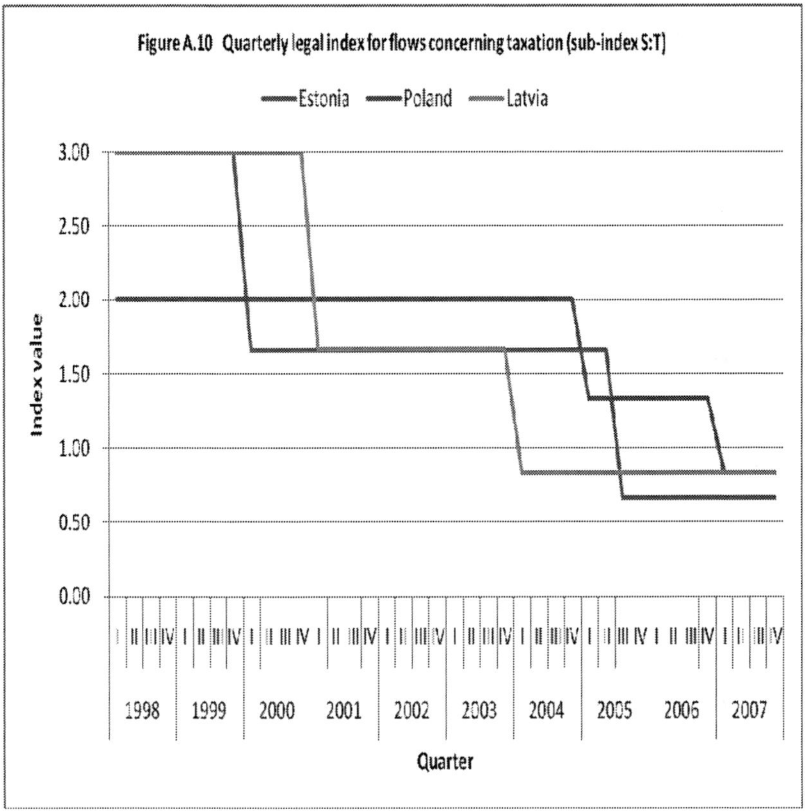
Figure A.10 Quarterly legal index for flows concerning taxation (sub-index S:T)
Estonia
Poland
Latvia
3.00
2.50
2.00
1.50
1.00
0.50
0.00
Index value
1998
1999
2000
2001
2002
2003
2004
2005
2006
2007
Quarter

Figure A.11 Quarterly legal index for flows concerning real property transfers (sub-index S:L)

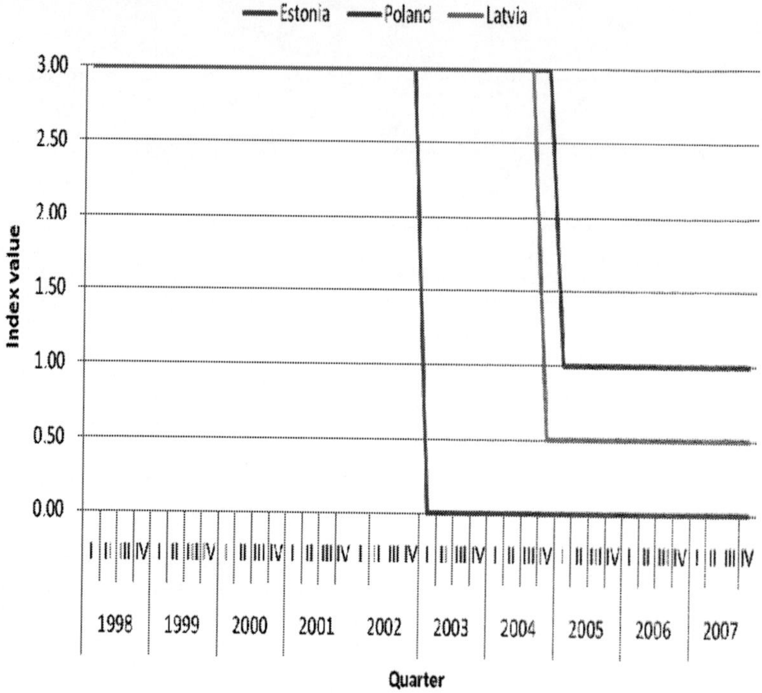

APPENDIX B

DATA TABLES FOR FIGURES 7-51 AND 7-52

Table B-1: Data table for Fig. 7-51[1]

FDI in Latvia (millions of lats)	2002	2003	2004	2005	2006	2007
Austria	2.2	1.8	7.1	12.2	10.1	59.1
Belgium	0.0	1.5	13.1	-2.2	7.2	6.7
Cyprus	-2.7	-0.2	14.9	14.4	77.2	79.3
Czech Republic	0.1	0.6	0.5	2.2	0.4	2.2
Denmark	7.8	-22.0	30.4	69.4	62.4	93.9
Estonia	8.7	14.4	74.0	54.5	157.0	250.6
Finland	10.0	29.7	30.4	12.5	31.4	69.8
France	0.3	3.1	3.0	1.5	3.9	3.0
Germany	3.2	4.5	40.9	-35.0	56.6	78.8
Great Britain	2.8	-2.9	21.1	7.9	46.7	38.8
Greece						
Hungary						
Ireland	-1.9	-3.9	-1.7	27.2	-20.6	0.9
Italy	3.3	4.6	-6.9	1.1	5.2	0.9
Lithuania	2.7	4.6	2.6	37.7	23.6	48.4
Luxembourg	0.9	2.1	-0.5	2.6	16.1	33.1
Malta	4.9	1.3	-0.2	-4.6	41.9	26.1
Netherlands	15.2	25.7	-23.5	-0.9	46.2	38.1
Poland						
Portugal						
Slovakia						
Slovenia						
Spain	0.3	0.7	-0.3	0.3	0.3	-0.7
Sweden	39.9	29.6	30.3	53.4	114.7	104.5

[1] Title and ownership of the data for each country in table B-1 remain with the Bank of Latvia. Title and ownership of the annual conversion rate data remain with Eurostat. In table B-1, 'other Member States' excludes Bulgaria and Romania.

EU total (excluding Bulgaria and Romania)	**97.7**	**95.2**	**235.2**	**254.2**	**680.3**	**933.5**
FDI from Latvia (millions of lats)	**2002**	**2003**	**2004**	**2005**	**2006**	**2007**
Austria	0.0	0.0	0.0	0.5	0.0	0.0
Belgium						
Cyprus	0.4	0.0	0.0	6.6	-0.9	-0.7
Czech Republic	0.0	0.0	0.0	0.3	0.0	0.2
Denmark	0.1	0.0	0.1	4.9	0.1	0.0
Estonia	-1.5	1.6	3.8	9.5	-1.5	-1.9
Finland	0.1	0.2	0.4	0.2	0.0	0.1
France	0.0	0.1	0.0	0.2	0.9	4.5
Germany	0.1	0.4	0.8	0.7	3.4	0.2
Great Britain	0.4	-0.1	1.7	-0.9	1.4	0.3
Greece						
Hungary						
Ireland	-0.1	0.0	0.0	0.0	0.0	0.2
Italy						
Lithuania	0.3	2.3	3.5	8.9	6.5	7.1
Luxembourg	0.0	0.0	0.0	0.0	0.0	-1.4
Malta	0.3	1.9	-3.0	-1.0	4.2	0.0
Netherlands	0.0	0.0	0.2	0.2	0.2	0.4
Poland	0.0	0.0	0.0	0.0	0.1	-0.3
Portugal	0.0	0.0	0.0	0.0	0.0	-0.5
Slovakia	0.2	0.4	0.5	0.1	-1.2	0.2
Slovenia	0.0	0.1	0.1	-0.7	0.7	-0.4
Spain	0.0	0.2	0.0	0.0	0.3	0.0
Sweden	0.1	0.2	1.2	-0.9	1.4	4.4
EU total (excluding Bulgaria and Romania)	**0.4**	**7.3**	**9.3**	**28.6**	**15.6**	**12.4**
	2002	**2003**	**2004**	**2005**	**2006**	**2007**
Annual conversion rate (lats to the Euro)	0.5810	0.6407	0.6652	0.6962	0.6962	0.7001
Data in millions of Euros	**2002**	**2003**	**2004**	**2005**	**2006**	**2007**
Annual change in FDI in Latvia from other Member States	168.2	148.6	353.6	365.1	977.2	1333.4
Annual change in FDI in other Member States from Latvia	0.7	11.4	14.0	41.1	22.4	17.7

Annual change total (gross) EU direct investment	168.8	160.0	367.6	406.2	999.6	1351.1
Annual legal index for intra-EEA flows (subsidiary index L:EEA)	2.44	2.38	1.69	1.19	1.19	1.19

Table B-2: Data table for Fig. 7-52[2]

Data in millions of Euros	2000	2001	2002	2003	2004	2005	2006
Annual change in FDI in Latvia from other Member States	288	75	169	150	353	365	978
Annual change in FDI in other Member States from Latvia	5	12	0	11	15	39	27
Annual change in total (gross) EU direct investment	293	87	169	161	368	404	1005
Annual legal index for intra-EEA flows (subsidiary index L:EEA)	3.00	2.69	2.44	2.38	1.69	1.19	1.19

[2] Title and ownership of the data for FDI inflows to, and FDI outflows from, Latvia in table B.2 remain with Eurostat. In this table, data are in millions of Euros and 'other Member States' excludes Bulgaria and Romania.

APPENDIX C

QUESTIONNAIRE AND LETTER FOR EACH SECTOR

Whilst there are only minor differences between the version of the questionnaire and covering letter sent to organisations in each business sector, all six letter variants and five questionnaire types are included in order to show what those enterprises received. The most significant difference is the omission of the two questions on the EU's regulatory framework from the questionnaire prepared for real property companies; in their professional business of transferring land and buildings, these organisations are outside the scope of the financial regulation Directives. The 'national law' definition in the letter is changed between Estonian, Polish and Latvian law as is appropriate to the recipient.

The order of presentation is as follows.

Investment fund management companies and investment service providers: letter.
Investment fund management companies and investment service providers: questionnaire.
Credit institutions: letter.
Credit institutions: questionnaire.
Life assurance service providers: letter.
Non-life insurance service providers: letter.
Life and non-life insurance service providers: questionnaire.
Insurance intermediaries: letter.
Insurance intermediaries: questionnaire.
Real property companies: letter.
Real property companies: questionnaire.

Mr. G. Baber,
Research Student, SOAS,
Marigold Cottage,
1, St. Mary's Close,
Aston, Herts.,
SG2 7EQ,
United Kingdom.

March/April 2008

Dear Sir/Madam,

I am conducting a survey as part of my research for the degree of Doctor of Philosophy (Ph.D.) at the School of Oriental and African Studies (SOAS), University of London. The survey consists of twelve questions, which investigate the effect of the European and national laws concerning the cross-border movement of capital on Estonian, Latvian and Polish businesses in four industrial sectors (investment, banking, insurance and property). I would be most grateful if you would complete the enclosed questionnaire, which is valuable to my research and would be of considerable interest to the European Commission in its role of initiator of European legal proposals.

Article 56 of the Treaty Establishing the European Communities (EC Treaty) states that all restrictions on capital movement and on payments between European Union (EU) Member States and between Member States and non-Member States shall be prohibited. This is a very bold and unequivocal statement, which provides EU businesses with considerable opportunities for trade and expansion not only within the EU, but also abroad. It is accompanied by a regulatory framework for the free movement of services and the freedom of establishment, which, for investment firms, is Directive 2004/39/EC. The application of these principles within Estonia, Poland and Latvia is the subject of my Ph.D. research.

The findings from the questionnaire will be treated in strict confidence, with no information being published about specific organisations and their

particular experience, unless these corporations wish to divulge particular facts. I shall be writing a report from the findings, and, if you wish to receive a copy of this report, please put your e-mail address on the space allotted on the questionnaire.

If you have any queries concerning the questions, I would be happy to answer them, and can be contacted at 209393@soas.ac.uk. Please answer as many questions as you can, and post the completed questionnaire to me at the address above.

With best wishes,

Yours sincerely,

Graeme Baber, M.A.(Oxon), LL.M., M.Sc., M.B.A., M.C.T.
Research Student, SOAS, University of London.

Post script: A note on definitions in the questionnaire

'National law' means 'Estonian legislation and regulations'.

'Movement of capital' and 'capital flows' include cash, cheque and electronic payments, shares, bonds, loans, investment units, deposits and financial instruments.

The 'European Union's regulatory framework' includes Directives 2004/39/EC for investment firms, 2006/48/EC for credit institutions, 73/239/EEC, 88/357/EEC and 92/49/EEC for insurance companies, 2002/83/EC for life assurance companies and 2002/92/EC for insurance intermediaries.

Question 1

Is the free movement of capital across national borders an issue for your business?

Yes ☐
No ☐

Question 2

Do you agree or disagree that national law in the investment sector causes a significant restriction on cross-border capital flows?

Agree ☐
Disagree ☐

Please give reasons for your answer, in the space below.

____
____
____
____
____
____

Question 3

What steps could be taken to improve the movement of capital across national borders in the context of your business?

____
____
____
____
____
____

Question 4

To what extent does the European Union's regulatory framework encourage or dissuade you from *providing investment services* to other European Economic Area (EEA) Member States?

Strongly encourage ☐
Mildly encourage ☐
Neither encourage nor dissuade ☐
Mildly dissuade ☐
Strongly dissuade ☐

Question 5
To what extent does the European Union's regulatory framework encourage or dissuade you from *establishing branches* in other EEA Member States?

Strongly encourage	
Mildly encourage	
Neither encourage nor dissuade	
Mildly dissuade	
Strongly dissuade	

Question 6
To what extent does *national law* encourage or dissuade you from *providing investment services* to other EEA Member States?

Strongly encourage	
Mildly encourage	
Neither encourage nor dissuade	
Mildly dissuade	
Strongly dissuade	

Question 7
To what extent does national law encourage or dissuade you from *establishing branches* in other EEA Member States?

Strongly encourage	
Mildly encourage	
Neither encourage nor dissuade	
Mildly dissuade	
Strongly dissuade	

Question 8
To what extent does national law encourage or dissuade you from providing investment services to *countries outside the EEA*?

Strongly encourage	
Mildly encourage	
Neither encourage nor dissuade	
Mildly dissuade	
Strongly dissuade	

Question 9
To what extent does national law encourage or dissuade you from establishing branches in countries outside the EEA?

Strongly encourage	
Mildly encourage	
Neither encourage nor dissuade	
Mildly dissuade	
Strongly dissuade	

Question 10
What is the *percentage of your total sales* arising from *outside the EEA*?

0%-10%	10%-20%	20%-30%	30%-40%	40%-50%	50%-60%	60%-70%	> 70%

Question 11
What is the percentage of your total sales arising from *other EEA Member States*?

0%-10%	10%-20%	20%-30%	30%-40%	40%-50%	50%-60%	60%-70%	> 70%

Question 12
Please give any other relevant comments, in the space below.

____
____
____
____
____
____

If you would like a copy of the report on the results of the survey, please put your e-mail address in the space below.

____

Mr. G. Baber,
Research Student, SOAS,
Marigold Cottage,
1, St. Mary's Close,
Aston, Herts.,
SG2 7EQ,
United Kingdom.

March/April 2008

Dear Sir/Madam,

I am conducting a survey as part of my research for the degree of Doctor of Philosophy (Ph.D.) at the School of Oriental and African Studies (SOAS), University of London. The survey consists of twelve questions, which investigate the effect of the European and national laws concerning the cross-border movement of capital on Estonian, Latvian and Polish businesses in four industrial sectors (investment, banking, insurance and property). I would be most grateful if you would complete the enclosed questionnaire, which is valuable to my research and would be of considerable interest to the European Commission in its role of initiator of European legal proposals.

Article 56 of the Treaty Establishing the European Communities (EC Treaty) states that all restrictions on capital movement and on payments between European Union (EU) Member States and between Member States and non-Member States shall be prohibited. This is a very bold and unequivocal statement, which provides EU businesses with considerable opportunities for trade and expansion not only within the EU, but also abroad. It is accompanied by a regulatory framework for the free movement of services and the freedom of establishment, which, for credit institutions, is Directive 2006/48/EC. The application of these principles within Estonia, Poland and Latvia is the subject of my Ph.D. research.

The findings from the questionnaire will be treated in strict confidence, with no information being published about specific organisations and their particular experience, unless these corporations wish to divulge particular facts. I shall be writing a report from the findings, and, if you wish to receive a copy of this report, please put your e-mail address on the space allotted on the questionnaire.

If you have any queries concerning the questions, I would be happy to answer them, and can be contacted at 209393@soas.ac.uk. Please answer as many questions as you can, and post the completed questionnaire to me at the address above.

With best wishes,

Yours sincerely,

Graeme Baber, M.A.(Oxon), LL.M., M.Sc., M.B.A., M.C.T.
Research Student, SOAS, University of London.

Post script: A note on definitions in the questionnaire

'National law' means 'Estonian legislation and regulations'.

'Movement of capital' and 'capital flows' include cash, cheque and electronic payments, shares, bonds, loans, investment units, deposits and financial instruments.

The 'European Union's regulatory framework' includes Directives 2004/39/EC for investment firms, 2006/48/EC for credit institutions, 73/239/EEC, 88/357/EEC and 92/49/EEC for insurance companies, 2002/83/EC for life assurance companies and 2002/92/EC for insurance intermediaries.

Question 1
Is the free movement of capital across national borders an issue for your business?

Yes ☐
No ☐

Question 2
Do you agree or disagree that national law in the investment sector causes a significant restriction on cross-border capital flows?

Agree ☐
Disagree ☐

Please give reasons for your answer, in the space below.

____
____
____
____
____
____

Question 3
What steps could be taken to improve the movement of capital across national borders in the context of your business?

____
____
____
____
____
____

Question 4
To what extent does the European Union's regulatory framework encourage or dissuade you from *providing financial services* to other European Economic Area (EEA) Member States?

Strongly encourage ☐
Mildly encourage ☐
Neither encourage nor dissuade ☐
Mildly dissuade ☐
Strongly dissuade ☐

Question 5
To what extent does the European Union's regulatory framework encourage or dissuade you from *establishing branches* in other EEA Member States?

Strongly encourage	
Mildly encourage	
Neither encourage nor dissuade	
Mildly dissuade	
Strongly dissuade	

Question 6
To what extent does *national law* encourage or dissuade you from *providing financial services* to other EEA Member States?

Strongly encourage	
Mildly encourage	
Neither encourage nor dissuade	
Mildly dissuade	
Strongly dissuade	

Question 7
To what extent does national law encourage or dissuade you from *establishing branches* in other EEA Member States?

Strongly encourage	
Mildly encourage	
Neither encourage nor dissuade	
Mildly dissuade	
Strongly dissuade	

Question 8
To what extent does national law encourage or dissuade you from providing financial services to *countries outside the EEA*?

Strongly encourage	
Mildly encourage	
Neither encourage nor dissuade	
Mildly dissuade	
Strongly dissuade	

Question 9
To what extent does national law encourage or dissuade you from establishing branches in countries outside the EEA?

Strongly encourage	
Mildly encourage	
Neither encourage nor dissuade	
Mildly dissuade	
Strongly dissuade	

Question 10
What is the *percentage of your total sales* arising from *outside the EEA*?

0%- 10%	10%- 20%	20%- 30%	30%- 40%	40%- 50%	50%- 60%	60%- 70%	> 70%

Question 11
What is the percentage of your total sales arising from *other EEA Member States*?

0%- 10%	10%- 20%	20%- 30%	30%- 40%	40%- 50%	50%- 60%	60%- 70%	> 70%

Question 12
Please give any other relevant comments, in the space below.

____

____

____

____

____

____

If you would like a copy of the report on the results of the survey, please put your e-mail address in the space below.

____

Mr. G. Baber,
Research Student, SOAS,
Marigold Cottage,
1, St. Mary's Close,
Aston, Herts.,
SG2 7EQ,
United Kingdom.

March/April 2008

Dear Sir/Madam,

I am conducting a survey as part of my research for the degree of Doctor of Philosophy (Ph.D.) at the School of Oriental and African Studies (SOAS), University of London. The survey consists of twelve questions, which investigate the effect of the European and national laws concerning the cross-border movement of capital on Estonian, Latvian and Polish businesses in four industrial sectors (investment, banking, insurance and property). I would be most grateful if you would complete the enclosed questionnaire, which is valuable to my research and would be of considerable interest to the European Commission in its role of initiator of European legal proposals.

Article 56 of the Treaty Establishing the European Communities (EC Treaty) states that all restrictions on capital movement and on payments between European Union (EU) Member States and between Member States and non-Member States shall be prohibited. This is a very bold and unequivocal statement, which provides EU businesses with considerable opportunities for trade and expansion not only within the EU, but also abroad. It is accompanied by a regulatory framework for the free movement of services and the freedom of establishment, which, for life assurance companies, is Directive 2002/83/EC. The application of these principles within Estonia, Poland and Latvia is the subject of my Ph.D. research.

The findings from the questionnaire will be treated in strict confidence, with no information being published about specific organisations and their

particular experience, unless these corporations wish to divulge particular facts. I shall be writing a report from the findings, and, if you wish to receive a copy of this report, please put your e-mail address on the space allotted on the questionnaire.

If you have any queries concerning the questions, I would be happy to answer them, and can be contacted at 209393@soas.ac.uk. Please answer as many questions as you can, and post the completed questionnaire to me at the address above.

With best wishes,

Yours sincerely,

Graeme Baber, M.A.(Oxon), LL.M., M.Sc., M.B.A., M.C.T.
Research Student, SOAS, University of London.

Post script: A note on definitions in the questionnaire

'National law' means 'Estonian legislation and regulations'.

'Movement of capital' and 'capital flows' include cash, cheque and electronic payments, shares, bonds, loans, investment units, deposits and financial instruments.

The 'European Union's regulatory framework' includes Directives 2004/39/EC for investment firms, 2006/48/EC for credit institutions, 73/239/EEC, 88/357/EEC and 92/49/EEC for insurance companies, 2002/83/EC for life assurance companies and 2002/92/EC for insurance intermediaries.

Mr. G. Baber,
Research Student, SOAS,
Marigold Cottage,
1, St. Mary's Close,
Aston, Herts.,
SG2 7EQ,
United Kingdom.

March/April 2008

Dear Sir/Madam,

I am conducting a survey as part of my research for the degree of Doctor of Philosophy (Ph.D.) at the School of Oriental and African Studies (SOAS), University of London. The survey consists of twelve questions, which investigate the effect of the European and national laws concerning the cross-border movement of capital on Estonian, Latvian and Polish businesses in four industrial sectors (investment, banking, insurance and property). I would be most grateful if you would complete the enclosed questionnaire, which is valuable to my research and would be of considerable interest to the European Commission in its role of initiator of European legal proposals.

Article 56 of the Treaty Establishing the European Communities (EC Treaty) states that all restrictions on capital movement and on payments between European Union (EU) Member States and between Member States and non-Member States shall be prohibited. This is a very bold and unequivocal statement, which provides EU businesses with considerable opportunities for trade and expansion not only within the EU, but also abroad. It is accompanied by a regulatory framework for the free movement of services and the freedom of establishment, which, for insurance companies, comprises Directives 73/239/EEC, 88/357/EEC and 92/49/EEC. The application of these principles within Estonia, Poland and Latvia is the subject of my Ph.D. research.

The findings from the questionnaire will be treated in strict confidence, with no information being published about specific organisations and their

particular experience, unless these corporations wish to divulge particular facts. I shall be writing a report from the findings, and, if you wish to receive a copy of this report, please put your e-mail address on the space allotted on the questionnaire.

If you have any queries concerning the questions, I would be happy to answer them, and can be contacted at 209393@soas.ac.uk. Please answer as many questions as you can, and post the completed questionnaire to me at the address above.

With best wishes,

Yours sincerely,

Graeme Baber, M.A.(Oxon), LL.M., M.Sc., M.B.A., M.C.T.
Research Student, SOAS, University of London.

Post script: A note on definitions in the questionnaire

'National law' means 'Estonian legislation and regulations'.

'Movement of capital' and 'capital flows' include cash, cheque and electronic payments, shares, bonds, loans, investment units, deposits and financial instruments.

The 'European Union's regulatory framework' includes Directives 2004/39/EC for investment firms, 2006/48/EC for credit institutions, 73/239/EEC, 88/357/EEC and 92/49/EEC for insurance companies, 2002/83/EC for life assurance companies and 2002/92/EC for insurance intermediaries.

Question 1
Is the free movement of capital across national borders an issue for your business?

Yes ☐
No ☐

Question 2
Do you agree or disagree that national law in the investment sector causes a significant restriction on cross-border capital flows?

Agree ☐
Disagree ☐

Please give reasons for your answer, in the space below.

____
____
____
____
____
____

Question 3
What steps could be taken to improve the movement of capital across national borders in the context of your business?

____
____
____
____
____
____

Question 4
To what extent does the European Union's regulatory framework encourage or dissuade you from *providing insurance services* to other European Economic Area (EEA) Member States?

Strongly encourage ☐
Mildly encourage ☐
Neither encourage nor dissuade ☐
Mildly dissuade ☐
Strongly dissuade ☐

Question 5
To what extent does the European Union's regulatory framework encourage or dissuade you from *establishing branches* in other EEA Member States?

Strongly encourage	
Mildly encourage	
Neither encourage nor dissuade	
Mildly dissuade	
Strongly dissuade	

Question 6
To what extent does *national law* encourage or dissuade you from *providing insurance services* to other EEA Member States?

Strongly encourage	
Mildly encourage	
Neither encourage nor dissuade	
Mildly dissuade	
Strongly dissuade	

Question 7
To what extent does national law encourage or dissuade you from *establishing branches* in other EEA Member States?

Strongly encourage	
Mildly encourage	
Neither encourage nor dissuade	
Mildly dissuade	
Strongly dissuade	

Question 8
To what extent does national law encourage or dissuade you from providing insurance services to *countries outside the EEA*?

Strongly encourage	
Mildly encourage	
Neither encourage nor dissuade	
Mildly dissuade	
Strongly dissuade	

Question 9

To what extent does national law encourage or dissuade you from establishing branches in countries outside the EEA?

Strongly encourage	
Mildly encourage	
Neither encourage nor dissuade	
Mildly dissuade	
Strongly dissuade	

Question 10

What is the *percentage of your total sales* arising from *outside the EEA*?

0%-10%	10%-20%	20%-30%	30%-40%	40%-50%	50%-60%	60%-70%	> 70%

Question 11

What is the percentage of your total sales arising from *other EEA Member States*?

0%-10%	10%-20%	20%-30%	30%-40%	40%-50%	50%-60%	60%-70%	> 70%

Question 12

Please give any other relevant comments, in the space below.

____

____

____

____

____

____

If you would like a copy of the report on the results of the survey, please put your e-mail address in the space below.

____

Mr. G. Baber,
Research Student, SOAS,
Marigold Cottage,
1, St. Mary's Close,
Aston, Herts.,
SG2 7EQ,
United Kingdom.

March/April 2008

Dear Sir/Madam,

I am conducting a survey as part of my research for the degree of Doctor of Philosophy (Ph.D.) at the School of Oriental and African Studies (SOAS), University of London. The survey consists of twelve questions, which investigate the effect of the European and national laws concerning the cross-border movement of capital on Estonian, Latvian and Polish businesses in four industrial sectors (investment, banking, insurance and property). I would be most grateful if you would complete the enclosed questionnaire, which is valuable to my research and would be of considerable interest to the European Commission in its role of initiator of European legal proposals.

Article 56 of the Treaty Establishing the European Communities (EC Treaty) states that all restrictions on capital movement and on payments between European Union (EU) Member States and between Member States and non-Member States shall be prohibited. This is a very bold and unequivocal statement, which provides EU businesses with considerable opportunities for trade and expansion not only within the EU, but also abroad. It is accompanied by a regulatory framework for the free movement of services and the freedom of establishment, which, for insurance intermediaries, is Directive 2002/92/EC. The application of these principles within Estonia, Poland and Latvia is the subject of my Ph.D. research.

The findings from the questionnaire will be treated in strict confidence, with no information being published about specific organisations and their

particular experience, unless these corporations wish to divulge particular facts. I shall be writing a report from the findings, and, if you wish to receive a copy of this report, please put your e-mail address on the space allotted on the questionnaire.

If you have any queries concerning the questions, I would be happy to answer them, and can be contacted at 209393@soas.ac.uk. Please answer as many questions as you can, and post the completed questionnaire to me at the address above.

With best wishes,

Yours sincerely,

Graeme Baber, M.A.(Oxon), LL.M., M.Sc., M.B.A., M.C.T.
Research Student, SOAS, University of London.

Post script: A note on definitions in the questionnaire

'National law' means 'Estonian legislation and regulations'.

'Movement of capital' and 'capital flows' include cash, cheque and electronic payments, shares, bonds, loans, investment units, deposits and financial instruments.

The 'European Union's regulatory framework' includes Directives 2004/39/EC for investment firms, 2006/48/EC for credit institutions, 73/239/EEC, 88/357/EEC and 92/49/EEC for insurance companies, 2002/83/EC for life assurance companies and 2002/92/EC for insurance intermediaries.

Question 1
Is the free movement of capital across national borders an issue for your business?

Yes ☐
No ☐

Question 2
Do you agree or disagree that national law in the investment sector causes a significant restriction on cross-border capital flows?

Agree ☐
Disagree ☐

Please give reasons for your answer, in the space below.

____
____
____
____
____
____

Question 3
What steps could be taken to improve the movement of capital across national borders in the context of your business?

____
____
____
____
____
____

Question 4
To what extent does the European Union's regulatory framework encourage or dissuade you from *providing insurance mediation* to other European Economic Area (EEA) Member States?

Strongly encourage ☐
Mildly encourage ☐
Neither encourage nor dissuade ☐
Mildly dissuade ☐
Strongly dissuade ☐

Question 5

To what extent does the European Union's regulatory framework encourage or dissuade you from *establishing branches* in other EEA Member States?

Strongly encourage	
Mildly encourage	
Neither encourage nor dissuade	
Mildly dissuade	
Strongly dissuade	

Question 6

To what extent does *national law* encourage or dissuade you from *providing insurance mediation* to other EEA Member States?

Strongly encourage	
Mildly encourage	
Neither encourage nor dissuade	
Mildly dissuade	
Strongly dissuade	

Question 7

To what extent does national law encourage or dissuade you from *establishing branches* in other EEA Member States?

Strongly encourage	
Mildly encourage	
Neither encourage nor dissuade	
Mildly dissuade	
Strongly dissuade	

Question 8

To what extent does national law encourage or dissuade you from providing insurance mediation to *countries outside the EEA*?

Strongly encourage	
Mildly encourage	
Neither encourage nor dissuade	
Mildly dissuade	
Strongly dissuade	

Question 9
To what extent does national law encourage or dissuade you from establishing branches in countries outside the EEA?

Strongly encourage	
Mildly encourage	
Neither encourage nor dissuade	
Mildly dissuade	
Strongly dissuade	

Question 10
What is the *percentage of your total sales* arising from *outside the EEA*?

0%-10%	10%-20%	20%-30%	30%-40%	40%-50%	50%-60%	60%-70%	> 70%

Question 11
What is the percentage of your total sales arising from *other EEA Member States*?

0%-10%	10%-20%	20%-30%	30%-40%	40%-50%	50%-60%	60%-70%	> 70%

Question 12
Please give any other relevant comments, in the space below.

____
____
____
____
____
____

If you would like a copy of the report on the results of the survey, please put your e-mail address in the space below.

____

Mr. G. Baber,
Research Student, SOAS,
Marigold Cottage,
1, St. Mary's Close,
Aston, Herts.,
SG2 7EQ,
United Kingdom.

March/April 2008

Dear Sir/Madam,

I am conducting a survey as part of my research for the degree of Doctor of Philosophy (Ph.D.) at the School of Oriental and African Studies (SOAS), University of London. The survey consists of twelve questions, which investigate the effect of the European and national laws concerning the cross-border movement of capital on Estonian, Latvian and Polish businesses in four industrial sectors (investment, banking, insurance and property). I would be most grateful if you would complete the enclosed questionnaire, which is valuable to my research and would be of considerable interest to the European Commission in its role of initiator of European legal proposals.

Article 56 of the Treaty Establishing the European Communities (EC Treaty) states that all restrictions on capital movement and on payments between European Union (EU) Member States and between Member States and non-Member States shall be prohibited. This is a very bold and unequivocal statement, which provides EU businesses with considerable opportunities for trade and expansion not only within the EU, but also abroad. It is accompanied by a regulatory framework for the free movement of services and the freedom of establishment, which mainly concerns companies in financial industries. The application of these principles within Estonia, Poland and Latvia is the subject of my Ph.D. research.

The findings from the questionnaire will be treated in strict confidence, with no information being published about specific organisations and their

particular experience, unless these corporations wish to divulge particular facts. I shall be writing a report from the findings, and, if you wish to receive a copy of this report, please put your e-mail address on the space allotted on the questionnaire.

If you have any queries concerning the questions, I would be happy to answer them, and can be contacted at 209393@soas.ac.uk. Please answer as many questions as you can, and post the completed questionnaire to me at the address above.

With best wishes,

Yours sincerely,

Graeme Baber, M.A.(Oxon), LL.M., M.Sc., M.B.A., M.C.T.
Research Student, SOAS, University of London.

Post script: A note on definitions in the questionnaire

'National law' means 'Estonian legislation and regulations'.

'Movement of capital' and 'capital flows' include cash, cheque and electronic payments, shares, bonds, loans, investment units, deposits and financial instruments.

Question 1

Is the free movement of capital across national borders an issue for your business?

Yes	
No	

Question 2

Do you agree or disagree that national law in the investment sector causes a significant restriction on cross-border capital flows?

Agree	
Disagree	

Please give reasons for your answer, in the space below.

____

____

____

____

____

____

Question 3

What steps could be taken to improve the movement of capital across national borders in the context of your business?

____

____

____

____

____

____

Question 4

To what extent does the European Union's regulatory framework encourage or dissuade you from *selling or leasing property* to citizens of other European Economic Area (EEA) Member States?

Strongly encourage	
Mildly encourage	
Neither encourage nor dissuade	
Mildly dissuade	
Strongly dissuade	

Question 5

To what extent does the European Union's regulatory framework encourage or dissuade you from *establishing branches* in other EEA Member States?

Strongly encourage	
Mildly encourage	
Neither encourage nor dissuade	
Mildly dissuade	
Strongly dissuade	

Question 6

To what extent does *national law* encourage or dissuade you from selling or leasing property to *citizens of countries outside the EEA*?

Strongly encourage	
Mildly encourage	
Neither encourage nor dissuade	
Mildly dissuade	
Strongly dissuade	

Question 7

To what extent does national law encourage or dissuade you from *establishing branches* in other EEA Member States?

Strongly encourage	
Mildly encourage	
Neither encourage nor dissuade	
Mildly dissuade	
Strongly dissuade	

Question 8

What is the *percentage of your total sales* arising from *outside the EEA*?

0%- 10%	10%- 20%	20%- 30%	30%- 40%	40%- 50%	50%- 60%	60%- 70%	> 70%

Question 9
What is the percentage of your total sales arising from *other EEA Member States*?

0%-10%	10%-20%	20%-30%	30%-40%	40%-50%	50%-60%	60%-70%	> 70%

Question 10
Please give any other relevant comments, in the space below.

____

____

____

____

____

____

If you would like a copy of the report on the results of the survey, please put your e-mail address in the space below.

____

APPENDIX D

VALIDATION STUDY REPORT FOR EXECUTIVES

Survey Methodology

In January 2008, a twelve question document was created and piloted on a class of Ph.D. students, which inquired into the effect of national law in Estonia, Poland and Latvia on the free movement of capital–one of the fundamental freedoms of the EU's Internal Market. This survey was part of the research for my Ph.D., which investigates the effect of legislation and regulation on the freedom of movement of capital in these Member States.

In February 2008, the questionnaire was sent in English to 220 organisations in the investment, banking, insurance and real property sectors of Estonia, Poland and Latvia, to the head offices of 10 large international banks, and to 23 companies that provided cross-border services to one or more of those countries. These enterprises (other than the major banks) were selected by stratified sampling from the Financial Services Authority lists in each country of registered investment, financial and insurance service providers. The real property companies were chosen from the import/export directories of Estonia and Latvia and from the British-Polish Chamber of Commerce list of registered real estate dealers.

The response rate to this batch of questionnaires was 5.3%–a total of 13 responses. This was an insufficient number of replies to produce a balanced sample. A follow-up e-mail with attached questionnaire produced no further replies.

The questionnaire was translated into Estonian, Polish and Latvian, and, in April 2008, a further 273 copies were sent to organisations in the investment, banking, insurance and real property sectors of these Member States. The response rate was 9.2%–a total of 25 responses. 38 replies were produced from the two batches–an overall response rate of 7.2% from 526 questionnaires. This was considered a sufficiently large number to be able to draw general conclusions from the replies.

The following table shows the breakdown of responses from both batches of questionnaires combined.

	Estonia		Poland		Latvia		Cross-border		**Total**		**Response rate**
	sent	replied	sent	replied	sent	replied	sent	replied	sent	replied	**%**
Investment fund management companies	16	**1**	31	**0**	14	4	9	**1**	**70**	**6**	**8.6**
Investment service providers	11	**1**	39	**3**	22	**0**	7	**0**	**79**	**4**	**5.1**
Credit institutions	16	**2**	62	**6**	21	**1**	3	**0**	**102**	**9**	**8.8**
Life assurance companies	7	**2**	24	**1**	11	**1**	0	**0**	**42**	**4**	**9.5**
Insurance companies	25	**3**	35	**4**	15	**0**	3	**0**	**78**	7	**9.0**
Insurance intermediaries	32	**3**	33	**1**	30	**0**	0	**0**	**95**	4	**4.2**
Real property companies	8	**1**	22	**1**	19	**0**	1	**0**	**50**	**2**	**4.0**
Total	**115**	**13**	**246**	**16**	**132**	**6**	**23**	**1**	**516**	36	**7.0**
Response rate %	**11.3**		**6.5**		**4.5**		**4.3**		**7.0**		
Head office of major international banks									**10**	**2**	**20.0**
Overall total response									**526**	**38**	**7.2**

Survey Results

The replies to each question are subdivided by industrial sector. The two responses from the headquarters of large international banks are classified as results from credit institutions. As one of these banks did not provide a sales profile, and since one investment fund management company did not state its sales to other EEA countries, questions 10 and 11 received 37 and 36 replies respectively. Questions 4 and 5 were not put to real property companies because such organisations are unaffected by the EU financial regulation Directives; consequently, these questions received 36 replies.

The key to the tables below is as follows:

InvF Investment fund management companies.
InvS Investment services providers.
CI Credit institutions.
InsS Insurance services providers (comprising both life and non-life insurance companies).
InsI Insurance intermediaries.
RP Real property companies.

Question 1

Is the free movement of capital across national borders an issue for your business?

	InvF	InvS	CI	InsS	InsI	RP	**Total**
Yes	1	3	7	4	0	0	**15**
No	5	1	4	7	4	2	**23**
Total	**6**	**4**	**11**	**11**	**4**	**2**	**38**

Question 2

Do you agree that national law in the [investment/banking/insurance services/insurance mediation/property] sector causes a significant restriction on cross-border capital flows?

	InvF	InvS	CI	InsS	InsI	RP	**Total**
Agree	1	1	3	3	1	0	**9**
Disagree	5	3	8	8	3	2	**29**
Total	**6**	**4**	**11**	**11**	**4**	**2**	**38**

Please give reasons for your answer in the space below.

Two replies state that international taxation is a problem; one specifies this in relation to cross-border mergers. Two responses in different sectors refer to limitations imposed by the national authorities. One insurance company mentions investment restrictions, and a property company identifies limitations on funds transferred to and from third countries. One bank states that barriers to cross-border capital flows have been significantly reduced due to increased cooperation among regulators, multijurisdictional agreements such as for underwriting shares and loans, and harmonisation of the regulatory framework.

Question 3

What steps could be taken to improve the movement of capital across national borders in the context of your business?

There are a variety of responses to this question. The suggestions with most consensus are 1) harmonisation of national laws and/or a supranational regulatory framework, 2) EU/third country cooperation agreements on the free movement of capital, especially with Russia and Ukraine, and 3) taxation simplification and/or harmonisation. The emphasis of these proposals is to reduce national differences in the conditions under which capital is transferred between EU Member States and between Member States and third countries. This is consistent with Article 56 of the EC Treaty, which, subject to a few exceptions, prohibits restrictions to the movement of capital and to payments between Member States and between such States and countries outside the EU.

Question 4

To what extent does the European Union's regulatory framework encourage or dissuade you from [providing investment services to/providing financial services to/providing insurance services to/providing insurance mediation to/selling or leasing property to citizens of] other European Economic Area (EEA) Member States?

	InvF	InvS	CI	InsS	InsI	**Total**
Strongly encourage	2	3	2	2	1	**10**
Mildly encourage	1	0	7	5	1	**14**
Neither encourage nor dissuade	3	0	2	4	2	**11**
Mildly dissuade	0	1	0	0	0	**1**
Strongly dissuade	0	0	0	0	0	**0**
Total	**6**	**4**	**11**	**11**	**4**	**36**

Question 5

To what extent does the European Union's regulatory framework encourage or dissuade you from establishing branches in other EEA Member States?

	InvF	InvS	CI	InsS	InsI	**Total**
Strongly encourage	1	1	2	2	1	**7**
Mildly encourage	1	0	7	2	0	**10**
Neither encourage nor dissuade	3	2	2	7	3	**17**
Mildly dissuade	1	1	0	0	0	**2**
Strongly dissuade	0	0	0	0	0	**0**
Total	**6**	**4**	**11**	**11**	**4**	**36**

Question 6

To what extent does national law encourage or dissuade you from [providing investment services to/providing financial services to/providing insurance services to/providing insurance mediation to/selling or leasing property to citizens of] other EEA Member States?

	InvF	InvS	CI	InsS	InsI	RP	**Total**
Strongly encourage	0	0	1	1	1	0	**3**
Mildly encourage	0	0	3	2	0	0	**5**
Neither encourage nor dissuade	6	4	6	5	3	2	**26**
Mildly dissuade	0	0	1	1	0	0	**2**
Strongly dissuade	0	0	0	2	0	0	**2**
Total	**6**	**4**	**11**	**11**	**4**	**2**	**38**

Question 7

To what extent does national law encourage or dissuade you from establishing branches in other Member States?

	InvF	InvS	CI	InsS	InsI	RP	**Total**
Strongly encourage	0	0	2	0	1	0	**3**
Mildly encourage	0	0	4	2	0	1	**7**
Neither encourage nor dissuade	5	3	4	6	3	1	**22**
Mildly dissuade	0	1	1	1	0	0	**3**
Strongly dissuade	1	0	0	2	0	0	**3**
Total	**6**	**4**	**11**	**11**	**4**	**2**	**38**

Question 8

To what extent does national law encourage or dissuade you from [providing investment services to/providing financial services to/providing insurance services to/providing insurance mediation to/selling or leasing property to citizens of] countries outside the EEA?

	InvF	InvS	CI	InsS	InsI	RP	**Total**
Strongly encourage	0	0	0	0	1	0	**1**
Mildly encourage	0	2	1	1	0	0	**4**
Neither encourage nor dissuade	4	1	6	6	1	1	**19**
Mildly dissuade	1	1	4	1	1	1	**9**
Strongly dissuade	1	0	0	3	1	0	**5**
Total	**6**	**4**	**11**	**11**	**4**	**2**	**38**

Question 9

To what extent does national law encourage or dissuade you from establishing branches in countries outside the EEA?

	InvF	InvS	CI	InsS	InsI	RP	**Total**
Strongly encourage	0	0	0	0	1	0	**1**
Mildly encourage	0	0	2	0	0	1	**3**
Neither encourage nor dissuade	4	2	6	5	1	1	**19**
Mildly dissuade	1	2	3	3	1	0	**10**
Strongly dissuade	1	0	0	3	1	0	**5**
Total	**6**	**4**	**11**	**11**	**4**	**2**	**38**

Question 10

What is the percentage of your total sales arising from outside the EEA?

	InvF	InvS	CI	InsS	InsI	RP	**Total**
0% □ 10%	4	4	7	11	4	0	**30**
10% □ 20%	1	0	1	0	0	0	**2**
20% □ 30%	0	0	0	0	0	1	**1**
30% □ 40%	1	0	1	0	0	0	**2**
40% □ 50%	0	0	1	0	0	1	**2**
50% □ 60%	0	0	0	0	0	0	**0**
60% □ 70%	0	0	0	0	0	0	**0**
> 70%	0	0	0	0	0	0	**0**
Total	**6**	**4**	**10**	**11**	**4**	**2**	**37**

Question 11

What is the percentage of your total sales arising from other EEA Member States?

	InvF	InvS	CI	InsS	InsI	RP	**Total**
0% □ 10%	2	2	5	6	2	1	**18**
10% □ 20%	1	0	1	1	2	0	**5**
20% □ 30%	0	0	0	0	0	0	**0**
30% □ 40%	0	1	2	0	0	0	**3**
40% □ 50%	0	0	0	0	0	0	**0**
50% □ 60%	1	0	1	1	0	1	**4**
60% □ 70%	0	0	0	0	0	0	**0**
> 70%	1	1	1	3	0	0	**6**
Total	**5**	**4**	**10**	**11**	**4**	**2**	**36**

Question 12

Please give any other relevant comments in the space below.

Two respondents refer to their business as being part of a large, international group–one specifies that the views expressed are those of the national unit. Two credit institutions and one investment fund management company mention other factors that affect the provision of cross-border services and the establishment of foreign branches. These are 1) the size and growth rate of a particular economy, 2) the fact that some Polish banks are controlled by foreign credit institutions means that these institutions and their investors influence capital flows, and 3) national laws in other EU Member States discourage the provision of investment services to those countries–specific areas mentioned are employment, marketing and taxation.

Comments and Conclusions

Many of the respondent executives do not consider the free movement of capital across national borders an issue for their business, and most state that national law in the industrial sector in which their organisation is placed does not cause a significant restriction to cross-border capital flows.

There is a positive response to the EU's regulatory framework, especially as an encouragement for providing services to other Member States. This is an endorsement of the financial regulation Directives, demonstrating that, in the opinion of directors of organisations in the financial and insurance sectors in Estonia, Poland and Latvia, these Directives make a constructive input to the free movement of services (and, to a lesser extent, to the freedom of establishment) within the framework of the Internal Market.

Most respondent executives are ambivalent to the effect of Estonian/Polish/Latvian law on the freedom to provide services to, and to found a branch in, another EEA state. This implies that national law does not inhibit or prevent the free movement of services or the freedom of establishment within the framework of the EU's regulatory framework. However, it also indicates that such law does not facilitate these freedoms. Since the cross-border supply of services and the establishment of a foreign branch involve capital flows, it follows that national law has no significant effect on the free movement of capital between EU Member States.

A majority of respondents state that their organisations make 0%-10% of their sales to other EEA states, although there are several enterprises with much greater turnover, including 6 with more than 70% of their sales to those countries. The fact that so many executives are in favour of the EU's regulatory framework indicates that they do not consider this an impediment to providing services outside their home country. It also indicates that respondents are aware of the Directives relevant to their organisation's business sector, even if this enterprise supplies 100% of its services locally.

Whilst many respondents state that Estonian/Polish/Latvian law neither encourages nor dissuades them from providing cross-border services to, or from opening a branch in, countries outside the EEA, a substantial number of executives reply that national law discourages them from pursuing these activities. The sales to third countries are mostly in the 0%-10% range, with all respondent organisations making less than 50% of their sales from those states. It appears that many directors are not concerned with the provision of services to countries outside the EEA, but that those which are so concerned may be discouraged by their national law from supplying such services.

If more executives of Estonian, Polish and Latvian companies are to contemplate the free movement of services to, and the freedom of establishment in, countries outside the EEA, then the national rules may need to be reconsidered. This is especially so in the light of Article 56(1) of the EC Treaty, which prohibits restrictions on the free movement of capital between EU Member States and third countries.

In summary, whilst the directors of Estonian, Polish and Latvian organisations in the sectors most affected by national rules restricting the free movement of capital do not consider the free movement of capital a major issue for their business, such free movement is required by Article 56 of the EC Treaty. It is also integrated with the free movement of services and the freedom of establishment within the EU's regulatory framework, which is welcomed by most executives.

The regulatory framework does not extend outside the EEA, but Article 56 requires the free movement of capital and payments between EU Member States and third countries. Consequently, national laws of Member States should permit such free movement. Estonian, Polish and Latvian companies tend to provide most of their services domestically, or, to a lesser extent, to other EEA states. The issue of the free movement of capital between the EEA and third countries is therefore not a significant concern of the directors of such companies, with a few notable exceptions (see question 3 above).

APPENDIX E

DETERMINANTS OF CROSS-BORDER CAPITAL FLOWS

Economic Indicators

There are several factors that alter the volume of cross-border capital flows, given that other things remain unchanged. 1) High real rates of return increase capital inflows and reduce capital outflows.[1] 2) Volatile interest rates lower capital inflows due to the high risk of small and unpredictable returns. 3) Low transaction costs, as in the 'Eurozone',[2] raise capital flows between the relevant countries. 4) A low inflation rate increases capital inflows and lowers capital outflows both because the real value of money is maintained and because the investment environment is generally considered to be stable and therefore attractive to risk-averse investors.[3] 5) Expectations of the national currency strengthening(/weakening) against a major currency and/or a basket of currencies may induce capital inflows(/outflows).[4] 6) Worsening terms of

---

[1] Fielding and Mizen (1997) state that *relative* real interest rates are the main determinant of capital inflows and outflows (*The Economic Journal*, 107, 431 and 438).

[2] The 'Eurozone' is the subset of Member States that have adopted the Euro as their currency, presently Austria, Belgium, Cyprus, Finland, France, Germany, Greece, Ireland, Italy, Luxembourg, Malta, the Netherlands, Portugal, Slovakia, Slovenia and Spain. Foreign exchange costs and risk are zero for financial flows between these States, and are low for flows between countries with stable exchange rates.

[3] It is established microeconomic theory that investors tend to be risk-averse. For instance, Katz and Rosen state "[I]n general, people are more likely to be risk averse than risk loving. An important piece of evidence for this proposition is the fact that riskier assets tend to pay higher rates of return than safe assets" ((1998), *Microeconomics*, 172).

[4] Walker and Punzi (2007) found that exchange rate expectations, substituted in their regressions and variance-at-risk analysis by exchange rate forecasts,

trade tend to lower capital inflows and raise capital outflows,[5] due to smaller revenues from exports and greater payments for imports respectively. The alternative outcome may occur if the price elasticities of export demand and import demand are high.[6]

Good Corporate Governance and Effective Institutions May Attract Capital Inflows

Positive shareholder rights and influence on company strategy raise management efficiency and investment performance, thereby enhancing economic growth and reducing investors' perceptions of risk.[7] Well-functioning national institutions and stable policies tend to attract investment from foreign banks; in particular, credit institutions may be unwilling to invest in countries with corrupt regimes, weak investor protection and tardy legal due process, and/or government ownership of the banks.[8]

Factors Affecting Gross Capital Flows

International diversification has increased in recent years, largely because there are fewer restrictions on the investments available to institutional investors. In addition, national barriers to trade in goods and services have fallen, causing the cross-border provision of, and payment for, these items to rise.[9]

---

positively affected capital inflows to the USA related to bonds from 1995-2001, but not in 2002-2006; they attributed this difference to reduced home bias in investment (*IMF Working Paper*, July 2007, 12-13, 15 and 19).

[5] In chapter 1 note 17, the 'terms of trade' are defined as the price of exports divided by the price of imports.

[6] The price elasticity of export(/import) demand is the negative of the percentage change in export(/import) quantity demanded divided by the percentage change in the price of exports(/imports).

[7] European Commission (2003), *The EU Economy: 2003 review*, 301.

[8] Papaioannou, E. (2005), *European Central Bank Working Paper Series*, No.437, 6.

[9] European Commission (2003), *EU Economy*, 279.

Factors Affecting Short-Term Net Capital Flows

A country with temporarily raised income runs a current account surplus in order to maintain higher consumption.[10] If a temporary productivity shock increases the return to domestic capital, foreign funds will be invested in the economy in order to make a profit.[11]

Factors Affecting Long-Term Net Capital Flows

The following factors affect long-term net foreign assets via global variables, such as the world real interest rate. 1) An increase in output per capita may improve the net foreign asset position through a falling domestic marginal product of capital, causing a rise in foreign investment, and also through an increase in the domestic saving rate, some of which is invested in foreign assets. 2) Higher levels of public debt may result in long-term capital outflows for debt service to foreigners. 3) Countries with an ageing population may anticipate a rise in the retiree to worker ratio by purchasing foreign assets to supplement domestic income.[12]

Drivers of Foreign Direct Investment

Cross-border mergers and acquisitions have contributed to FDI flows, especially between developed countries. The decline in merger and acquisition activity in 2001 and 2002 partly explains the fall in global FDI flows in these years.[13]

Proximity and trade openness increase FDI flows. A large share of FDI in OECD countries is between geographically close states and among those with regional trade agreements. For instance, EU Member States tend to have higher capital inflows from each other than from third countries, and much of the FDI to Canada and Mexico is from the USA.[14]

---

[10] Ibid. The 'current account surplus' is the excess of export revenues over the sum of import revenues and net transfers abroad.

[11] Ibid., 280.

[12] Ibid.

[13] Ibid., 287.

[14] Ibid., 288. In the section 'Drivers of Portfolio Investment' below, there is an inverse relationship between distance and equity capital inflows that is partly attributed to information transmission. It would be informative if the studies performed on the proximity/information link were to be applied also to capital inflows relating to other securities and to FDI.

Country-specific dummy variables were significant in regressions explaining FDI inflows.[15] Furthermore, country risk hindered investments of German organisations in six South American and eight Asian developing countries from 1990-1999.[16] These dummy variables may have captured some of the institutional and structural variation between states.[17]

Indeed, an effective infrastructure may encourage inbound direct investment. Biswas (2002) found that infrastructure had a significant, positive effect on FDI from the USA to 44 countries during 1983-1990.[18] This author reported that democracies attracted more inward FDI than autocracies, and that regime duration had a significant, negative influence on inflows of direct investment.[19] The International Country Risk Guide property rights index had a significant, positive effect on FDI inflows, indicating that the protection of these rights was important to investing US multinationals.[20]

In their single market commodity model of FDI inflows, Baniak et al. (2005) found that an increase in the variability of the host country's exchange rate or in marginal production costs raised the expected utility from investing there.[21] The more risk-averse investors were, the less likely they were to fund projects.[22] These authors explained the effect of other determinants of inward direct investment indirectly through their action on exchange rate variability, marginal costs and risk; for instance, infrastructure improvements may lower production, transportation or communication costs.[23]

---

[15] Biswas (2002), *Review of Development Economics*, 6(3), 492. Yasmin et al. (2003), *Pakistan Economic and Social Review*, 41(1)-41(2), 59.

[16] Wezel (2003), *Economic Research Centre of the Deutsche Bundesbank*, Discussion Paper 11/03, 30 and 33.

[17] Yasmin et al. (2003), *Pakistan Economic and Social Review*, 41(1)-41(2), 59.

[18] *Review of Development Economics*, 6(3), 499. Biswas' infrastructure variables are per capita installed capacity of electricity generators and the number of telephone lines per 100 persons (ibid., 496).

[19] Ibid., 500.

[20] Ibid. Since democracies tend to maintain property rights more effectively than autocracies (ibid., 497), the regime type dummy variable and the property rights index may be correlated.

[21] *Problems of Economic Transition*, 48(2), 20.

[22] Ibid., 22.

[23] Ibid., 23. These are interesting ideas–it would be useful for the authors to empirically test their model's predictions.

Drivers of Portfolio Investment

Portes and Rey (2000) showed that information transmission, whose substitutes in the regressions were the volume of telephone calls and the number of bank branches, had a significant, positive effect on bilateral equity flows from 1989-1996,[24] and that the former proxy captured some of the inverse effect of distance on such cross-border capital movements.[25] Portes and Rey (2005) confirmed these results.[26] They found market size, technology efficiency and distance to be the main determinants of equity transaction flows.[27]

Walker and Punzi (2007) reported that the interest rate spread on US bonds significantly changed capital flows into the USA connected with the transfer of such bonds during 2002-2006, but not from 1995-2001.[28] These authors also stated that the expansion of the domestic financial market, substituted in the analysis by own-country GDP growth, had a significant, positive impact on US bond capital inflows in both periods, but that the level of significance increased substantially in 2002-2006.[29] Exchange rate expectations had a positive but declining effect on these flows.[30] Walker and Punzi concluded that the elasticity of substitution between US and foreign bonds had risen,[31] and explained that this may have been "attributable to a reduction in home bias".[32]

Tille and Wincoop (2008) constructed a two-country dynamic stochastic general equilibrium model of portfolio choice for cross-border capital movements.[33] In the model, capital flows were affected by portfolio growth and reallocation components, the latter including "time-varying second moments".[34] Portfolio growth captured the capital movements over time of a particular allocation of saving to investment, and portfolio reallocation represented the capital flows resulting from a

---

[24] *Center for International and Development Economics Research at the University of California*, Paper C00-111, 2.

[25] Ibid., 16.

[26] *Journal of International Economics*, 65, 290.

[27] Ibid., 270.

[28] *IMF Working Paper*, July 2007, 14, 17 and 19.

[29] Ibid., 14 and 19. In the variance-at-risk analysis, GDP growth had a positive but insignificant influence on US bond capital inflows in both periods (ibid., 17).

[30] See note 4.

[31] (2007), *IMF Working Paper*, July 2007, 14 and 21.

[32] Ibid., 14.

[33] *CEPR Discussion Papers*, No.6705.

[34] Ibid., 19 and 23.

change in portfolio composition;[35] time-varying second moments showed inflows and outflows due to changes in risk that affected optimal portfolio shares.[36]

Although the authors did not empirically test the forecast of capital flows made by their model, they found the portfolio reallocation effect to be consistent with the work of Hau and Rey (2008).[37] Tille and Wincoop stated that the observation of Hau and Rey, that mutual funds purchased foreign stock following a rise in the relative return of domestic to foreign stock,[38] was consistent with the model's prediction of active reallocation to Foreign stock after a positive income shock for Home investors.[39]

Capital Flows to Developing Countries

The World Bank stated in its World Development Report for 1985 that rates of return on investment tended to be higher in developing countries, but that private funds to them were underprovided due to restrictive capital market regulations there, sovereign risk, lack of foreign exchange from earnings there, lack of information concerning opportunities for investment, and the unwillingness of banks to lend in the long-term.[40] By contrast, an implication of Mundell's two commodity two country model is that protectionist policies in both developed and developing countries have substantially increased capital flows from developed to developing economies.[41]

Alfaro et al. (2005) identified asymmetric information and lack of other factors, such as human capital and land, as reasons why capital tended not to flow from developed (capital abundant) to developing (capital scarce) countries, but empirically found low institutional quality in

---

[35] Ibid., 19.

[36] Ibid., 46.

[37] *CEPR Discussion Papers*, No.6901. This was an unpublished paper at the time of writing of Tille and Wincoop (2008), *CEPR Discussion Papers*, No.6705.

[38] Hau and Rey (2008), *CEPR Discussion Papers*, No.6901, 2.

[39] Tille and Wincoop (2008), *CEPR Discussion Papers*, No.6705, 24-25 and 30; Home and Foreign are the two countries in the model.

[40] Eaton (1989), *Handbook of Development Economics*, Volume II, 1308.

[41] Ibid., 1321. In Mundell's model, an import tariff on a capital-intensive good in one country raises the rate of return to capital in this state, thereby increasing its capital inflows (ibid., 1320).

the latter to be the main explanation for this lack of investment.[42] Fedderke and Liu (2002) stated that a stable, transparent policy environment attracted capital flows.[43]

Capital Flows to the Former Socialist Economies of Eastern Europe Acceding to the EU

The privatisation of state-owned enterprises is nearing completion. Consequently, the sale of parts of those entities to foreigners, which is a driver for FDI, will decline. Nonetheless, the balance of payments in these countries will reflect the rising supply and profitability of foreign investment.[44] An increase in the size of the countries' financial sectors and in their "standards of prudential supervision" will attract further capital inflows.[45]

During 1991-2001, most foreign capital invested in the economies of Eastern Europe and the former Soviet Union was concentrated in the countries at more advanced stages of transition. Greater reform and higher income raised both FDI and portfolio investment flows. Macroeconomic stability and pending EU Membership increased FDI, whilst less flexible exchange rate regimes tended to attract portfolio investment.[46]

---

[42] *University of Houston Working Papers*, November 2005, 2, 5-7 and 21. These authors used Ordinary Least Squares and Instrumental Variables regression techniques for 58 countries from 1970-2000.

[43] *Economic Modelling*, 19(3), 419. These authors modelled the determinants of capital flows to/from South Africa from 1965-1990.

[44] Rising foreign investment is a capital inflow, which is a positive entry in the balance of payments.

[45] European Commission (2003), *EU Economy*, 298.

[46] Assenov (2003), *Osaka Economic Papers*, 53(1), 99.

APPENDIX F

STUDIES BY LA PORTA ET AL. AND SIEMS' CRITIQUE

The three 'La Porta et al.' studies described in this appendix construct indices to analyse the effect of legal factors, including investor protections and law enforcement, on the depth and performance of stock markets. They are influential and much cited in the literature,[1] but have been criticised by Dr. Mathias Siems for the alleged arbitrariness of the methodology.

La Porta et al. (2003a)

La Porta et al. (2003a)[2] (LP1) categorises 49 countries' legal regimes into French, German and Scandinavian civil law, and common law, systems.[3] It assigns three variables to measure the size of equity markets: 1) the ratio of each country's stock market capitalisation held by minorities to its gross national product (GNP) for 1994, 2) the ratio of the number of listed domestic companies to population for 1994, and the ratio of the number of initial public offerings of equity (IPOs) to population for July 1995 to June 1996. A country's debt market size is provided by the ratio of the sum of the total face value of corporate bonds and private

[1] Subsequent studies have adapted the statistical methodology of the 'La Porta et al.' articles. An example is Berkowitz et al. (2003), *American Journal of Comparative Law*, 51, 163–203, which built a 'legality index' to look at the effectiveness of legal institutions in the context of legal transplants and development.

[2] *International Financial Integration Volume II, The International Library of Critical Writings in Economics*, 156(2), 415–434. This paper was first published in 1997.

[3] Civil law systems have developed from Roman law and are codified. The French, German and Scandinavian families have different origins. Common law systems are modelled on English law and use the doctrine of judicial precedent for legal development.

sector bank debt to GNP in 1994. Each of these four measures is the dependent variable in the four regression groups.[4]

There are two independent control variables in all the regressions: 1) historical GDP growth, which may affect stock market valuations and breadth, and 2) the logarithm of real GNP, because larger economies may have bigger capital markets. The other independent variables are a dummy variable for each of French, German and Scandinavian legal origin and for 'one-share = one-vote', which is 1 if the country's law states that ordinary shares have one vote per share and 0 otherwise, and three legal indices: antidirector rights, creditor rights and rule of law.

The antidirector rights index aggregates shareholder rights. It ranges from 0 to 5, adding 1 if the country provides one of the following rights: 1) proxy voting by post, 2) no requirement to deposit shares before the General Shareholders' Meeting, 3) cumulative voting, 4) an oppressed minorities procedure, and 5) 10% ownership of share capital is sufficient to call an Extraordinary Shareholders' Meeting.

The creditor rights index combines creditor rights. It extends from 0 to 4, adding 1 for each of these national rights: 1) filing for re-organisation carries restrictions, such as creditors' consent, 2) secured creditors can obtain their security once the reorganisation petition has been accepted, 3) the debtor cannot administer its property before the re-organisation is resolved, and 4) secured creditors are the first recipients of the proceeds from the sale of a bankrupt company's assets.

The rule of law index changes the 0 to 6 scale from the International Country Risk Guide's Law and Order index to 0 to 10.[5] It assesses law and order in each country,[6] and is the average of the April and October readings of the monthly index between 1982 and 1995.

The first three sets of ordinary least squares (OLS) regressions measure equity market size, with external stock market capitalisation / GNP, number of listed domestic companies / population, and number of IPOs / population as the dependent variable in each set.[7] There are five regressions in each group, all of which include GDP growth, log real GNP and the rule of law index. Other independent variables in each regression are:

regression 1 antidirector rights index;
regression 2 one-share = one-vote;

[4] See below in this section.
[5] The PRS Group, 15 August 2007.
[6] The Law subcomponent considers the legal system's impartiality and strength; the Order element assesses public compliance with the law (ibid).
[7] See above.

regression 3 French origin, German origin, Scandinavian origin (F,G&S);
regression 4 antidirector rights index, F,G&S;
regression 5 one-share = one-vote, F,G&S.

The inclusion of the shareholder rights variables both with and without the legal origin dummies enables the authors to ascertain how much change in the dependent variable is due to the former and how much due to a separate 'legal family effect'.

The fourth set of OLS regressions measures debt market size. The dependent variable is debt / GNP .[8] The three regressions include GDP growth, log real GNP and the rule of law index. Other independent variables are:

regression 1 creditor rights index;
regression 2 F,G&S;
regression 3 creditor rights index, F,G&S.

The placement of the creditor rights index and the legal origin dummies in separate regressions and together enables separation of a credit rights affect on debt market size from any legal family effect. LP1 concludes

> "French and Scandinavian civil law countries do have more narrow debt markets than common law countries, a difference not adequately captured by our creditor rights index".[9]

This conclusion is based on the creditor rights index coefficient being significant at the 10% level in regression 1 and insignificant in regression 3, the test statistic for the French origin dummy variable being significant at the 5% level in regression 2 and insignificant in regression 3, and the coefficient for the Scandinavian origin dummy variable being significant at the 5% level in both regressions 2 and 3, with the creditor rights index coefficients being positive and the other coefficients negative.[10] Another

[8] See above.

[9] La Porta et al. (2003a), *International Financial Integration*, 430.

[10] Significance tests were performed on all independent variable coefficients in all the regressions. LP1 does not describe how the authors performed the significance tests, but, assuming that they used a Normal distribution because the sample size > 30, and assuming that the tests are two-tailed, I reproduce the test on the French origin dummy in regression 2. Coefficient = -0.1516; standard error = 0.0740; null hypothesis: the coefficient is not significantly different from zero. z-statistic = (-0.1516 – 0) / 0.0740 = -2.049. 1.96 (5% level) < |z| < 2.33 (1% level), so the null hypothesis is rejected; French origin is significant at the 5% level, as stated in LP1 (ibid., 429).

notable result is that the rule of law index coefficient is at least 10 % significant in 17 of the 18 regressions, which enables the authors to state that "good law enforcement has a large effect on the valuation and breadth of both equity and debt markets".[11]

La Porta et al. (2003b)

La Porta et al. (2003b)[12] (LP2) measures the legal protections for investors in common law countries and in French, German and Scandinavian civil law nations. It uses a similar approach to LP1, including several legal indices and the methods employed by the earlier study.

One particular aspect of interest in LP2 is the two-stage OLS regression used to test the effect of poor investor protection on ownership concentration of shares. The dependent variable is 'mean ownership', which is the average percentage of ordinary shares held by the three largest shareholders in the ten biggest privately-owned non-financial companies in each country. The independent control variables are 1) log GNP per capita, since the ownership patterns of richer and poorer countries may differ, 2) log total GNP, because larger economies may contain bigger firms with a lower ownership concentration, and 3) the country's Gini coefficient,[13] since societies with less equal income distribution may contain companies with a greater ownership concentration.

The authors first regress mean ownership against French, German and Scandinavian legal origin dummy variables and the control variables. The French origin and log total GNP coefficients are significant at the 1% level, and the Gini coefficient is significant at the 10% level. The other coefficients are insignificant. The authors state: "this regression confirms the sharply higher concentration of ownership in the French-civil-law countries."[14]

---

[11] Ibid., 430.

[12] *International Financial Integration Volume II, The International Library of Critical Writings in Economics*, 156(2), 435–477. This paper was first published in 1998.

[13] The study uses the 1990 Gini coefficient (or the most recent available) for each country. If a graph is plotted of 'percentage of income' against 'percentage of income recipients' for the country concerned (the Lorenz Curve), then the Gini coefficient is equal to the area between 45° line from the origin (the line of equality) and the Lorenz Curve divided by the area under the line of equality (Meier and Rauch (2000), *Leading Issues in Economic Development*, 380).

[14] La Porta et al. (2003b), *International Financial Integration*, 472.

The second regression adds several measures of legal protection as independent variables: rule of law, accounting standards, antidirector rights, mandatory dividend, legal reserves required and creditor rights indices, and the 'one-share = one vote' dummy variable.[15] The log total GNP coefficient remains significant at the 1% level, but the Gini coefficient becomes insignificant. The antidirector rights and legal reserves required coefficients are significant at the 5% level. The accounting standards and mandatory dividend coefficients are significant at the 10% level. The other coefficients are insignificant.

The French origin coefficient turns insignificant in the second regression, "which suggests that our measures of investor protections actually capture the limitations of the French-civil-law system".[16] The authors state that some of the independent variables may be endogenous.[17] They provide accounting standards as an example of an endogenous variable, because countries with small stock markets and concentrated ownership may "have little use for good accounting standards, and so fail to develop them".[18] This does not affect the positive influence of French legal origin on mean ownership, since "the only true exogenous variable in these regressions in the legal origin".[19]

---

[15] The rule of law and creditor rights indices and the 'one-share = one-vote' dummy variable are explained in the section 'La Porta et al. (2003a)'. The antidirector rights index is from 0 to 6, adding the test of whether shareholders have pre-emptive rights that are removable only by a shareholders' vote to LP1's antidirector rights index (see the section 'La Porta et al. (2003a)'). The other indices are not described here.

[16] La Porta et al. (2003b), *International Financial Integration*, 472.

[17] An endogenous variable is "one whose value is determined inside the model" (Dougherty (1992), *Introduction to Econometrics*, 322). The coefficient of an endogenous variable is correlated with the regression's disturbance term, and is therefore biased. There are techniques to improve the estimates of these coefficients in simultaneous equation models, such as indirect least squares (ILS) and 2-stage least squares (2SLS) regression, but LP2 does not introduce simultaneous equations for the endogenous terms.

[18] La Porta et al. (2003b), *International Financial Integration*, 472.

[19] Ibid., 473. An exogenous variable is "one whose value is determined outside the model and is therefore taken as given" (Dougherty (1992), *Introduction to Econometrics*, 322).

La Porta et al. (2006)

La Porta et al. (2006)[20] (LP3) investigates the impact of securities laws governing IPOs on market development, which is represented by a selection of dependent variables in the regressions. These include: 1) the ratio of the average stock market capitalisation, excluding the three largest shareholders, of each country's ten largest non-financial companies to GDP, 2) the logarithm of the ratio of the number domestic firms to GDP, and 3) the ratio of equity issued from 1996–2000 to GDP.

The study uses several legal indices for securities laws; the main ones are disclosure requirements, liability standards and public enforcement indices.[21] They are calculated and compared for 49 countries, which are categorised as common law, French-civil-law, German-civil-law and Scandinavian-civil-law nations.[22]

Methods include the calculation of t-statistics of mean difference in order to make comparisons between legal families, OLS regressions, the calculation and testing for significance of correlation coefficients, and 2SLS regressions. Correlation coefficients show associations between variables, and are a helpful step prior to the regressions. The use of 2SLS is a development from LP2,[23] and is described in this section.

LP3 uses OLS regression to estimate all 7 dependent variables that represent market development. Since each of these variables is measuring the same attribute, this is not a simultaneous equation system but seven separate regressions. Each takes the following form.
Dependent variable = α + β1(disclosure requirements index) + β2(liability standards index) + β3(public enforcement index) + β4(antidirector rights index) + β5(ln GNP per capita) + β6(efficiency of the judiciary index) + disturbance term, where α and βi are coefficients to be estimated by the regression.

The authors state two reverse causality arguments: 1) governments may enact better securities laws in states with active financial markets, and 2) regulators are attracted to large securities markets in order to benefit financially. Hence, the legal indices are endogenous. In the 2SLS regression procedure, 'investor protection', which "accounts for roughly

[20] *The Journal of Finance*, 61(1), 1–32. This paper was first published in 2004.
[21] See the section 'Siems' Critique' for Siems' criticism of these indices.
[22] LP1, LP2 and LP3 use the same countries and classify them identically for legal origin.
[23] See note 17.

70% of the variation in disclosure, liability standards, and antidirector rights",[24] is used as an instrumental variable for these three indices.[25]
The first (OLS) regression is:
Investor protection = γ + δ1(common law dummy variable)[26] + δ2(efficiency of the judiciary index) + δ3(ln GDP per capita) + disturbance term, where γ and δi are regression coefficients.
The second (OLS) regression is:
Dependent variable = ε + ζ1(investor protection) + ζ2(antidirector rights index) + ζ3(ln GNP per capita) + ζ4(efficiency of the judiciary index) + disturbance term, where ε and ζi are regression coefficients.

In the first regression, the coefficient of the common law dummy variable is significant at the 1% level, which indicates that investor protection is higher in common law countries than in civil law countries. In the second regression, the coefficient of investor protection is significant at the 10% level in one instance, at the 5% level in three cases and at the 1% level in two instances. In the seventh case, this coefficient is insignificant. For six of the seven dependent variables that represent market development, therefore, higher investor protection increases such development.

The authors conclude: "These results should partially mitigate endogeneity concerns".[27] This is true, as the substitution of a suitable instrumental variable for endogenous terms improves the accuracy of regression coefficient estimates in large samples.[28] However, the authors' 2SLS regressions have the following shortcomings.

1. There is no formal system of economic equations in which exogenous and endogenous variables can be identified.
2 The standard 2SLS procedure uses the estimator of each endogenous variable from its reduced form equation as an

---

[24] La Porta et al. (2006), *Journal of Finance*, 27.
[25] The aim is to replace the endogenous variables in the OLS regression with a proxy (the instrumental variable) which varies with the dependent variable in a similar way to these endogenous terms, but, unlike them, does not vary with the disturbance term. In practice, a large sample size is needed to remove this correlation. LP3's sample size of 49 is sufficiently large to use 2SLS regression.
[26] The dummy variable is 1 if the country's legal origin is common law, and 0 otherwise. The authors believe this to be the only exogenous variable in the entire system.
[27] La Porta et al. (2006), *Journal of Finance*, 27.
[28] See note 25.

instrumental variable in the second regression.[29] LP3 combines three legal indices identified as endogenous into one instrumental variable, 'investor protection', which is not defined other than to say that it accounts for 70% of the variation in these three terms.[30] There is a loss of accuracy in using 'investor protection' as an equivalent to the reduced form estimators of the three endogenous indices.

Siems' Critique

Dr. Siems suggests deficiencies in the approach taken in LP3.[31] These are as follows.

1. *Home bias*. LP3's foundations and questions show an approach to securities' law based wholly on US law without considering alternative systems. For instance, the disclosure index does not incorporate alternative methods of protection not based on disclosure, such as approval by independent directors, shareholders or a supervisory board.
2. *Rules with the same index rank are not identical.* Legal culture, background and micro-structure are ignored. For example, liability rules (which are used to construct LP3's liability index) are often connected to the law of tort, which has distinct requirements in each country that may affect its particular concept of 'negligence'. Further, a statistic on judicial efficiency is too elementary to substitute for an enquiry into national civil procedure.
3. *The indices do not consider different legal solutions.* In constructing their legal indices, La Porta et al. ask whether specific legal rules exist in different countries, disregarding other legal solutions with a similar effect but with a different method for accomplishing it. Legal principles, case law and extra-legal factors are ignored.
4. *Categorisation of legal systems into common law and civil law families does not capture differences in national securities' laws.* Most securities' laws follow similar historical paths. In many

---

[29] A reduced form equation is one that estimates the value of an endogenous variable by regressing it using OLS against all the predetermined (exogenous and time-lagged endogenous) variables in the system.

[30] See above in this section.

[31] Siems (2005a), *International Company and Commercial Law Review*, 16(7), 300–305.

countries, they are described by a combination of statutes and case law.

5. *LP3 shows weak methodological awareness.* La Porta et al. make an incomplete attempt to incorporate quantitative analysis into legal research.

Despite these penetrating criticisms, Siems considers arguments in favour of numerical comparative law in another paper,[32] and offers guidelines therein on how to consider using it. His reasons for this methodology are 1) comparative law's practical role is raised by reducing complexity, and its aims (such as to assist legislation, law reform and legal interpretation) depend on clear results; 2) quantitative methods are used in fields which, like law, concern human behaviour, including economics, psychology, political science and sociology; 3) comparative law has several techniques, the choice of which depend on the research objective.[33]

Siems' guidelines for using numerical comparative law are as follows.[34]

1. *Necessity.* Traditional comparative law techniques are difficult to implement if many provisions or countries need to be assessed.
2. *Methodological awareness.* Statistical results may be less clear than apparent. One must consider the methodological problems.
3. *Transparency.* It must be clear how data is assembled and what it means.
4. *Comparability.* Cultural, economic and social differences make statistical comparisons less valuable.
5. *Functional equivalents.* Indices should include measures containing functional equivalents in order to prevent home bias and hidden benchmarking against the comparatist's domestic national laws.
6. *Reflections.* It may be impossible to draw accurate conclusions from the statistical analysis.

---

[32] Siems (2005b), *Cardozo Journal of International and Comparative Law*, 13, 521–540. Siems (2005b) also puts arguments against numerical comparative law, but his critique on La Porta et al.'s methodology is more pertinent (see above in this section).

[33] Ibid., 534–538. This concurs with Professor Palmer's comments (see the subsection '*Comment*' in section 1.3.2).

[34] Ibid., 539–540.

Comment

La Porta et al.'s numerical approach to comparative securities' law is a pioneering one, and is a valuable addition to the techniques available. However, their statistical analysis would be improved by 1) the prior statement of formulae corresponding to the theory; 2) the inclusion of regression equations before the results, and 3) a consideration of the problems that may arise in OLS regressions, which make the coefficients biased and/or inefficient (i.e. with artificially large standard errors). These difficulties include endogeneity,[35] heteroscedasticity,[36] spatial correlation,[37] non-normality,[38] and multicollinearity.[39] These issues must be identified and addressed, so that OLS regressions give best linear unbiased estimators and so that t-tests and F-tests are valid, especially in small samples.

Siems' comments are a cautionary note on the use of numerical comparative law, pointing to the need to take care. Of particular importance are his guidelines as to methodological awareness and data transparency.[40] He criticises La Porta et al.'s home bias in their legal indices. His comment on the simplicity of a statistic on judicial efficiency points to another problem with La Porta et al.'s use of indices: they are not sufficiently adapted to the comparison that they intend to make. Several indices, especially in LP3, are taken directly from the International Country Risk Guide, which provides a comparison between countries at a general level. In addition, these authors use many legal indices, some or all of which may be considered arbitrary, non-specific and US-law based. Narrower research objectives and fewer indices would introduce more statistical accuracy.

---

[35] Endogeneity is present in a regression if an explanatory variable is endogenous i.e. determined within the system of equations and correlated with the disturbance term (see note 17). The 2SLS regressions in LP3 address the issue of endogeneity of the disclosure requirements, liability standards and antidirector rights indices (see the subsection 'La Porta et al. (2006)').

[36] Heteroscedasticity is present in a regression if the disturbance term has unequal variance amongst observations.

[37] Spatial correlation is present in a regression if the disturbance term is associated in cross-sectional observations (LP1, LP2 and LP3 use cross-sectional data). There may also be serial correlation of the disturbance term in time series data.

[38] Non-normality is present in a regression if the disturbance term is non-normally distributed amongst observations.

[39] Multicollinearity is present in a regression if the explanatory variables are linearly related to each other.

[40] See the section 'Siems' Critique'.

BIBLIOGRAPHY

Books, Articles and Reports

Alfara, L., Kalemli-Ozcan, S., and Volosovych, V. (2005), 'Why doesn't Capital Flow from Rich to Poor Countries? An Empirical Investigation', *University of Houston Working Papers, November 2005* (Houston: University of Houston).

Arnull, A., Dashwood, A., Dougan, M., Ross, M., Spaventa, E., and Wyatt, D. (2006), *Wyatt and Dashwood's European Union Law*, 5th edn. (London: Sweet and Maxwell Limited).

Assenov, I. (2003), 'Market Reforms and Foreign Investment: What Drives Capital Flows to Transition Economies?', *Osaka Economic Papers*, 53(1), 99–118.

Baniak, A., Cukrowski, J., and Herczyński, J. (2005), 'On the Determinants of Foreign Direct Investment in Transition Economies', *Problems of Economic Transition*, 48(2), 6–28.

Bank of Estonia, 'Report on the Adoption of the Euro', May 2007.

Basel Committee on Banking Supervision, 'Core Principles for Effective Banking Supervision', October 2006.

—. 'International Convergence of Capital Measurement and Capital Standards: A Revised Framework – Comprehensive Version', June 2006.

Berkowitz, D., Pistor, K., and Richard, J.-F. (2003), 'The Transplant Effect', *American Journal of Comparative Law*, 51, 163–203.

Betham, M. (1795), 'Invitation To JBC', *in* Breen, J. *ed.* (1992), *Women Romantic Poets 1785–1832: An Anthology* (London: J. M. Dent & Sons Ltd)

Biswas, R. (2002), 'Determinants of Foreign Direct Investment', *Review of Development Economics*, 6(3), 492–504.

Boyd Jr., H. W., and Walker Jr., O. C. (1990), *Marketing Management: A Strategic Approach* (Boston, Massachusetts: Richard D. Irwin, Inc.).

Campos, N. F., and Horváth, R. (2006), 'Reform Redux: Measurement, Determinants and Reversals', *CEPR Discussion Papers, No.5673* (London: Centre for Economic Policy Research).

Cardoso, E. A., and Dornbusch, R. (1989), 'Foreign Private Capital Flows', *in* Chenery, H., and Srinivasan, T. N. *eds.*, *Handbook of*

Development Economics, Volume II (Amsterdam: Elsevier Science Publishers B.V.).

Channell, W. (2005), 'Lessons Not Learned: Problems with Western Aid for Law Reform in Postcommunist Countries', *Carnegie Working Papers, No.57* (Washington D.C.; Carnegie Endowment for International Peace).

Commission on European Contract Law (1999), 'The Principles of European Contract Law'.

Cuddington, J. (1986), 'Capital Flight: Estimates, Issues and Explanations', *Princeton Studies in International Finance No.58*, 1–40.

Cypher, J. M., and Dietz, J. L. (2004), *The Process of Economic Development*, 2nd edn. (Abingdon, United Kingdom: Routledge).

Dąbrowska, K., and Gruszczyński, M. (2002), 'Foreign Capital in the Polish Banking Sector and the Effectiveness of Monetary Policy', *22nd NBP Conference "Monetary Policy in the Environment of Structural Changes": Session 1 "Structural Changes and the Effectiveness of Monetary Policy".*

De Bono E. (1977), *Lateral Thinking* (Harmondsworth, United Kingdom: Penguin Books Ltd.).

Dougherty, C. (1992), *Introduction to Econometrics* (New York: Oxford University Press, Inc.).

Eaton, J. (1989), 'Foreign Public Capital Flows', *in* Chenery, H., and Srinivasan, T. N. *eds., Handbook of Development Economics, Volume II* (Amsterdam: Elsevier Science Publishers B.V.).

Edwards, S. (1985), 'Stabilization with Liberalization: An Evaluation of Ten Years of Chile's Experience with Free-Market Policies, 1973–1983', *Economic Development and Cultural Change*, 33, 223–254.

European Bank for Reconstruction and Development (1994), *Transition report: October 1994* (London: European Bank for Reconstruction and Development).

—. (2007), *Transition report: November 2007* (London: European Bank for Reconstruction and Development).

European Commission Directorate General for Economic and Financial Affairs, 'The EU economy: 2003 review', No.6/2003.

Eurostat (2002), 'Statistical Classification of Economic Activities in the European Community NACE Revision 1.1'.

Ewald, W. (1995), 'Comparative Jurisprudence (II): The Logic of Legal Transplants', *American Journal of Comparative Law*, 43, 489–510.

Fedderke, J. W., and Liu, W. (2002), 'Modelling the Determinants of Capital Flows and Capital Flight: With an Application to South African Data from 1960 to 1995', *Economic Modelling*, 19(3), 419–444.

Fielding, D., and Mizen, P. (1997), 'Investment, Output and Interest Rate Policy when Capital is Mobile', *The Economic Journal*, 107, 431–440.

Frankowski, S. *ed.* (2005), *Introduction to Polish Law* (The Hague: Kluwer Law International).

Glenn, H. P. (2006), 'On the Use of Biological Metaphors in Law: The Case of 'Legal Transplants'', *Journal of Comparative Law*, 1, 124–130.

Hart, H. L. A. (1961), *The Concept of Law* (Oxford: Oxford University Press).

Hau, H., and Rey, H. (2008), 'Global Portfolio Rebalancing under the Microscope', *CEPR Discussion Papers, No.6901* (London: Centre for Economic Policy Research).

Havrylchyk, O., and Jurzyk, E. (2006), 'Profitability of foreign banks in Central and Eastern Europe: Does the entry mode matter?', *BOFIT Discussion Papers, No.5* (Helsinki: Bank of Finland Institute for Economies in Transition).

International Monetary Fund (1993), *Balance of Payments Manual*, 5th edn. (Washington D.C.: International Monetary Fund).

Katz, M. L., and Rosen, H. S. (1998), *Microeconomics*, 3rd edn. (Irwin/McGraw Hill: New York).

Kierzkowski, D., Miller, J., and Wiśniewski, A. W. *eds.* (2000), *The Polish Civil Code* (Warszawa: Tepis Publishing House of the Polish Society of Economic, Legal and Court Translators).

Klau, M., and Fung, S. S. (2006), 'The new BIS effective exchange rate indices', *BIS Quarterly Review*, March 2006, 51–65.

La Porta, R., Lopez-de-Silanes, F., Schleifer, A., and Vishny, R. W. (2003a), 'Legal Determinants of External Finance', *in* Eijffinger, S. C. W., and Lemmen, J. J. G. *eds.*, *International Financial Integration Volume II, The International Library of Critical Writings in Economics*, 156, 2, 415–434 (Cheltenham, United Kingdom: Edward Elgar Publishing Limited).

—. (2003b), 'Law and Finance', *in* Eijffinger, S. C. W., and Lemmen, J. J. G. *eds.*, *International Financial Integration Volume II, The International Library of Critical Writings in Economics*, 156, 2, 435–477 (Cheltenham, United Kingdom: Edward Elgar Publishing Limited).

La Porta, R., Lopez-de-Silanes, F., and Schleifer, A. (2006), 'What works in Securities Laws?', *The Journal of Finance*, 61(1), 1–32.

Legrand, P. (2006), 'Comparative Legal Studies and the Matter of Authenticity', *Journal of Comparative Law*, 1, 365–460.

Lora, E. (1997), 'A Decade of Structural Reforms in Latin America: What Has Been Reformed and How to Measure It', *Inter-American*

Development Bank Working Papers, No.348 (Washington D.C.: Inter-American Development Bank).

McFarlane, G. (1984), *The Layman's Dictionary of English Law* (London: Waterlow Publishers Limited).

Meier, G. M., and Rauch, J. E. (2000), *Leading Issues in Economic Development*, 7th edn. (New York: Oxford University Press, Inc.).

Mountjoy, A. B. *ed.* (1987), *Readers Digest Guide to Places of the World* (London: The Readers Digest Association Limited).

Palmer, V. V. (2005), 'From Lerotholi to Lando: Some Examples of Comparative Law Methodology', *American Journal of Comparative Law*, 53, 261–290.

Papaioannou, E. (2005), 'What Drives International Bank Flows? Politics, Institutions and Other Determinants', *European Central Bank Working Paper Series, No.437* (Frankfurt am Main: European Central Bank).

Pilbeam, K. (2006), *International Finance*, 3rd edn. (Basingstoke, United Kingdom: Palgrave Macmillan).

Portes, R., and Rey, H. (2000), 'The Determinants of Cross-Border Equity Flows: The Geography of Information', *Center for International and Development Economics Research at the University of California, Paper C00-111* (Berkeley: University of California).

—. (2005), 'The determinants of cross-border equity flows', *Journal of International Economics*, 65, 269–296.

Randall, M. D. V., and Urquhart, F.M. *eds.* (2007), *Martin Randall Travel 2007* (London: Martin Randall Travel Limited).

Roberts, J. M. (1996), *The Penguin History of Europe* (London: Helicon Publishing Limited).

Sarno, L., and Taylor, M. P. (1999), 'Hot money, accounting labels and the permanence of capital flows to developing countries: an empirical investigation', *Journal of Development Economics*, 59, 337–364.

Siems, M. M. (2005a), 'What does not work in comparing securities laws: a critique on La Porta et al's methodology', *International Company and Commercial Law Review*, 16(7), 300–305.

—. (2005b), 'Numerical Comparative Law: Do We Need Statistical Evidence in Order to Reduce Complexity?', *Cardozo Journal of International and Comparative Law*, 13, 521–540.

Tille, C., and van Wincoop, E. (2008), 'International Capital Flows', *CEPR Discussion Papers, No.6705* (London: Centre for Economic Policy Research).

Twining, W. (2006), 'Diffusion of Law: A Global Perspective', *Journal of Comparative Law*, 1, 3–26.

Walker, W. C., and Punzi, M. T. (2007), 'Financing of Global Imbalances', *IMF Working Paper, July 2007* (Washington D.C.: International Monetary Fund).

Weatherill, S., and Beaumont, P. (1999), *EU Law*, 3rd edn. (London: Penguin Books).
Wezel, T. (2003), 'Determinants of German Foreign Direct Investment in Latin American and Asian Emerging Markets in the 1990s', *Economic Research Centre of the Deutsche Bundesbank, Discussion Paper 11/03* (Frankfurt am Main: Deutsche Bundesbank).
Yasmin, B., Hussain, A., and Chaudhary, M. A. (2003), 'Analysis of Factors Affecting Foreign Direct Investment in Developing Countries', *Pakistan Economic and Social Review*, 41(1)-41(2), 59–75.
Zweigert, K., and Kötz, H. (1998), *An Introduction to Comparative Law*, 3rd edn. translated by Weir T. (Oxford: Clarendon Press).

Legislation

European Union legislation

Act concerning the conditions of accession of the Czech Republic, the Republic of Estonia, the Republic of Cyprus, the Republic of Latvia, the Republic of Lithuania, the Republic of Hungary, the Republic of Malta, the Republic of Poland, the Republic of Slovenia and the Slovak Republic and the adjustment to the Treaties on which the European Union is founded (2003).
Consolidated Version of the Treaty Establishing the European Community (2002).
Consolidated Version of the Treaty on the Functioning of the European Union (2008).
Council Directive 88/361/EEC of 24 June 1988 for the implementation of Article 67 of the Treaty.
Council Directive 90/434/EEC of 23 July 1990 on the common system of taxation applicable to mergers, divisions, transfers of assets and exchanges of shares concerning companies of different Member States.
Council Directive 90/435/EEC of 23 July 1990 on the common system of taxation applicable in the case of parent companies and subsidiaries of different Member States.
Council Directive 92/49/EEC of 18 June 1992 on the coordination of laws, regulations and administrative provisions relating to direct insurance other than life assurance and amending Directives 73/239/EEC and 88/357/EEC (third non-life insurance Directive).
Council Directive 93/22/EEC of 10 May 1993 on investment services in the securities field.
Council Directive 2003/123/EC of 22 December 2003 amending Directive 90/435/EC on the common system of taxation applicable in the case of parent companies and subsidiaries of different Member States.

Directive 97/5/EC of the European Parliament and of the Council of 27 January 1997 on cross-border credit transfers.

Directive 2000/12/EC of the European Parliament and of the Council of 20 March 2000 relating to the taking up and pursuit of the business of credit institutions.

Directive 2002/83/EC of the European Parliament and of the Council of 5 November 2002 concerning life assurance.

Directive 2002/92/EC of the European Parliament and of the Council of 9 December 2002 on insurance mediation.

Directive 2003/48/EC of the European Parliament and of the Council of 3 June 2003 on the taxation of savings income in the form of interest payments.

Directive 2004/39/EC of the European Parliament and of the Council of 21 April 2004 on markets in financial instruments.

Directive 2005/60/EC of the European Parliament and of the Council of 26 October 2005 on the prevention of the use of the financial system for the purpose of money laundering and terrorist financing.

Directive 2006/48/EC of the European Parliament and of the Council of 14 June 2006 relating to the taking up and pursuit of the business of credit institutions.

Directive 2006/49/EC of the European Parliament and of the Council of 14 June 2006 on the capital adequacy of investment firms and credit institutions.

Directive 2007/64/EC of the European Parliament and of the Council of 13 November 2007 on payment services in the internal market amending Directives 97/7/EC, 2002/65/EC, 2005/60/EC and 2006/48/EC and repealing Directive 97/5/EC.

Directive 2009/138/EC of the European Parliament and of the Council of 25 November 2009 on the taking-up and pursuit of the business of Insurance and Reinsurance (Solvency II).

First Council Directive 73/239/EEC of 24 July 1973 on the coordination of laws, regulations and administrative provisions relating to the taking-up and pursuit of the business of direct insurance other than life assurance.

Regulation (EC) No 2560/2001 of the European Parliament and of the Council of 19 December 2001 on cross-border payments in euro.

Second Council Directive 88/357/EEC of 22 June 1988 on the coordination of laws, regulations and administrative provisions relating to direct insurance other than life assurance and laying down provisions to facilitate the effective exercise of freedom to provide services and amending Directive 73/239/EEC.

Treaty on European Union – Declaration on Article 73 D of the Treaty establishing the European Community (1992).

Estonian legislation

Commercial Code, RT I 1995, 26/28, 355; consolidated text RT I 2005, 63, 481. Amended by RT I 2005, 68, 525; RT 2006, 7, 42; RT I 2006, 55, 407; RT I 2006, 55, 412; RT I 2006, 61, 456.

Credit Institutions Act, RT I 1999, 23, 349; consolidated text RT I 2005, 8, 32. Amended by RT I 2004, 86, 582; RT I 2005, 13, 64.

Eesti Pank Governor's Decree, 14 May 2001 No 2, Confirmation of instructions for settlement of payments, RTL 2001, 62, 861.

Financial Supervision Authority Act, RT I 2001, 48, 267. Amended by RT I 2002, 23, 131; RT I 2002, 105, 612; RT I 2003, 81, 544; RT I 2004, 36, 251.

Forest Act, RT I 2006, 30, 232.

Income Tax Act, RT I 1999, 101, 903; consolidated text RT I 2001, 11, 49. Amended by RT I 2001, 16, 69; RT I 2001, 50, 283; RT I 2001, 59, 359; RT I 2001, 79, 480; RT I 2001, 91, 544; RT I 2002, 23, 131; RT I 2002, 41, 253; RT I 2002, 44, 284; RT I 2002, 47, 297; RT I 2002, 62, 377; RT I 2002, 111, 662; RT I 2003, 18, 105; RT I 2003, 58, 387; RT I 2003, 82, 549; RT I 2003, 88, 587; RT I 2003, 88, 591; RT I 2004, 36, 251; RT I 2004, 37, 252; RT I 2004, 45, 319.

Income Tax Act, RT I 1999, 101, 903; consolidated text RT I 2004, 59, 414. Amended by RT I 2004, 84, 568; RT I 2004, 89, 604; RT I 2005, 22, 148; RT I 2005, 25, 193; RT I 2005, 36, 277; RT I 2005, 54, 430; RT I 2005, 57, 451; RT I 2006, 7, 40; RT I 2006, 7, 41; RT I 2006, 26, 193; RT I 2006, 28, 208.

Insurance Activities Act, RT I 2004, 90, 616.

Investment Funds Act, RT I 2004, 36, 251.

Land Taxes Act, RT I 1993, 24, 428; consolidated text RT I 1996, 41, 797. Amended by RT I 1996, 89, 1589; RT I 1997, 82, 1398; RT I 1999, 27, 381; RT I 1999, 95, 840; RT 2000, 95, 612; RT I 2001, 102, 666; RT I 2002, 44, 284; RT I 2003, 71, 472; RT I 2003, 88, 587; RT I 2003, 88, 589; RT I 2003, 88, 591.

Law of Property Act, RT I 1993, 39, 590; consolidated text RT I 1999, 44, 509. Amended by RT I 2001, 34, 185; RT I 2002, 93, 565; RT I 2002, 47, 297; RT I 2002, 53, 336; RT I 2002, 99, 579; RT I 2003, 13, 64; RT I 2003, 17, 95; RT I 2003, 78, 523; RT I 2004, 20, 141; RT I 2004, 37, 255; RT I 2005, 39, 308; RT I 2005, 59, 464.

Law of Property Act Implementation Act, RT I 1993, 72/73, 1021; consolidated text RT I 1999, 44, 510. Amended by RT I 2000, 51, 325; RT I 2000, 88, 576; RT I 2001, 31, 171; RT I 2001, 42, 234; RT I 2001, 94, 582; RT I 2002, 47, 297; RT I 2002, 53, 336; RT I 2002, 99, 579; RT I 2003, 13, 64; RT I 2003, 51, 355; RT I 2003, 78, 523; RT I 2003, 81, 546; RT I 2004, 14, 91.

Local Taxes Act, RT I 1994, 68, 1169. Amended by RT I 1996, 49, 953; RT I 1999, 16, 269; RT I 1999, 101, 903; RT I 2000, 33, 196; RT I 2000, 81, 515; RT I 2002, 44, 284; RT I 2002, 110, 654; RT I 2003, 88, 591; RT I 2004, 45, 319.
Private International Law Act, RT I 2002, 35, 217.
Regulation No.73 of the Minister of Finance of 19 November 1997, RTL 1997, 194/195, 1022.
Restrictions on Transfer of Immovable Property Ownership to Aliens, Foreign States and Legal Persons Act 1996, RT I 1996, 39, 766.
Securities Market Act, RT I 2001, 89, 532. Amended by RT I 2002, 23, 131; RT I 2002, 63, 367; RT I 2002, 102, 600; RT I 2002, 105, 612; RT I 2003, 81, 544; RT I 2003, 88, 591; RT I 2004, 30, 208; RT I 2004, 36, 251; RT I 2004, 37, 255; RT I 2005, 13, 64; RT I 2005, 39, 308; RT I 2005 59, 463; RT I 2005, 59, 464.
Social Tax Act, RT I 2000, 102, 675. Amended by RT I 2001, 50, 285; RT I 2001, 59, 359; RT I 2001, 79, 480; RT I 2001, 91, 544; RT I 2001, 95, 587; RT I 2002, 44, 284; RT I 2002, 62, 377; RT I 2002, 111, 662; RT I 2003, 82, 549; RT I 2003, 88, 587; RT I 2003, 88, 591; RT I 2004, 37, 252; RT I 2004, 84, 568; RT I 2004, 89, 604; RT I 2005, 9, 34; RT I 2005, 25, 193.
Taxation Act, RT I 2002, 26, 150. Amended by RT I 2002, 57, 358; RT I 2002, 63, 387; RT I 2002, 99, 581; RT I 2002, 110, 660; RT I 2002, 111, 662; RT I 2003, 2, 17; RT I 2003, 48, 341; RT I 2003, 71, 472; RT I 2003, 82, 554; RT I 2003, 88, 591; RT I 2004, 2, 7; RT I 2004, 28, 188; RT I 2004, 28, 189; RT I 2004, 30, 208; RT I 2004, 45, 319; RT I 2004, 56, 403; RT I 2004, 84, 568; RT I 2004, 84, 569; RT I 2005, 13, 66; RT I 2005, 25, 193.

Finnish legislation

Act on the Financial Supervision Authority, 27.6.2003/587. Amended by 2.4.2004/227, 30.7.2004/706, 3.12.2004/1041, 21.12.2004/1232, 30.12.2004/1295, 30.12.2004/1311, 13.5.2005/299, 23.6.2005/449, 8.6.2006/444.

Latvian legislation

Activities of Insurance and Reinsurance Intermediaries Law, 17.03.2005, Latvijas Republikas Augstākās Padomes un Valdības Ziņotājs, 2005, No.8.
Administrative Procedure Law, 13.06.2002, Latvijas Vēstnesis, 2002, No.97 (2672). Amended by Latvijas Vēstnesis, 2003, No.96 (2861); LV, 2004, No.12 (2960); LV, 2005, No.74 (3232).

Cabinet Regulation No.793: Procedures for the Application of the Norms of the Law On Personal Income Tax, 26.09.2006, Latvijas Vēstnesis, 2006, No.156 (3524). Amended by Latvijas Vēstnesis, 2007, No.121 (3697).

Credit Institution Law, 05.10.1995, Latvijas Republikas Augstākās Padomes un Valdības Ziņotājs, 1995, No.23. Amended by Latvijas Vēstnesis, 1996, No.49 (534); LV, 1996, No.100/101 (585/586); LV, 1996, No.183 (668); LV, 1997, No.296/297 (1011/1012); LV, 1998, No.167/169 (1228/1230); LV, 2000, No.223/225 (2134/2136); LV, 2002, No.64 (2639); LV, 2002, No.161 (2736); LV, 2003, No.73 (2838); LV, 2003, No.175 (2940); LV, 2003, No.182 (2947); LV, 2004, No.90 (3038); LV, 2004, No.180 (3128); LV, 2005, No.92 (3250); LV, 2005, No.99 (3257); LV, 2006, No.103 (3471); LV, 2007, No.40 (3616); LV, 2007, No.85 (3661).

Finance and Capital Market Commission: 2002-08-15 Regulations on the Issue of Credit Institution and Credit Union Operating Licences, 24.05.2002, Latvijas Vēstnesis, 2002, No.81 (2656). Amended by Latvijas Vēstnesis, 2004, No.75 (3023); LV, 2004, No.191 (3139).

Financial Instrument Market Law, 20.11.2003, Latvijas Vēstnesis, 2003, No.175 (2940). Amended by Latvijas Vēstnesis, 2005, No.68 (3226); LV, 2005, No.99 (3257); LV, 2006, No.100 (3468); LV, 2007, No.62 (3638).

Law On Enterprise Income Tax, 09.02.1995, Latvijas Vēstnesis, 1995, No.32 (315). Amended by Latvijas Vēstnesis, 1995, No.168 (451); LV, 1996, No.46 (531); LV, 1996, No.108 (593); LV, 1997, No.83/84 (798/799); LV, 1997, No.309/310 (1024/1025); LV, 1998, No. 75/76 (1136/1137); LV, 1998, No.282 (1343); LV, 1999, No.52/53 (1512/1513); LV, 1999, No.416/419 (1876/1879); LV, 2000, No.125/126 (2036/2037); LV, 2000, No.448/449 (2359/2360); LV, 2001, No.26 (2413); LV, 2001, No.178 (2565); LV, 2003, No.101 (2866); LV, 2004, No.206 (3154); LV, 2005, No.179 (3337); LV, 2005, No.198 (3356); LV, 2006, No.207 (3575); LV, 2007, No.85 (3661).

Law On Insurance Companies and Supervision Thereof, 10.06.1998, Latvijas Vēstnesis, 1998, No.188/189 (1249/1250). Amended by Latvijas Vēstnesis, 1999, No.133/135 (1593/1595); LV, 2000, No.230/232 (2141/2142); LV, 2002, No.80 (2655); LV, 2003, No.58 (2823); LV, 2003, No.175 (2940); LV, 2004, No.101 (3049); LV, 2004, No.208 (3156); LV, 2005, No.99 (3257) LV, 2005, No.198 (3356); LV, 2007, No.106 (3682).

Law On Insurance Contracts, 10.06.1998, Latvijas Vēstnesis, 1998, No.188/189 (1249/1250). Amended by Latvijas Vēstnesis, 2000,

No.230/232 (2141/2142); LV, 2002, No.161 (2736); LV, 2007, No.56 (3632).

Law On Investment Companies, 18.12.1997, Latvijas Vēstnesis, 1997, No.342/345 (1054/1057). Amended by Latvijas Vēstnesis, 2000, No.230/232 (2141/2142); LV, 2002, No.165 (2740); LV, 2004, No.54 (3002); LV, 2007, No.51 (3627).

Law On Land Reform in the Cities in the Republic of Latvia, 20.11.1991, Latvijas Republikas Augstākās Padomes un Valdības Ziņotājs, 1991, No.49. Amended by Latvijas Vēstnesis, 1993, No.22; LV, 1994, No.47 (178); LV, 1994, No.145 (276); LV, 1995, No.169 (472); LV, 1997, No.126/127 (841/842); LV, 1999, No.136/137 (1596/1597); LV, 2001, No.166 (2553); LV, 2004, No.174 (3122); LV, 2005, No.108 (3226); LV, 2006, No.95 (3463); LV, 2007, No.103 (3679).

Law On Personal Income Tax, 11.05.1993, Latvijas Republikas Augstākās Padomes un Valdības Ziņotājs, 1993, No.22/23. Amended by Latvijas Vēstnesis, 1994, No.7 (138); LV, 1994, 130 (261); LV, 1995, No.34 (317); LV, 1995, No.93/94 (376/377); LV, 1996, No.46 (531); LV, 1997, No.1/2 (716/717); LV, 1997, No.265/267 (980/982); LV, 1997, No.315/316 (1030/1031); LV, 1999, No.416/419 (1876/1879); LV, 2000, No.40/41 (1951/1952); LV, 2000, No.452/453 (2363/2364); LV, 2001, No.178 (2565); LV, 2002, No.34 (2609); LV, 2003, No.99 (2864); LV, 2003, No.182 (2947); LV, 2004, No.69 (3017); LV, 2004, No.206 (3154); LV, 2005, No.48 (3206); LV, 2005, No.179 (3337); LV, 2006, No.95 (3463); LV, 2006, No.166 (3534); LV, 2006, No.207 (3575); LV, 2007, No.1 (3577); LV, 2007, No.62 (3638); LV, 2007, No.85 (3661).

Law On Ports, 22.06.1994, Latvijas Vēstnesis, 1994, No.80 (211). Amended by Latvijas Vēstnesis, 1996, No.94 (579); LV, 1997, No.93 (808); LV, 1997, No.167/168 (882/883); LV, 1999, No.397/398 (1857/1858); LV, 2000, No.197/200 (2108/2111); LV, 2001, No.56 (2443); LV, 2001, No.77 (2464); LV, 2002, No.165 (2740); LV, 2003, No.103 (2868); LV, 2003, No.156 (2921); LV, 2003, No.159 (2924); LV, 2005, No.104 (3262); LV, 2005, No.181 (3339).

Law On Private Pension Funds, 05.06.1997, Latvijas Vēstnesis, 1997, No.150/151 (865/866). Amended by Latvijas Vēstnesis, 1997, No.334/335 (1049/1050); LV, 1998, No.265/266 (1326/1327); LV, 1999, No.186/189 (1646/1649); LV, 2000, No.230/232 (2141/2142); LV, 2002, No.156 (2731); LV, 2003, No.175 (2940); LV, 2004, No.54 (3002); LV, 2005, No.51 (3209); LV, 2005, No.189 (3347).

Law On Privatization of Land in Rural Areas, 09.07.1992, Latvijas Republikas Augstākās Padomes un Valdības Ziņotājs, 1992, No.32. Amended by Republikas Augstākās Padomes un Valdības Ziņotājs, 1993, No.8; Latvijas Vēstnesis, 1993, No.22; LV, 1993, No.130; LV,

1994, No.148 (279); LV, 1995, No.162 (445); LV, 1996, No.111 (596); LV, 1996, No.225 (710); LV, 2001, No.154 (2541); LV, 2003, No.58 (2823); LV, 2005, No.191 (3349); LV, 2007, No.102 (3678).

Law On State Funded Pensions, 17.02.2000, Latvijas Republikas Augstākās Padomes un Valdības Ziņotājs, 2000, No.7. Amended by Latvijas Vēstnesis, 2002, No.169 (2744); LV, 2003, No.175 (2940); LV, 2004, No.54 (3002); LV, 2005, No.78 (3236); LV, 2006, No.162 (3530); LV, 2007, No.78 (3654).

The Civil Law, 28.01.1937; consolidated text: Latvijas Republikas Augstākās Padomes un Valdības Ziņotājs, 1992, No.29. Amended by Latvijas Republikas Augstākās Padomes un Valdības Ziņotājs, 1993, No.1; Latvijas Vēstnesis, 1994, No.75 (206); LV, 1997, No.112 (827); LV, 1997, No.286 (1001); LV, 1998, No.153/154 (1214/1215); LV, 1998, No. 184/185 (1245/1246); LV, 1998, No.280/281 (1341/1342); LV, 2002, No.187 (2762); LV, 2004, No.161 (3109); LV, 2005, No.49 (3207), LV, 2006, No.24 (3392); LV, 2006, No.107 (3475); 2007, No.40 (3616).

The Commercial Law, 13.04.2000, Latvijas Vēstnesis, 2000, No.158/160 (2069/2071). Amended by Latvijas Vēstnesis, 2000, No.473/476 (2384/2387); LV, 2001, No.52 (2439); LV, 2001, No.101 (2488); LV, 2002, No.34 (2609); LV, 2004, No.72 (3020); LV, 2005, No.104 (3262); LV, 2006, No.53 (3421).

The Free Port of Riga Law, 09.03.2000, Latvijas Vēstnesis, 2000, No.111/112 (2022/2023). Amended by Latvijas Vēstnesis, 2001, No.117 (2504); LV, 2003, No.85 (2850).

The Free Port of Ventspils Law, 19.12.1996, Latvijas Vēstnesis, 1997, No.1/2 (716/717). Amended by Latvijas Vēstnesis, 2001, No.117 (2504); LV, 2003, No.85 (2850).

Polish legislation

Act of 24 March 1920 on the Acquisition of Immovable Properties by Foreign Persons; consolidated text: Dziennik Ustaw 2004, No.167, item 1758. Amended by Dziennik Ustaw 2005, No.94, item 788; 2005, No.183, item 1538.

Act of 26 July 1991 on Natural Persons' Income Tax; consolidated text: Dziennik Ustaw 2000, No.14, item 176. Amended by Dziennik Ustaw 2000, No.22, item 270; 2000, No.60, item 703; 2000, No.70, item 816; 2000, No.104, item 1104; 2000, No.117, item 1228; 2000, No.122, item 1324; 2001, No.4, item 27; 2001, No.8, item 64; 2001, No.52, item 539; 2001, No.73, item 764; 2001, No.74, item 784; 2001, No.88, item 961; 2001, No.89, item 968; 2001, No.102, item 1117; 2001, No.106, item 1150; 2001, No.110, item 1190; 2001, No.125, items

1363 and 1370; 2001, No.134, item 1509; 2002, No.25, item 253; 2002, No.74, item 676; 2002, No.89, item 804; 2002, No.135, item 1146; 2002, No.141, item 1182; 2002, No.169, item 1384; 2002, No.181, item 1515; 2002, No.200, items 1679 and 1691; 2002, No.240, item 2058; 2003, No.7, item 79; 2003, No.45, item 391; 2003, No.65, item 595; 2003, No.84, item 774; 2003, No.90, item 844; 2003, No.96, item 874; 2003, No.122, item 1143; 2003, No.135, item 1268; 2003, No.137, item 1302; 2003, No.166, item 1608; 2003, No.202, item 1956; 2003, No.222, item 2201; 2003, No.223, item 2217; 2003, No.228, item 2255; 2004, No.29, item 257; 2004, No.54, item 535; 2004, No.93, item 894; 2004, No.99, item 1001; 2004, No.109, item 1163; 2004, No.116, items 1203, 1205 and 1207; 2004, No.120, item 1252; 2004, No.123, item 1291; 2004, No.162, item 1691; 2004, No.210, item 2135; 2004, No.263, item 2619; 2004, No.281, items 2779 and 2781; 2005, No.25, item 202; 2005, No.30, item 262; 2005, No.85, item 725; 2005, No.86, item 732; 2005, No.90, item 757; 2005, No.102, item 852; 2005, No.143, items 1199 and 1202; 2005, No.155, item 1298; 2005, No.164, items 1365 and 1366; 2005, No.169, items 1418 and 1420; 2005, No.177, item 1468; 2005, No.179, item 1484; 2005, No.180, item 1495; 2005, No.183, item 1538; 2006, No.46, item 328; 2006, No.104, items 708 and 711; 2006, No.107, item 723; 2006, No.157, item 1119; 2006, No.183, items 1353 and 1354.

Act of 15 February 1992 on Legal Persons' Income Tax; consolidated text: Dziennik Ustaw 2000, No.54, item 654. Amended by Dziennik Ustaw 2000, No.60, items 700 and 703; 2000, No.86, item 958; 2000, No.103, item 1100; 2000, No.117, item 1228; 2000, No.122, items 1315 and 1324; 2001, No.106, item 1150; 2001, No.110, item 1190; 2001, No.125, item 1363; 2002, No.25, item 253; 2002, No.74, item 676; 2002, No.93, item 820; 2002, No.141, item 1179; 2002, No.169, item 1384; 2002, No.199, item 1672; 2002, No.200, item 1684; 2002, No.230, item 1922; 2003, No.7, item 79; 2003, No.45, item 391; 2003, No.96, item 874; 2003, No.137, item 1302; 2003, No.180, item 1759; 2003, No.202, item 1957; 2003, No.217, item 2124; 2003, No.223, item 2218; 2004, No.6, item 39; 2004, No.29, item 257; 2004, No.54, item 535; 2004, No.93, item 894; 2004, No.116, item 1203; 2004, No.121, item 1262; 2004, No.123, item 1291; 2004, No.146, item 1546; 2004, No.171, item 1800; 2004, No.210, item 2135; 2004, No.254, item 2533; 2005, No.25, item 202; 2005, No.57, item 491; 2005, No.78, item 684; 2005, No.143, item 1199; 2005, No.155, item 1298; 2005, No.169, item 1420; 2005, No.179, item 1484; 2005, No.180, item 1495; 2005, No.183, item 1538; 2006, No.94, item 651; 2006, No.107, item 723; 2006, No.157, item 1119; 2006, No.183, item 1353.

Act of 29 August 1997: Banking Law; consolidated text: Dziennik Ustaw 2002, No.72, item 665. Amended by Dziennik Ustaw 2002, No.126, item 1070; 2002, No.141, item 1178; 2002, No.144, item 1208; 2002, No.153, item 1271; 2002, No.169, items 1385 and 1387; 2002, No.241, item 2074; 2003, No.50, item 424; 2003, No.60, item 535; 2003, No.65, item 594; 2003, No.228, item 2260; 2003, No.229, item 2276; 2004, No.64, item 594; 2004, No.68, item 623; 2004, No.91, item 870; 2004, No.96, item 959; 2004, No.121, item 1264; 2004, No.146, item 1546; 2004, No.173, item 1808; 2005, No.83, item 719; 2005, No.85, item 727; 2005, No.167, item 1398; 2005, No.183, item 1538; 2006, No.104, item 708; 2006, No.157, item 1119; 2006, No.190, item 1401.

Act of 27 July 2002: Foreign Exchange Law, Dziennik Ustaw 2002, No.141, item 1178. Amended by Dziennik Ustaw 2003, No.228, item 2260; 2004, No.91, item 870; 2004, No.173, item 1808; 2006, No.157, item 1119.

Act of 22 May 2003 on Insurance Activity, Dziennik Ustaw 2003, No.124, item 1151. Amended by Dziennik Ustaw 2004, No.91, item 870; 2004, No.96, item 959; 2005, No.48, item 447; 2005, No.83, item 719; 2005, No.143, item 1204; 2005, No.167, item 1396; 2005, No.183, item 1538; 2005, No.184, item 1539; 2006, No.157, item 1119.

Act of 22 May 2003 on Insurance Mediation, Dziennik Ustaw 2003, No.124, item 1154. Amended by Dziennik Ustaw 2004, No.96, item 959; 2005, No.48, item 447; 2005, No.167, item 1396; 2005, No.183, item 1538; 2006, No.157, item 1119.

Act of 28 February 2004 on Freedom of Economic Activity, Dziennik Ustaw 2004, No.173, item 1807. Amended by Dziennik Ustaw 2004, No.281, item 2777; 2005, No.33, item 289; 2005, No.94, item 788; 2005, No.143, item 1199; 2005, No.175, item 1460; 2005, No.177, item 1468; 2005, No.178, item 1480; 2005, No.179, item 1485; 2005, No.180, item 1494; 2005, No.183, item 1538; 2006, No.17, item 127; 2006, No.144, items 1043 and 1045; 2006, No.158, item 1121; 2006, No.171, item 1225.

Act of 27 May 2004 on Investment Funds, Dziennik Ustaw 2004, No.146, item 1546. Amended by Dziennik Ustaw 2005, No.83, item 719; 2005, No.183, items 1537 and 1538; 2005, No.184, item 1539; 2006, No.157, item 1119.

Act of 29 July 2005 on Public Offers and the Conditions for Introducing Financial Instruments to the Organised Trading System, and on Public Companies, Dziennik Ustaw 2005, No.184, item 1539. Amended by Dziennik Ustaw 2006, No.157, item 1119.

Act of 29 July 2005 on Trading in Financial Instruments, Dziennik Ustaw 2005, No.183, item 1538. Amended by Dziennik Ustaw 2006, No.104, item 708; 2006, No.157, item 1119.

Regulation of the Minister of Finance of 3 September 2002 on General Foreign Exchange Permits, Dziennik Ustaw 2002, No.154, item 1273. Amended by Dziennik Ustaw 2004, No.73, item 658.

Cases decided by the ECJ

Albore, C-423/98, [2000] ECR I-5965.
Analir and Others, C-205/99, [2001] ECR I-1271.
Barbier, C-364/01, [2003] ECR I-15013.
Blanckaert, C-512/03, [2005] ECR I-7685.
Bouanich, C-265/04, [2006] ECR I-923.
Burtscher, C-213/04, [2005] ECR I-10309.
Campus Oil, 72/83, [1984] ECR 2727.
Commission of the European Communities v Belgium, C-478/98, [2000] ECR I-7587.
—. v Belgium, C-503/99, [2002] ECR I-4809.
—. v France, C-483/99, [2002] ECR I-4781.
—. v Hellenic Republic, 305/87, [1989] ECR 1461.
—. v Italy, C-174/04, [2005] ECR I-4933.
—. v Portugal, C-367/98, [2002] ECR I-4731.
—. v Spain, C-463/00, [2003] ECR I-4581.
—. v United Kingdom, C-98/01, [2003] ECR I-4641.
Costa v ENEL, 6/64, [1964] ECR 1141.
D., C-376/03, [2005] ECR I-5821.
Denkavit International and Denkavit France, C-170/05, [2006] ECR I-11949.
Eglise de Scientologie and Scientology International, C-54/99, [2000] ECR I-1335.
Kerckhaert and Morres, C-513/04, [2006] ECR I-10967.
Konle v Austria, C-302/97, [1999] ECR I-3099.
Lankhorst-Hohorst GmbH v Finanzamt Steinfurt, C-324/00, [2002] ECR I-11779.
Lenz, C-315/02, [2004] ECR I-7063.
Manninen, C-319/02, [2004] ECR I-7477.
Meilicke and Others, C-292/04, [2007] ECR I-1835.
Ospelt and Schlössle Weissenberg Familienstiftung, C-452/01, [2003] ECR I-9743.
Reisch and Others, Joined Cases C-515/99, C-519/99 to C-524/99 and C-526/99 to C-540/99, [2002] ECR I-2157.
Salzmann, C-300/01, [2003] ECR I-4899.
Simmenthal, 106/77, [1978] ECR 629.
Skatteverket v A, C-101/05, ECR I-11531.
Trummer and Mayer, C-222/97, [1999] ECR I-1661.

Van Duyn v Home Office, 41/74, [1975] ECR 1337.
Van Gend en Loos v Nederlandse Tariefcommissie, 26/62, [1963] ECR 1.
Van Hilten-van der Heijden, C-513/03, [2006] ECR I-1957.
Verkooijen, C-35/98, [2000] ECR I-4071.
Von Colson v Land Nordrhein-Westfahlen, 14/83, [1984] ECR 1891.
Weidert and Paulus, C-242/03, [2004] ECR I-7379.

Statistical Sources

Bank for International Settlements (2008). Statistics homepage: http://www.bis.org/statistics/index.htm.
Bank of Estonia (2008). Statistics homepage (English): http://www.bankofestonia.info/pub/en/dokumendid/statistika/.
Bank of Latvia (2008). Statistics homepage (English): http://www.bank.lv/eng/main/all/statistics/.
Central Statistical Bureau of Latvia (2008). Data area homepage (English): http://www.csb.gov.lv/csp/content/?lng=en&cat=244.
Central Statistical Office of Poland (2008). Homepage (English): http://www.stat.gov.pl/english/index.htm.
Estonian Financial Supervision Authority (2008). Market data homepage (English): http://www.fi.ee/?id=581&PHPSESSID=fa078cdb896c4f45f57f799df75b9a30.
Eurostat (2008). Homepage (English): http://epp.eurostat.ec.europa.eu/portal/page?_pageid=1090,30070682,1090_33076576&_dad=portal&_schema=PORTAL.
Latvian Financial and Capital Market Commission (2008). Statistics homepage (English): http://www.fktk.lv/en/statistics/credit_institutions/annual_reports.
National Bank of Poland (2008). Homepage (English): http://www.nbp.pl/Homen.aspx.
Polish Financial Supervision Authority (2008). Homepage (English): http://www.knf.gov.pl/en/.
Statistics Estonia (2008). Statistics homepage (English): http://www.stat.ee/statistics.
World Bank (2008). Statistics homepage: http://web.worldbank.org/WBSITE/EXTERNAL/DATASTATISTICS/0,,menuPK:232599~pagePK:64133170~piPK:64133498~theSitePK:239419,00.html.

World Wide Web Pages and Other Resources

Committee of European Banking Supervisors (CEBS): Guidelines on the Application of the Supervisory Review Process under Pillar 2 (CP03 revised).

Communication from the Commission to the Council, the European Parliament and the Economic and Social Committee, 'Tax policy in the European Union – Priorities for the years ahead' /* COM/2001/0260 final */.

Communication from the Commission to the Council and the European Parliament concerning a New Legal Framework for Payments in the Internal Market (Consultative Document)/* COM/2003/0718 final */.

Communication from the Commission to the European Parliament, the Council, the European Central Bank, the European Economic and Social Committee and the Committee of the Regions, 'Ninth Report on the practical preparations for the future enlargement of the euro area' /* COM/2009/692 final */.

Estonian Financial Supervision Authority (2007), 'Affiliated Branches of Foreign Credit Institutions' (online) (cited 14 February 2007). Available from http://www.fi.ee/index.php?id=1774&PHPSESSID=72a36a374a76dcd7ec00838d090.

Estonian Financial Supervision Authority (2007), Unpublished letter: The compatibility of certain provisions of the Insurance Activities Act 2004 with EU law, and the legal status of Regulation No.73 of the Minister of Finance of 19 November 1997.

Estonian Legal Language Centre (2006), 'Background of ELTC' (online) (cited 8 November 2006). Available from http://www.legaltext.ee/avalik/yldinfo/180___In_brief.htm.

Estonian Ministry of Justice (2007), Unpublished letter: The absence of international provisions in the Law of Property Act 1993 and Law of Property Implementation Act 1993, and the legal status of the Restrictions on Transfer of Immovable Property Ownership to Aliens, Foreign States and Legal Persons Act 1996.

EUbusiness.com (2007), 'High inflation means no euro in Latvia before 2011' (online) (cited 28 June 2007). Available from http://www.eubusiness.com/Euro/latvia-euro.43/.

Implementing the Community Lisbon programme – Proposal for a Directive of the European Parliament and of the Council on payment services in the internal market amending Directives 97/7/EC, 2000/12/EC and 2002/65/EC {SEC(2005) 1535} /* COM/2005/0603 final – COD 2005/0245 */.

Latvian Translation and Terminology Centre (2007), 'Strategic plan' (online) (cited 4 October 2007). Available from http://www.ttc.lv/?print=41.

Memorandum of Understanding between the Finantsinspektsioon (Estonian Financial Supervision Authority) and the Bundesaufsichtsamt für das Kreditwesen (German Federal Banking Supervisory Office) concerning their cooperation in the field of supervision of banks and investment firms.

Memorandum of Understanding between the Insurance Supervisory Authority of Estonia as a Member of CEIOPS (Committee of European Insurance and Occupational Pensions Supervisors) and the Insurance Supervisory Authority of Switzerland Regarding Cooperation and Exchange of Information.

Mr. Thomas Auväärt, Ministry of Finance of Estonia (2008), Unpublished e-mail: Date of implementation of Regulation No.73 of the Minister of Finance of 19 November 1997.

Ms. Anna Wlostowska, National Bank of Poland (2008), Unpublished e-mail: Methodology for compilation of Polish balance of payments statistics.

Ms. Daiga Gaigala-Lizbovska, Bank of Latvia (2008), Unpublished e-mail: Methodology for compilation of Latvian balance of payments statistics.

Ms. Ingrid Mitt, Bank of Estonia (2008), Unpublished e-mail: Methodology for compilation of Estonian balance of payments statistics.

Polish Office of the Committee for European Integration (2007), 'History of the EU: Stepping stones to enlargement' (online) (cited 22 October 2007). Available from http://www1.ukie.gov.pl/WWW/en.nsf/0/D809DBFA2BFB5681C1256ED20047E7C6?Open.

Professor Māris Baltiņš, Latvian Translation and Terminology Centre (2007), Unpublished e-mail: References for laws in Latvijas Vēstnesis.

The PRS Group (2007), 'ICRG Methodology' (online) (cited 15 August 2007). Available from http://www.prsgroup.com/ICRG_Methodology.aspx.

United Nations Statistics Division (2007), 'Social indicators' (online) (cited 21 June 2007). Available from http://unstats.un.org/UNSD/demographic/products/socind/inc-eco.htm.

White Paper from the Commission to the Council, 'Completing the Internal Market' /* COM/85/310 final */.

World Trade Organization (2007), 'Understanding the WTO: The Organization – Members and Observers' (online) (cited 17 November 2007). Available from http://www.wto.org/english/thewto_e/whatis_e/tif_e/org6_e.htm.

INDEX